Illinois Central College
Learning Resources Center

The Psychology of

PERSUASIVE
SPEECH

BOOKS BY **Robert T. Oliver**

ROBERT T. OLIVER *TARBELL, 1909-*

THE PENNSYLVANIA STATE UNIVERSITY

The Psychology of

PERSUASIVE

SPEECH

New Impression

DAVID McKAY COMPANY, INC.

New York

THE PSYCHOLOGY OF PERSUASIVE SPEECH

SECOND EDITION JANUARY 1957

REPRINTED SEPTEMBER 1960

AUGUST 1962
AUGUST 1963

NEW IMPRESSION 1968

LIBRARY OF CONGRESS CATALOG CARD NUMBER 57-7093

Printed in the United States of America

VAN REES PRESS   •   NEW YORK

DEDICATED TO

My wife and two sons

I HAVE TRIED TOO IN MY TIME TO BE
A PHILOSOPHER; BUT... CHEERFULNESS
WAS ALWAYS BREAKING IN.

—Boswell's Johnson

Preface

THE FIRST EDITION OF *The Psychology of Persuasive Speech* (1942) announced in its preface, "The aim of this book is to help its readers to become more effective motivators of human conduct." A most gratifyingly widespread use of the first edition over a span of fourteen years indicates that many teachers and students concur in this aim and have felt it was fairly well achieved. For this revision, the aim remains the same.

What is attempted in this revision is to incorporate in one volume the best features of both *The Psychology of Persuasive Speech* and *Persuasive Speaking: Principles and Methods* (1950). The first book dealt in some depth with problems of human motivation as encountered in audience situations. The latter book was much more directly functional for immediate speech situations. The author always felt that the two books constituted a basic unity—and in this edition the two are joined.

In order to avoid excessive length, and in view of the considerable new writing incorporated, some sections of both earlier books are eliminated. It is hoped, however, that not only have their strong features been retained, but that they gain added usefulness in the integration.

In this edition great stress has been placed upon the ethical responsibilities of the speaker—both in relation to his social responsibilities and to the wholesome development of his own personality.

In addition to a specific chapter devoted to this theme, the ethical point of view is basic to the entire text.

Nevertheless, the author has not permitted any considerations to interfere with the purely scientific approach of depicting what appears to be genuinely persuasive. In the imperfect universe in which we live, practices not sanctioned by the highest ethical considerations do, under many circumstances, prove effective motivators of human conduct. It has seemed wise to maintain a clear conception of *what works,* both to avoid corruption of persuasion as a science and to provide students with the knowledge they require to analyze persuasion that is directed toward them from multiple sources.

Within the limits of tenable space, the attempt has been made to present a well-rounded and complete purview of oral persuasion. It may be that in some classes time will not permit the full discussion of all the chapters, but it is felt that any student engaging in the study of persuasion should have available before him a unified presentation of the entire complex field.

Neither has the author deviated from his view that persuasion is an advanced course in Speech. For example, in the chapters on delivery and organization, it is presumed that students will already have studied these topics on an elementary level in beginning courses. Rather than repeating what they ought already to know, the chapters carry them forward to specialized considerations applying especially to persuasive discourse.

Readers who note the lack of chapters on style and on development of ideas may fear that these important topics are ignored. However, a reading of the book indicates that the author considers them so important as to be incorporated into many of the other chapters. They are presented as integral processes, essential in many (if not all) stages of preparing and presenting oral persuasion.

In the planning and writing of this volume, the author has drawn heavily not only upon the work of many persons in many fields—including a great number of objective experiments—but also upon his own experience in directing for the federal government a national program of persuasion (for the prevention of food waste) during

World War II and upon his ten years of participation in the public relations work of the Republic of Korea. With *practicality* as the primary standard of judgment, the effort is made in these pages to present to students a philosophy and methodology of persuasion that really prove effective.

In any such work as this, the direct and indirect assistance of many individuals is indispensable. Specific acknowledgments to sources consulted are made in the chapter bibliographies. Grateful appreciation is expressed to the authors and publishers who have authorized quotations from published works. In addition, warm thanks are due to many teachers in all sections of the country who have used the earlier editions of *The Psychology of Persuasive Speech* and *Persuasive Speaking,* and who have generously sent to the author their reactions and suggestions. More particularly, gratitude is expressed to Professor Holle DeBoer and Mr. James Lewis, who have read large portions of this revision and have made many helpful comments upon it. I am particularly grateful to Dr. Iline Fife, who, besides reading the manuscript, has borne (in my absence abroad) the responsibility for reading and correcting the proof. My appreciation is also extended to Professor Harold P. Zelko, who very kindly prepared the index during my absence from the country. Finally, and with deep appreciation, the author thanks his wife and two sons, who have shown tolerant understanding of the pains and demands of authorship while this revision has been in preparation. For the errors and shortcomings of this work, the author must, of course, accept full responsibility.

ROBERT T. OLIVER

State College, Pennsylvania

Contents

Illustrative Speeches

PART 1

Motivation in Human Affairs

Of the modes of persuasion furnished by the spoken word there are three kinds. The first depends on the personal character of the speaker; the second on putting the audience into a certain frame of mind; the third on the proof, or apparent proof, provided by the words of the speech itself. Persuasion is achieved by the speaker's personal character when the speech is so spoken as to make us think him credible. We believe good men more fully and more readily than others: this is true generally whatever the question is, and absolutely true where exact certainty is impossible and opinions are divided . . . [the speaker's] character may almost be called the most effective means of persuasion he possesses. Secondly, persuasion may come through the hearers, when the speech stirs their emotions. Our judgments when we are pleased and friendly are not the same as when we are pained and hostile. . . . Thirdly, persuasion is effected through the speech itself when we have proved a truth or an apparent truth by means of the persuasive arguments suitable to the case in question.

—ARISTOTLE, *Rhetoric,* Book I, Chapter 2

The Need for Persuasion

OUR OWN AGE, PERHAPS MORE THAN PREVIOUS TIMES, has become very strongly persuasion-minded. In part this is because we live in a time when industrialization has made the production of goods relatively easy, thus placing increased emphasis upon the persuasive art of salesmanship to stimulate consumption. In part, we are persuasion-minded because propaganda has been added to war (and may even be in process of replacing war) as a principal means of competition among rival nations. Whatever the full reasons may be, the tendency is for people to seek means of solving problems in human relationships by persuasion rather than by force. This is true in the schoolroom—where the "motivated assignment" has been replacing the teacher's switch; in our system of handling criminals—whereby we now seek to rehabilitate rather than merely to punish; in labor-management relations—where mediation is often successful; in family life—where the former iron discipline exercised by the father has given way to consideration of the needs and opinions of both parents and children.

Why study persuasion?

Thomas Mann, the great German novelist, has written that "Speech is civilization," by which he apparently meant that discussion and persuasion are the only civilized ways by which to settle differences. History is a long, intermittent, often discouraging, slow progression

3

from brute force to the evolution of more and more ways in which disputes may be settled through discussion.

Nor is the value of persuasiveness limited to national and international situations. No one of us goes through a single day without real need for the ability to speak persuasively. Favors are to be sought, mistakes are to be excused, help is to be solicited, opinions are to be changed—thus the flow of persuasive situations continues. No one escapes the need for persuasiveness; those who do not have it pay a continuing price.

Just how valuable to the ordinary individual is skill in persuasive speech? The answer begins to become apparent to the infant in his cradle. He is constantly trying to persuade his mother to minister to his immediate desires, while she seeks to subordinate them to considerations of his eventual welfare. On through the growing complexity of childhood wants, of adolescent problems, and of adult responsibilities, the individual is seldom free from desires, needs, and opinions which clash either with objective reality or with the desires, needs, and opinions of other individuals or groups. The chief need for persuasive skill is to enable one to conclude a fair proportion of these clashes in his own favor.

The constant demands for persuasive skill may be illustrated by a glance into a typical day of Mr. Smith, a mythical representative businessman. While dressing in the morning he wonders how he can divert his wife from the conviction that a bowl of hot cereal is a daily necessity for healthy living. While eating the cereal (for his wife is the better persuader!) he listens to his teen-age son's reasons for wanting a car of his own, and puts off the decision until later. On the train he silently marshals his own arguments while Jones pours forth a flood of eloquence in support of the "wrong" political party. At the office he discovers that the feud which has been long developing between his two best salesmen has broken out into open quarreling and must somehow be mediated. A letter on his desk threatens a damage suit over an automobile accident in which Smith is convinced the blame actually lay on the driver of the other car. The telephone rings and Smith is informed that the Zhorst Company will buy its supplies elsewhere unless certain price concessions are forthcoming. A life insurance salesman and a wholesaler's agent are waiting to see him. Sometime during the day he will have to get in touch with the income tax collector to try to justify the $500 deduction which has been challenged. The sales manager wants his opinion on the merits of a proposed advertising campaign. As a deacon of his church he must attend a committee meeting to consider means of increasing Sunday attendance. The Grand Master of his lodge calls to appoint him chairman of a committee to raise funds for the repair of the Cozy Camp Orphanage. If someone should invite Mr. Smith to consider the principles of persuasive speech, he would be too busily in need of them to have time to study them!

Quite aside from the consideration of possible vocational and social advantages, everyone is entitled to the satisfaction of at least occasionally ending an amiable controversy with the warm glow of success in having won acceptance for his belief. This satisfaction is not too much to hope for. But if it is to be attained, it must also be worked for; and most of us have a long way to go in mastering persuasive skills.

Persuasive ineptitude

Our persuasive ineptitude is often startling. Widely as persuasion is practiced, and strong as are the incentives to use it well, the evidence is overwhelming that in this fundamental aspect of human relationships there is a vast amount of psychological illiteracy.

For example, it is not uncommon for a college student to say, "The reason I cut your class, Professor, was that I had to study for a test in another course." Does he expect special consideration for an absence that he flatly declares was caused by his giving precedence to another obligation? In an argument one may often hear, "Can't you understand what I'm getting at?" Does not this attack upon the intelligence of the auditor practically force him to strengthen his opposition to the proposal? The complaint is frequently heard that "the best men are not elected to public office." Why not? Do they lack the skill in appealing to voters which is possessed by less worthy but more successful candidates? "If you had read more widely on the subject," you may find yourself saying, "you would see what I mean." The auditor is forced to sharpen his disagreement now, to save his self-respect.

When we are surrounded by countless examples of such persuasive blunders as these that have been cited, is there any reason to wonder at the need that most people feel for greater understanding of human motives and for increased mastery of persuasive techniques?

Practical value of persuasion

In business and industry, persuasive speaking has been found to have a dollars and cents value. Of course, the role of the salesman has long been recognized. More recently, businesses have experimented with discussion groups within their own companies to try to persuade their employees to meet more effectively their responsibility to the company. After a five-year trial of such persuasive discussions, General Electric Company found the following startling results: (1) its direct labor costs were reduced by one third; (2) waste was cut two thirds; (3) absenteeism was reduced 80 per cent; and (4) accident frequency was cut by 85 per cent. In presenting these results, General Electric concluded: "It is pointless to ask how much of the progress shown has been due to the communications program alone; these results were achieved by dynamic and aggressive leadership, and the communications techniques described here have been the means by which this leadership was made felt throughout the unit."

Driving home the value of persuasiveness in employee-management relations, Arthur W. Pearce, editorial director of *Modern Industry,* wrote in 1951:

When an executive develops a good idea, he's half-way to performing a valuable service to his company and to himself as well. The other half consists of getting the idea into action. The pay-off comes, for both company and individual, when other people understand the idea, accept it, and help put it into effect. This is true whether the executive is a top man, giving leadership to the whole company, or a subordinate making a report and recommendation to the top man. A scholar or a technical expert can often work up good ideas. A good salesman can sell them. *The man at the top, or one heading for the top, should be able to do both, if he's a real leader.*

These are considerations that will motivate your own study of persuasion.

Setting your goal

As you enter into this study of persuasive speaking, it is not new to you, in the sense that trigonometry is new to students just entering that course. You have been using persuasion frequently all your life— and have also been subject to a constant flow of persuasive influences. It is probably right to assume that you have commenced the study of persuasion because you are fully aware of its importance and desire to deepen your understanding of its nature and to sharpen your skill in employing its techniques. Happily, no human being can ever become perfectly persuasive; for this would be a power far too great for anyone to be trusted with. Nevertheless, you may indeed expect to increase markedly your own persuasive effectiveness, as you study the factors of motivation and the means of utilizing them. Above all, you will be entering into a study of the realities of human nature—a study that should enable you to know better both yourself and your fellows. And therein is the chief reward you should find from your labors.

What persuasion is

In a broad sense, persuasion is any form of discourse that influences thought, feelings, or conduct. In this sense, all speech is persuasive—for all speech is influential. Even soliloquies influence the speaker himself; and such commonplaces of utterance as "Good morning" and "Isn't it a nice day?" may on occasion be influential. It is surely true that no speech that truly informs listeners can avoid influencing their judgment and hence their future behavior. It is also true that a speech of entertainment influences human conduct—and such a speech might conceivably have far-reaching effects, such as inducing a husband and wife who have been drifting apart to cease their quarreling and to view their differences thereafter in a spirit of greater good humor. For such reasons the generally utilized threefold division of public speeches into those designed to inform, to persuade, and to entertain may be difficult to maintain.

The fundamental basis for distinguishing persuasion from other forms of discourse is the conscious *purpose of the speaker*. If the president of the Interfraternity Council calls a meeting and presents information on the extent of cheating in the University with the deliberate purpose of shaming the students into more honest behavior, he would be said to be making a persuasive speech characterized primarily by its factual content. If he spoke throughout the speech in humorous vein, keeping his audience in recurrent laughter with witty and comic representations of methods of cheating, again with the deliberate intent of so ridiculing the practice that his listeners would be led to renounce it, he would be considered to be making a persuasive speech consisting of humorous devices. Or, he might deliver an avowedly persuasive speech constructed of arguments and moral appeals. The content of the three speeches would vary markedly, but in each instance the speaker would be making a calculated effort to *change the psychological orientation of the listeners*. His purpose in speaking would be to render the audience different—in belief, in attitude, in feeling, or in conduct—as a direct result of his speech. It is only thus (through a determination of the purpose of the speaker) that persuasion may truly be distinguished as a special mode of discourse.

Obviously, this approach to a definition of persuasion provides a better method for a speaker to use in classifying his own speeches as being persuasive or nonpersuasive than it does for an auditor to make a similar judgment—for it is notoriously difficult to be sure of someone else's intent. This will become evident if a group of individuals should try to classify any ten speeches (as printed, for example, in *Vital Speeches*) as being persuasive or informative. It may be suspected that oftentimes a speaker is not really absolutely certain in his own mind whether he is seeking merely to inform, or to effect a change of judgment in his listeners by the kinds of information he presents. What can properly be recommended is that whenever you prepare a speech you should give most careful attention to precisely what you do wish to achieve by it. This process is most successful if you make an invariable practice of writing down your purpose in a single clear statement—and then use this statement of purpose thereafter as the severe standard for determining what you shall say and how you shall say it.

Actually, persuasion takes many forms and is of many degrees. The meaning of persuasion will be clearer if it is understood that persuasive speeches are those that aim at the following goals, singly or in combination:

1. To create favorable interest in a cause or in a speaker. This is a "preparation" stage through which every new movement and aspiring leader must go.

2. To win a following for a speaker, as in an election campaign.

3. To win active support for a cause, such as world federation.

4. To dissipate or lessen hostility to a cause or to a speaker, as in a political speech to members of a rival party.

5. To secure immediate action from an audience, as in an appeal for funds, or for support in a vote about to be taken.

6. To secure acceptance of a speaker's belief, point of view, or opinion, as in a speech supporting the principle of free trade.

Persuasion versus *argument*

As we have seen, persuasion is that form of discourse which attempts to influence human conduct, belief, or feelings. Another related (but much more restricted) form of discourse is *argument*. The chief distinction between persuasion and argument is one of method. Both seek to achieve influence; but persuasion utilizes (in Aristotle's phrase) "all available means"—whereas argument is "reasoned discourse," which attempts through facts and logic to influence the mind, the judgment, the reasoning faculties. Thus, the first clear distinction between them is that argument makes its appeal to the thinking abilities of the listeners; while persuasion appeals through facts, logic, emotions, and rationalization.

Another significant difference is that argument typically (though not necessarily) starts with a definite and clear statement of what the speaker wishes to achieve; whereas persuasion often (though not invariably) seeks to lead the reactions of the audience in a favorable direction before revealing the speaker's goal. Many examples of this difference are found in our everyday experience.

For instance, one type of argumentative discourse is the *debate,* in which the affirmative and negative sides are definitely established in relation to a stated proposition, such as, "Resolved, that: the voting age should be reduced to eighteen." Another example is found in the law courts, where one lawyer prosecutes a charge against a defendant, while another lawyer defends him. On the other hand, a typical persuasive situation arises when a son wishes to influence his father to permit and assist him to study law, or when a daughter seeks permission to stay out late for a date. In such situations, the son or daughter may typically "lead up to" the "proposition" by carefully laying a groundwork of appeals before informing the father of the purpose of the discussion. In persuasion, "bluntness" is often a handicap.

A third difference in method is that argument (despite its appeal to logic) often becomes "heated"; whereas persuasion (despite its emotional overtones) typically is noncontroversial. Since the "arguers" know from the first that they are in direct opposition, they tend to use their arguments as weapons with which to batter one another into submission. Persuasive speakers, on the contrary, use their appeals as "baits," or "lures," or as inducements in an attempt to win a willing and unforced acceptance. When we describe one individual as "argumentative" we generally mean he is combative in social talk; and when we speak of another as "persuasive," we mean it is difficult to find reasons for wanting to disagree with him.

Both argumentation and persuasion have decided values as educational devices for the speaker. Training in argumentative discourse is valuable in learning how to analyze subject matter, evaluate evidence, organize logical reasons, balance advantages against disadvantages. If you are trying to decide whether to buy or rent a home, training in argumentation will help you to get to the heart of the problem and to balance the pertinent evidence on each side. On the other hand, training in persuasion assists you in evaluating problems in terms of the probable reactions of other persons who may be involved. If you are trying to decide whether you should rent rather than buy, your work in persuasion should enable you to understand better the probable factors that will be present in the mind of your fiancée or wife. Argument is largely subject-centered; persuasion, audience-centered. Each has its own values, just as each has its own limitations.

If argument is in many respects like war, persuasion is more akin to commerce—which the economists define as an exchange of goods, services, or tokens of wealth in which both parties to the transaction are the gainers. So it is when one man pays $20,000 for a house; both buyer and seller get what they most desire and each considers himself a winner. Precisely so it is in a persuasive discourse: son gets the use of the family car, and father gets a renewed pleasure in the fine relationship established between himself and his boy. Or the politician gets the votes and the voters get the satisfaction of seeing the man of their choice supported. Or the Community Chest gets the donations, and the donors get the warm reward of a sense of community approval. Or the group of citizens gains an enlarged understanding of America's Asian policies, while the speaker has the gratification of winning new converts to his own position on the subject.

Persuasion aims not at applause for the display of logical and verbal versatility, but for the less scintillating but solider satisfaction of actually changing the attitudes, opinions, feelings, or conduct of those who are addressed. An argument frequently is between two or several contestants, each trying to influence an audience but seldom trying to convert one another. Persuasion consists of an honest endeavor to influence the thinking of the one or several to whom the remarks are addressed. Argument is a piling up of reasons buttressed by facts. The methods of persuasion vary greatly, including "all available means." The argumentative individual, far from being well on the road to success as a persuasive speaker, probably is in greatest need of having his own personality and speech methods changed, before he can expect to achieve much persuasive success. The two modes of discourse should never be confused.

Persuasion operates in two directions

In studying persuasive speech, the tendency is to center attention upon means of becoming a more persuasive speaker. It is evident, however, that this approach satisfies only a portion of our persuasive needs. For the persuasive influences through which society exists surround us on every side. We are *recipients* of persuasion to a far greater degree than we are persuasive agents. The study of persuasive methods and factors will serve us not only as we attempt to express our own influence, but also as we analyze and judge the persuasive appeals with which we are daily deluged.

As we walk down the streets we pass window displays of goods artfully arranged to arouse a desire to buy them. Billboards and posters catch our attention with appeals to our opinions, votes, and pocketbooks. In the casual interplay of conversation are suggestions, appeals, arguments, and facts that may alter our program for the day or our plans for the future. The speeches we hear, the books we read, the newspapers we scan, the movies we see, the radio and television programs we tune in are but a few examples of the flow of persuasion to which we are continually subjected. In no other age in human history has so much time, money, and skill been expended in the effort to influence belief and conduct. An education is sadly ineffective which does not fit us to analyze and judge the nature of the appeals surrounding us. We need to understand what persuasion is and how it occurs for defense as well as for offense: as a means of self-protection, as well as a means of exerting our own influence.

When we consider that democracy is actually a way of life in which persuasive speech has come to be accepted as a substitute for force, it is evident that every member of society should become as skilled in persuasion as his abilities permit. We require persuasive insights both to win votes and to decide among the appeals made to us by different candidates and political parties; both to buy wisely and to sell effectively; both to choose our own associates and form our own loyalties, and to win others to causes and convictions which we believe to be sound. The study of persuasion, then, should fit us to analyze and weigh the persuasion exerted upon us, as well as to improve our ability to win support for our own aims and ideas.

A source of persuasive effectiveness

Since persuasion is so intimately interwoven into the very fabric of human society, it is obvious that it cannot be interpreted as merely a system of techniques. Properly considered, persuasion is more than a system: it is a way of life. The truly persuasive individuals are those who represent in their own characters and personalities the best traits of the society in which they live. They both represent and transcend the accepted characteristics of their group. The best persuasive speakers are those who represent in their own persons both what their auditors *are* and what they *desire to become*. The views of such speakers tend to prevail to the extent that they synthesize and express in themselves the attributes which their auditors, more or less consciously, are striving to acquire.

For three thousand years students of speech have insisted that a persuasive speaker must first of all be a *good man*. "The man who can really play his part as a citizen and is capable of meeting the demands both of public and private business, the man who can guide a state by his counsels, give it a firm basis by his legislation and purge its vices by his decisions as a judge," such a man, wrote Quintilian about A.D. 90, "is assuredly no other than the orator of our quest." This is far indeed from the shallow point of view sometimes encountered that mastery of persuasion depends upon skillful utilization of a bagful of special tricks. He who would master the art of persuasive speech must first of all master himself. For his influence will depend upon all that he is, in word, in thought, and in deed.

The concept of the "good man" as a persuasive speaker needs to be considered in a social as well as in a moral sense. The speaker who is effective with a particular group is the one who truly represents the values and attitudes of that group. "Set a thief to catch a thief." All parents learn how deeply their children are affected by the standards and reactions of their playmates. Fraternity members, labor union members, professional soldiers, Ku Klux Klansmen, farmers, lawyers, Italian-Americans—any definitive group you can imagine will most likely be more easily influenced by one of its own kind than by an outsider. The "good man," then, is in part one who exemplifies in himself the qualities admired by the group to which he belongs.

In many popular ways this requirement of "belonging" is stressed. When we grant the accolade of the treasured phrase, "a regular fellow," to one of our associates, we mean that he really is one of us— a being whom we admire and like because he possesses the qualities we either have or wish we had. "Birds of a feather flock together" is a proverb conveying much the same point of view. Group loyalty and group solidarity are more than high virtues—they are deeply significant persuasive factors. The deep strength of Abraham Lincoln's power over his own and succeeding generations lay in the fact that he was "a man of the people." But he remains one of history's great orators because his basic "goodness" made him also a "man of the ages." In his great speeches, in his movingly simple and honest letters, and in his person he expressed the ideals toward which as a nation we are inclined. Far more than any special system of persuasive techniques, this quality of both exemplifying and transcending the group is the fundamental source of persuasive power.

Necessity of mastering skills

What has been said may seem to imply that any study of speech skills may be not only unnecessary but even actually harmful. "Just be a good fellow, be one of the group, go along with the crowd," may be one interpretation of the foregoing section. Little reflection is needed, however, to reveal the falsity of any such conclusion. The truly persuasive speaker, according to a long tradition in rhetoric, is "a good man trained in the arts of speech." Every group—including the various ones you belong to—contains many members who meekly and ineffectively "go along with the crowd." They accept the characteristics of the group much as a blotting paper soaks up ink. They vote with the majority, obey the leadership, and never raise their voices to say "Nay." They may appear to represent what the group stands for, but in reality they do so largely on a passive plane. Far from both representing and *transcending* the group, they are over-awed and dominated by it. Even in faithfully obeying the dictates of the group, they are far from exemplifying what the members most admire. Every group seeks within itself the elements of growth and leadership. The really "representative" political figure is not the meek party hack but the outspoken leader who phrases and fights for the program around which the party is organized. In every segment of society the ability to express what the other members only partially comprehend and feel is the attribute most admired. It is this that Robespierre meant when he said, "He who can phrase it can lead it."

The advertising expert is one who makes a profession of studying what people want and how they feel, so that he can phrase their wants for them. "Reach for a Lucky instead of a sweet" was effective because it built on the current dread of getting fat. Leadership has sometimes been defined as understanding how the group feels and what it wants just a little bit before the group does itself. This type of social insight is not something that every Tom, Dick, or Harry automatically possesses. It does not come simply from a willing sub-mersion of oneself in the standards of the crowd. It depends, rather, upon a sensitively sympathetic personality, assisted by training in analysis. The truly persuasive speaker, in these terms, is a "good man" who has been trained "in the arts of speech."

Synthesis of insight and skill

In all kinds of persuasion, then, the fundamental approach must be found in the essential nature of the people to whom the persuasion is addressed. Whether in advertising, in public speaking, in parental relations with children, or in any other type of persuasive problem, effectiveness is achieved directly in terms of the ability to perceive and formulate what are often the unspoken and sometimes even the unsensed desires and needs of those who are being addressed. In any analysis of persuasion, it is certain to be found that the funda-mental source of persuasive influence is the identity of the persuader with the inmost and deepest characteristics of the individuals and groups which he influences.

It should not be concluded, however, that the persuader is an opportunist who cannily watches social trends and tries to be among the first to express them. Such a habit of mind is most likely to lead to a superficial shiftiness that arouses only distrust and dislike. He who is willing to be a weather vane cannot hope to be able to shift ahead of the wind.

Quite on the contrary, the truly persuasive individual is one who is honestly and deeply attached to the underlying ideals of his social *milieu*. He values them so deeply and understands them so truly that they come alive in his mind and feelings, and there grow and develop. Such an individual will be in the forefront of the deep movements of social change, neither lagging behind nor going off on unrelated tangents. Being truly a part of his group, he grows out of it, rather than straying away from it. With insight drawn from his sympathetic relationship with the group, he can guide it onward along the path of its best potential development more rapidly than it otherwise would go. Like a doctor diagnosing a patient's state of health, the effective persuader diagnoses the emotional and mental health of the people, and speaks to them on the basis of their own perhaps dimly realized convictions.

As one remarkably successful automobile salesman explained, "I always talk to a prospect with a sympathetic understanding of the fact that he already very much wants to possess a new car. My function is to help him to become consciously aware of that fact, and to show him how to realize his own desires." This is a far different approach from that which the tyro might use, of trying through argument or appeal to beat down opposition and force acceptance of the salesman's product. The individual who uses argument as though it were a club to beat down opposition may balance many failures with occasional success. But it is not persuasion in which he engages; it is aggression. The nature of persuasion is to lead, not to drive. The closer we stay to that fundamental concept, the more effective our persuasion will be.

Conclusion

It should now be evident that in order to improve your ability as a persuasive speaker, you will be studying not only techniques of speaking but also the fundamentals of human nature and of social organization. Such a study will not be easy and must not be allowed to be superficial. *First of all,* you will be required to become increasingly effective in your power of analysis: of your own purpose and goals, of the needs, desires, and characteristics of those you seek to influence, and of the factual, emotional, and logical elements of the subject matter you choose to discuss. *Secondly,* you will be learning more about the means of presenting your ideas in a manner that will "invite" rather than "force" acceptance; you will practice speech that is disarming and appealing, rather than argumentative and combative. *Thirdly,* you will be expected to attain increased objectivity of thinking—the rare and precious ability to see, sense, and feel from the other fellow's point of view. And, *finally,* you will be helped to utilize these insights in various forms of public address, subject to the difficult limitations of time and the demands of the occasion, and still further handicapped by the fact that most of the audiences to be addressed cannot be fully analyzed or perfectly understood. Your mastery of persuasion will certainly never become complete, but by systematic endeavor it should surely be steadily improved. And to sustain your spirits through the difficulties of studying the art of persuasion, you can be assured that few if any other skills you may ever attain will offer you as great a reward as the ability to be persuasively effective. It is an attribute worthy of your utmost endeavors.

Exercises

1. Make a list of at least ten ways in which you are subjected to persuasion in a typical week. From what sources does the persuasion come? How do you tend to react to it? To what extent does persuasion shape your activities, determine your beliefs, and influence your feelings? What kinds of persuasion do you resist and resent? What kinds do you welcome as: (1) bringing you new ideas and impulses; or (2) aiding you in making difficult decisions?

2. Make another list of typical ways in which you attempt to exercise persuasion in a typical week. What motives impel you to each of these persuasive efforts? What methods of persuasion do you use? In general, how do you rate your own persuasive effectiveness in terms of the influence exerted upon your associates?

3. Describe an instance in which you wished very much to achieve a persuasive result but failed. Indicate the goal you sought to achieve, and the barriers that prevented success. So far as possible, describe a strategy different from the one you used which might have had a better effect.

4. Think of two individuals whom you know personally, one of whom you regard as being effectively persuasive, the other as persuasively ineffective. Analyze differences in the personalities of the two individuals. To what extent is each one representative of the basic characteristics of his own social group? What skills does the former possess which the latter lacks?

5. Discuss the dual characteristics of "representing and transcending" the group, as illustrated in the personalities of various national or local leaders.

6. Prepare and deliver a speech of from three to five minutes on one of the following topics:
  a. A persuasive (or unpersuasive) person of my acquaintance.
  b. One of my significant successful (or unsuccessful) persuasive efforts.
  c. The values (or evils) of persuasion in contemporary life.
  d. Characteristics that make a person liked and respected.
  e. Characteristics that create dislike and distrust.
  f. An incident where force might better have been replaced by persuasion.

7. For students who wish to broaden their understanding of the nature of persuasion and its influence in society, the following readings are recommended:

David K. Berlo and H. E. Gulley, "Some Determinants of the Effect of Oral Communication in Producing Attitude Change and Learning," *Speech Monographs,* XXIV (March, 1957), 10-20.
Eric Berne, *Games People Play: The Psychology of Human Relationships* (New York: Simon and Schuster, 1965).
Kenneth E. Boulding, *The Image* (Ann Arbor: University of Michigan Press, 1961).
J. A. C. Brown, *Techniques of Persuasion from Propaganda to Brain-washing* (Baltimore: Penguin Books, 1964).

Roger Brown, *Social Psychology* (New York: The Free Press, 1965), particularly Chapters 2 and 7.

————, *Words and Things* (Glencoe: The Free Press, 1958).

Arthur R. Cohen, *Attitude Change and Social Influence* (New York: Basic Books, 1964).

Gary Lynn Cronkhite, "Toward a Real Test of Dissonance Theory," *Quarterly Journal of Speech,* 52 (April, 1966), 172-178.

W. R. Dresser, "Effects of 'Satisfactory' and 'Unsatisfactory' Evidence in a Speech of Advocacy," *Speech Monographs,* XXX (August, 1963), 302-306.

Hugh D. Duncan, *Communication and Social Order* (New York, Bedminster Press, 1962), particularly Chapters 16, 17, 20, and 31.

L. Festinger, *A Theory of Cognitive Dissonance* (Evanston: Row, Peterson, 1957).

Wallace C. Fotheringham, *Perspectives on Persuasion* (Boston: Allyn and Bacon, 1966).

S. I. Hayakawa (ed.), *Our Language and Our World* (New York: Harper, 1959).

Carl I. Hovland, Irving L. Janis, and Harold H. Kelley, *Communication and Persuasion: Psychological Studies of Opinion Change* (New Haven: Yale University Press, 1953).

Robert B. Huber, *Influencing through Argument* (New York: David McKay, 1963).

Abraham Kaplan, *The Conduct of Inquiry: Methodology for Behavioral Science* (San Francisco: Chandler, 1964).

Herbert C. Kelman, "Processes of Opinion Change," *Public Opinion Quarterly,* XXV (Spring, 1961), 57-79.

R. D. Luce and H. Raiffa, *Games and Decisions* (New York: Wiley, 1957).

Milton Rokeach, *The Open and Closed Mind: Investigations into the Nature of Belief Systems and Personality Systems* (New York: Basic Books, 1960).

Jurgen Ruesch, *Therapeutic Communication* (New York: Norton, 1961).

Thomas C. Schelling, *The Strategy of Conflict* (Cambridge: Harvard University Press, 1960).

Hans Sebald, "Limitations of Communication: Mechanisms of Image Maintenance in Form of Selective Perception, Selective Memory and Selective Distortion," *Journal of Communication,* XII (September, 1962), 142-149.

Stephen Toulmin, *The Uses of Argument* (Cambridge: Cambridge University Press, 1958).

ॐ 2.

The Ethics of Persuasion

NO ONE CAN STUDY PERSUASION CONSCIENTIOUSLY without becoming deeply and seriously concerned with its ethics. Is it *moral* for any individual to attempt to change the beliefs, feelings, and conduct of others—unless he is absolutely certain that his view is right and theirs is wrong? And considering the limitations of our imperfect knowledge and the very elusive nature of ultimate truth, what mortal dares to assert such certainty? Philosophically, is persuasion ever justified?

Perhaps the best practical answer to this question has been suggested by Professor W. Norwood Brigance. Considering that people are going to have to make choices, regardless of the philosophical consideration of whether absolute certainty is possible, Brigance sensibly pointed out: "Whether men shall pursue an immediate want or a remote one, whether they shall accept the satisfaction of a high idealistic desire or of a low material one, has always been, and so long as this planet supports human life will continue to be, dependent in part on how vividly and impellingly these alternatives are revealed to them by leaders, thinkers, writers, and speakers."

The ethical indictment

Plato was incensed against the Sophists of ancient Athens, who consciously sought to develop the ability "to make the worse appear the better reason." Shakespeare enshrined in one of his penetrating

The republics that have maintained themselves in a regular and well-modelled government, such as those of Lacedaemon and Crete, held orators in no very great esteem. Aristotle did wisely define Rhetoric to be a science to persuade the people; Socrates and Plato, an art to flatter and deceive. And those who deny it in the general description verify it throughout in their precepts. The Mahometans will not suffer their children to be instructed in it, as being useless; and the Athenians, perceiving of how pernicious consequence the practice of it was, being in their city of universal esteem, ordered the principal part, which is to move affections with their exordiums and perorations, to be taken away. 'Tis an engine invented to manage and govern a disorderly and tumultuous rabble, and that never is made use of but like physic to the sick, in the paroxysms of a discomposed estate. In those republics where the vulgar or the ignorant, or both together, have been all powerful, and able to give the law—as in those of Athens, Rhodes, and Rome—and where the public affairs have been in a continual tempest of commotion, to such places have the orators always repaired.

In short, Montaigne observed that where democracy is the form of government, there will be found agitation, demagogic appeals to mob prejudice, and disruptive public discussion. He did not know, as we do, that democracy is also the form of government that gives opportunities for improvement to the average individual and on occasion produces a Lincoln, a Wilson, a Churchill.

Seeking a balance

It is impossible to dismiss lightly the ethical criticisms of persuasion. What must not be lost sight of is that persuasion is an art, which may be used for either good or evil. Medical skill may be used either to perform abortions or to save life. The ability to write clear political analyses may produce both a Machiavelli and a John Locke. Scientific research may develop hydrogen bombs and bacteriological warfare along with mass production of consumers' goods and penicillin. Surely we must remind ourselves most soberly that persuasion can be and often has been an instrument of evil in some instances as well as of great good in others. But we must not be swept into a tide of condemnation of persuasive skill to the extent that we forget the role of Alexander Hamilton in persuading the New York State Convention

phrases the distaste we all very properly have for "that glib and
art, to speak and purpose not." Thomas Carlyle devoted the very
portant occasion of his inauguration as Lord Rector of Edinbu
University to emphasize what he considered a basic question in hun
relationships: "A dishonest man . . . does nothing but darken coun
by the words he utters. . . . For, if a 'good speaker,' never so eloque.
does not see into the fact, and is not speaking the truth of that, b
the untruth and the mistake of that, is there a more horrid kind
object in creation?" And he was answered in part by one of his note
contemporaries, Thomas Babington Macauley, who observed: "W(
see doctrines, which cannot bear a close inspection, triumph perpetu-
ally in drawing rooms, in debating societies, and even in legislative
or judicial assemblies."

In our own day, Angelo M. Pellegrini, a speech professor at the
University of Washington, sadly concluded that "Public speaking is
ordinarily regarded as an instrument of power over others for the
achievement of personal ends." Sinclair Lewis satirized this common
view when he had his unheroic hero, George Babbitt, exclaim: "It
certainly is a fine thing to be able to orate. I've sometimes thought
that I had a little talent that way myself, and I know darn well that
one reason why a four-flushing old back number like Chann Mott can
get away with it in real estate is just because he can make a good
talk, even when he hasn't got a doggone thing to say." We cannot but
wonder whether this pragmatic observation is not a principal reason
for the widespread interest among adults in taking Speech courses.
Nor can we avoid the conclusion of Professor Carl Dahlstrom that
"Society does not need more individuals who have ways and means
of selling themselves, of taking advantage of the ignorant and the
sentimental, of putting something over on gullible people, of vainly
seeking even a noble end *via* stinkingly corrupt means; but society is
sadly in need of men and women who can become proficient and
known in their professions without loss of personal integrity or sacrifice of self-respect."

Montaigne noted that historically persuasive speaking has always
labored under this ethical indictment. He wrote,

to ratify the Constitution of the United States or the inspiring words of Winston Churchill in rallying the people of England and of the free world to resist the tyranny of Hitler.

The problem of the conflict between honesty and dishonesty is always with us. It is not in any special way involved in persuasive speaking. Shall we lie or shall we tell the truth? Shall we attempt to gain a livelihood by robbing banks, by selling shoddy merchandise, and by pandering to vice; or shall we earn our living by constructive and socially desirable productivity? Shall we indulge in petty tyranny over individuals under our authority, or shall we seek the common good through co-operative endeavor? A list of such questions as these might be indefinitely extended to reach into all aspects of human life and thought. Ethics are of vital concern in all our activities— including persuasive speaking. The ethical problems of persuasion may be isolated only in part from the broader question of morality in general.

Finding an ethical basis

The difference between "right" and "wrong" seems very simple as a generalization, and often very difficult when applied to specific situations. It is wrong to lie; but perhaps it may be right to tell your hostess you had an enjoyable evening, even though you were bored. So often do situations of this kind arise that we have had to invent the "white lie" label to justify frequent "permissible" deviations from the truth. One should tell the truth—but should a lawyer for the defense tell "the whole truth" when he knows something that is detrimental to the cause of his client? Sometimes the answer is clear; sometimes not. It is wrong to violate an agreement; but what if you should discover you have been unfairly tricked into making the agreement in the first place? Most people in our society have been reared to believe they should always do what is right—yet we all know how perplexing it becomes on occasion to determine what the right is.

Part of the problem arises from the disagreement that is evident in our age as to whether standards of ethics are "absolute" or "relative." *Absolute ethics* are eternal and immutable, applying with equal force in all times, to all peoples, under all circumstances. An example is the Ten Commandments. *Relative ethics* are dependent upon the customs and culture of the people concerned; hence they vary widely in different times and different places. For example, American Indians believed it was ethically right to steal horses from their enemies. In our own day there is a strong tendency to defend such behavior as social drinking, divorce, and gambling on the relativistic ground that such conduct is now socially approved.

Absolutist ethics are based on one of two hypotheses: (1) that God ordained certain ethical laws; or (2) that human beings have certain immutable and innate characteristics which make some kinds of action forever right and others forever wrong. Relativistic ethics have developed chiefly from recent theorizing in the social sciences, especially sociology, anthropology, and social psychology. Anthropologists have discovered that all peoples in all ages have had fixed moral codes that have been rigorously enforced, but that these codes differ greatly among different groups. Sociologists are concerned with the impact of social conditions upon individuals; and in the course of their studies they encounter facts which lead them to believe that criminal behavior, for example, may sometimes be a direct result of communal inequalities and injustices. As a result, we live in a time when it is far less fashionable to "blame" wrongdoers of many types than it was a few generations ago. Accordingly, the dividing line between "right" and "wrong" has become less definite.

One notable attempt to re-establish a firm basis for ethical judgments is the formulation of *the principle of social effects*. What is good for society as a whole, in the long run, is ethical (according to this concept); what is detrimental to society is unethical.

This *principle of social effects* readily lends itself for application to persuasive speaking. If one speech on racial segregation arouses increased hatred between the races and hardens the attitudes of intolerance of the listeners, its "social effect" is unethical—regardless of whether the purpose of the speaker was to maintain or to end segregation. On the other hand (and again regardless of the specific purpose of the speech), if another speaker sends his audience from the meeting with a deepened feeling of respect for all people and with renewed determination to work out a just and humane solution, the "social effect" of his speech is ethical.

One interesting development of this principle of social effects is found in Aldous Huxley's *The Devils of Loudun* (1952), in which he says we ought not only to condemn "the mere magic of words and a golden voice" used to persuade an "audience of the rightness of a bad cause," but "We ought to feel the same dismay whenever we find the same irrelevant trick being used to persuade people of the rightness of a good cause." The key phrase here, of course, is *irrelevant trick*. As Huxley adds, "The belief engendered may be desirable, but the grounds for it are intrinsically wrong." Let us not, he pleads, be "guilty of pandering to the least creditable elements of human nature." An audience that is induced to accept shoddy reasoning or falsification of facts to support a right conclusion has, at the same time, suffered the adverse effect of becoming habituated to false pleading. This cannot help making these listeners more vulnerable, on another occasion, to demagoguery exercised in a bad cause. In such manner should we apply the principle of social effects.

The twofold problem in persuasion

For students of persuasion, it is helpful to make a clear-cut distinction in their thinking between *what is effective* and *what is ethical*. If we are to have a science of persuasion, it can be developed only as we keep our attention centered upon the single question: what actually does achieve persuasion? Is it persuasively effective to use emotional appeals, rationalization, and a careful selection of facts which reflect favorably upon the speaker's proposal? This question can be tested by the experimental presentation to matched audiences of such types of speeches; while to other similar audiences are presented speeches advocating the same purpose, but composed solely of relevant facts and pure logic. Whether one type of speaking is more or less ethical than the other is indeed a very important question, but a wholly different one from the question of what actually does result in persuasion.

Some pragmatic rhetoricians, such as Machiavelli, in *The Prince*, and Adolf Hitler, in *Mein Kampf,* have devoted themselves single-mindedly to the question of "what works." We may, and do, condemn them for lack of ethics; but this must not blind us to the desirability of at least determining what is scientifically effective in changing human conduct, and what is not. Atomic physicists, for example, devoted themselves to the single question of how to divide (and afterwards how to fuse) the atom with explosive effect, and the result was the development of the atomic and the hydrogen bombs. This does not mean there is no ethical problem involved in the production of means by which the human race could be utterly destroyed. What it does mean is that the question of *how* to produce the bombs and the question of *whether* they should be produced are separate questions.

Similarly, if you were working in an advertising agency, and were assigned responsibility for developing a series of advertisements that would sell more automobiles of a certain make, you would doubtless be aware of the apparent fact that more cars can be sold through the use of photographs taken at angles which emphasize the length of the car; through photographs which show very little of the car but do high-light an attractive young woman standing beside it; through presentation of television shows which are highly enjoyable but which have no relation to the product of the sponsor. The question you would confront would be: what kind of advertising campaign can we conduct that will sell more of these automobiles? Of course you will be constrained within certain ethical limits by law. You may also be still further constrained by your own standards of what is ethical. But we are face to face with the fact that if you objected to printing a picture which showed only a tiny portion of the car, while standing by it is a most enticingly beautiful girl, you might very well lose your job. Again, this is not to say that the ethical considerations are unimportant, but only to indicate that within the context of our culture strictly ethical factors are often not the only bases for many of our conclusions.

What, then, should be the point of view from which we approach the problem of the ethics of persuasion? Should a textbook in persuasive speaking describe only persuasive methods that are absolutely ethical? If so, by what standard (absolutist or relative) should the selection be made? Should unethical factors in persuasion also be presented? If not, by what means can you be prepared to resist being influenced by them when they are used by others? Should a textbook in persuasion be written solely to present what is known of the *science of persuasion* (how to persuade) or should it concentrate chiefly upon differentiating between methods that are moral and those that are immoral?

In this book the effort is made to present the means of persuasion as fully as our present knowledge of this difficult science permits. Assuredly, the author does not advocate in any instance the use of unethical means of persuasion. The whole educational process (in the home, school, church, and community) has as a central purpose the inculcation of ethical standards. It is hoped that this is the point of view that will govern the reading of all the chapters that follow.

The adaptation dilemma

One principal problem of ethics that is especially germane to the study of persuasive speaking is the question of how to manage the necessity of adaptation to the audience. It is a fundamental principle of public address that a speech should be "audience-centered"; that it should be developed from the point of view of audience interests, needs, and capabilities. Speakers are advised to note that a speech on a given topic will be quite different if delivered to a woman's club from that presented to a high school assembly. The problems of the speaker are how to "adapt" sufficiently to the audience so that he will be effective in influencing it, while, at the same time, remaining true to his own concept of the truth he seeks to present.

A potent warning of the danger in this situation has been given by Glenn Frank, late President of the University of Wisconsin, who was an effective author, editor, educator, and popular speaker. He said,

Many lecturers who began their careers with worthy standards have permitted the acid of applause to eat the value out of their service. One night the lecturer strikes a certain string that vibrates easily; thereafter he finds it difficult to avoid striking that string again and again, not because it gives the note needed, but because there he is assured of ready response from his audience. He discovers that the anecdote gets response more easily than does analysis; straightway he multiplies his anecdotes. He finds that it is easier to storm the emotions than to convince the reason; he sets about adding pathos to his technic. He sees that an epigram galvanizes the attention of an audience; forthwith he peppers his lecture with epigrams, although the average epigram is only half true. The dwindling of his audience would imperil his income. His audience is to him what the tiger is to its trainer; he must become either the master or the victim of its moods. Unconsciously he allows the instinct of self-preservation to dictate his assertions. His mind becomes a weathercock, nervously sensitive to the automatic applause of flattered prejudice.

This warning by Dr. Frank is so detailed and circumstantial that it needs no elaboration. The danger is clear. What should be done about it? Edmund Burke, one of England's greatest thinkers and orators, set forth what he believed to be the right procedure in a speech which he gave to his constituency in Bristol. If, in the following quotation, we substitute "speaker" for "representative," and "audience" for "constituency," we shall have a classic statement of the moral position from which a speaker should approach the problem of audience analysis. Burke said:

Certainly, gentlemen, it ought to be the happiness and glory of a representative to live in the strictest union, the closest correspondence, and the most unreserved communication with his constituents. Their wishes ought to have great weight with him; their opinion high respect; their business unremitted attention. It is his duty to sacrifice his repose, his pleasures, his satisfactions, to theirs; and, above all, ever, and in all cases, to prefer their interest to his own. But his unbiased opinion, his mature judgment, his enlightened conscience, he ought not to sacrifice to you, to any man, or to any set of men living. These he does not derive from your pleasure; no, nor from the law and the constitution. They are a trust from Providence, for the abuse of which he is deeply answerable. Your representative owes you, not his industry only, but his judgment; and he betrays instead of serving you, if he sacrifices it to your opinion.

In his own parliamentary career Burke sought to live up to the standard that he here described; he lost his bid for re-election, but has been acclaimed in history for his high principles. This, too, is a choice speakers must often make: between immediate and long-range effectiveness.

For most speakers, the immediate reaction of their listeners to a speech is of less consequence than the long-range effects. If you should give a speech at your local Rotary Club in which you aroused a storm of applause for your heated denunciation of "graft and favoritism" in the local government, this temporary approval would be of far less significance than the permanent lack of confidence that would result from the gradual discovery by members of your audience that you had been guilty of gross exaggeration and misstatement. Many a time a speaker is well advised (from the standpoint even of his own selfish interests) to "soft pedal" his remarks and not permit himself to be swept away by the "intoxication of his own eloquence," simply because in the fervor of his speech he may be led to go beyond the facts. A good rule to keep in mind is to aim your speech toward the reaction you hope will persist, rather than to seek only for an immediate result. By this rule your adaptation will tend to be to the more solidly reasoned aspects of the thinking of your audience, rather than to their inflammable emotions.

Fundamental ethical standards

Considered philosophically, the problem of ethics in speaking is inescapably difficult. Yet there are some simple moral principles that are readily identifiable and should be easily practiced. For example:

1. *Do not falsify or misrepresent evidence.* Do not misquote an authority, or tear something he has said out of context, so it seems to mean something other than he intended. Do not "invent" a significant element in a specific example you may use—for example, do not tell your audience that the reason a man killed his wife was because he was drunk, if he was not. Be true to the facts as you know them.

2. *Do not speak with assurance on a subject on which you are actually uninformed.* John M. Mecklin, in *An Introduction to Social Ethics,* writes of "the moral obligation of being intelligent," which he calls "moral thoughtfulness." It is, in this view, immoral to condemn

a political regime for dishonesty when you actually know little about it; similarly, it is unethical to try to persuade the audience to approve of a program (such as socialized medicine) unless you have studied it thoroughly enough to be honestly assured you know how to balance its defects against its merits. "Ignorance of the law is no excuse," and ignorance of the facts is not a moral justification for advocating a point of view that is really untenable. In other words, be sure to earn the right to advocate a policy by first of all understanding it.

3. *Do not seek approval from your audience for a policy or a program by linking it in their minds with emotional values (such as patriotism or sympathy for the underprivileged) with which it has no actual connection.* Irrelevancy may often befog the judgment of listeners who have no opportunity to examine your subject fully. But, as an ethical speaker, you have an obligation to talk about the subject —not around it.

4. *Avoid confusing the minds of the audience about the worthiness of a point of view by "smear" attacks upon the leadership associated with it.* All through history the *argumentum ad hominem* has, unhappily, been found to be effective; but this does not mean it is honest. Chauncey Depew, in his autobiography, *My Memories of Eighty Years,* tells of a conversation he had with the great orator, Wendell Phillips, after Phillips had made a vitriolic attack in a speech upon Caleb Cushing. Phillips defended himself as follows: "I have found that people, as a rule, are not interested in principles or in their discussion. They are so absorbed in their personal affairs that they do very little thinking upon matters outside their business or vocation. They embody a principle in some public man in whom they have faith, and so that man stands for a great body of truth or falsehood, and may be exceedingly dangerous because a large following connects the measure with the man, and, therefore, if I can destroy the man who represents a vicious principle, I have destroyed the principle." This same line of reasoning accounts for the bitterness that commonly characterizes political campaigns. Experience teaches that *ad hominem* attacks frequently achieve immediate results—but at the cost of the destruction of many worthy reputations, including, often, the ultimate repu-

tation of the speaker. Sometimes, too (as in Hitler's Germany) the cost may extend to the very destruction of the state.

5. *Do not delude yourself into feeling that the end justifies the means.* Even if you have a most worthy purpose to accomplish, it is dangerous and surely unethical to seek to establish acceptance for it by dishonest means. Should the dishonesty of your methods later become known, it is all too likely that the worthy purpose you advocate may be then condemned. Also, your own later effectiveness will surely be lessened or destroyed.

6. *If you are activated in advocating a proposal by self-interest or by your allegiance to a particular organization, do not conceal that fact and pretend an objectivity you do not possess.* It is far sounder ethically, and in the long run more effective, to tell your audience frankly that "I am hired to oppose socialized medicine by the American Medical Society. Naturally, you should be on guard against the biases that I cannot help having. However, I intend to discuss this subject very factually, and I believe the facts will speak for themselves." Frankness is in itself very disarming and often opens the way toward conviction, especially if the case you support is really sound.

7. *Do not advocate for an audience something in which you yourself do not believe.* One reason was mentioned by Quintilian, when he wrote, "For however we strive to conceal it, insincerity will always betray itself, and there was never in any man so great eloquence as would not begin to stumble and hesitate so soon as his words ran counter to his inmost thought." Similarly, Carl Sandburg relates an instance in which Lincoln said to a prospective client, "You'll have to get some other fellow to win this case for you. I couldn't do it. All the while I'd be talking to that jury I'd be thinking, 'Lincoln, you're a liar,' and I believe I should forget myself and say it out loud." Quintilian and Lincoln were pointing out that insincerity cannot often succeed. But Demosthenes condemned it even when successful. In his famed "Oration on the Crown," he asked: "What greater crime can an orator be charged with than that his opinions and his language are not the same?" It is well to remember that you may fool other people (part of the time) but that you can rarely fool yourself.

The foundation of conviction

Toward the end of 1955, Senator John F. Kennedy published a book entitled *Profiles in Courage,* in which he analyzed the careers of selected public figures who had fought courageously for unpopular causes. His book achieved popularity primarily because so many readers admire courage that will support a minority opinion, despite condemnation. Another Senator, William Edgar Borah, exclaimed to his Idaho constituents, in the campaign of 1912: "God pity the miserable creatures sailing upon that turbulent political sea at Washington without convictions for a compass! I have seen them, and there is nothing more despicable in all the world besides. Men without poise and purpose, without convictions and determination, who do not stand ready to fight for their views regardless of who opposes them upon all these great questions are the miserable instruments by which men of sinister purposes accomplish their design."

Sincerity of conviction is a tremendous asset in persuasion and one that is at once ethical and effective. It is a truism of salesmanship that you cannot sell a product unless you are first sold on it yourself. In all fairness, it should also be pointed out that you can be ever so sincere and still fail to achieve the result you desire. Demosthenes, for example, often cited as the world's greatest orator, lost his oratorical battle to persuade the Greek states to unite in their opposition to Philip. Yet Thomas Carlyle, in *Heroes and Hero Worship,* was doubtless right in his insistence that every man of genuine force in the world must be sincere. The fervor of conviction is not easily counterfeited even once, let alone over an extended period.

As a persuasive speaker, you have your own choice of subjects. You should never yield to any temptation to speak on behalf of a point of view in which you do not believe simply because it will be readily accepted. There is no justification for speaking except to win audience agreement with a policy or program you feel to be important. For example, you may try to persuade your audience to spend more time in studying, even though you may anticipate resistance. The very fact that that point of view is resisted is the chief reason you would wish to advocate it! "Audience adaptation" is never a reason for modifying your viewpoint, only for giving careful consideration of how to achieve it.

Of course, if the audience you address is strongly opposed to your point of view, you may well limit what you hope to achieve in a single speech. For example, if you wish to convert the Young Republican Club to support a Democratic candidate for the presidency, you could scarcely expect to accomplish that purpose in one talk. You might be wise to speak in defense of the principle of nonpartisanship, trying to establish the single point that in selecting a president the quality of the man is more important than his political label. Many persuasive goals require not one speech, but an extensive campaign; this point will be discussed further in Chapter 21. This, however, is a matter of tactics; it never means the abandonment of a fundamental conviction merely because it is unpopular with the audience.

A word of final caution

Undeniably, public speaking is too often marked by exaggeration and half-truths. Exaggeration may occur in the heat of enthusiasm, so that the speaker says more than he really means simply through an earnest desire to be as emphatic as possible. What often happens is that he defeats his own purpose by convincing his audience that his judgment is unbalanced and undependable. Precision of statement and specificity of support are no less important in speaking than in writing. They are necessary both for the self-respect of the speaker and to win the credence of the audience.

Half-truths are inevitable in any discourse (written or spoken) simply because the whole truth is almost always so involved and far-reaching that it cannot be compressed into any unified and coherent discussion. (For example, this chapter on ethics is far from complete and could scarcely be made so. To cover the subject adequately would mean writing a textbook in ethics as well as one in persuasion, and uniting them with hosts of detailed examples.) The speaker must always face the inevitability of selecting significant portions of the total truth about his subject and doing his best to keep his own judgment and that of the audience in balance. However, the ethical danger confronting a speaker is that he may be tempted deliberately to select half-truths about his subject which he feels can be foisted upon an audience which knows far less about the subject than he does himself. The simple fact is that this is a form of lying. It will be avoided by ethical speakers merely because it is immoral. And those who are not deterred by this consideration will find that usually it won't work.

Conclusion

Simple honesty seems not too much to ask of any speaker, yet it often is difficult to achieve. Honesty of motive, however, is always the least we may demand of ourselves and of those to whom we listen. There is no excuse for deliberate deceit, for intentionally misleading an audience. If you always speak out of honest convictions, if you earn the right to your convictions by thorough understanding of the subject of which you speak, and if you present your viewpoints solidly buttressed with facts and expressed with tempered restraint, your persuasive speeches should be ethically sound. And if they are not ethically sound, the price you will have to pay may well include not only the failure of that particular speech but also the lasting loss of respect. The price is far too high for what may appear to be a cheap means of winning a temporary success.

Exercises

1. Read Ralph Waldo Emerson's two essays on "Eloquence." Present to the class a five-minute speech interpreting his views on the ethics of speech.

2. Read "Joe McCarthy, Brief Case Demagogue," by Barnet Baskerville, and "Huey Long: Analysis of a Demagogue," by Ernest G. Bormann, in *Today's Speech,* II (September 1954), 8-20. A class discussion may profitably be conducted on these and other current examples of demagoguery, with the aim of clarifying the unethical aspects of the speaking of demagogues and of pointing out the harmful social effects.

3. What is meant by making a speech "audience-centered"? What ethical problems are, or may be, involved? How can you secure the advantages of adaptation to an audience without stumbling into ethical pitfalls?

4. Discuss the seven "fundamental ethical standards." Do you see any particular problem in using any of them as a guide to your own speech preparation?

5. Why, in the words of Glenn Frank, is the relation of a speaker to an audience like that of a circus trainer to a tiger? By what means should a speaker defend himself from being "destroyed" by the audience? When may "success" in speaking be a moral "failure"?

6. Read through (or browse intelligently in) any book on ethics. (Those by Mecklin, Dewey and Tufts, Cabot, and Tsanoff may be recommended.) As a result of this reading, what additional ethical considerations would you propose to the class as having direct relevance to persuasive speaking? Are you personally in favor of "absolute" or "relativistic" ethical standards? What are the advantages and disadvantages of each?

7. Should an individual be willing, if necessary, to be martyred for his beliefs? Would you personally endorse the statement by Socrates that "I would rather speak after my manner and die than after your manner and live"? Is this question of martyrdom for personal convictions a real problem in our contemporary society?

8. Read and evaluate for the class Walter Lippmann's "The World Outside and the Pictures in Our Heads," Chapter I, of *Public Opinion,* (New York: Macmillan, 1922). What are its ethical implications for the persuasive speaker?

9. For depth exploration of the ethics of persuasion, the following readings are recommended:

Kurt Baier, *The Moral Point of View: A Rational Basis of Ethics* (Ithaca: Cornell University Press, 1958).

B. J. Diggs, "Persuasion and Ethics," *Quarterly Journal of Speech,* 50 (December, 1964), 359-373.

Douglas Ehninger, "The Debate about Debating," *Quarterly Journal of Speech,* 44 (April, 1958), 128-136.

R. T. Eubanks and V. L. Baker, "Toward an Axiology of Rhetoric," *Quarterly Journal of Speech,* 48 (April, 1962), 157-168.

Erich Fromm, *Man for Himself: An Inquiry into the Psychology of Ethics* (New York: Rinehart, 1947).

———, *The Art of Loving* (New York: Harper Colophon Books, 1962).

J. N. Garver, "On the Rationality of Persuading," *Mind,* 69 N. S., No. 274 (April, 1960), 163-174.

Franklin S. Haiman, "A Re-examination of the Ethics of Persuasion," *Central States Speech Journal,* III (March, 1952), 4-9.

———, *Freedom of Speech: Issues and Cases* (New York: Random House, 1965).

John Harding, Bernard Kutner, Harold Proshansky, and Isidor Chein, "Prejudice and Ethnic Relations," in Gardner Lindzey (ed.), *Handbook of Social Psychology,* II Vols. (Cambridge: Addison-Wesley, 1954), II: 1021-1061.

Walter Kaufmann, "Truth, Language, and Experience," in *Critique of Religion and Philosophy* (New York: Doubleday Anchor Books, 1961), pp. 62-99.

E. MacRae, "A Test of Piaget's Theories of Moral Development," *Journal of Social and Abnormal Psychology,* 49 (1954), 14-18.

William Lee Miller, "The Debating Career of Richard M. Nixon," *The Reporter,* XIV (April, 1956), 11-17.

Richard Murphy, "The Ethics of Debating Both Sides," *Speech Teacher,* VI (January, 1957), 1-9.

Thomas R. Nilsen, "Free Speech, Persuasion, and the Democratic Process," *Quarterly Journal of Speech,* 44 (October, 1958), 235-243.

————, *The Ethics of Speech Communication* (Indianapolis: Bobbs-Merrill, 1966).

Robert T. Oliver, "Ethics and Efficiency in Persuasion," *Southern Speech Journal,* XXVI (Fall, 1960), 10-15.

Robert T. Oliver and Dominick A. Barbara, *The Healthy Mind in Communion and Communication* (Springfield, Ill.: Charles C Thomas, 1962).

Vance Packard, *The Hidden Persuaders* (New York: David McKay, 1957).

Paul E. Pfuetse, *Self, Society, Existence* (New York: Harper Torchbooks, 1961).

Melvin Rader, *Ethics and the Human Community* (New York: Holt, Rinehart and Winston, 1964).

Jurgen Ruesch, *Disturbed Communication* (New York: Norton, 1957).

F. Redl and D. Wineman, *Controls from Within: Techniques for the Treatment of the Aggressive Child* (New York: The Free Press, 1954).

Edward A. Shils, "Social Inquiry and the Autonomy of the Individual," in Daniel Lerner (ed.), *The Human Meaning of the Social Sciences* (New York: Meridian Books, 1959, pp. 114-157).

Karl R. Wallace, "An Ethical Basis of Communication," *Speech Teacher,* IV (January, 1955), 1-9.

Harry L. Weinberg, *Levels of Knowing and Existence* (New York: Harper, 1959), particularly Chapters II and V.

✒ 3.

Human Motivation

PERSUASION IS FAR MORE THAN A SET OF TECHNIQUES. No one can learn to be persuasive merely by mastering methods of organization, or by learning a variety of means of developing ideas, though these are modes of presentation that are in their own way indispensable. The foundation for persuasion, however, is the study of human motivation. What is it that makes people tick? This is the necessary preliminary question before a speaker can begin to devise ways of inducing them to tick in harmony with his own proposals. It is to this inquiry that the present chapter is directed.

Need to understand human nature

"To study persuasion intensively," wrote Charles Henry Woolbert, one of the founders of the modern Speech profession, "is to study human nature minutely. Without a guide to men's action probabilities, without appreciating and understanding their action grooves, a speaker or writer works in a vacuum and so has no possible basis for insuring success. . . . More than half of success in winning men is in understanding how they work."

It would be difficult to name a field in which a knowledge of human nature and skill in motivating it would not be a positive asset. Armies, for instance, are noted for their iron discipline, their rules and formulas, their mechanization, and the impersonality that governs the official relations of officers and men. Yet the noted British tactician,

General Sir Archibald Wavell, writing on "The Art of Generalship," declared that these aspects of military science are merely the "skeleton," without the "flesh and blood."

To learn that Napoleon won the campaign of 1796 by manœuvre on interior lines or some such phrase is of little value. If you can discover how a young unknown man inspired a ragged, mutinous, half-starved army and made it fight, how he gave it the energy and momentum to march and fight as it did, how he dominated and controlled generals older and more experienced than himself, then you will have learned something. Napoleon did not gain the position he did by so much a study of rules and strategy as by a profound knowledge of human nature in war. A story of him in early days shows his knowledge of psychology. When an artillery officer at the siege of Toulon he built a battery in such an exposed position that he was told he would never find men to hold it. He put up a placard, "The Battery of Men Without Fear," and it was always manned.

Whether it be drilling an army or coaching football, organizing a Community Chest campaign or selling shirts, teaching algebra or directing traffic, the most successful practitioners are the ones who best understand the "action grooves" of the people with whom they deal. The most persuasive speakers in any field are the experts in human nature. Regardless of how much other knowledge may be demanded of them, their real field of specialization is human motivation.

In essence, the science of persuasion must be the science of motivation. When the aim is to direct the reactions of audiences, the first and basic inquiry must be directed to their stimulus possibilities. We must seek to understand *why* men act, *what* stimuli are effective, and *how* they may be utilized in a persuasive speaking situation.

Basic patterns of motivation

The simplest motivational pattern found among living organisms is an automatic stimulus-response relationship. When you touch a worm with a straw, the worm tends to curl up; when a dog touches a very hot object, he withdraws his paw. As forms of life increase in complexity, the stimulus-response pattern becomes less automatic, less predictable, and increasingly complex.

Levels of response. The simplest kind of stimulus-response pattern is the tropism, which takes its name from the Greek *trope,* "a turning." A tropism consists of an involuntary adjustment of a simple organism in a direction that will provide for its maximum well-being. A fine example of tropism is seen in a cellar in which a pile of potatoes sends out thin white tendrils many feet long toward a tiny patch of sunlight.

A more complex reaction pattern is the *reflex,* which requires the stimulation of a receptor, the flow of a nerve impulse to the spinal cord, and the resultant action of an effector muscle or gland. A typical reflex action is the blink of an eye when it is disturbed.

A third level in the chain of increasingly complex response patterns is the *synergy,* or a combination of reactions which may be set off by a reflex, as in sneezing, coughing, or involuntary laughing.

A fourth level of response consists of the *semiautomatic activities* of the body, such as breathing and the formation of specific speech sounds. These reactions are voluntary, but generally are not consciously directed.

On the fifth level are the *habits,* which are voluntary in their inception but become semiautomatic, and are often so compelling that they resist the strongest efforts of the mind to control them. Smoking and drinking are habits of great strength; weaker but still important response patterns are such habits as regular brushing of teeth, reading, attending movies, scratching one's head, and many other acquired habitual actions.

The sixth step brings us to the level of *cortical control,* including all the deliberate activities of an individual, voluntarily and consciously directed. It should not be assumed, however, that these reactions are purely intellectual. They are complicated and confused by the presence of innumerable stimuli and response possibilities, which are prone to supplement, or be substituted for, the original, primary, adequate connection.

Varieties of primary stimuli. Among the several kinds of primary stimuli, we look first for the *immediate, external stimulus*—such as a loud noise, a bright light, a taste, an odor—which gives rise to a reaction. From the moment the infant is born into what William James called the "blooming, buzzing world of confusion," he is surrounded continually by hundreds of such external stimuli, impinging upon some one or several of his five major sensory receptors. But these are not the only stimuli operating upon the individual.

Through the operation of *associative memory* he is subjected to the influence of former stimuli, such as the pleasant recall of a beautiful scene, a successful experience, or a friendly smile—or the more unpleasant memories of real or fancied indignities, deprivations, humiliations, or accidents. These are the stimuli which "give us pause" and frequently intervene to prevent a direct reaction. "A child once burned dreads the fire." "We learn by experience." "I'll never do that again!" In such expressions we dramatize the effect of former stimuli upon our present actions.

Furthermore, every individual is subjected to the influence of constant metabolic changes caused by *internal bodily processes,* such as the digestion of food or the ache of a bruised muscle. We are all acutely aware of what a difference in our reaction to any situation may be caused by a headache, hunger, or a cold in the head.

Finally, the direct stimuli operating upon an individual include the *normal resolutions of one physiological state into another.* Thus there is a tendency to feel sleepy after eating, or tired after strenuous exercise. To interfere with this normal succession of bodily states is to court trouble. Indigestion and drowsiness are foes hard for any persuasive speaker to combat, whether he finds them in himself or in his audience.

Some of these four types of stimuli might be single and relatively simple; others, such as the recollection of former experiences, are invariably multiform and complex. It is safe to say that in the combination of all four types of stimuli there is set up a body of influences operating upon any given decision in such a fashion that the ultimate action is invariably the result of *some,* and usually the result of *many* considerations wholly irrelevant to the problem itself. This fact is of vast significance to the persuasive speaker.

Conditioned responses. To complicate further the problem of the persuasive speaker, it is essential to note that we are subjected not only to these various types of primary stimuli, but also to conditioned stimuli, or, to adopt the customary phraseology, we have all developed a great many conditioned responses. Pavlov, the Russian scientist who contributed most largely to our knowledge of this field, experimented with dogs to show that the salivary flow indicating hunger could be induced by the sight of food (a primary stimulus); then by the sight of food and the concurrent ringing of a bell (a combination of a primary stimulus with a wholly irrelevant stimulus); and finally by the ringing of the bell alone (a conditioned stimulus).

In our everyday experience we are conscious of a great variety of conditioned responses. We feel very differently toward a Gideon Bible in a hotel room than we do toward the family Bible which has come down to us through several generations. We may have a wholly irrational dislike for a new acquaintance who bears a name to which we have been adversely "conditioned." A point of view which we might otherwise readily accept may be rejected because it is expressed by an individual whom we do not like. Some persons are "conditioned" to accept and others to reject whatever sentiments might come from the pulpit of a given church. A great many of our responses are thus wholly or partially "conditioned," with or without our knowledge, and with sometimes surprising effects upon our tastes, judgments, attitudes, and prejudices.

To the original difficulty, then, of comprehending—to say nothing of controlling—the tangled skein of primary stimuli, there is added for the persuasive speaker this further barrier to success: a stimulus to which one auditor will give a primary response will arouse in another a wholly irrelevant, frequently unpredictable conditioned response.

Stimulus-meaning-response

The fact to note especially is that among human beings the associational centers of the cortex intervene between most stimuli and their responses, and (for a wide variety of reasons, some of which may be identifiable in a situation and some not) cause a wide variation in the nature of the response. Fundamentally, what happens is that the external stimulus is taken into the brain as a *symbol*—and it is to that symbol, rather than to the actual reality of the original stimulus, that we react. This means that we live in a symbolic world, often far removed from the world of actuality. As Walter Lippmann expressed it in *Public Opinion,* "For the most part, we do not first see, and then define, we define first and then see." In other words, we hear a stick snap in the forest; but instead of interpreting this simply as the breaking of a stick, our brain conjures up a picture of a bear or other animal stepping on a stick, and our reaction is one of fear of a bear, rather than simply awareness of sound. Or, in listening to a speech, we hear a word mispronounced, but our brain reminds us that a former teacher warned us that mispronunciation is an indication of low social status. Instead of simply recording in our minds the fact of a variation from the accepted norm of pronunciation, we marshal a complex attitude of critical rejection of the speaker. For us, then, the "meaning" may be of far greater import than the inmmediate "stimulus" in determining the nature of our response.

Sources of stimuli. One further fact should be considered relative to the stimulus situation in a persuasive speech. As may be readily seen from the foregoing comments, the man on the platform delivering the speech is not the sole source of the stimuli that are operating upon the audience. Some of the stimulation they receive comes from what he says and presumably works together into a pattern leading toward the desired response. But other stimuli come from his clothing, appearance, vocal quality, name, the position he holds, his complexion—from a score of sources connected with the speaker, but irrelevant to the message he has to deliver. Also, the audience is stimulated by the nature of the occasion, by the seating arrangement in the hall, by the appearance of the hall itself, by the lighting, by the temperature, by possible distractions from without. Furthermore, every member of the audience is stimulated by the other persons in the audience around him. And finally each auditor is stimulated from within: by the conditioning which he has received to the various stimuli that operate upon him, by his memories and habits, by his internal bodily conditions and processes. The part the speaker plays in "initiating, activating, and directing" his responses may frequently be surprisingly small.

Mental reactions. The variety in the stimuli which operate upon an individual is matched by the variety in the types of mental responses which may be made to any proposition presented for consideration. Six types of mental responses may profitably be distinguished for the consideration of the persuasive speaker.

1. His auditors may feel compelled to accept his proposal, if its validity seems to be overwhelmingly established by previous experience or present observation.

2. His auditors may willingly accept what he says, if there has been nothing in previous experience to cast doubt upon the assertion.

3. His auditors will eagerly accept a contention, if previous experience and present desire both favor it.

or

4. His auditors may receive an argument tentatively and suspiciously, if it is partly supported but partly undermined by portions of their experience and some of their desires.

5. His auditors may refuse to render a judgment on the proposal until they can subject it to further observation, experience, or consideration.

6. Finally, his auditors may find reasons in past experience or present preferences for positively rejecting the persuasive plea.

The aim of the persuasive speaker should always be toward one of the first three of these types of responses, and as far as possible away from the last three.

Conclusions. Out of these considerations of the types of stimuli and their responses operative in the persuasive-speaking situation, two conclusions of importance for the speaker should be emphasized. First, in many instances persuasion is impossible. No one should be surprised or discouraged that failure must accompany many of his best, most skillful persuasive appeals. Second, it is crystal clear that persuasion which depends upon logic alone will generally fail. The total reasons-for-acting pattern of any listener is composed only in part of his respect for logic and fact. His entire galaxy of motives deserves the speaker's most careful study. If it is difficult to secure the desired response from a listener when you are closely attentive to his slightest reactions, then how much smaller is the chance of success when the speaker deliberately turns away from the listener, mentally, to concentrate wholly upon his subject and his own reactions to it.

Attitudes

Stimuli are independent and immediate incitements to action. But each stimulus, in addition to calling forth a direct response, also leaves a greater or lesser lasting influence that helps to shape the subsequent response to a similar situation. Eventually there is established a general reaction pattern called an *attitude*. For instance, the stimulus of the smell of cigar smoke might call forth a response of discomfort. A second similar experience would evoke the same discomfort, enforced by memories of the first time. In successive experiences, this discomfort would be accentuated by an active dislike of cigar smoking, which might be termed an attitude.

The attitude thereafter is in itself a stimulus of a preparatory nature. That is, it prejudges a situation and prepares the body to react in the habitual manner. Thus, to continue the foregoing illustration, once an attitude of dislike for cigar smoking has been established, the mere sight or even the thought of cigar smoke will prepare the individual having this attitude to react strongly against the first whiff of smoke and the smoker.

An attitude may be briefly defined as a pre-established readiness to act in given situations toward a predetermined goal. A large part of a normal individual's thinking and acting is conditioned by his attitudes. In other words, about many aspects of life our minds are made up. This is an inevitable residue of experience.

We have attitudes toward our work, our family, our friends, the community in which we live, different nationalities and races, drinking, education, and many other objects, activities, and situations. By definition an attitude is relatively fixed, and thus it not only helps us to understand present and past actions, but it also provides a reasonably dependable basis for predicting future actions. Much of our social conduct is guided by our knowledge of our friends' attitudes toward religion, politics, dancing, card playing, musical comedy, and the like. We know in a general way what will please and what will offend them. It is evident that a persuasive appeal which fits in with an established attitude is much more likely to succeed than one which opposes it.

Fortunately for the persuasive speaker, persons having like attitudes tend to congregate together. Many organizations exist simply to promote attitudes which have been definitely formulated. Most reform groups, such as the Anti-Saloon League and the Society for the Prevention of War, are of this type. Temporary organizations are continually springing up to foster the expression and spread of attitudes on topics of current controversial interest. In addition to these organized formulations of attitudes, there is a tendency for unorganized but like-minded persons to draw together. Thus one public meeting is apt to have a predominance of liberals in the audience, another of conservatives. The religious and the irreligious are apt to assemble in separate groups when religion is to be discussed. Similarity of attitude seems to have the same power over people that a magnet has over iron filings. "Birds of a feather flock together." Herein is one of the greatest simplifying factors in the problem of persuasive speaking. It is a unifying influence which helps to offset the diverse factors within an audience.

In analyzing the possible effects of an audience's attitudes in terms of the persuasive-speaking situation, there are three considerations that the speaker must keep in mind. The first is the fact that *although attitudes are relatively constant, they sometimes seem to be subject to surprisingly sharp variations.* This may be due to the concurrent existence of two or more opposing attitudes. Thus members of a family or an organization may quarrel violently among themselves, but defend one another against outside attack. An individual may be liberal in one situation and conservative in another; argue sometimes for religion, sometimes against it; speak for the administration in some conversations, against it in others.

If an individual's attitudes always change either to agree with his listeners (the "yes man") or to oppose them (the "born arguer"), there is reason to distrust his intellectual stability if not his integrity.

But changes of expressed attitudes may result not from (*a*) the urge to conform, or (*b*) the urge to argue, but from (*a*) changes in external circumstances, or (*b*) changes within the individual himself. For instance, one's attitude toward prohibition may have been affected by its repeal, or by a personal experience having an embittering, liberalizing, or broadening tendency. A study by L. W. Doob indicated that 25 per cent of possible attitudinal changes on twenty-two different subjects among a group of one hundred seventy-six college students did occur in a period of ten weeks. Sixty-five per cent of the changes in attitude were attributed to changes in external circumstances (such as the communist conquest of China). A variation as large as 25 per cent is certainly a factor to be kept in mind. It indicates at least that it is not an entirely hopeless task to try to change an audience's attitude on a given subject, although the chances for success are small.

A second most important consideration is the fact that *any given attitude varies in intensity under different circumstances*. A person will regard roast beef with much less gusto just after a hearty meal than he does before eating. One's fondness for another individual may vary greatly with time, place, and degree of propinquity. Partisan enthusiasm flames much higher during a campaign than it does between elections. A reformer's zeal may be all-consuming in an evening meeting, but lack the strength to draw him away from his ordinary activities the next day. The attitude of self-confidence rises and falls like the mercury in a thermometer. The wise persuasive speaker will attempt to adjust his plea to these variations in attitude intensity. "There is a tide in the affairs of men," wrote Shakespeare, "which, taken at the flood, leads on to fortune."

A third consideration of significance is the fact that *an attitude which has been expressed becomes an opinion*. Once this has occurred, it will be much more stubbornly clung to than before. For instance, in the study by Doob previously referred to, only 52 per cent of the students whose responses showed a change of attitude would admit that the change was "real." Forty-eight per cent refused to recognize the change which they themselves had recorded. This tendency to cling to an opinion occurs for two reasons: first, because the expression tends to define the attitude more clearly and to bring it into sharper focus in the mind than it was before; and second, because an opinion publicly expressed must be upheld for the sake of one's reputation and self-regard. Much depends, of course, upon the circumstances of the expression of opinion. If it has been stated privately, casually, and tentatively, it is more subject to voluntary change than if it has been stated publicly, deliberately, and dogmatically. The persuasive speaker should make every effort to discourage the expression by his audience of attitudes which oppose his aim, while encouraging the expression of every favorable attitude.

Figuratively speaking, an attitude may be likened to a powerful stream. It is perhaps possible to row against the current, but much easier either to go with it or to pull the boat toward one bank so the oarsman can proceed upstream without bucking the flow. Whatever alternative is finally adopted, it would be a foolish boatman who planned a river trip without taking the currents into account. Just so should the persuasive speaker chart his course with the attitudes of his audience in mind.

Self-interest and belief

The basic factor in persuasion might be formulated briefly as follows: *To control the unfettered behavior of his auditors, a persuasive speaker must base his conclusion upon their desires.* His effective speaking will all be pointed directly or indirectly to that end. The propositions by which his conclusion is supported will be bound together by no other essential connection than that they all combine to make his auditors wish to accept what the speaker says. When facts and logic serve this purpose, they should be used; when they do not, substitutes for them must be found. As the logician John Stuart Mill observed, if man had found the facts of geometry troublesome, he would long ago have found them false. "He that complies against his will, is of his own opinion still." We are all very much like the woman who told Jane Addams at Hull House, "I don't want to eat what I'd ought; I want to eat what I'd ruther."

To sharpen one's perception of what people would "ruther" do, and to lead them toward that and away from what they "ought," is persuasive speaking at its lowest moral ebb. But to acquire the ability to make people "ruther" do what they "ought" is a high and worthy goal any speaker might be proud to pursue.

Nevertheless, regardless of how idealistic is the motive of the speaker, his success in winning an audience to accept and adopt his exalted goal will depend primarily upon this fundamental fact: *people can only be induced willingly to do what they desire to do.* They will see what they wish to see, hear what they wish to hear. Out of a babble of unintelligible sounds, one will pick out his own name, or any word affecting his own welfare. If this "law" seems extreme, there is at least much in every individual's experience to support it. In further support of this law, two of Zillig's classic experiments and one by Thorndike will be cited.

Zillig had her elementary-school pupils ballot to select the best-liked and the least-liked members of the class. Without revealing the results of the balloting, she then asked ten students, supposedly chosen at random but actually consisting of five who were most popular and five who were least liked, to stand in the front of the room, arranged in alternate order. Privately she instructed the well-liked pupils to do the opposite of what she would command. Then she clearly directed all ten subjects to raise their right hands. The five who were least liked did so; the well-liked students raised their *left* hands. Zillig asked the remainder of the class to list the names of all who did the exercise incorrectly. Then she instructed the class in the need for the utmost care in observation and the importance of correct testimony in their listing of the names. After this instruction she had the exercise repeated four times, each time with the least-liked pupils always doing as she asked and the most-liked pupils always disobeying her commands. When she gathered up the papers recording the judgments of the class, she found that the most popular students (who were always wrong) had been credited with a higher percentage of correctness than the least-liked (who actually had been always right). Such evidence is eloquent testimony to the subjectivity of our thinking.

In another experiment, Zillig secured from eighteen teachers the names of two of their students whom they liked best and the two whom they liked least. Then she secured copies of a spelling test from all these students, in which the errors in spelling had been marked by the teachers. She found that the teachers *overlooked* 38.7 per cent of the errors made by the best-liked pupils and only 12.3 per cent of the errors made by the least-liked pupils. Thus, it appeared that teachers, as well as their elementary-school pupils, permit their likes and dislikes to have a decisive effect upon their judgment.

E. L. Thorndike, attempting to discover the influence of subjectivity in thinking, devised a test of the validity of opinions regarding the worth of various cities. He "computed for each of 117 cities a factual index, which is a composite of 23 items of fact each of which would be regarded by all competent persons as indicative of the goodness of life for good people." He then collected opinions concerning "the quality of the government, schools, morals, culture, public spirit, and humanity" of such of the cities as those queried knew about on the basis of their own direct experience. He stressed the fact that he did not wish to have judgments expressed unless the subjects were confident that their opinion was well founded. The judgments regarding the factors considered for each city were recorded on a sliding scale of six responses, ranging from very good to very bad. The subjects who were asked to record their opinions were distinctly above average in ability. They included ninety-seven educators, seventy-two clergymen and social workers, ninety-nine businessmen, seventeen public health experts, and thirty-one reformers, or a total of two hundred sixty-eight persons. In analyzing their judgments, Professor Thorndike concluded that "Their opinions are too much influenced by the life the cities provide for people of financial and social status like their own and too little by the life of the entire population." In comparing their judgments with the factual index, he secured the following correlations:

97 educators	.59
31 reformers	.51
entire group	.42
72 clergymen and social workers	.36
99 businessmen	.27

The testimony of the public health experts, which was surprisingly bad, he decided not to classify in view of the small number participating. The clergymen, social workers, and businessmen were notably lacking in objectivity. For the whole group, the evidence is strongly in support of the theory that their thinking was governed by subjectivity.

Any inference is, by definition, an *assumed relationship* between facts. It is a belief regarding the meaning of data. This belief is something apart from the facts themselves: it is an addition to them—it is the whole which is greater than the sum of its parts. Th"s belief is always subjective. It is the reaction of the self (from within) to what is observed without.

If left to its own unfettered will, the self would doubtless always formulate its beliefs exactly in accordance with its desires. Children and adults of primitive psychical development tend to do just this. But they inevitably suffer frequent and keen disappointments, as their beliefs, so formulated, are undermined by objective reality. The situation for normal adults has been well described by one of the earlier students of the psychology of belief, G. F. Stout, in his *Manual of Psychology*.

Belief depends on subjective tendencies, just because these tendencies cannot work themselves out without it. Ends can only be realized by the use of means; but in order to use means we must have some belief in their efficacy; hence the impulse to pursue an end is also an impulse to form beliefs which will make action for the attainment of the end possible. But it is not within the range of our arbitrary selection to determine *what* means will lead up to a given end, and what will not. This depends on the nature of the real world in which we live. There must therefore in the framing of a belief be always some endeavour to conform to conditions other than, and independent of, our own subjective tendencies. Our inability to attain ends otherwise than through certain means constitutes a restriction of mental activity within more or less definite channels.

The relationship between belief and desire—the subjective influence on the judgment of objective data—has been measured by F. H. Lund in a series of experiments involving several hundred individuals of more than high school education. Presumably they should rank higher than average in objectivity. To each of them a series of propositions was given to be rated on a scale of "belief strength" or certainty; later, when they had supposedly forgotten their previous ratings, he had them rate the same propositions on a scale of "desirability." The correlation between these two ratings is well over + .80—far too high to be explained by chance. It offers a striking testimony that we believe what we want to believe.

Resistance to change

One way in which self-interest operates in our thinking is by inducing a preference for the status quo. When a satisfactory position has once been achieved, there is a strong tendency to cling to it, without any active efforts to determine whether other positions might not be better. Furthermore, this attraction to what is established affects our reaction to wholly new experiences and ideas. C. K. Trueblood, in his study entitled, "Beliefs and Personality," concluded that, "Of beliefs espoused by the adult mind, those are most easily accepted which most resemble, or are logically or psychologically most closely related to powerful existing convictions."

This conservative trend is not instinctive, however. Our native tendency, Trueblood found, is always to accept whatever is present in the mind. Defenses which we have erected against accepting everything that is presented to us are: (1) a general skepticism, or sophistication—which is one mark of the mature mind; (2) beliefs already held which contradict, directly or indirectly, the new presentation; (3) active or latent dislike of the agent presenting the new concept. All these defenses against the new beliefs militate in favor of the old ones.

Trueblood also discovered three positive reasons for favoring the conclusions which have become established in the mind. In the first place, they have the prestige which comes from their past success. They would never have been accepted initially if they had not induced satisfaction. Secondly, by the mere fact of their favorable retention in the mind they have become an object of interest, and therefore their continuation is favored. Finally, any belief established in the mind is interwoven with habits of thought, attitudes, and purposes in a web which can be broken only with difficulty and discomfort. The per-

suasive speaker is, thus, more successful generally in appealing to the
old than to the new.

Woodrow Wilson, in speaking to a salesmen's conference at Detroit
in July, 1916, emphasized this point on the basis of his own wide
experience:

> I have had a great deal more resistance of counsel, of special counsel,
> when I tried to alter the things that are established than when I tried to do
> anything else. We call ourselves a liberal nation, whereas as a matter of
> fact we are one of the most conservative nations in the world. If you want
> to make enemies, try to change something. You know why it is. To do
> things today exactly the way you did them yesterday saves thinking. It does
> not cost you anything. You have acquired the habit; you know the routine;
> you do not have to plan anything, and it frightens you with a hint of
> exertion to learn that you will have to do it a different way tomorrow.
> Until I became a college teacher I used to think that the young men were
> radical; but college boys are the greatest conservatives I ever tackled in
> my life, largely because they have associated too much with their fathers.

Oftentimes the persuasive speaker can utilize this conservative
tendency by showing that his proposal, though it may seem to be new,
really has its roots firmly fixed in the past. At other times it is necessary to launch boldly forth into a new field of action and to try to take
an audience to a new position. In this same address to the salesmen,
Wilson gave his formula for leading auditors on to fresh conclusions.

> What you have to do with them is to take them upon some visionary
> height and show them the map of the world as it is. . . . Let them see the
> great valleys teeming with laborious people. Let them see the great struggle
> of men in realms they never dreamed of. Let them see the great emotional
> power that is in the world, the great ambitions, the great hopes, the great
> fears. Give them some picture of mankind . . . and they will sometimes
> see that the item [which the speaker is attacking] is not properly related to
> the whole, and what they will get interested in will be to relate the item
> to the whole, so that it will form part of the force, and not part of the
> impediment.

One final consideration regarding the role of self-interest in the
formation of beliefs is important. We sometimes fail to do what we want
to do, or believe what we want to believe, for reasons wholly outside

our own control. We are hedged in by laws, by customs, by force and the threat of force. A speaker may try to lead our decision toward peace, which is naturally based upon our desire. But the reply may be Patrick Henry's "Peace, peace! There is no peace! An appeal to arms, and to the God of hosts, is all that is left us." A salesman may build upon our desire for his product when, as a matter of fact, we lack the means of buying it. A speaker may present a point of view so radical that its acceptance would result in social ostracism for the auditors. In all these instances, the persuadees are not free to follow their desires to the speaker's conclusion. On the other hand, occasions are frequent when an audience is constrained by law, by custom, or by external circumstances to accept a decision which it finds distinctly unpalatable. In such instances, the speaker can safely launch his proposal directly into the teeth of its desires and still feel confident of a favorable decision. A famous example is the acceptance with which the English people greeted the affirmation of Winston Churchill, as he assumed the prime ministry of England in the dark aftermath of the fall of Norway, on May 10, 1940: "I have nothing to offer but blood, toil, tears and sweat." There was no pleasanter alternative for them to choose.

Self balanced by sentiment

If it seems to be beyond dispute that much human activity is motivated by self-interest, it also seems to be true that many reactions are relatively or completely unselfish. Sacrifice seems to have just as definite an existence as self-seeking. Innate egocentricity is partly offset by innate sympathy. Children cry over the misfortunes of their playmates, as well as over their own troubles. The urge to help, to comfort, to share is evidenced in many ways. Sentiment limits, and to an extent counterbalances, the demands of self.

Types of relationship

The relations of self and sentiment in human affairs fall into three types. First, *there are the very considerable areas in which sentiment is dominated or suppressed by self-interest.* Thus, coldly calculating, unscrupulous financial transactions may be justified by the explanation that "business is business." Frequently the comment is heard, "If you don't look out for yourself, no one else will." "Every man for himself," runs the old proverb, "and the devil take the hindmost." Out of nine-teenth-century philosophy have come the popular aphorism, "Self-preservation is the first law of life," and the Nietzschean doctrine of the Superman. The evolutionary formula of "the survival of the fittest" appears to be generally interpreted as meaning that only the self-seeking have a chance for survival. Our age is the era of the "self-made man," of the "go-getter," whose constant aim is to "get ahead" and whose chief virtue is his vigilance in searching for "the main chance."

Second, *there are areas in human affairs in which self-interest has actually resulted in the creation and maintenance of sentiment.* This situation is illustrated by the prevalence of such slogans as: "Turn about is fair play," "Honesty is the best policy," and "Loyalty breeds loyalty." "You be decent and others will be decent to you" seems to be the essence of this point of view. It was crudely stated by Artemus Ward as, "You scratch my back and I'll scratch yourn." This attitude is selfish in its inception, but largely unselfish in its results. Much of the sentiment which operates in human affairs is of this sort.

Third, *there are examples of sentiment which appear to rise superior to the demands of self-interest* and to be genuinely unselfish in origin as well as in effect. In this class are instances of heroic sacrifice, such as the risk of life in saving individuals from drowning or from burning buildings. Also included in this category are the anonymous contri-butions, sometimes wholly unsolicited, to charity. It may be argued that self-interest actually motivates these acts, too, inasmuch as the one who sacrifices doubtless feels a sense of satisfaction in his good deeds. At least it would appear to be evident that in many instances individuals are willing to sacrifice more than the concomitant gain. These examples of the complete or relative triumph of sentiment over self may be due to idealism, to enlightened selfishness, or to sublima-tion. The task of the persuasive speaker will be easier as he under-stands how to appeal to each of these limitations upon self-interest.

The ideal and the practical

The conflict between self-interest and sentiment is utilized by persuasive speakers in questioning idealism. To call a proposal idealistic or impractical is a potent form of attack. What this frequently means is that it is too unselfish to win adherents. Most persuasive speakers indicate their judgment of the relative strength of these two appeals by claiming to be practical—even though they may conclude with an appeal to idealism. Thus Charles A. Lindbergh started his speech to a New York audience on April 23, 1941, by saying:

There are many viewpoints from which the issues of this war can be argued. Some are primarily idealistic. Some are primarily practical. One should, I believe, strive for a balance of both. But, since the subjects that can be covered in a single address are limited, tonight I shall discuss the war from a viewpoint which is primarily practical. It is not that I believe ideals are unimportant, even among the realities of war; but if a nation is to survive in a hostile world, its ideals must be backed by the hard logic of military practicability. If the outcome of war depended upon ideals alone, this would be a different world than it is today.

Most of his speech was indeed "practical," in that it was devoted primarily to the theme: "We in this country have the right to think of the welfare of America first." However, the last third of the speech sought to link the speaker's theme with idealism, as though he sensed that only on that basis could the point he desired be established. He concluded with a highly idealistic plea:

The security of a nation lies in the strength and character of its people. ... There are times when we must sacrifice our normal interests in life in order to insure the safety and the welfare of our nation. ... We ask you to share our faith ... and to contribute to the progress of mankind.

An even more striking combination of the practical and the ideal is found in an opening paragraph of Herbert Hoover's speech on "America and the Famine in the Five Little Democracies," delivered at Poughkeepsie, New York, on November 15, 1940, where he said:

I am asking for no gifts, no government appropriations, no use of American ships. I am not going to discuss ideologies, or who is to blame.

I simply wish to present the case of these people to America. I will suggest that their lives and infinite suffering can be saved. And I will suggest that we have a moral responsibility.

Here in very brief space the speaker proceeded from the assurance that no sacrifice would be asked to the conclusion that there was a moral responsibility to act.

The mingling of these appeals is very well seen in the historian Prescott's summary of a speech Cortes addressed to his men as he started upon the conquest of Mexico. Selfishness and religious principles are closely interwoven in his appeal to them for support:

I hold out to you a glorious prize, but it is to be won by incessant toil. Great things are achieved only by great exertions, and glory was never the reward of sloth. If I have labored hard and staked my all on this undertaking, it is for the love of that renown which is the noblest recompense of man. But, if any among you covet riches more, be but true to me, as I will be true to you and to the occasion, and I will make you masters of such as our countrymen have never dreamed of! You are few in number, but strong in resolution; and, if this does not falter, doubt not but that the Almighty, who has never deserted the Spaniard in his contest with the infidel, will shield you, though encompassed by a cloud of enemies; for your cause is a *just cause,* and you are to fight under the banner of the Cross. Go forward, then, with alacrity and confidence, and carry to a glorious issue the work so auspiciously begun.

Enlightened selfishness

The phrase "enlightened selfishness" has become popular in diplomatic circles. It is the duty of a statesman to work for the best interests of his own country, but in many instances idealism triumphs through a demonstration that in the long run the country's own interests will be best served by an act of sacrifice. In this category are the restoration by the United States of Cuban independence and our return to China of the indemnity it paid us after the Boxer Rebellion, to be used for the education of Chinese youths in America. "The white man's burden," celebrated by Kipling, was the duty of improving the lot of Asiatic and African natives, on the theory that they would one day become profitable customers. In the sphere of personal relations, enlightened selfishness governs much social and business activity. It is perhaps based upon the Biblical injunctions: "Cast thy bread upon the waters: for thou shalt find it after many days." and, "Give, and it shall be given unto you."

Enlightened selfishness might be defined as selfishness plus intelligence. It consists of taking the long view rather than the short view—of judging in terms of ultimate rather than immediate goals. It is comparable to the making of investments, in that something is "put in" with the definite expectation of "taking out" a satisfactory profit. For this reason, bank accounts are built up, taxes are paid, donations are given to the Community Chest. The use that a speaker might make of this concept is illustrated in an experience of Dr. Mary Wolf, during the campaign for woman suffrage, when she was speaking to a group of frugal Pennsylvania Dutch farmers. Sensing that her plea for equal rights was having no effect, she ended her speech with the declaration that the fight would go on, year after year, until it was won; that it was an expensive fight in time, energy, and money; but that the expense was borne in reality by the men, inasmuch as they had almost all the money, and the time the women spent was taken away from their home duties. "Wouldn't it be better," she asked, "to pass this bill, to give women the rights they are seeking, and to end this expensive agitation?" This plea won votes; the men were willing to surrender some of their prerogatives if in the long run they profited thereby.

The lesson for the persuasive speaker is clear: when selfishness blocks the acceptance of his proposal, the auditors should be "enlightened" to see that their own interests are in reality furthered by what the speaker has to propose.

Sublimation

Freudians and other psychologists who accept with reservations the importance of the sex drive in human activity have popularized the concept of sublimation. According to this theory, sex energy may be and often is diverted to other ends Laurance F. Shaffer, in *The*

Psychology of Adjustment, presented a standard psychoanalytic explanation of sublimation when he wrote:

> The most normal of the fulfillment dynamisms is *sublimation.* By this process the libidinal urges are transformed into interests and activities described as "aim-inhibited," in that their object is no longer sexual. The origins of vocational interests, hobbies, civic activities and religion are traced to sublimation. Although sublimated activities are in many instances remote from the original urges, they show in other cases their original sexual derivation.

The term *sublimation* is much older than psychoanalysis, and is still frequently used to mean any diversion of a low aim to one that is ethically higher. One definition is: "any refining or purifying process; elimination of base or impure elements; purification; refinement." Thus, it might be said that the pugnacious tendency of an individual may be sublimated into a heroic devotion to duty. John B. Gough, a drunkard, became one of the most effective temperance reformers. Ignatius Loyola, a soldier, founded one of the great religious bodies, the Jesuit order. Martin Niemoeller, a submarine commander in World War I, became a religious martyr under the Nazis. It is evident that "base or impure" motives *can* be "refined or purified." One avenue, then, that the persuasive speaker might follow in his appeals for action is the picturing of high moral duties to take the place of more selfish aims.

Conclusion

"To study persuasion intensively . . . is to study human nature minutely." A persuasive appeal acquires its motivational effectiveness by suggesting to the listeners that agreement with the speaker will satisfy their own needs, desires, and aspirations. In order to achieve this effect, the appeal gains strength by being aligned with their attitudes and by being presented in terms of their subjective interpretation of the subject. We find no reason to doubt that people can only be induced *willingly* to do what they *desire* to do.

However, this does not mean that all thinking and conduct are selfish. Observation and experience are replete with examples to the contrary. It is also true that one of the things we most treasure is the good will and approval of our associates. We value highly praise for such qualities as sympathy, understanding, idealism, brotherhood, self-sacrifice, co-operativeness. It is obvious that our motivation is not focused alone upon self-interest, but that in fact it is organized around the two poles of *self-interest* and the *sentiment of sociability*. We are interested not only in what belongs to us—but also in making sure that we belong to the group. Man is at once egocentric and social. The sources of motivation lie in both of these disparate poles. The wise persuasive speaker makes sure that he appeals to both.

Exercises

1. Dr. Victor Heiser spent a third of a century in carrying the doctrine of medical purity to forty-five nations representing the most hygienically backward peoples in the world. As is the lot of every reformer, his chief task was to persuade the peoples to accept his reforms. Typical of his difficulties was the fight he had to win adoption of his sanitation program for the Philippine Islands. In *An American Doctor's Odyssey* he tells the story of this and of many another persuasive struggle. In the following passage, taken from page 64 of that book, note his method. Does it conform to the principles set forth in this chapter? Is it a method which would generally be useful in persuasive speaking? What does Dr. Heiser gain by seeing the problem from the Filipinos' point of view?

President McKinley had once promised that the United States would do nothing to interfere with Filipino habits and customs. But the Bureau of Health was constantly doing this very thing, and any measure proposed which the Filipinos did not like was *ipso facto* not one of their customs. I could sympathize with them; it was doubtless unpleasant to be ordered about by sanitary officers and nurses.

Popular hostility was naturally reflected in the press, and even the doctors joined in the hue and cry when I submitted a sanitary code for Manila. I was invading the privacy of the home. After they had delayed its passage for a year, I called them into conference and asked, "Gentlemen, what corrections would you like to make?" They submitted their proposals. I agreed they were excellent, but needed only a few slight changes here and there of a purely technical nature. I then rewrote the code, essentially as it had been before, and everybody was happy.

I used this same system often in the legislature, where hostility could be converted into active co-operation by the simple expedient of saying to the most violent objector, "Will you draft this bill for me?" His opposition would evaporate instantly, and he would eagerly accept the commission. When he brought it back, I would agree that his version was excellent, and then recast the entire bill. As the bill thereafter bore his name, the theoretical author and I would remain faithful allies forever.

2. What is the significance for persuasive speaking of this statement from Stuart Chase? "A thermometer measures temperature now; a man responds to the same situation with memories of when he last froze his toes!"

3. Listen to a persuasive speech over the radio and answer the following questions regarding it.

   a. What was the speaker's proposal?
   b. Did he speak with a full appreciation of his auditors' point of view?
   c. Did he appeal to the auditors' self-interest? If so, how?
   d. Did he incorporate an appeal to sentiment in his speech? If so, how?
   e. Could you improve his speech by revising his appeals to self-interest and to sentiment—or by inserting them if he left them out?

4. Discuss the following:

   a. Define: self-interest, sentiment, enlightened selfishness, sublimation, and idealism.
   b. In what sense is all knowledge subjective?
   c. Are speeches which attempt to force agreement truly persuasive? Cite examples of such speeches. Do they ever have a legitimate purpose?
   d. Why do we tend to cling to our established beliefs? Are young people prone to radicalism? Are any particular groups in society more or less radical than others? What reasons can you find for these differences?
   e. Why do we sometimes accept distasteful conclusions? Are we apt to have mental reservations in such cases? Is complete unselfishness possible?

5. The following readings will be helpful for a further analysis and understanding of problems of human motivation:

J. A. C. Brown, *Techniques of Persuasion* (Baltimore: Penguin Books, 1963), particularly Chapters 3 and 8.

Kenneth Burke, *A Grammar of Motives* (Englewood Cliffs, N.J.: Prentice-Hall, 1945).

C. N. Cofer and M. H. Appley, *Motivation Theory and Research* (New York: Wiley, 1964).

Melvin DeFleur and Frank Westie, "Verbal Attitudes and Overt Acts: An Experiment on the Salience of Attitudes," *American Sociological Review*, 23 (1958), 667-673.

Jon Eisenson, J. Jeffrey Auer, and John V. Irwin, *The Psychology of Communication* (New York: Appleton-Century-Crofts, 1963), particularly Chapter 14, pp. 227-252.

Leon Festinger, "Behavioral Support for Opinion Change," *Public Opinion Quarterly*, 28 (Fall, 1964), 404-417.

Kenneth D. Frandsen, "Effects of Threat Appeals and Media of Transmission," *Speech Monographs*, 30 (June, 1963), 101-104.

R. Barry Fulton, "Motivation: Foundation of Persuasion," *Quarterly Journal of Speech*, 49 (October, 1963), 295-307.

H. Gilkinson, S. F. Paulson, and D. E. Sikkink, "Conditions Affecting the Communication of Controversial Statements in Connected Discourse," *Speech Monographs*, XX (November, 1953), 253-260.

Calvin S. Hall and Gardner Lindzey, *Theories of Personality* (New York: Wiley, 1957).

S. I. Hayakawa (ed.), *Language, Meaning, and Maturity* (New York: Harper, 1964), particularly Carl R. Rogers, "Communication: Its Blocking and Its Facilitation," pp. 53-60; and Raymond Rogers, "The Gonks and the Tiger," pp. 303-314.

Sigmund Koch, "The Current Status of Motivational Psychology," *Psychological Review*, 58 (1951), 147-154.

Richard T. LaPiere, "Attitudes versus Actions," *Social Forces*, XIII (December, 1934), 230-237.

Thomas R. Nilsen, "Interpersonal Communication: A Conceptual Framework," *Central States Speech Journal*, XV (February, 1964), 31-35.

Carolyn W. Sherif, Muzafer Sherif and Roger Nebergall, *Attitude and Attitude-Change: The Social Judgment-Involvement Approach* (Philadelphia: Saunders, 1965).

Raymond G. Smith, "Motivation and Communication Theory," *Central States Speech Journal*, XV (May, 1964), 96-99.

E. L. Thorndike, "Facts vs. Opinions: An Empirical Study of 117 Cities," *Public Opinion Quarterly*, II (January, 1938), 85-90.

Otis M. Walter, "Toward an Analysis of Motivation," *Quarterly Journal of Speech*, 41 (October, 1955), 271-278.

M. Zillig, "Einstellung und Aussage," summarized in William H. Burnham, *The Wholesome Personality* (New York: Appleton, 1932), pp. 93-97.

✍ 4.

The Speaker and His Audience

THE PRECEDING CHAPTER DISCUSSED BASIC ELEMENTS of motivation or motivation in general. But persuasive occasions are always particularized. There is a particular type of speaker, addressing a particular kind of audience, on a specific occasion, to achieve a goal that is in some way a special goal. So diverse are these various factors that there sometimes seems no better advice to give than to "analyze the audience and adapt to it." However, there are fairly well-defined factors to be taken into account, such as the speaker's qualities and attitudes, the representative nature of the speaker, the sociopsychological relations between a speaker and his audience, the categories of audiences, and the means by which audiences may be effectively analyzed. As a general introduction to our consideration of *personality effects in persuasion,* we shall examine a specific instance—the political effects of the personality of President Dwight D. Eisenhower.

Eisenhower: a case study

There is abundant evidence from a continuing series of polls by Gallup and others that Eisenhower has been an unusually popular president. There is also wide agreement that his popularity stems not so much from what he has done as from the qualities of the man himself. James Reston, the acute head of *The New York Times* Washington Bureau, in an article in the September 28, 1952, issue of the *Times,* quoted Eisenhower himself on this very point: "It's not what

62

you say that matters. Question is, do you leave an impression of sincerity; do they believe you when you leave?" We may wish it were otherwise, but from Aristotle to the present, students of persuasion have found there is a large element of truth in this observation.

Reston, in this same article, went on to conclude that Eisenhower's chief political attribute is the trust that he inspires:

> The people of this country had a very vivid image of General Eisenhower when he came back from Europe. He was a heroic figure. He was a "fighter for the right." The important thing about General Eisenhower's personal appearances is that, regardless of what the intellectuals think of what the general says, he confirms the original image for the people who see him.
>
> When you talk to the people in these crowds about Ike, you get the impression that they distrust words, that they are willing to put their trust more in the look of a man's face than in the words he may read out to them from a piece of paper.
>
> General Eisenhower does not ask them to think very much; as a matter of fact, one gets the impression from talking to the people at the back end of the train that they do not want him to ask them to think, they have tried that or think they have, and the complexities of the big issues have left them baffled and looking, not for a detailed program they can understand and approve, but for a man they can trust. And this is what the general manages to portray.

Justification for Reston's analysis is found in the following complete text of a brief speech delivered by Eisenhower in Detroit, on June 14, 1952. The talk has nothing to say about issues but makes a strong and apparently successful appeal for personal trust. It is a fine example of how a speaker may enhance the persuasiveness of his own personality:

> Ladies and gentlemen, I think sometimes my military training may not have been as thorough as it could have been, because one of the principles of military life is never to be surprised. I am touched, astonished and surprised this morning, and I expect it is due to deliberate intent on the part of my associates, now normally labeled as political advisers.
>
> They get some inkling of the way I get tired of my own voice, and so I think they conceal from me at times that I am expected to battle again with one of these microphones.

In any event, as you know, I am scheduled for two talks here today; for a simple fellow like myself that is quite a chore.

I am delighted that such a group as this should invite me to their breakfast hour to give me a chance to say to them, "Thank you for coming," and to express my almost amazement that they are interested in the views I may hold about today's life and problems, and to give me a chance to meet just some more Americans, always something that is valuable and instructive to any of us.

I am going to tell you one thing about my talks today, in which you may have some interest.

When I told Mr. Summerfield [Arthur E. Summerfield, Republican National Committeeman from Michigan] that I would come out here, I began to think as would anyone else, what message could I bring that was worth while to the people of Detroit, and I worked pretty hard on numbers of drafts of ideas and putting them together, and during the past week I have been going through an experience that for me, if not for you, is certainly strange, and it has been again very instructive, and I have listened to many questions that people have asked me, and so, finally, coming down on the train last night and this morning, I made a decision to this effect:

All my prepared speeches are thrown out of the window. Today, whatever I do, I am going to try to take the questions that have been coming to me over the past week and do my best to show to you and to the people of this city how I feel about them as a matter of conviction.

On many of them I have no details of solution. I am not a medicine man and I have no panaceas for anything. All I can do, therefore, is to show how I would approach these problems. I can show by them my basic concern for, and my love of, America.

If what I have got to offer in the way of honest, decent approach, as I see it, for Americans, to this problem, is not enough, there is nothing more I can do. Such as I have is yours and all the rest of America's to use freely, and that is exactly what I intend to try to say today, without benefit of paper, and I am telling you, and I see among you some of my intimate friends, if I make blunders I know my friends will excuse it. I hope the others will realize at least that I am sincere.

I have used the vertical pronoun very much in this little talk and I don't like it, but at least let me say again, thank you very much indeed for coming here and letting me meet with you for this brief moment. Thank you.

What the speaker represents

It is readily observed that the persuasive problems (and hence methods) of the speaker with great prestige or of undoubted authority are distinctly different from those of the neophyte. We also realize from experience and observation that the known or presumed motives and connections of speakers have striking effects on the audience reaction to what they say. Other influential prestige factors include the confidence and bearing of the speaker, and the stability or continuance of his advocacy. Representing the pertinent factors in the form of a table, we see that the use a speaker may make of persuasion will depend upon his character and representative function in the situation in which he speaks. Does he represent:

a. Himself alone or a minor, unrecognized group;	*or*	b. A major group or institution?
c. Inexperience or lack of expertness;	*or*	d. An established reputation as an authority?
e. Desire for personal advantage;	*or*	f. Devotion to unselfish service?
g. Temporary advocacy;	*or*	h. Permanent advocacy?
i. Uncertainty and awkwardness;	*or*	j. Confidence and poise?

It would seem apparent that as a general rule greater influence will be exerted with less effort by speakers representing the factors in the second column. It is also obvious that such a rule is not invariable. If it were, no rebel (*a*) [1] would ever overthrow an established government or other organization (*b*); no new theorist (*c*) would ever supplant a traditional belief (*d*) (as Einstein in basic respects revised Newtonian physics); private *entrepreneurs* (*e*) would always tend to be poorer than charitable institutions (*f*); advocates of war (*g*) would always yield to the established advocates of peace (*h*); and unskilled speakers (*i*) would never prevail over skilled platform masters (*j*), regardless of the respective merits of their causes. Without asserting

---

[1] These parenthetical keys refer to items in the foregoing table.

any dogmatic rules, however, there is much to learn about persuasion from examining the status of various types of speakers.

A speaker representing himself alone. Most of us, when we speak, speak only for ourselves. "I, John Doe, present the facts [adapted as well as he can to the audience] and let you judge for yourselves." Normally such a lone voice has a hard time making itself heard and a harder time getting its message heeded. A notable example is Norman Thomas, who is widely recognized to have enjoyed the advantages of being (*d*) an established authority on national and international affairs; who has been generally considered (*f*) devoted to the public welfare; who certainly for a long lifetime has remained (*h*) in the public eye as a permanent advocate; and who by general agreement represents (*j*) a high standard of confidence and poise as a speaker. Yet he has time and again been defeated by men who were able to speak as representatives of (*b*) large and widely accepted political parties and other major groups. The famous General "Billy" Mitchell, lone and unavailing advocate during his lifetime of increased air power, is another well-known example of a man who was both right and powerful in his pleas, yet failed largely because he stood alone (*a*), unrepresentative of any established and respected organization.

A speaker representing a major group. Many an unknown man has suddenly had his persuasive effectiveness multiplied by being selected as president of a university or of the local Rotary Club. The ordinary persuasive speaker may have no such opportunity to add to the weight of his words. However, it is extremely valuable as a persuasive device to identify yourself so far as you properly can with established institutions. Thus, when you advocate any proposition to your audience, you may well find it helpful to state, "The views I am presenting to you are not merely my own. What I am urging is precisely the program of . . ." and then name such prestige-bearing organizations or groups as (when appropriate to your message) "the Founding Fathers," "the Christian Church," "the men who conducted the atomic research." In a great many instances you may find that if you do not actually speak *for* an established group, you may at least in all propriety speak *with* one. And to the extent that you can do so, your persuasiveness will increase.

An inexpert speaker. To have to talk on a subject you know little about is an undoubted handicap. Yet it often happens that a persuasive speaker wishes to support a particular candidate, even though he is no expert in political affairs; or he may seek to obtain donations to the Red Cross without having acquired firsthand knowledge of its multifarious activities. In all such cases, the speaker will gain in persuasiveness to the extent that he convinces his audience he has drawn his facts and conclusions from authoritative sources. In such speeches it is well to stress the reliability of your sources of information, and to buttress your own recommendations with precise quotations from established authorities.

A recognized authority. Who would be inclined to resist conclusions about physics presented by Albert Einstein or to denounce batting techniques advocated by Ted Williams? The value of being a recognized authority is readily understood. What students of persuasion might properly deduce from this fact is the great advantage they may secure to themselves by studying their subject matter so thoroughly that they fairly "bristle" with information about it. Even if you must start your speech with no reputation whatever as an authority in the field you are discussing, you can gain some of the prestige and advantages of expertness by demonstrating to the audience that you have, indeed, mastered the topic on which you are venturing to offer advice.

A speaker seeking his own advantage. "Let the buyer beware" is an old formulation of the point of view that auditors should be wary when a speaker tries to "sell" them an idea or a project from which he, personally, will gain. Many speakers of this type have found it useful to state very candidly the amount and kind of advantage they themselves will receive if the audience agrees with their proposals. From this point they can go on to show how the audience, too, will gain. Thus, a speaker may say, "Of course one reason I want to sell you an automobile is because I make my living from commissions on the cars I sell. So does any other car salesman, so there is no difference in that respect. There is, however, a difference in the value you, as a buyer, will receive. The chief advantages you will get from buying this car instead of another car are as follows. ..." Usually it does little good, and may do much harm, to try to conceal or deny the degree of self-interest you, as the speaker, may have in the proposition you want the audience to accept.

An unselfish speaker. It is obvious that if a man asks you for a donation for the Community Chest you will give it to him more readily than if he requests money to buy cigars for himself. It should follow as a matter of course that when you are speaking on behalf of some community project or humanitarian reform you will take care to let your audience know, unobtrusively but unmistakably, that you are advocating the welfare of society, rather than seeking any gain for yourself.

A temporary advocate. Audiences have learned by experience not to be overly influenced by the pleas of a speaker who is known to take up any passing fad or to serve as a mouthpiece for any special interest that may from time to time request his help. A cause so insignificant that it cannot hold the loyalties of an advocate scarcely seems deserving of public support. Moreover, there is a natural feeling that merely temporary advocates of any program are unlikely to be fully informed about it. Persuasion often is a slow and long-term undertaking, operating gradually upon the sensibilities of a community, just as little drops of water eventually wear away a stone. As the biographies of the great persuasive advocates show, many worthy causes have required a lifetime, and often several generations, before they succeed. The persuasive speaker who has a genuine program to develop cannot afford to be impatient.

A permanent advocate. Abolition of slavery, women's rights, prohibition, control of child labor, improvement in the lot of labor, and all other social causes have been of slow growth. We honor the men and women who devoted their lives to such enterprises, and in honoring them we willingly subject ourselves to the influence of their persuasive appeals. It is a well-known maxim of advertising that unless an advertising campaign can be continuous over a long period of time, it is hardly worth while at all. The same generalization often applies to persuasion. The only persuasive goals you can hope to achieve in single brief speeches are those that are extremely limited and that are closely geared to existing beliefs and desires. In persuasion, as in much else, the more you hope to achieve, the longer it will take.

An uncertain and awkward speaker. Actually there is seldom a necessary correlation between confidence and correctness. Dr. Johan Obrink, of Uppsala, Sweden, put this question to the test by giving objective examinations to groups of children and adults. In addition to the answers, he asked them to indicate whether they were "sure" or "unsure" of their answers. He found that: (1) "Those who were sure when they were right, also were sure when they were wrong"; and (2) children were more sure than adults. Whatever the facts may be, however, it is readily observed that speakers who are well poised and confident generally transmit this confidence to their audiences and accordingly are more readily believed. Especially on subjects about which the audience itself is uninformed, there is a natural tendency to "lean upon" the apparent sureness of a speaker who gives overt evidence of mastery.

A confident and poised speaker. Since confidence and poise in speaking situations derive largely from training and practice in speech —rather than simply from specialized knowledge of the subject matter—it would seem that all who desire skill in persuasion would willingly submit themselves to the discipline of mastering the skills of delivery. The speaker who will not work hard to attain the personal qualities that will help gain acceptance for his ideas can scarcely be thought to have a genuinely sincere desire to accomplish the goals he professes to seek.

The speaker's qualities

There is no absolute agreement as to what personality is. The root meaning of personality, from *per sonare,* is "to speak through." *Persona* was the name given to the mask worn by an actor in Roman drama. The *persona* had a triple function; for it attracted attention to the actor, revealed the type of character he represented, and, with a built-in megaphone, made his speech more easily audible.

In modern usage personality is sometimes defined vaguely as "that which makes one effective," or "one's social stimulus value"; sometimes inclusively as "the sum total of all the biologically innate dispositions, impulses, tendencies, appetites, and instincts of the individual, and the acquired dispositions and tendencies"; and sometimes technically as "the dynamic organization within the individual of those psychophysical systems that determine his unique adjustments to his environment." From the standpoint of its function in persuasive speaking, personality may be defined simply as *those qualities of an individual which are recognized in his social relationships as constituting his real self.*

Character. Deliberate wrongdoing is the shortest route to loss of public sympathy and esteem. Mistakes of the heart are much less easily forgiven than mistakes of the head. Not everyone can do right, but it is demanded of everyone that he at least try. This high regard for ethics is partly sentimental, but largely practical. Character is the foundation stone upon which society rests. As Dr. Samuel Johnson told Boswell, modern civilization would be utterly impossible if we could not trust one another. Through countless generations of social conditioning, mankind has come to regard character as perhaps the ultimate value in life. So highly is it regarded that its possession is an "open sesame" to many of life's choicest rewards.

A spotless character is for the persuasive speaker his magic armor. If he has it, no opponent can wound him; through all controversies he can move serenely, personally unscathed. His defenses are impregnable. And in attack his opposition is weakened by the assurance that he is motivated only by the highest regard for what is right. "His strength is as the strength of ten, because his heart is pure." If this is true of the conflict of the battlefield, how much truer is it in the forum, on the platform, and in the market place! The greatest single asset that a persuasive speaker can have is a character that is known to be beyond reproach.

Reputation. Reputation is the stereotyped impression by which an individual is known. It is an oversimplification of his entire personality. It is like the brand name of a commercial product, and it is just as important to the persuasive speaker as to the manufacturer that his brand be widely and favorably known. Publicity is a highly persuasive factor. A well-known radio commentator can command large audiences and high fees, whereas an unknown academic expert will scarcely even be listened to. Frequently publicity builds an impression of expertness. It is likely to be assumed that any man who is well known is *knowing*. For a persuasive speaker to give no thought to his reputation would be as foolish as for him to neglect any other important aspect of the motivational problem.

Appearance. Appearance should be considered in two categories, which may be designated as natural and assumed. In the first are included such factors as height, weight, and general comeliness. The latter category covers carriage and the neatness and appropriateness of dress. A number of studies that have been made of the relationship of physique and success seem to indicate that size is an important factor. Large men, for instance, are more apt to hold executive positions than are small men. A representative study, made by E. B. Gowin, is summarized in the following table.

TABLE SHOWING RELATION OF PHYSIQUE TO POSITION HELD

Classes of men	Weight	Difference (pounds)	Height	Difference (inches)
1. Bishops	176.4		5:10.6	
2. Small-town preachers	159.4	17	5: 8.8	1.8
3. University presidents	181.6		5:10.8	
4. Presidents of small colleges	164	17.6	5: 9.6	1.2
5. City school superintendents	178.6		5:10.4	
6. Small-town principals	157.6	21	5: 9.7	.7
7. Presidents of State Bar Associations	171.5		5:10.5	
8. County attorneys	162.4	9.1	5:10	.5
9. Sales managers	182.8		5:10.1	
10. Salesmen	157	25.8	5: 9.1	1
11. Railroad presidents	186.3		5:10.9	
12. Station agents	154.6	31.7	5: 9.4	1.5

The evidence showing the correlation between large size and social effectiveness is impressive, but in such a field as this the exceptions are at least as important as the general trend. It is not only well to know that large men have a natural persuasive advantage over small ones, but it is just as valuable to note that this advantage is very often offset by the many other factors involved in the total personality. A large man who slouches awkwardly and appears ill at ease is doubly handicapped, whereas many a small man manages to look "every inch a king." The great Southern orator, Alexander Hamilton Stephens, weighed only ninety pounds and was barely five feet tall. Napoleon Bonaparte measured five feet two inches; Lenin, five feet three inches; Stalin, five feet five inches; Mussolini and Hitler each five feet six inches. Billy Rose, the master showman, is five feet four inches tall. The important consideration in so far as physique is concerned seems to be whether one manages to look impressive.

Daniel Webster's appearance made a tremendous impression upon his contemporaries. An Englishman, upon seeing him for the first time, exclaimed, "No man can be as great as Daniel Webster looks!" He was familiarly known in his time as "the godlike Daniel." One admirer wrote of him that "he was so big and strong, so large in every way, that people sank into repose in his presence, and felt rest and confidence in the mere fact of his existence." His head was large and his brain was one of the two or three largest that have ever been measured. But otherwise his proportions were quite ordinary. The important fact was that he bore himself as one who demanded respect as his due.

The effect of personal cleanliness, neatness, and dress that is appropriate and unobtrusive can scarcely be overemphasized. In all these respects the individual is master of his own appearance. Appearance is sometimes spoken of as the index to personality. This is a particularly appropriate analogy in that it is the most available means by which casual associates can determine what may lie within. The women of America spend over a billion dollars yearly upon cosmetics; the men, if they would be persuasively effective, must at least spend time and thought upon how they appear to others.

Social ease. Closely allied in its effect to appearance is the quality of social ease. Emerson wrote half seriously that "God may forgive sins ... but awkwardness has no forgiveness in heaven or earth." Tension and uneasiness in a speaker are contagious. They breed unrest, uncertainty, and discomfort in his audience. On the other hand, speakers who appear to be at ease, composed, and self-confident inspire confidence and trust.

Edwin G. Flemming had two hundred of his psychology students rate one another for the qualities of pleasantness of personality, steadiness or reliability, expressiveness, and social adjustment. Upon correlating the results, he found that social adjustment provided the best measure of pleasing personality. No other factor proved "nearly as important as a general social adaptability." Through a series of similar studies he reached the following conclusion: "if an individual's fear ratio is low, if his social intelligence is high, if he is expressive and emotionally steady, that individual will have a pleasing personality."

The quality of social ease is certainly aided by a good sense of humor and by what is closely allied to it, a sense of proportion. Individuals who "blow up" over a misplay in bridge or wax scathingly sarcastic over an accidental tardiness in keeping an appointment are difficult to live with. On the other hand, the ability to smile over slight mishaps, to recuperate easily from disappointments, to avoid feeling hurt by myriads of fancied social slights are all ingredients of the well-balanced, persuasively effective personality. They all contribute their bit to that comfortable and comforting attribute known as social ease.

Sincerity. Great earnestness generates real power behind an idea. If we don't like the idea, we are apt to term the power fanaticism; if we do, we call it sincerity. In either case it might be described as a sense of mission. No real leadership is possible without it. We recognize it in the minister's "call," in the reformer's zeal. The poet William Cowper described it in these words:

> No wild enthusiast ever yet could rest,
> Till half mankind were like himself possessed.

Lord Nelson, the hero of Trafalgar, wrote that the mission to serve king and country was always "before my mind's eye as a radiant orb that courted me onward to renown." Sometimes this drive consists of general ambition, as seems to have been the case with Woodrow Wilson, who confided to his wife in 1894 that he was "hungry—too hungry—for reputation and influence."

Always it is an insistent belief by the individual that his task is important, that his contribution is urgently needed, that what he is doing is unquestionably worth while. It is directly contrary to the feeling of the English Lord who yawned himself down in the midst of his speech because he felt too bored to go on! It is contrary, too, to the habit of qualification which some speakers develop—the habit of smothering their ideas beneath a blanket of such phrases as "on the whole," "to a certain extent," or "in a manner of speaking." Sometimes such phrases as these are proper intellectual safeguards, but frequently they are merely cushions for an intellect which is too lazy to discover whether the alleged facts it is bandying about are really true.

The dull, phlegmatic, feelingless speech is always ineffective. But there are two types of speeches that are fired with enthusiasm, one of which must be regarded with suspicion. The first is simply *emotional intensity,* which may easily be confused by both speaker and audience with an honest depth of feeling. It is comparatively easy to "get steamed up" for an occasion. An imaginative individual might well work himself into a state of crusading zeal for a proposal which he presents one evening, and might conceivably express real indignation at its enormities the next day. Every speaker is acquainted with the phenomenon of "becoming intoxicated with his own eloquence" to the point of being swept along to the expression of much more extreme statements than were originally intended. This emotional type of emphasis can be turned on and off almost at will; its real worth is fairly well assessed in the story of the radio entertainer who, just finishing a heart-rending children's tale, and thinking the microphone had been turned off, declared feelingly, There, I guess that'll hold the little devils for a while!

Real sincerity is based upon *profound intellectual conviction*. It is
not a hothouse flower that springs into being overnight. It is compounded of toilful examination and earnest thought. It results in what
is known as "moral thoughtfulness"—a certitude that cannot be
shaken, for it is founded upon an exhaustive consideration of the facts.
Darwin's sincere devotion to his theory of evolution was based on a
lifetime of accumulating data and rigorously evaluating their meanings. As the old Arabian proverb has it, "Blessed is the man who
knows and knows that he knows—he is a leader; follow him." When
a persuasive speaker is warmly asserting the merits of a proposal, his
audience should subject him to the test of intellectual conviction proposed by Dr. Samuel Johnson: "Do you *think* you are right or do you
know?"

The speaker's attitudes

An important part of the speaker's personality consists of his attitudes toward his audience, his subject, and himself. Does he respect
his auditors? Does he consider them as mature individuals with minds
of their own, with points of view that are just as important to them as
his are to him? Or does he present his proposal with arrogant presumption, as though he felt himself to be a sage casting crumbs of
enlightenment before children? Adlai Stevenson has often been cited
as a speaker who aims at a high level of listener intelligence; some
think at too high a level. However, it is always true that a speaker
who does not respect his audience will never be respected by it. One
cannot "talk down" to a group of people and receive their respectful
concurrence in return. Unless the speaker thinks of his speech as a
meeting of minds between himself and his audience, as a give-and-take
conversation, as a sharing of attitudes and beliefs, he is creating by his
own attitude a barrier to his success.

Similarly, the speaker's effectiveness will be greater if his audience
senses that he has an attitude of genuine humility toward his subject
matter. Truth is an elusive phantom not easily corralled. It is seldom
indeed that all the truth is on the speaker's side. Nor can a speaker
often honestly say that he has examined every aspect of his subject to

its ultimate extent. It is well, then, to follow the practice of Benjamin Franklin in avoiding irritating assertions of certainty. There is point in the popular definition of dogmatism as "being mistaken at the top of one's voice."

Finally, the speaker's attitude toward himself should be well balanced. Calm assurance lies in the realm between arrogance and uncertainty. It is born of the speaker's knowledge that he is giving his audience the best fruits of his most thoughtful consideration, and that his proposal is consequently based upon moral thoughtfulness and not upon mere emotional intensity.

Some very interesting conclusions regarding the importance to a persuasive speaker of his attitudes were indicated by a study conducted by Ray H. Simpson at Barnard College. Using one hundred eighty-five women college students of psychology as subjects, Simpson attempted to discover what factors cause participants in group discussion to be influential and what factors cause them to be influenced. With twenty-four of the girls in a control group, the other one hundred sixty-one each engaged in four fifty-minute discussions, and each took a total of nine hours of personality and intelligence tests. Before discussion the attitude of each participant toward the topic was secured; this was checked with the attitudes after the discussion was completed, and was checked again after an interval of time had elapsed. Thus was determined (1) which individuals had been most influenced; (2) which had been most influential; (3) whether the influence was lasting. By correlating these data with the personality scores, Simpson sought to determine the answers to the following questions:

1. Are individuals who are relatively more intelligent than others in the group also more influential in that group?
2. Do pencil and paper tests of dominance give any indication of dominance in a specific situation, such as that presented by the discussion situation?
3. Are the self-sufficient as measured by personality tests most influential in discussion?
4. Are radical members of discussion groups most influential?
5. Is religious background a factor of importance in determining the influence an individual will have?

6. Are students who are best liked by classmates most influential?

7. Do individuals with artistic judgments most similar to those of experts tend to have most influence in discussion?

8. What types of individuals are most influenced by discussion?

He found a reliable correlation between intelligence and both immediate and lasting influence; between self-confidence and immediate (but not lasting) influence, and between radicalism, as measured by the Social Attitudes Inventory, and both immediate and lasting influence. His study merits the most careful examination. In general, it indicates that of all the possibly persuasive factors listed in the eight questions, the attitudes held by the speaker are among the most important.

The speaker-audience relationship

The social influence upon individuals comes to a focus in the desire that we all have for status. Status may be defined as "position in society," or "recognition by one's fellows." The order of precedence in diplomatic, or social, or academic functions is exceedingly important. College professors sacrifice hours of leisure in the writing of scholarly articles for which they receive no tangible rewards, but which they hope will improve their "professional standing." Students will endure all sorts of hazing in order to be considered "good fellows." In the so-called highly practical realm of business, many a man prefers to work at a poorly paid white-collar job rather than accept a position as a skilled machinist with a higher salary but with lower social standing. In America we pride ourselves upon having no social classes, but it is nonetheless true that all of us are keenly conscious of the position we hold in the regard of our fellows. Our concern for fashion is one evidence of this consciousness. As Thorstein Veblen has observed, it is by no means unusual for an individual to go ill clad in cold weather in order to appear well dressed.

Another evidence of our concern for status is the high regard in which we hold common sense. It is actually true that common sense is no more than the untrained interpretation of partial data which have been casually and accidentally accumulated. But it is nevertheless highly thought of precisely because it is the *common* sense. Agreement with one's fellows is frequently preferred to being right but solitary.

The appearances we make upon public platforms for the purpose of exhibiting ourselves, our ideas, or our skills are relatively infrequent. Everyone is well aware of the role of the audience in the preparation and delivery of a speech. The experienced speaker selects his subject and develops his illustrations with his audience in mind. He dresses to conform to the audience's standards. He is careful of the impression he will make as he enters the hall, ascends the platform, and sits awaiting his time to speak. And his speech itself is presumably completely audience-centered. We are less aware of the role that the audience plays in our ordinary life, but it is large. Not only the speaker, but every auditor as well, is audience conscious. Futhermore, this consciousness exists not only in the auditorium or in the presence of a group, but in almost all that one does.

This fact becomes clearer if we think of *audience* in an inclusive sense as comprising all the people whom we wish to impress favorably, or of whose regard, favorable or not, we are conscious. The group may be large or small. When Margaret Fuller died, Emerson wrote, "I have lost in her my audience." Some people try to please everyone; others try to please only a small group. But no normal person is unconscious of some audience. When we note an individual who is out of step with society, we should try to find with what group he is in step and we shall have the key to his actions. A radical living in a conservative community may seem to flout all public opinion, but in reality the public he cares for is a group of fellow radicals who may be miles away.

Most of our actions, thoughts, and attitudes are either entirely caused or decisively influenced by our regard for our audiences. Certain bodily changes seem to occur without regard for one's fellows; thus, we become sleepy, tired, or hungry as a result of internal conditions. Or do we? Is it not true that we habitually become sleepy at our customary hour of retirement and that this hour varies according to the custom of those among whom we live? One may feel very sleepy indeed, but become wide-awake upon the appearance of well-liked friends. Similarly, we become hungry frequently out of sheer boredom; and, on the other hand, we can be stimulated by company to the point of forgetting food. Hunger strikers go for days without eating, upborne by the consciousness of the sympathetic or disturbed reactions of their audience. We know, too, how fatigue is affected by social considerations. A young lady who is "tired out" may feel strangely revived by an unexpected invitation to a dance.

These illustrations could be easily extended. But they deal with the effects of an audience upon our physiological reactions. As we depart from this realm to a consideration of all the other multitudinous aspects of our lives, we see how intimately and intensely our activities are shaped by our social consciousness. Our ambitions, our fears, our attitudes, our beliefs, our loyalties, our dislikes, our friendships and enmities, our work and play are all organized around two poles: ourselves and society. "Keeping up with the Joneses," "Our set doesn't do that," and "It's outside the pale" are phrases frequently upon our lips and much more often in our thoughts. They are at least subconscious factors in determining how an audience responds to a speech.

William James, whose keen insight into the realities of human nature amounted to genius, commented upon the horror of being completely unnoticed.

If no one turned round when we entered, answered when we spoke, or minded what we did, but if every person we met "cut us dead," and acted as if we were non-existent things, a kind of rage and impotent despair would ere long well up in us, from which the cruelest bodily tortures would be a relief; for these would make us feel that, however bad might be our plight, we had not sunk to such a depth as to be unworthy of attention at all.

Acting, perhaps, upon this hint, H. G. Wells wrote a novel entitled *The Invisible Man,* which describes just such a condition and just such a result as James indicated. It is well worth the reading by anyone who doubts the need of an audience, or its effects upon human reactions. The speaker who can threaten social ostracism or promise social approval has a powerful weapon in his hands.

Audience analysis and adaptation

Adaptation to an audience does not always mean specific shaping of the speech to fit the particular individuals who will hear it. This is the ideal when it is possible, but often it cannot be done. Many audiences consist of such varieties of auditors that little more can be done in classifying them than to list them as Americans with, for instance, a Middle West background. Woodrow Wilson faced this problem when, in September, 1919, he traveled across the continent, making thirty formal addresses in support of the League of Nations. Auditors of all kinds poured out in great crowds to hear him, and each address had a further large audience through the newspapers. As a consequence, he concentrated in his speeches on the deep, underlying motives which all his auditors had in common—the urge for national self-preservation, the loyalty to America, the feelings of decency, and the sentiments of idealism. Only through brief introductory comments on the local scene (and these in but a few of the speeches) did he aim his pleas specifically at his particular hearers. The failure of his tour may be a poor recommendation for his method, but it is doubtful if he could have done much more through an attempt to fit each speech to the extremely heterogeneous audiences who heard him.

General adaptation does not, however, mean that the audience is ignored: far from it. Such a situation demands the utmost care in so constructing the speech that it *does* touch upon the fundamental, underlying, universal motives that will appeal to all the varied types of persuadees whom the speaker will try to influence. And for its successful use, the speaker must always be alert to make any specific changes which the occasion seems to demand.

When the speaker prepares a speech for a particular audience (and the overwhelming majority of speakers do just this), he should try to discover the following information about the prospective audience situation:

Physical Characteristics

Of the audience:
1. How large will it be?
2. What age groups will be present—and in what proportions?

   3. Which sex will predominate—and to what extent?
   4. What will be the physical status of the auditors?
     a. Will they be tired from a day of hard labor?
     b. Will they be tired from a long preceding program?
     c. Will they be lethargic from having just eaten heartily?
     d. Will they be alert and excited—eager for action?

Of the occasion:
   1. In what kind of auditorium will the meeting be held?
     a. What is the actual size?
     b. What is the size in relation to the number of auditors?
     c. What is the shape?
     d. Where will the speaker stand in relation to the auditors?
     e. How are the acoustics?
     f. Will the speech be delivered from a platform?
     g. What kinds of symbols, if any, will be in the auditorium?
   2. What kind of program will precede (and follow) the speech?
     a. What will be its length?
     b. What will be its type (music, games, speeches, movies)?
     c. What will be the audience's participation in it?
   3. What is the purpose of the meeting?
     a. To celebrate an anniversary or an event?
     b. To constitute one unit of a campaign or series of programs?
     c. Specifically to hear the invited speaker?

Of the speaker:
   1. Will he be physically fit?
     a. Could he rest prior to the meeting, or will he have to speak while tired from traveling or working?
     b. Will he have eaten lightly or not at all during the two or three hours preceding the speech?
   2. Will he be physically impressive?
     a. Because of his own physique? *or*
     b. Because of the height or arrangement of the rostrum?

Psychological Characteristics

Of the audience:
   1. What is the mental ability of the audience—and with what variation?
     a. General intelligence level?
     b. General educational level?
     c. General background of experience?
     d. Special knowledge of the speaker's subject matter?

2. What predisposing tendencies will influence the audience?
    a. Special beliefs?
    b. General and specific attitudes?
    c. Group loyalties?
    d. Previous relationships with the speaker?
    e. The probable mood of the audience?
    f. Degree of liberalism, or flexibility of mind?
        (1) How directly is the self-interest of the audience involved in the proposal?
        (2) Does the audience believe its self-interest will be affected favorably or unfavorably?
    g. How much and what kind of public opinion have been evidenced regarding the proposal?

Of the occasion:
1. Who are the sponsors of the meeting?
    a. What prestige do they have in the community?
    b. What, if any, relationship do they have to the speaker's proposal?
    c. What is their attitude toward the speaker and his proposal?
2. How appropriate will the speech be to the function of the meeting?
    a. In subject matter?
    b. In aim?
    c. In general tone or style of composition and delivery?
3. What relationship is the speech expected to have to the function of the meeting?

Of the speaker:
1. What is the prestige of the speaker with this particular audience?
2. Is the speaker fully prepared?
    a. Intellectually?
    b. Emotionally?

Purposive adaptation

Whether the speaker's adaptation is to human nature in general or to a specific body of listeners, his purpose should be most carefully formulated with the potential persuadees in mind. The speaker should ask himself how the essence of his proposal can be so stated as to provide the maximum attraction for his desired audience. If the audience consists of twelve local farmers, the proposal should be phrased so that their acceptance of it will be facilitated. If the audience is the whole population of the United States, or of the world, it should be phrased to take advantage of the broad interests, needs, and loyalties represented by all the hearers. In general, the following characteristics should be inherent in a proposal to make it generally acceptable. For special audiences, the special needs of the hearers will have to be taken into account.

1. The probable results of the proposal should be definitely stated. When we launch forth into a new undertaking, we want to know what will be (or at least what may be) accomplished. The speaker should talk very largely in terms of results—and picture them in very concrete terms. Salesmen are advised, for instance, not to sell a product, but to sell its utility. "Don't sell a car—but the pleasure of driving into the countryside"; "Don't sell a house—but a home."

2. Its results should be lasting. While an audience may make some effort to secure a purely temporary advantage, it is much more likely to respond when long-term benefits are evident. Chamberlain, recognizing this fact, came back from his Munich meeting with Hitler in 1938 proclaiming that he had won "Peace in our time." The cry became a slogan which popularized the policy of appeasement of the Axis powers. Salesmen find that one great aid in selling their products is a long-term guarantee. People like to buy a "lifetime" pen. One deep-seated desire which people have is to make an impression which will outlive them and thus provide a tangible sort of immortality. On this basis Gutzon Borglum sold the United States Government his project of carving in the "eternal granite" of the Black Hills a monument to Washington, Jefferson, Lincoln, and Theodore Roosevelt which should last through untold ages.

3. Its results should be impressive. The *first,* the *largest,* the *greatest* are descriptive terms of apparently high persuasive value. Innumerable are the towns that advertise that they have such attractions as "The largest apple packing plant in the world"; or, "The oldest university west of the Mississippi River." The continual striving to be impressive is well exemplified in the advertising of motion pictures: each one is said to be more stupendous, magnificent, breath-taking, or awe-inspiring than its predecessors. The effects of such a persuasive

technique may be indicated by the fact that although professional critics of the motion picture industry usually complain about the low quality of the pictures, nevertheless, some eighty million admissions weekly are sold for movies in the United States.

The use of impressiveness by a persuasive speaker is illustrated in the passage by which John Adams, according to Daniel Webster, stated his support of the Declaration of Independence:

> Sir, before God, I believe the hour is come. My judgment approves this measure and my whole heart is in it. All that I have, and all that I am, and all that I hope in this life, I am now ready here to stake upon it; and I leave off as I began, that, live or die, survive or perish, I am for the Declaration. It is my living sentiment, and by the blessing of God it shall be my dying sentiment—Independence now, and INDEPENDENCE FOREVER!

4. Its results should be attractive. The speaker should plan how he can make his auditors want to accept his proposal by showing how their welfare will be advanced by it. People never want to abandon the status quo unless it is for something better. Stated crudely, they ask of every proposal, "What shall we get out of this?" They may get some material benefit, or the satisfaction of aiding a good cause—but the speaker must show that they will get something. On a low plane this characteristic of a satisfying proposal is simply a promise of value to be received for effort expended; on a high plane it is a call to labor for worthy ideals. In this spirit President Franklin D. Roosevelt recommended his program of reforms to a terribly depressed nation, in his first inaugural address:

> We face the arduous days that lie before us in the warm courage of national unity: with the clear consciousness of seeking old and precious moral values; with the clean satisfaction that comes from the stern performance of duty by old and young alike. We aim at the assurance of a rounded and permanent national life.

Any proposal that has clearly manifested these four characteristics should prove satisfying to its audience. A speaker who takes care to make them clear in his phrasing of his central speech purpose is taking careful and accurate aim at his target. If he backs his missile with sufficient motive power, it should hit its mark.

Types of Audiences

For a long time, audiences have been classified as favorable, indifferent, or unfavorable. A popular modern refinement has presented this same basic classification on a fivefold scale:

| HIGHLY FAVORABLE | MILDLY FAVORABLE | INDIFFERENT | MILDLY OPPOSED | STRONGLY OPPOSED |

This fivefold division of audience attitudes is elementary and fundamental. Every persuasive speech should be planned to fit whichever of these attitudes its audience will have. Furthermore, it should be noted that the attitudes are directed toward both the speaker and his proposal. It happens sometimes that an audience is favorably inclined toward a speaker, but hostile to his proposal. In other instances, popular proposals are presented by unpopular speakers. In either case, the speaker should attempt to keep his audience's thinking occupied with what they do like—either the proposition or the speaker. When the speaker uses this method, the unpalatable element is likely to be accepted by the audience after merely incidental attention. The process is similar to the sugar-coating of a bitter pill.

A. POLARIZATION

Besides noting the attitude of an audience, the speaker should take account of its degree of polarization, or receptivity to persuasive appeals. A question of great importance to the speaker is just how receptive his audience is likely to be. This is at least as important as whether its initial attitude is favorable or not.

H. L. Hollingworth, in *The Psychology of the Audience,* has done valuable pioneer work in deducing a classification of audiences based upon their degree of polarization. He offers a five-step scale, from the completely nonpolarized to the highly suggestible audiences. With the thought that he has left out of consideration one important type of speaking situation, the group discussion, his classification is presented here with the number of steps increased to six. The addition to Hollingworth's list is number three in the following series:

1. The *pedestrian audience* consists of casual and accidental listeners, such as those a street-corner orator may attract. Under these circumstances, the problem of the speech is like that of a show window or an advertisement: to catch the attention and quickly build up enough interest to hold the auditors while the speaker proceeds with his message. The task of the speaker is to mold a group of individuals who have assembled without purpose and with only transient and superficial interest into a real, unified, homogeneous audience. Sensationalism is the most successful ingredient of speeches aimed at this kind of audience. The sideshow barker, the sidewalk vendor of patent medicines and trick contrivances, the street-corner orator, the itinerant evangelist, and the auctioneer disposing of the products of a bankrupt jewelry store—all have techniques that are based upon a large amount of bodily action, strong vocal force and wide variety, exaggeration, dramatic illustrations, direct personal appeals, and crude slapstick comedy. Their speeches are like newspaper headlines, and the two are subject to the same condition: everything else must be subordinated to the need of securing attention.

2. The *passive audience* is one that has assembled for a debate, lecture, or other performance, without much more motive than idle curiosity or the desire to be amused. Sometimes such an audience is present only because it has to be, as at a compulsory chapel program. Initial attention will readily be given, but the development of interest and the achievement of persuasion depend entirely upon the speaker. The audience feels no compulsion to concentrate upon the speech. If it is dull, they are apt to think, "We've drawn a blank today," and they settle down to read, write letters, or whisper to one another. If the speaker does not want his auditors to take their leave mentally, he will have to maintain a high level of interest in his speech. Speakers frequently assert that a school assembly is a hard audience to address, and in this sense it is: the students have been summoned to attend,

and feel no responsibility to meet the speaker halfway. Like any passive audience, they will respond gladly and warmly to an interesting speech, but will display obvious boredom at a dull one.

3. The *discussion audience* consists of speakers as well as listeners, such as those at a forum, round table, or parliamentary session. All the members potentially and many of them actually combine both roles. The attention is frequently shifted from one participant to another, and what one speaker partly achieves may be undermined by the next. The very nature of the discussion situation presupposes an active difference of opinion among the members of the group, and as any one participant speaks, the minds of at least a portion of his audience are busily engaged in considering contrary alternatives to his proposal. Under these circumstances, no speaker can hope to hold close attention for long, as every auditor is conscious of the desire of other participants to get the floor. The most successful discussion speakers are those who minimize differences of opinion, who speak in a conciliatory manner, and who use the common ground approach.

4. The *selected audience* consists of members who are all assembled with a common interest, as at a meeting of a lodge, a service club, a labor union, or a church. There may be many different points of view represented by the auditors, but at least they all cluster around a common core of interest. The speaker may ordinarily take the interest of such an audience for granted, if he has something to say of genuine importance on a topic appropriate to the purpose of the meeting. The auditors do feel a responsibility to give their close attention to the speaker, but they demand in return evidences of careful preparation and thoughtful consideration of the purpose which led them to assemble. They attended the meeting for a purpose, and the speaker is expected to help them achieve it.

5. A *concerted audience* is one in which all the auditors are bent upon achieving the same end, such as raising funds for the Community Chest, improving the local school system, selecting a new minister, or deciding upon a suitable gift for the senior class to leave to its Alma Mater. Sometimes in such a group there are strongly divergent opinions as to how the end desired by all is to be achieved. There are

different methods of conducting a drive for funds, different opinions as to what will be an improvement for school systems, contending candidates for pastorates, and a wide variety of possible gifts. A speaker, in presenting his own idea, should minimize his differences with others, should appeal strongly to common loyalties, should willingly yield on all but essential points, and would do well to present his proposal as the choice of many, rather than as his own particular plan.

6. An *organized audience,* finally, is one united on a specific program or loyally attached to its chosen leader. For example, a nominating convention is *concerted* upon the task of picking a nominee; after that has been done, it is *organized* to work for his election. Debate ceases entirely or is minimized; differences are either settled or ignored. The majority has spoken, a program has been decided upon, a leader has been chosen, and there is little left to do but for each auditor to pledge his loyal support. The speaker in such a situation emphasizes the common bonds that bind all together, stresses the importance of their joint endeavor, presents a definite plan for action, and makes a strong plea for sacrificial and united effort to put their program into effect.

To the speaker it makes every difference which type of audience he is to address. If he is wise, in the early stages of preparation for his speech he will make the best estimate he can of the attitude of his audience toward himself and toward his proposal: whether favorable, indifferent, or opposed; and he will decide upon which of these six levels of polarization his audience will probably be found. The kinds of motive appeals he should use depend to a considerable extent upon his determination of these two points. They give him his best answers to the questions: How large and what kind of a persuasive problem does this particular occasion present?

B. HOMOGENEITY OF AUDITORS

The importance of homogeneity in an audience differs with different types of persuasive speeches. It is relatively unimportant to a speaker that his audience may be composed of widely divergent types of auditors when the following circumstances prevail:

1. The speaker seeks a unified, social response;
2. Social pressure favors the speaker's proposal;
3. Little sacrifice is demanded of the persuadees.

When the first condition is combined with both the second and the third, the speaker's proposal is almost certain to prevail. When the first is combined with either the second or the third, the proposal is likely to be accepted. And when any one of the three conditions exists by itself, there is a predisposing tendency for the audience to accept the speaker's point of view. All three conditions are met when the speaker calls upon his audience to rise and salute the flag or attend a mass meeting to pay honor to a popular hero. The first condition is exemplified in a speaker's plea for everyone to turn out to vote on election day. The second condition is met when the speaker is backed by a strong majority opinion, as when he asks his audience to buy Defense Bonds in time of war. Illustrations of the third condition are found when an audience is simply asked to express its opinion when there is nothing practical that it can do. An example is from a speech by Senator Pat McCarran in the Senate on August 6, 1951. "We need a fighting policy, aiming at the soonest possible collapse of the Red hierarchy," the Senator said, "and we need techniques of psychological warfare to match such a policy." It was especially easy for his auditors to agree, since no direct action of their own was required.

These three circumstances that have been described all tend to lighten the speaker's persuasive task; it is for that reason that he is able to overcome the difficulty of a heterogeneous audience. But this difficulty will be too great, and therefore homogeneity is all but essential, when he speaks under the following circumstances:

1. The speaker seeks an individualized response;
2. Social pressure is lacking or is opposed to the proposal;
3. Personal sacrifice or action is required of the persuadees.

An individualized response means that each auditor is to make up his mind on the basis of his own relationship to the proposal. It is the goal of speeches made to high school students on the merits of a college education, for instance. Some will go to college, some not; of those who go, some will desire chiefly vocational training, some a cultural education; part of the audience will be able to afford the expense of a college course—others will need scholarship aid or be wholly unable to go. Another type of speech that seeks an individualized response is a sales talk. The motives that lead one auditor to buy may have no effect on the others. Every salesman knows how greatly his sales problem is complicated when someone or several persons join his single auditor.

When public opinion opposes the speaker's plan, or when he advances something new and unheard of, he meets suspicion and unwillingness to act. This sense of caution is heightened by any feeling among the auditors that they are strangers to one another. The feeling of "What will people think?" is then reinforced by the question, "What are these people around me thinking?" Any visible response to the speaker's proposal would be very hard to secure; and without the contagious power of increasing evidences of open and avowed approval, a reserved audience can hardly be won to favorable partisanship.

If the speaker's proposal entails the making of sacrifices by his auditors, he is also greatly handicapped by marked diversity among them. Sacrifice is most easily secured under conditions of marked group loyalty or strong emotional excitement, and with a heterogeneous audience neither of these conditions is to be expected. Furthermore, in a divergent audience, the degree of sacrifice demanded of the individual varies. When volunteers are requested to make a canvass of the town for charitable contributions, each auditor is likely to think, "So-and-so can spare the time much more easily than I can"; or, "So-and-so has much more ability at that sort of thing than I have." "Passing the buck" is easier than when the members of the audience are all of one type.

Conclusion

As is indicated in the quotation selected to introduce these opening chapters on motivation, Aristotle nominated "the personal character of the speaker" as the first of the three modes of persuasion. This chapter has outlined ways in which an audience is influenced by the representative nature, the qualities, and the attitudes of the speaker. Also discussed are the two-way relationships that exist between a speaker and his audience—including the "larger audience" of the total community. The nature of the audience itself is analyzed, with an indication of what the speaker should look for when he is preparing to adapt what he has to say to audience needs, interests, and desires. Unlike the customer, the audience is not "always right." But in seeking to set the audience right in relation to his proposal, the speaker needs to know a great deal about the characteristics of those to whom he speaks. This is fundamental to persuasion.

Exercises

1. Using the *Readers' Guide to Periodical Literature* as a guide to source materials, report orally on the persuasive personality of one of the following: John F. Kennedy, Robert Kennedy, Edward Kennedy, Lyndon B. Johnson, Hubert Humphrey, Ronald Reagan, Eugene McCarthy, Nelson Rockefeller, Martin Luther King, Stokely Carmichael, Billy Graham, Oral Roberts, U Thant, Mao Tse-tung, Charles de Gaulle, Richard Nixon.

2. Write a one-sentence definition of personality. Thinking of two acquaintances, one of superior and one of inferior personality, does your definition serve as a suitable standard for assessing their differences? How would you rate them in accordance with the qualities of the speaker discussed in this chapter?

3. Select an effective persuasive speaker—local or national, living or dead—and analyze him in terms of the tenfold types of representation, as discussed in this chapter. What is the relation of his persuasiveness to his representative functions?

4. In terms of a particular subject on which you might speak to your classroom audience, what would be your own representative functions? What can you do to improve upon them?

The Psychology of Persuasive Speech

5. The following references will enable you to broaden your understanding of the speaker's personality and his relationship with his audience:

K. Anderson and T. Clevenger, Jr., "A Summary of Experimental Research in Ethos," *Speech Monographs,* XXX (June, 1963), 59-78.

Eldon E. Baker and W. Charles Redding, "The Effects of Perceived Tallness in Persuasive Speaking: An Experiment," *Journal of Communication,* XII (March, 1962), 51-53.

Barbara Lieb Brilhart, "The Relationship between Some Aspects of Communicative Speaking and Communicative Listening," *Journal of Communication,* XV (March, 1965), 35-46.

Jon Eisenson, J. Jeffrey Auer, and John V. Irwin, *The Psychology of Communication* (New York: Appleton-Century-Crofts, 1963), particularly Chapter 16, "Psychology of Public Address," pp. 271-309.

Robert J. Ferullo, "The Self-Concept in Communication," *Journal of Communication,* XIII (June, 1963), 77-86.

Alvin Goldberg, "An Experimental Study of the Effects of Evaluation upon Group Behavior," *Quarterly Journal of Speech,* 46 (October, 1960), 274-283.

Bradley S. Greenberg and Gerald R. Miller, "The Effects of Low-Credibility Sources on Message Acceptance," *Speech Monographs,* 33 (June, 1966), 127-136.

Franklyn S. Haiman, "An Experimental Study of the Effects of Ethos in Public Speaking," *Speech Monographs,* 16 (September, 1949), 190-202.

L. S. Harms, "Listener Judgment of Status Cues in Speech," *Quarterly Journal of Speech,* 48 (April, 1961), 164-168.

M. A. Hewgill and G. R. Miller, "Source Credibility and Fear-arousing Communications," *Speech Monographs,* 32 (June, 1965), 95-101.

Paul D. Holtzman, "Confirmation of Ethos as a Confounding Element in Communication Research," *Speech Monographs,* 33 (November, 1966), 464-466.

Carl I. Hovland and Irving Janis, *Personality and Persuasability* (New Haven: Yale University Press, 1959).

C. I. Hovland, I. Janis, and H. H. Kelley, *Communication and Persuasion* (New Haven: Yale University Press, 1953), particularly Chapter II, "Credibility of the Communicator," pp. 19-55.

C. I. Hovland and W. Mandell, "An Experimental Comparison of Conclusion-Drawing by the Communicator and by the Audience," *Journal of Abnormal and Social Psychology,* 47 (1952), 581-588.

C. I. Hovland and W. Weiss, "The Influence of Source Credibility on Communication Effectiveness," *Public Opinion Quarterly,* XV (1951), 635-650.

F. Craig Johnson and George R. Klare, "General Models of Communication Research: A Survey of the Developments of a Decade," *Journal of Communication,* XI (March, 1961), 13-26 and 45.

Franklin H. Knower, "A Study of Speech Attitudes and Adjustments," *Speech Monographs,* V (1938), 130-203.

James C. McCroskey, "Scales for the Measurement of Ethos," *Speech Monographs,* 33 (March, 1966), 65-72.

James C. McCroskey and Robert E. Dunham, "Ethos: A Confounding Element in Communication Research," *Speech Monographs,* 33 (November, 1966), 456-463.

Gerald R. Miller, *Speech Communication: A Behavioral Approach* (Indianapolis: Bobbs-Merrill, 1966).

Lawrence B. Rosenfeld, "Teaching Impromptu Speaking," *Speech Teacher,* XV (September, 1966), 232-234.

Paul I. Rosenthal, "The Concept of Ethos and the Structure of Persuasion," *Speech Monographs,* 33 (June, 1966), 114-126.

Thomas M. Scheidel and Laura Crowell, "Feedback in Small Group Communication," *Quarterly Journal of Speech,* 52 (October, 1966), 273-278.

Ray H. Simpson, *A Study of Those Who Influence and Those Who Are Influenced in Discussion* (New York: Columbia University Press, 1938).

——, "Attitudinal Effects of Small Group Discussions: Shifts on Certainty-Uncertainty and Agreement-Disagreement Continua," *Quarterly Journal of Speech,* 46 (December, 1960), 415-418.

An Overview of the
Persuasive Process

THE INESCAPABLE FUNDAMENTAL THESIS OF PERSUA-
sion is that it is a process of influencing the behavior of the persons
who are being addressed. This means that it is above all "audience-
centered." Ethically, the speaker is bound to do his utmost to present
his own view of truth, rather than to pander to audience desires or
prejudices; and he should avoid using any means which will undermine or weaken that purpose. Logically and philosophically, the
speaker is bound to exercise the utmost carefulness in research and
in thinking to insure that the decision he wishes his audience to accept
is sound. But so far as persuasion itself is concerned, the task with
which he is confronted is how to win the agreement of his listeners.

This understanding of persuasion was evidenced in a rather unusual
quarter when, at the Mathematical Colloquium of Columbia University, on October 13, 1913, one of the country's leading mathema-
ticians, addressing other experts in mathematics, in an address entitled,
"The Human Worth of Rigorous Thinking," emphasized this same
concept of audience-centering: "What is it," Dr. Keyser asked, "that
our speaker will be obliged to deal with first? I do not mean obliged
logically nor obliged by an orderly development of his subject. I mean
obliged by the expectation of his hearers."

To ask the persuasive speaker to turn his eyes away from the subject matter and toward his audience does not mean that we are advis-

ing shallow thinking or demagogic trickery. The good persuasive speaker does need a wide background of general information. He needs to know what the best reference sources are and how to use them. He needs to be trained in close observation and in logical analysis and argument. He needs to be able to think problems through with scientific objectivity. He needs to be imbued with a passionate love of truth. And he should learn how to organize his materials in a logical brief that will enable him to test carefully the degree to which his conclusions are supported by convincing evidence. Without these abilities and characteristics, he will be unable to reach the right conclusions himself, and in his persuasive speaking would be as a blind guide trying to lead the blind. It is quite proper that most educational efforts should be directed toward the increase of knowledge and the improvement of judgment.

But if we are to go beyond the stage of formulating conclusions to investigate the methods of getting those conclusions adopted by others; if we are, in short, to have a science of persuasion, it must be based squarely upon an understanding of human nature. This is a task which calls for thinking that is not shallow and tricky; it is intellectual labor of the hardest sort. An individual engaged in formulating a judgment is enacting the role of a scientist or a logician. But when his own mind is made up, he must turn his attention to a problem very different, more complex, and more difficult; namely, how to persuade others to accept his conclusion.

It is at this point that he becomes a student of persuasive speech. His thinking subsequently is not subject-centered, but audience-centered. The question he brings to the study of persuasion is not, "How can I reach a right conclusion?" but, "How can a given audience be influenced to accept my conclusion?" This point of view deserves the sharpest emphasis it can receive, for it is the catalytic which precipitates the principles set forth in this book.

A persuasive sample

Let us hypothecate a speech by a man named Joe. He is not a nationally known expert, but just a home town lawyer giving the local

Rotary Club the usual annual appeal for Community Chest Donations. But this speech we are imagining turned out not to be so usual, for Joe decided to climb out of the routine rut and warm up the nerves that guide the hands of his listeners toward their pocketbooks. He titled his speech, "We Don't Get Mad Often Enough," and set out to crack the shell of indifference that shuts in the normal man's kernel of philanthropy. Said Joe:

You and I have done a lot for this town, and it has done a lot for us. We're the meat and television boys who help our fellow citizens get their hands on the goods and services that make their families the most comfortable people on earth. We bid low, build well, and sell cheap, so that they can afford to maintain the highest standard of living in the world. And we make a decent profit for ourselves while we do it. This is what we mean by the American system, and right here at home we can see around us every day in the year that it is the best system ever developed.

We feel pretty happy about it, and we ought to. For in all the five thousand years of civilization, and among all the two and a quarter billion people alive today, this high standard of living we enjoy has never been equaled or even approached. The Communists and the Socialists and the dictators around the world can propagandize all they please about "planned equality," but we're the folks who really deliver the goods. We have every right to feel good about it—and I hope we do.

We're in good shape in every respect but one. And I want to put that one problem squarely up to you so we can see it and solve it. Our problem is that we don't get mad often enough.

By this time Joe's audience was really sitting up and listening to what he had to say. They had come to the meeting with an air of resignation. They knew this was the week to launch the drive for the Community Chest, and they expected to be told the need was great and that they must give to support the Red Cross, the Boy Scouts, and all the rest. They fully expected to drowse through the familiar appeal and then write the usual minimum check. If everyone did his duty, the quota would finally be met and they could get back to planning the spring bridge tournament and forget the whole thing for another year. But Joe wasn't palming the job off as a chore to be done and forgotten. His voice was vibrant with real feeling and his eyes had a warm glow as he gripped the back of his chair and talked his way through the crust and right down into their hearts.

We don't get mad often enough. My wife has a cleaning woman who comes twice a week, and she has a son who is a pal of my own boy in high school. This boy makes good grades, plays on the school football team, and all the fellows think he's a pretty good guy. But he's not planning to go on to college and law school, as my own son is. He's thinking, instead, of what kind of job he can get after high school ends. There'll be a job waiting for him, and he'll probably make out all right in a mediocre sort of way. He'll earn a living and raise a family and be a decent citizen in our community. But I'm mad about what is going to happen to that boy—for he's an intelligent lad with real promise. He ought to have the same chance our own sons have to climb up the ladder and be a real success. He has a right to aim for the top, and if he makes it we'll all benefit from everything he achieves. That's the real American system, and that's the way it ought to be.

Joe paused for a long moment while he looked slowly around the room at the men who were leaning forward in their chairs to hear him. Then he went on:

In a lot of countries around the world those who are at the top do their level best to hang onto every advantage they can get. They're afraid of competition from the masses down below. They don't want any more people squeezing their way into the professions or the business field. They've got a good thing, and their whole idea is to build a fence around it and protect their monopoly.

Well, they've been following that philosophy for a good many centuries, and look what it's got them. There they are, away down the scale of the standard of living—far below us, and still struggling to hold on. We Americans know a lot better than that. We know that what keeps our prosperity rolling along is the great, surging drive of all the people to climb closer to the top. We've discovered a new formula for genuine success—new in the whole history of the world. And what makes me mad is that we don't carry it far enough and live it right up to the hilt.

Once again Joe stopped and shifted his position. He realized his voice had climbed up to a high pitch and that some of his listeners might think he was letting his feelings run away with his common sense. So he dropped his pitch down again, and when he resumed speaking it was in a slow and matter-of-fact tone.

I'm not trying to say we ought to walk right through the front door into Utopia. I know, just as well as you do, that in any population of one hundred and sixty-five million people there have to be a lot of guys who'll spend their lives digging ditches and cleaning sewers and pumping gasoline into our cars. Of course the great majority are going to be common laborers. We need their work, and under our system we keep their work week short and pay them well. There's no need for anyone to worry about that.

But I'm not concerned this evening about the hundred and sixty-five million people in the United States. I'm concerned about the folks right here in our own home town. And I'm not interested in trying to make room at the top for every youngster who attends our public schools. What I do want—and I'm sure you all want it, too—is to keep the channels open so the boys and girls we all know can have the same chance we had ourselves to make the most of their abilities and to have the best opportunities we can give them to lead useful and happy lives.

Joe went right on talking for another ten minutes, telling his audience in human terms about how the other half lives, about what it means to battle without resources against cold and hunger and disease, and above all how the whole community would benefit if everyone in it had a chance to make the most he could out of himself. And he ended with a serious appeal directed to every man in the hall.

You know and I know that things won't get any better by accident. Our progress comes from planning, and hard work, and a feeling of responsibility by every one of us to do his part. We've got a plan here in our town that's been worked out by a body of experts who really make community service their life careers. They work hard to do the job for our people that we need done and want done. We're lucky to have them, and they're lucky to have us. They work for us, and we're not the type to let them down.

We've built our own success on the basis of investing heavily in order to make a good return. I know we're going to invest heavily in this common job of building a better home town. The pledge blanks for this Community Chest drive have all been distributed and are lying right there before you, beside your plates. What I'm asking you—and I'm sure we're all asking one another the same thing—is to make this pledge the biggest and the most meaningful you possibly can. If we all get into this thing the right way, and do more than we ever thought we could, we'll lift this town right up onto a new level of prosperity and happiness for the good of us all. I'll leave you now to the pledge cards and your fountain pens—

and I hope you'll write out your pledge with the vision in your eyes of the kind of home town we all want this to be.

The speaker was not an orator but just a man named Joe—a member of the Rotary Club who took a routine job and determined to make it a success. He knew what persuasive speaking really is, and he knew what it can accomplish. The results were not only more money for the Chest but a better feeling of comradeship and unity in the Club—and, incidentally, a further boost toward leadership for this speaker named Joe. If he wanted the office of District Attorney, or a seat in the legislature, or more clients for his law office, he was headed toward these goals by the right path. For we all value the men among us who can stand up and speak with effective persuasiveness in behalf of the ideals we all profess but (except when we are nudged in the right direction) do not invariably support. We can put ourselves on the right track, but it takes effective leadership to keep us there and to keep us moving along it toward the promised goal.

Persuasion and leadership

As was pointed out in Chapter 1 (and it is important enough to merit re-emphasis) persuasive speaking is a form of leadership. Both leadership and persuasion arise from the same sources and are composed in large part of the same qualities. There is a tendency to think of them both as a type of dominance exercised by one person over many. Actually, in psychological terms, both consist of a circular response: that is, they consist of many stimuli that not only go out from one to many, but also of stimuli that come back from the many to the one. In a sense the process is like the old dream of perpetual motion, for each action causes an equal or greater reaction—a back kick that keeps the whole process moving along.

Abraham Lincoln was this kind of leader, a man of the people, so much like the great mass of Americans that he felt as they felt, thought as they thought, and tried to accomplish what they wanted done. Yet at the same time he felt more keenly than they could feel, understood the problems more clearly, and phrased the solutions far more eloquently. As a result, what he said—"This government cannot endure permanently half slave and half free"; ". . . care for him who shall have borne the battle, and for his widow and his orphan"; "government of the people, by the people, for the people, shall not perish from the earth"—was not only what the people believed, but was so fine a statement of their beliefs that his proposals became the goals toward which succeeding generations have been irresistibly led.

The leader, and the persuasive speaker (who is the best kind of leader), draws his power from his understanding of people and uses that power to draw them on to the achievement of their own best hopes and ideals. He lives right, plans right, and speaks right, because he draws his persuasiveness from his perception of the nature and the needs of the people with whom he talks, as well as from his best understanding of the facts of the case.

Identification of speaker and audience

It would be easier to master persuasion if speech were merely a set of tools any man could acquire and learn to use. But persuasion is more than a skill; it is a way of life. The old Roman, Publius Syrus, expressed this concept cogently when he wrote: "Speech is a mirror of the soul; as a man speaks, so is he." No one can persuade others to his beliefs unless he honestly and sincerely believes that what he says is right. Nevertheless, self-assurance alone can become vanity, and egotism, and argumentative arrogance. To speak effectively to others it is essential to have their welfare at heart, to respect their thinking, to share their faith.

When our hypothetical man named Joe spoke to his fellow townsmen, he was not trying to destroy their sets of values and lead them to accept his. Rather, he restated for them their own convictions and recreated for them a warm and glowing vision of their own beliefs. At no point in his speech did he berate them for being duller or less generous or more self-centered than he was himself. He spoke in terms of *you and I,* of what we all know, of what we plan together, of the hopes we share. With confidence that he understood them rightly, he dared to speak with enthusiasm of the commonality of their march forward toward a better community. His contagious sincerity was solidly based on the certainty that his own analysis was right, and that he was correct in believing his audience was motivated by feelings very much like his own.

"Trust yourself," wrote Ralph Waldo Emerson, "every heart vibrates to that iron string." Then Emerson went on to write his famous essay on "Self-Reliance," in which he showed that self-fulfillment arises only from full participation in the aspirations and sense of values of mankind generally. Self-respect and respect for others are not two opposites that may on occasion happily concur. They are even more closely united than opposite aspects of one basic quality. They are inextricably intertwined, like the warp and the woof of a piece of cloth. Neither can truly exist without the other. The man who pities or despises his fellows cannot really think well of himself. Nor can the self-doubter have unquestioning faith in the qualities of his associates. Leadership belongs to those who sense within themselves values that are shared by all. Out of this awareness comes the fundamental effectiveness of persuasive speech. Water flows into oil, but oil and water never mix. The speaker who considers himself to be significantly different from his audience is failing to keep open the channels through which they may be influenced.

You can't get very far by writing down, thinking down, or speaking down to the people whom you address. Condescension is not a pathway to co-operation. But neither can you be persuasively effective if you feel you must think up and speak up to them. Leadership is too heavy a load to be pushed uphill. Ideas and influence, like water, find their own levels. They flow back and forth most easily between equals. They achieve their effect when spoken by a speaker with self-respect to an audience he respects. This is one of the basic requirements for mastery of persuasive speech—simple to state, easy to accept, and indispensable to success; yet sometimes, for some persons, hard to achieve.

Planning the speech

A second basic requirement for persuasion is that the speech be carefully planned. Even a poor plan is better than none. Wendell

Johnson, author of *People in Quandaries,* has said that "The chief problem in education is to get people to delay their response to any stimulus long enough to think about it." Think before you speak! Think even before you decide what to talk about, or what point of view to uphold. It seems simple, but many an individual has got himself into hot water by popping out an immediate retort to a question, only to find himself presented with the ego-necessity of defending an indefensible position that he should never have assumed in the first place. The steps to the educational goal proposed by Professor Johnson were long ago outlined by Aristotle when he stated, very simply, in his *Poetic* that every composition should have a Beginning, a Middle, and an End.

Before you adopt (much less publicly proclaim) a proposal which you will have to uphold, stop and think whether it has real value and whether it will be worth the trouble it will cost. For ideas, like other commodities, have their price tags, even if they seem to be conjured up out of thin air. In an evening's conversation you may be moved by someone's reckless criticisms to announce firmly, "I am in favor of the administration's foreign policy!" If all you care about is some lively verbal gymnastics, plunge right in and let the sparks fly.

But if you want to be persuasive (either to convince your companions or to give yourself some exercise in genuine persuasion) stop and take a long look at the tremendous burden of proof your statement would saddle you with. American foreign policy is so complex that it is quite possible you yourself (and your companions) may not know what it is in all respects. Furthermore, the foreign policy of any nation (our own included) never can be drawn up in ideal fashion at any one time by any administration. Like Topsy, it just grows. It springs from Yalta as one source, the Oriental Exclusion Acts of 1916 as another, the 1928 Smoot-Hawley Tariff as another, the oil contracts of the Middle East, the 1900 Open Door Policy toward China, the Monroe Doctrine, the Korean truce, and hundreds of other prior events and decisions. To leap into the *Beginning* of a persuasive situation with the sweeping assertion that you "approve" of our entire foreign policy would be akin to stepping into a waterfront brawl with the offer to take on all comers.

A better opening statement might be, "Let's see if we can agree with one another on what America's foreign policy really is?" This leaves you every opportunity to defend any and every aspect of it that you may wish, without the liability of being prepledged to support parts of it which most certainly could not be present in your mind when you assume your initial position. The old advice not to bite off more than you can chew might well be restated as: don't bite off more than you need to chew. Nothing is going to prevent your swallowing the whole meal if you choose, but it is more healthful and much better etiquette to take it in manageable bites.

But let's not get lost in our analogy. The point is this: before you attempt any feat of persuasion, whittle the job down to size. Even if you want finally to accomplish *everything,* you still have to start with *something.* Then you can move on from that point to a whole series of somethings else. You get to your destination by passing through all the way stations along the route.

Another reason for being extremely careful in stating what it is you want to accomplish by your persuasive appeal is that persuasion is far better accomplished by avoiding opposition than by arousing it. Argument generates heat but seldom warmth of mutual accord. If you start by declaring, "I stand here and you stand there," you widen the gulf and make it harder to cross. Note how Joe started his talk to the Rotary Club—by telling his audience that "You and I have done a lot. . . . We make a decent profit. . . . We feel pretty happy about it." *We are working together for things in which we all believe.* Unless this is true, final agreement on specific programs will be difficult if not impossible. If this is true, start out by stressing the fact.

The proper function for the *Beginning* of any persuasive speech is to demonstrate that not much persuasion is needed; we're all the same kind of people; we all have the same kinds of problems; we're bound together by common aims and common hopes. Remember: leadership depends upon identification of the leader with the group. Unless the listeners accept the claimant to leadership as one of themselves, they won't truly listen—and he won't lead. Solomon may have had this in mind in writing that there is nothing new under the sun. There are many new ideas (and upon their backs humanity advances) but people won't advance with the idea-man unless he makes it clear that this *newness* is a natural outgrowth from the system of values and ideals they already cherish. Change is painful and is resisted; fulfillment is easy and desired.

The *Middle* that Aristotle spoke about is different for every subject and every situation. It is the body of the persuasive speech. It's the part of Joe's talk to the Rotary Club which we didn't follow word for word, but merely summarized. It's the combination of facts and appeals that make sense to an audience after a right beginning has shown them the speaker is one of their kind, working with them, to help them achieve a goal they want to reach. One of America's most successful salesmen (winner for three successive years of Chevrolet's national sales contest among its dealers) summarized his own formula for developing the *Middle* of his sales talk by saying, "I help the prospect find reasons for buying a new car that will satisfy his wife, his mother-in-law, and his banker." Once a proper introduction of the topic insures that your listeners will want to follow along with you to your conclusion, your method is not to argue with them but to suggest ways in which their own beliefs and desires converge toward the chosen goal. There will be more about the *Middle* in later chapters, especially in Part IV.

As every salesman knows, the close of a sales presentation, what Aristotle called the *Ending,* is a vital point. The object is to make agreement as easy as possible and opposition as unthinkable as you can. Not, "Will you buy?" but "Which of these models suits you best?" is the standard close of the skilled salesman. You will recall that Joe ended by calling attention to the pledge cards which had already been distributed and were lying right beside the plates of the Rotary Club members. He took their pledge for granted, but asked them to write it with "a vision in your eyes of the kind of home town we all want this to be."

If you remember the unsuccessful persuasive speeches you have heard, it is likely that many of them ended with the speaker gloating over his triumph in proving that he was right and the audience had been wrong. "Therefore, I hope you will now agree with me that the old system you have been following is wrong and that it should be replaced with the superior method I have presented to you." The effective persuasive speeches, on the other hand, end with a demonstration that the audience has been right all along, and can now proceed to vote, or to buy, or to decide with the clear and happy knowledge that the speaker has helped to set up the goal they all want to reach.

Confronting opposition

It is likely that you have found little in the preceding pages with which to disagree, but you may have an uneasy feeling that they have not dealt broadly enough with the whole problem of persuasion. Emphasis constantly has been upon avoidance of arguments—yet we all know that we are on occasion brought face to face with opposition that is flatly stated. We may learn to avoid using such terms as "I am right and you are wrong," but others do and will use them when talking to us. What, then, is good persuasive practice in dealing with opposition that is unmistakably direct? This is a real situation which certainly does arise on occasion. When it does, there are three methods that might be recommended for converting the discussion from an argument to a persuasive situation.

A. AVOIDANCE OF DIRECT ATTACK

The first suggestion is to avoid returning the direct attack upon the individual whose views you want to change. If his ego is attacked, his first thought is to defend it, and thus an argument develops. This fact is illustrated every day in the heated discussions in which the only thought of the arguers seems to be to beat down and humiliate one another. Abraham Lincoln, addressing a temperance society on February 22, 1842, found his auditors in the mood for savage attack upon the drinker, and he gave them this wholesome advice:

... assume to dictate to his judgment, or to command his action, or to mark him out as one to be shunned and despised, and he will retreat within himself, close all the avenues to his head and heart; and though your cause be naked truth itself, transformed to the heaviest lance, harder than steel, and sharper than steel can be made, and though you throw it with more than herculean force and precision, you will be no more able to pierce him than to penetrate the hard shell of a tortoise with a rye straw. Such is man, and so must he be understood by those who would lead him even to his own best interests.

One of the most successful statesmen, diplomats, and businessmen in American history, a master of persuasion—Benjamin Franklin— testified in his autobiography as to the single most effective persuasive technique that he ever developed. In sum, it was a careful consideration of the feelings of the people whom he sought to persuade.

I made it a rule to forbear all direct contradiction to the sentiments of others, and all positive assertion of my own. I even forbid myself ... the use of every word or expression in the language that imported a fix'd opinion, such as *certainly, undoubtedly,* etc., and I adopted, instead of them, *I conceive, I apprehend,* or *I imagine* a thing to be so or so; or it *so appears to me at present.* When another asserted something that I thought an error, I deny'd myself the pleasure of contradicting him abruptly, and of showing immediately some absurdity in his proposition; and in answering I began by observing that in certain cases or circumstances his opinion would be right, but in the present case there *appear'd* or *seem'd* to me some difference, etc. I soon found the advantage of this change in my manner; the conversations I engag'd in went on more pleasantly. The modest way in which I propos'd my opinions procur'd them a readier reception and less contradiction; I had less mortification when I was found to be in the wrong, and I more easily prevail'd with others to give up their mistakes and join with me when I happened to be in the right.

And this mode, which I at first put on with some violence to natural inclination, became at length so easy, and so habitual to me, that perhaps for these fifty years past no one has ever heard a dogmatical expression escape me. And to this habit (after my character of integrity) I think it principally owing that I had early so much weight with my fellow-citizens when I proposed new institutions, or alterations in the old, and so much influence in public councils when I became a member; for I was but a bad speaker, never eloquent, subject to much hesitation in my choice of words, hardly correct in language, and yet I generally carried my points.

B. CAMOUFLAGE OF NECESSARY ATTACK

If attack were never needed, neither would there be much need for persuasion. Persuasion has been lightly defined as the process of moving an opponent from his non-sense to your sense. Often it is unavoidable to disagree with a persuadee's stated position before you can start moving him toward your own. When this situation arises, remember that it is not only the Orientals who desire to "save face." This desire is universal. Accordingly, any attack which proves necessary should be so camouflaged that it will hardly appear as an attack at all.

This fact is so fundamental that it has proved of value even to animal trainers. Larry Trimble, Hollywood motion picture director, and trainer of the famous dog star, Strongheart, and other animal actors, owed his success to his understanding of the value of preventing humiliation.

He knows that every animal wants to think well of itself, wants to be understood, wants to be appreciated, and wants to find and be its best self. But he also knows how sensitive animals are to the mental atmosphere around them, and how arresting to their growth it is to hurt their feelings, to ridicule them, to look down upon them with contempt, or to correct them in the wrong way. One of his basic rules is always to permit an animal to "save face"; that is, never to embarrass it, no matter what the animal may have done or neglected to do.[1]

If this principle is necessary in dealing with animals, it surely is of value in saving the much more highly developed sensitivity of human beings. Ten methods may be suggested for saving the pride of a persuadee with whom you must directly disagree.[2]

1. Agree with him in principle. "As a general rule you are quite right, but the particular circumstances of this case are such that. . . ."

2. Make it clear that he is not to be blamed for being wrong. "Of course, this sort of problem doesn't arise in your type of work."

---

[1] J. Allen Boone, *Letters to Strongheart* (New York: Prentice-Hall, 1939), p. x.

[2] These methods have been adapted from *The Psychology of Dealing with People,* by Wendell White.

3. Admit that many persons agree with him. "What you say seems to be the general opinion of the matter, but. . . ."

4. Agree with part of his statement, or with his reason for making it. "In large part what you say is true, but. . . ."

5. State your desire to agree if you could. "That point of view certainly appeals to me, too, but. . . ."

6. Take time to examine and evaluate his idea carefully—thus proving your respect for it. "This requires thought. Let's see how it would work. . . ."

7. Agree, then raise objections as an afterthought. "Yes, that seems to be right. But, have we taken into account the fact that. . . ."

8. Restate his idea in a form which is acceptable to you, assuming that that is what he meant all the time. "I see. Then your position is that. . . ."

9. Praise the individual before attacking his idea. "That's good! That's the sort of work we have learned to expect from you. Now, let's look at some of the minor details. . . ."

10. Attack your own ego before deflating his. "I wish I had half your fluency and ease, but I always have to stumble around to get an idea expressed. What I tried to say is. . . ."

C. DIRECTING APPEAL TO SELF-INTEREST

Since belief seems inevitably allied to self-interest, a third suggestion for the persuasive speaker is undoubtedly to appeal directly to the desires of the audience. Sometimes this can be done bluntly and directly, as it is in the sermon which Jonathan Swift is said to have preached from the text of *Proverbs* XIX:17: "He that hath pity upon the poor lendeth unto the Lord; and that which he hath given will he pay him again." The preacher's entire commentary on this scriptural passage was: "Brethren, you have heard the condition; if you like the security, down with the dust."

More frequently the appeal to self-interest needs elaboration and some degree of indirectness. Its use is admirably illustrated in the following passage from Hartzell Spence's fine biography of his father, entitled *One Foot in Heaven.* It describes a method of personal evangelism used during a revival meeting:

One night, when the hammering of rain on the tabernacle's wooden roof echoed across many empty seats, Major Cooper spied a vaguely familiar face in the congregation. He finally placed it as that of Reuben Wright, once a regular churchgoer but now never seen. The major hobbled up the aisle and slid into Wright's pew.

"I haven't seen you in some time."

"I haven't been here." Reuben Wright scowled.

"Have you been out of town?"

"No."

"Have you been sick?"

"Let me alone," Wright said.

The major sat silently beside him for a long time. The altar call continued. The music swelled. Mr. Keeler's son played softly on his trombone an old hymn: "Jesus is tenderly calling, today. Calling, oh sinner, come home."

Wright stirred. "I haven't heard that for a long time," he said.

The major nodded.

"I was just thinking that, too."

"Do you remember," Wright asked, "how Westley Carmichael used to play it on the cornet in Sunday School?"

"So he did," the major recalled. "Why, that's fifteen years ago!"

"Yes," Wright replied, "it's been a long time."

"But it would be good to hear him again," the major said. "I wonder if we could get him to play it Sunday? If we could, would you come?"

Wright hesitated. "The church has outgrown me. It doesn't want me around any more."

The major remembered now. Wright had stopped attending church when the choir had been reorganized eight years before. Wright's voice was gone, they had said. A flicker of sympathy came into the major's eyes.

"They don't need me, either," he said, humbly. "I no longer do anything except attend the Sunday service. And I get mighty lonely, sitting there by myself. Why don't you come out next Sunday and join me? It would help. Maybe we could organize an old duffers' Bible class, and you could teach. You used to discuss the Scriptures wonderfully, I remember."

Reuben Wright looked at the major for the first time. "Do you think we could?"

"Why not?" the major asked. "There must be others, like us, who have grown away."

"There's the Widow Jordan," Wright said. "She hasn't been to church since Albert died. There's Harry Gray—you remember him—"

"And Lizzie Carson," the major added, "whatever happened to Lizzie Carson?"

"We ought to find out," Wright suggested.

"Let's do it."

It was Wright now who sought the major's hand.

"You know," he said, "I've been hoping for years that I could get back to my church. I've missed it."

A moment later they walked up the aisle together. Father knew from their faces that something extraordinary had happened and gave them a special blessing.

Conclusion

This chapter concludes the introductory unit of five chapters dealing with the total process of human motivation. Later chapters will elaborate and refine portions of what has been thus far presented, and will offer further guidance in the application of motivational principles in various forms of persuasive speech. As you conclude this part of the book, you will find much to review, and it is hoped you will keep in mind a large part of the detailed presentation on motivational problems and appeals. In an effort to help you in selecting broad and fundamental principles to serve as guides to further persuasive effectiveness, the following seven injunctions are suggested:

1. Be sure to exercise a sound and reasonable self-respect, based upon what you know you can do well and upon a candid and demonstrable consideration of what you have accomplished. Be fair to yourself as well as others. Hold your head up and keep the light of self-confidence in your eyes.

2. Increase your regard for your fellow men by measuring their behavior not in terms of an impossible ideal but in terms of the selfish motives and base impulses which you know from self-analysis and observation are unquestionably a part of human nature. Make a point of appreciating human nature by realizing how much better mankind is than our primal urges might lead anyone to expect.

3. Develop the habit, in conversation as well as in public speeches and business conferences, of starting whatever you have to say from

the point of view of your listeners. Your enthusiasm can't become theirs unless you start with their interests and their understanding of the situation.

4. Express your own ideas in a way that will lead to your own conclusion, but do so by processes of reasoning, explanation, and illustrative anecdotes that make sense in terms of your listeners' experiences. You can persuade others to do far more than they originally intended to do, but only if you help them guide themselves along *their route* toward *your conclusion*. In public speaking this demands constant and alert sensitivity to the reactions of your audience. In conversation and conferences it means that you should talk less and listen more.

5. When you come to the point of asking for a decision, don't let an active ego (we all have it) spoil what you have accomplished by insisting upon a triumphant display of your own superior smartness. Sometimes it's well to ask your listeners for more than you hope (or want) to get, so that you can conclude your remarks with a retreat to a position your listeners will accept as a partial surrender to their own desires. Do you know a wife anywhere who doesn't use this technique in dealing with her husband?

6. When you are speaking don't try to be different from what you really are. Whatever you say and however you say it have to grow out of your personality, your convictions, and your character. Try to analyze yourself honestly and get help from observing what others think of you.

7. None of the principles of persuasion can be memorized in an afternoon and put to work with unvarying success that evening. It takes a lot of climbing to reach the heights. But the only way to get there is to start out and then keep going. This chapter should be reread and its principles practiced. The following chapters lead through various essential way stations toward the goal of genuine persuasive effectiveness.

Exercises

1. The hypothetical speech by Joe may be used as a framework for review and class discussion of the motivational factors set forth in the preceding four chapters. The class may be divided into four groups, with group one assigned to test it in accordance with Chapter 1, group two with Chapter 2, and so forth. In this manner, the generalized considerations set forth in the introductory chapters can all be brought to a concrete test.

2. By this time, members of the class will each have given one or more persuasive speeches. Class members may be asked to write an evaluation of the persuasive techniques and effectiveness of any one member in the class, in accordance with the prescriptions set forth in these first five chapters. If the instructor assigns each class member to criticize in this fashion one specific classmate, all of them may thus be analyzed. These critiques should be helpful to the members receiving them and the preparation of the critiques will serve as a guided review of the chapters.

3. Each member of the class may be asked to present a brief persuasive speech advocating support for the Boy Scouts, the blood-donation program of the Red Cross, or any other local community project.

4. For students wishing to investigate problems in the over-all pattern of persuasion, the following readings will be helpful:

D. K. Berlo and H. E. Gulley, "Some Determinants of the Effects of Oral Communication in Producing Attitude Change and Learning," *Speech Monographs,* XXIV (March, 1957), 10-20.

W. Norwood Brigance, "A Genetic Approach to Persuasion," *Quarterly Journal of Speech,* 17 (June, 1931), 329-339.

Paul D. Holtzman, Robert E. Dunham, and Richard E. Spencer, "Direct Assessment of Effectiveness of Student Speakers," *Journal of Communication,* XVI (June, 1966), 126-132.

W. J. McGuire, "Inducing Resistance to Persuasion: Some Contemporary Approaches," in L. Berkowitz (ed.), *Advances in Experimental Social Psychology* (New York: Academic Press, 1964), I: 191-229.

W. J. McGuire and D. Papageorgis, "The Relative Efficacy of Prior Belief-Defense in Producing Immunity to Persuasion," *Journal of Abnormal and Social Psychology,* 62 (March, 1961), 327-337.

Wilbur Schramm, "How Communication Has an Effect," in Jane Blankenship and Robert Wilhoit (eds.), *Selected Readings in Public Speaking* (Belmont, Calif.: Dickenson, 1966), pp. 227-233.

W. E. Utterback and H. F. Harding, "Some Factors Conditioning Response to Argument," *Speech Monographs,* XXII (November, 1955), 303-308.

PART II

Principles of Persuasion

Among the presentations filing in a continuous series across the threshold of the mind, or appealing for its recognition all at once, some are singled out and given consideration; others are neglected, or pass on with scant attention.

—CHARLES S. GARDNER

The working of suggestion is dependent upon the impulsive, dynamic nature of ideas. . . . We conceive of ideas as being nothing more than formal, inert reasons and assume that to secure action we must add to our ideas the activity of the will. As a matter of fact . . . ideas are the most live things in the universe. They are dynamic and lead to action.

—WALTER DILL SCOTT

Audience adaptation seems to be primarily the product of the speaker's personality. A communicator succeeds only to the extent to which he can build up a useful image of the person with whom he is communicating. To do this he must try to put himself into the "role of the other," in order to know what to expect in the behavior of the other. . . . Success in many situations, then, depends largely on the number of roles the speaker has adequately integrated into his own personality which he can recognize in the individuals with whom he is communicating.

—ORDEAN NESS

✠ 6.

Attention

NORBERT WIENER, WHO HAS ATTRACTED WIDESPREAD interest in the "science of the transfer of information," which he calls *cybernetics,* made the trenchant observation in his book, *The Human Use of Human Beings,* that, "speech is a joint game between the talker and the listener against the forces of confusion." The "major opponent" of "normal communicative discourse," he declared, "is the entropic tendency of nature itself." Entropy, as your dictionary defines it, is "a mathematical measure of unavailable energy." There is, then, Wiener claims, a vast amount of natural energy that is simply unavailable to us. In terms of persuasive speaking, as Wiener makes clear, "it is not the quantity of information that is sent that is important for action, but rather the quantity of information which can penetrate into a communication and storage apparatus sufficiently to serve as the trigger for action."

Does this sound abstruse and complex? Actually, it is the very stuff of common sense. The mind of man is complex far beyond comprehension. But one thing we do know about it is that a vast amount of information gets to the fringes of our attention without ever penetrating "sufficiently to serve as the trigger for action." Writing on, "What Is Memory?" in the September, 1953, issue of *Scientific American,* Ralph W. Gerard points out that tests of perception indicate that each one tenth of a second is a "frame of reference" for the human brain, and that in each of these fractional intervals of time our brains are capable of receiving as many as one thousand units of information. In seventy years of waking time, your brain and mine may be bombarded with fifteen trillion units of information. Since the human brain is estimated to consist of ten billion nerve cells, this means we receive in a lifetime over one thousand times more units of information than we have nerve cells by which they can be interpreted, associated, and stored. No wonder we fail to be consciously aware of so much that goes on around us! No wonder different individuals in any situation observe what is happening in so many different ways, and leave the scene (of an automobile accident, for example) with such varying impressions!

What this means for persuasion was stated by James Albert Winans a generation ago, when he wrote, "Persuasion is the process of inducing others to give fair, favorable, or undivided attention to propositions." Stated somewhat differently, persuasion is the process of devising the means of making clear and emphatic the particular elements of a situation which will induce the listeners to note and recall as "the trigger of action" precisely those factors that will lead them to the conclusion desired by the speaker.

The selection of attention

How we live depends upon what we notice. We see what we see only because we miss everything else. The contact that we have with the world about us is made possible only through our selective attention. The attention of the artist selects certain features of a landscape to observe; the attention of the farmer selects others. Both then deal with those parts to which they attend. Each is what he is partly by virtue of not being the other.

As Murphy, Murphy, and Newcomb point out in their *Experimental Social Psychology,* "To be human is not to be diffusely stimulable in all directions; it is to be selective, to be oriented toward particular classes and modes of stimulation."

The attention of the infant is given only to a small number of pressing needs and desires. As the child develops, his interest gradually becomes engaged in particular types of activity, and he indulges in them to the partial or complete exclusion of others. In his educational experience he finds his teachers attempting to extend his attention into various realms which are thought to be good for him. To a greater or less extent his education and growing maturity combine to "broaden" his mind to a fairly extensive body of attention-arousing factors. The "well-rounded" man willingly gives his attention to many phases of life; the "narrow" man to but few. Yet the environment of both is crowded with much more that they do not notice than with that which they do.

The chief task of the persuasive speaker is to serve as a "selector" of his audience's attention. Among the techniques the speaker must learn, the most basic and vital are those that enable him to gather in the wandering thoughts of his auditors and to concentrate them upon his proposal. If he can induce them to give it their "fair, favorable, or undivided attention," he may be assured of success. But to the extent that their attention wanders, he is certain to fail.

The job of the salesman is to divert the attention of his prospects away from any potential needs or desires except those which may be satisfied by the purchase of his product. Let their attention be centered upon it and they will buy. The trial lawyer will attempt to concentrate the thinking of the jury upon aspects of the case favorable to his client. The politician, the preacher, the reformer, the general advocate are all successful speakers just to the extent that they are able to capture and direct the attention of their auditors. Whatever catches interest influences conduct. The persuasive speaker, in trying to influence the conduct of his auditors *toward* his proposal and *away* from its alternatives, will find that control of their attention is the most vital step.

Anyone who has ever groaned and squirmed under the inescapable thralldom of a dull speaker, or who has ever sat in an audience with his mind wholly absent on business more intriguing than the speech that was being droned against his ears, can present personal testimony to the central position of the ability to command attention in the technique of speech. An audience will struggle against many of the persuasive efforts of a speaker and will seek to defend its judgment from the pressure he tries to exert upon it. But every audience has a vulnerable spot—a veritable Achilles' heel—in its longing to be interested. If the speaker is doing his best to hold the attention and interest of his audience, he may be sure that the audience is at least as eager as he is to find the speech interesting, rather than boring.

The attractive elements in a speech may be likened to the siren song which lured the sailors of mythology off their course. Though it meant the abandonment of their judgment, of their enterprise, even of their lives, the sailors eagerly followed the sweet allure of the music. Just so do auditors eagerly follow the train of interestingness in a speech. If a speaker can command the siren song—if he has the elements of interest in his speech—the auditors will gladly surrender their closest attention to him. And, as shall be pointed out, with their attention goes their belief, their willingness to act, their acceptance of the speaker's point of view. A modern psychologist's paraphrase of Solomon might well read, "Where the attention is, there the heart is also."

It may not be possible for every speaker to master this art of grasping and holding attention. At least, it is certain that many speakers would profit much from learning what attention is and how to control it, and from gaining familiarity with the types of interest. In the following pages these topics are discussed.

The nature of attention

A. ATTENTION DEFINED

Attention is the process of concentrating the receptive resources of the organism. Watch someone straining to hear a distant voice. The whole body is focused in the direction of the sound. The listener leans toward it, his muscles taut, his eyes intent, his ears strained, his very breathing stopped. At such a time the organism is most fully alive. Latent powers are brought to bear upon the solution of the task; the hearing is actually keener than it normally is. Yet other sounds that ordinarily would be distinctly heard fade into the background of consciousness or out of it entirely. The mind becomes an ellipse, stretching itself narrower and narrower as it reaches out toward the object of its attention. It is no wonder that the concentration of attention may result in the solution of problems that otherwise seem too difficult to attempt.

The nature of attention may be clarified if we think of it as a state of *tension,* or readiness, a tending toward the expected. Its converse might be stated as "relaxed and indifferent," a phrase in which the terms are not accidentally combined. But when the mind attends to a stimulus, it goes out to seek it, to explore it, to take it in. It is like an army advancing to capture its objective, with the entire resources of the organism mobilized to assist its advance. Other bodily processes temporarily slow down or stop. The organism makes an "all out" effort to encompass the object of its attention.

Consciousness may be defined not inaccurately as the process of paying attention. One is conscious of those things to which he attends. Consciousness may sink to a very low level as one bathes in the sun, half asleep, on a drowsy, sultry July afternoon. Or one's consciousness may be acutely alert as he awakens in the middle of the night with a sense of danger lurking somewhere in the surrounding dark.

The power to attend is the power to live; one lives in relation to those things to which he attends. Some attend to many things and live in a constant stream of shadowy, half-sensed impressions. Others attend to but few and develop a zealous interest in them to the exclusion of other potential relationships. In either case, the nature of their attention determines the nature of their lives. It is the best measure of consciousness we have.

Attention and interest are twin words that, although not synonymous, are always in company. Whatever we attend to is interesting, and to whatever is interesting we freely give our attention. It is true that the attention may be forced for a time to objects that are uninteresting. But when this occurs, one of two things happens: either the object takes on interest or the attention ultimately wanders from it. Interest grows with acquaintance, with knowledge, with prolonged attention. The elements of interest are the aspects of experience which attract attention. The attentive values of an object are those characteristics of it which arouse interest. The two terms are inseparably intertwined.

B. HOW ATTENTION OPERATES

The selective nature of attention has already been indicated. The selection occurs through a process that is partly physical and partly mental. The respiratory, circulatory, and digestive functions are subordinated. Attention becomes "breathless"; the pulse rate accelerates. The endocrine glands increase their secretions; the muscles become taut. The recall of ideas associated with the present stimulus is accelerated, while other mental activity is depressed. The feeling tone is one of curiosity, expectancy, anticipation. Body and mind alike are characterized by a readiness to act in relation to the stimulus upon which they are concentrated and by a lack of efficient relationship with competing stimuli.

In a speech situation, an audience closely attending to the speaker will be leaning forward in its seats, with its eyes fastened upon him, its hearing so concentrated upon his words that it will hear little else. Other activity in the audience ceases, as it concentrates on the speech. As the muscles of the auditors tighten, their faces may assume strange expressions, their bodies awkward postures. Their consciousness is drawn, as by centripetal power, toward the focal point of the speech. If on the other hand, the auditors are bored and inattentive, their eyes wander, they listen to distracting sounds, their bodies slump in their seats, their minds are occupied with other thoughts. They may read, write, whisper, squirm, or shuffle. A speaker who does not know whether his audience is with him or not is a poor observer indeed.

C. LIMITING FACTORS

Even under the most favorable circumstances the attention tends to wander. Variety is said to be the spice of life. We are seldom indifferent to the different. Monotony, on the other hand, is the begetter of boredom, which leads to either restlessness or indifference. One of the principal problems of the speaker is to hold the audience's interest long enough for him to present his case. Even when an audience gives its most willing attention to a speaker, the length of time that attention can be maintained is limited by several factors.

The limit of absolute attention is only a few seconds. When psychologists wish to test the number of objects that can be taken in in a single perception, they expose them for only one fifth of a second; for if a longer interval of time is allowed, the observer may shift his attention. If you look at such an object as a key, your attention does not remain fixed upon its entire form, but ranges back and forth over its details. Just so the attention of the auditors demands variety; unless the speaker provides it in abundance for them, they will seek it outside his speech. There are always distractions and counterattractions to which they may turn for relief.

Other limiting factors come from within the auditors themselves. Each one has his own problems that are more or less pressing. Some may be inattentive because of fatigue, drowsiness, or overeating. Some may have special antipathies to the speaker's message, or person, or mannerisms, and prefer to turn their attention aside. The interests of the auditors vary, so that what appeals to some will only bore others. One man finds stamp collecting a fascinating hobby; another thinks it is childish.

In all these combined factors there is so much limitation upon the attention span that it has become a commonplace that good speeches must be short ones. Brevity is the soul of wit, we are told. No souls are saved after the first twenty minutes, it is commonly said. Program chairmen are apt to tell their speakers, "Talk as long as you wish—up to twenty minutes!" Lincoln's Gettysburg Address and the Lord's Prayer are pointed to as models of how long a speech should be.

The truth is that most great speeches have been long—some of them running to four or five hours or more. If a speaker can hold his auditors for a few minutes only, it is a sign not of wit, but of sterility. A speaker may wear out his audience in twenty minutes or he may hold it fascinated for an hour. The point at which interest is lost is the limit to which he should continue. Said Ruth Bryan Rhode, "If you don't strike oil in two minutes, stop boring!" But if the speaker can himself provide sufficient elements of interest to hold his audience for an hour, his speech will probably be the better for the increased time he has had for the development of his points. The safest advice is: When you plan your speech, take the factors that limit the attention span into very serious account, and be prepared to be brief if you see signs that these factors are overcoming your best efforts to keep interest alive.

Controlling the attention of an audience

In view of the importance of attention, the methods of controlling it deserve thoughtful consideration. It is well for a speaker to realize (1) the attention values a stimulus may have; (2) the subjective factors affecting his audience's attention span to which he may appeal; (3) the means he may employ to induce attention; (4) the qualities of a stimulus which tend to imbed it in the auditors' memories; (5) the means of emphasis by which he can implant artificially an idea in the memory.

A. ATTENTION VALUES

If two or more stimuli are presented in an individual's field of attention, to which will he turn first? This is a problem that has been frequently and fruitfully explored. As a result of numerous tests, it has been fairly well agreed upon that the attention values a stimulus may have are: (1) intensity—vividness, loudness, brightness; (2) extensity—size or amount; (3) impressivity—duration or repetition; (4) velocity or movement; (5) variety—change or contrast. A bright light will attract attention more quickly and surely than a dim one; a loud noise more than a low one; a sharp taste more than a flat one. Similarly, a large object has a greater initial attention value than a small one. The importance of duration or repetition is illustrated by an alarm clock. A noise that is ignored at first will demand attention if it continues or is repeated. This is a factor, however, for which there is distinctly a law of diminishing returns. If a stimulus persists regularly and monotonously, it loses its attention value. In fact, the sudden cessation of a continuous sound or of any long-continued stimulus will of itself attract the attention. The value of movement in grasping the attention may readily be illustrated by a glance out the window. The objects that will first be noticed are the ones that are moving, and they are also the ones to which the attention is most apt to return. Any change or contrast likewise compels attention. The eye is caught by a fleck of tomato juice on a white shirt front; the ear picks up the drone of a beetle coming through the quiet evening air; and the tongue is instantly conscious of a foreign taste in food that is being eaten.

All these factors can and should be used in persuasive speaking. One is using these attention values when he speaks with penetrating intensity of tone; when he talks in a loud voice; when he pronounces a sentence with unusual deliberation, or repeats it; when he emphasizes what he says with a gesture or change of position; and when he varies his mood, his vocal rate, force, or pitch, or changes his speaking style. He may vary his short sentences with a long one, his declarative sentences with several questions, his commonplace vocabulary with some striking words. Such rhetorical variety was provided in a radio talk by General Hugh Johnson, when in trespassing upon the time of the Columbia Symphony Orchestra, he said, "To infringe politically upon these great musical programs is like tin-canning a dog in the apse of a cathedral."

B. SUBJECTIVE FACTORS

What will get and hold attention is affected to a very considerable degree by two subjective factors that lie within the auditors: their attention habits and their personal interest. Everyone develops positive and negative habits of attention. Parents, for instance, may sleep through the rumbling passage of a train, the honking of automobile horns, the blaring of the radio from the house next door—yet awaken instantly if a tiny sound emanates from their child's room. Women who sort fruit in the canneries soon accustom their eyes to detecting instantly spoiled specimens that to the casual eye would be lost among the sound ones. But just as we become accustomed to reaching out for certain stimuli, and thus become abnormally sensitive to them, so do we develop negative habits of shutting out certain others. A worker in a steel mill, for instance, will scarcely notice the noise. A farm laborer becomes immune to the odors of the barnyard.

These attention habits are partly caused and are strongly reinforced by the factor of personal interest. An individual will pick out of any body of stimuli the one that closely affects his own welfare. He will see his own name as his eye runs hastily over a page of newsprint. In a walk through the business district, he will be drawn insensibly toward the window that displays books, or fishing tackle, or whatever else he may especially be interested in. These are attention values given to an object by one's experience with it. The speaker should find out in part what they are for his particular audience as he learns something of its background.

<h3 style="text-align:center">C. METHODS OF INDUCING ATTENTION</h3>

In capturing the attention of a group, it is well to appeal to it through some sensory channel that is not in use. For instance, if the auditors are chatting busily with one another, it is difficult for a speaker to attract their attention by using his own voice. A professor who had had some difficulty in getting his class to obey the call to order with which he ordinarily opened the hour secured results when, one day, he simply stepped to the board and commenced writing upon it. The eyes of the students were much more open to his appeal than were their ears. If a speaker must compete for attention through a sensory channel already in use (that is, if his auditors' eyes and ears are occupied), he should produce a stimulus as distinct as possible from those to which they are responding. At a recent gathering the chairman failed in his attempt to call the meeting to order simply by arising and standing before the group. This method might have been effective if he had chosen to use the platform; but he stood in front of it, on the audience level, and thus did not stand out sharply enough from the others to make any appreciable imprint upon their attention.

After the attention has once been secured, it needs to be held. To aid the speaker in doing this, various attempts have been made to determine the *elements of interest,* or the factors so essentially interesting that they may be counted upon to hold a typical audience's attention. These elements of interest arise out of the attention values a proposal may have and out of the subjective attention factors that lie within the auditors. Hence, they have already been touched upon indirectly; here they are listed, with brief discussion, as the speaker might employ them in his speeches. They include the concrete, conflict, the combination of the familiar and the unusual, humor, the varied, and the vital.

1. *Concreteness.* When a speaker concludes a passage of abstractness and generality with a concrete illustration, it is as though he stepped from a dark room into the light. The audience that before had been able to perceive his meaning but dimly can now see it with luminous clarity. This is one of the most persuasive effects of concreteness. What the mind can take in, it tends to keep in. What it cannot comprehend, it cannot believe. An appreciation of this truth made Abraham Lincoln a great speaker. He said that when he was a child nothing disturbed him more than being unable to understand the meaning of the conversation of the adults whom he heard talking to one another. He determined that in his own speaking he would never say anything that could not easily be understood by a little child. He consequently filled his speeches with anecdotes and illustrations and became so skilled in their use that he could convert an audience with a story when another man would fail with an elaborate argument. In his practice he demonstrated the fact that any speaker can utilize to the extent of his powers; namely, that concreteness allures attention, cements interest, and instills belief.

2. *Conflict.* Interest in conflict is demonstrated by the avidity with which people follow war news, by the attendance at athletic contests, by the unquestioned strength of the competitive urge. Just so does an audience love a speaker who is a good fighter. Winston Churchill's fervent attacks upon the German war leaders were frequently interrupted by delighted shouts of, "Give it to them, Winnie!" Similarly, Truman won the 1948 election with an undignified but effective

"Give 'em hell!" whistle-stop campaign. In a somewhat different way, the persuasive speaker can make effective use of the conflict appeal by calling on his audience to join in his battle. Using this technique, Wendell Willkie arose through the presidential campaign of 1940 from being a political nonentity, to capture the nomination of the Republican Party, and to come within a very narrow margin of votes of winning the election from the most popular President in recent history. With hair rumpled, arms waving, and voice charged with earnestness, he spoke to hundreds of audiences during the three-month campaign, calling on the American people to join him in his crusade. A fair illustration of his use of this appeal is the conclusion of his speech at Coffeyville, Kansas, on September 16, 1940:

> I call upon you, therefore, to help me fight this battle of America. I call upon you to awaken your fellow citizens to these moral and spiritual values without the exercise of which our democracy must inevitably contract into dictatorship. I call upon you to exact of every man in government office the same standards of courage, of honesty, of thrift, of enterprise and of humanity that you exact of yourselves.
>
> And I turn to that vast, mistaken, deluded government of ours in Washington, and I say: Give our country back to us. We want it. We love it. We should like to share the burden of it among ourselves. We should like, if necessary, to suffer for it, so that we may pass it on intact to other generations.

3. *The familiar-unusual combination.* It has been frequently observed that neither the completely old nor the completely new is interesting. The speaker who simply presents "old stuff" is not only boring but also insulting, as he implies that his audience is ignorant of what are really familiar facts. And on the other hand, a speech that consists of entirely novel material has no point of contact with the auditors' minds. They wonder, "What has this to do with us?" And since it has nothing to do with them—with their interests, their experience, their needs—they soon give their attention to something else.

It is the intermingling of the new and the old that is interesting: familiar facts seen in a new light, or the unusual presented in contrast or in comparison with the well known. Clarence K. Streit, in offering his daring new plan for a federal union of all the world's democracies, has been very careful to stress over and over again the essentially *conservative* nature of his proposal.

Why is it that even now we Americans, our government, our leaders and experts, are doing so little to explore the possibilities of applying beyond our shores these 100 per cent American principles which our fathers carried steadily on, from shore to shore? Why not make at least one more attempt to do it before saying that we can't? Why not call another Constitutional Convention in Independence Hall, invite at least the other English-speaking democracies, try to work out with them another definitive Federal Union Constitution? Why not transfer from our national democracies to this new Union democracy those same five powers which the thirteen states transferred to the Union—defense, free trade, money, communications, and citizenship—since we have proved for a hundred and fifty years that this transfer makes for peace and prosperity and freedom for everyone?

Here in every sentence the old and the new are linked; the appeal is to extend old and tried principles into new areas. It is sound technique.

4. *Humor* is a means of inducing attention to which everyone pays lip service, but that persuasive speakers use too little. Speakers are likely to catalogue humor in their minds as "entertainment," and feel it has no use in serious persuasion. The result is that persuasive speeches often are fanatically (and hypnotically) intense, with far too little variation of mood. Such intensity builds up resistance in the listeners, who feel they are being "pushed" into a conclusion against their will. Humor can shift their attention from self-defense to pure enjoyment of what the speaker is saying. Then, being disarmed and losing their suspicion, they become much more receptive to his message. An excellent example of an effective persuasive speech marked by considerable use of humor is that by Bruce Barton, "Which Knew Not Joseph," printed at the end of Chapter 13.

5. *Variety.* Monotony is sleep-inducing; counting sheep is a favorite remedy for insomnia. Similarly, monotonous speakers are chiefly effective in putting their audiences to sleep. The speaker should use variety in his action, his voice, his mood, and in the content of his speech. Movement has already been noted as an attention value, but

the regular swing of a pendulum attracts little notice. It is the unexpected action that is compelling. Gestures should never be allowed
to fall into habitual patterns. The speaker needs a wide repertoire
of bodily action. As for the voice, it is a pretty accurate index of what
is going on in the mind. If the speaker is actually in lively communication with his audience, his voice will have abundant variety. If he
speaks in a monotone, the audience will be lulled to drowsiness by
its mechanical qualities and invited to inattention by the positive evidence in the speaker's voice that he is paying little attention to his
hearers.

Monotony of mood is similarly ineffective. Earnestness is a good
persuasive quality; but the continual drive of an unvaried attack carries far less assurance than the easy, confident, skillful shift from
argument to humor, from exposition to satire, from frontal attack to
playful ridicule. The variation of mood is not only a means of holding
interest, but, in its sure demonstration that the speaker's emotions are
under strict control, it creates confidence in his judgment. In these
respects of action, voice, and mood, the speaker is dependent upon
his skill in delivery; hence, he is dependent in part upon the exigencies
of the moment.

The content of the speech, however, can deliberately be shaped,
at the speaker's leisure, to insure variety. Such a powerful evangelist
as Billy Sunday used what many critics might consider a ludicrous
amount of variety in his speeches. He kept a continual stream of
images moving across the canvas of his auditors' minds, so that his
speeches read almost like a stream-of-consciousness novel. But, appealing as he did to relatively childlike minds, he managed with his
variety to hold their closest attention and thereby to win their acceptance of his plea. A typical example of his method is the following
paragraph, which he used many times:

I had a friend who was a brilliant young fellow. He covered the Chino-
Japanese war for a New York paper. He was on his way home when he
was shipwrecked, and the captain and he were on an island living on roots
for a week and then they signalled a steamer and got started home. He
got word from the New York *Tribune* and they told him to go to 'Frisco,

so he went, and they told him to come across the arid country and write up the prospects of irrigation. And as he walked across those plains, he thought of how they would blossom if they were only irrigated. Then he thought of how his life was like that desert, with nothing in it but waste.

Aside from the constant variety, it is instructive to note the concentration of persuasive appeals in this brief paragraph: the association of the speaker with a "brilliant" reporter who travels widely and is shipwrecked with no less a personage than the captain; the appeal to romance and adventure in the desert island, war, and travel items; the appeal to the urge of workmanship in the description of what might be accomplished through irrigation; the disarming quality of the argument-free narrative; and the final stunning effects of the suggestive analogy in the concluding sentence. It is apparent that Billy Sunday did not become the greatest evangelist of his generation by accident.

One caution must be noted regarding the value of variety. As will be seen in the next chapter, some types of monotony, skillfully and purposefully used, have their own elements of value in persuasion. But creating interest is not one of them.

6. *The vital.* Two propositions may be noted here: first, nothing is really persuasive to an audience which is not in some degree vital to it; second, nothing is really vital unless it is personal. Both propositions can be paraphrased in the statement that we react deeply to situations only when our own physical, social, or mental welfare is affected. This may appear to be a harsh judgment. It is illustrated, however, on every side. As this was written, the news from abroad told of miseries, injustices, and danger in Asia, the Middle East, North Africa, and Eastern Europe. People in the writer's community, as elsewhere, talked much of the communist menace, and felt themselves to be deeply moved by it. But when two well-liked volunteer firemen were killed in fighting a blaze in a local store, the wave of horror that swept through the crowd of spectators demonstrated vividly what a difference there is in our feelings when aroused by a major tragedy of which we read or by a minor tragedy that touches us personally. Whatever other elements of interest are used, the greatest advantage

lies with the speaker who can say: "This is your problem. You will suffer if the alternative side triumphs; you will benefit in the acceptance of my plan."

D. MEMORY VALUES

In the great mass of experimentation regarding the operation of memory, there is some guidance on the problem of holding attention. What-is-best-attended-to and what-is-most-firmly-implanted-in-the-memory are all but synonymous terms. It is significant that not very much of all that passes through the mind remains available for future use. Radossawljewitsch found that his twenty-nine subjects retained only an average of 47.4 per cent of the nonsense syllables they learned, after an interval of eight hours; after one hundred twenty days, only 3 per cent could be recalled. The speaker's problem is to attach the strongest possible memory values to the points he chiefly wants his audience to keep in mind. If he thinks that very much of what he says will be remembered, he is simply unaware of how memory operates.

In rapid summary of some of the studies which are listed in the bibliography at the end of this chapter, the following conclusions of value to the persuasive speaker may be noted: (1) Ballard found the memory of nine-year-old subjects superior, that of twelve- and sixteen-year-olds median, and that of twenty-one-year-old subjects significantly lower; (2) Luh discovered that overlearning is advantageous in assisting recall after a four-hour interval, but is slightly detrimental in affecting the amount that can be remembered after a one- or two-day interval; (3) Lyon found that meaningful material is recalled much better than nonsense syllables; (4) Shaffer summarized some thirty-five studies of the recall of pleasant and unpleasant material and concluded that pleasantness is a positive factor in lengthening the memory span; (5) Thorndike noted that rewards for remembering and punishment for forgetting likewise have a notable effect; (6) finally, Jersild has proved that the method of presentation of material has a significant effect on how well it is recalled.

Out of these studies, several principles can profitably be kept in mind for impressing material so well on the minds of the auditors that it will have a maximum chance of being remembered.

1. What is best understood is most apt to be recalled. One reason why we forget the names of people to whom we are introduced is that they are only half heard in the first place. Similarly, no one remembers a speech he doesn't understand.

2. What is interesting is apt to be recalled. Many an audience remembers nothing a speaker says except his jokes or striking illustrations.

3. Rhythm and rhyme are memory aids. There is value in the apt quotation of poetry.

4. Within limits, we remember what we want to remember. Any actual motivation is an attention getter and memory fixer.

5. The technique of the speaker is a considerable factor in influencing the memory of his auditors. The persuasive speaker needs to master the best means of emphasis.

E. MEANS OF EMPHASIS

The means of emphasis have been a favorite topic of rhetoricians ever since the science of composition was first studied. But more questions regarding it have been raised than have been settled. Position is important—but is the first or the last part of the speech most emphatic? Amplitude is a factor—but at what point do elaboration and illustration cease to emphasize an idea and begin to smother it? The type of statement given an idea is influential—but what kind should it be? Delivery may be effective—but how?

A. T. Jersild undertook to discover precise answers to such questions as these. He prepared a fictional narrative speech, which was memorized and delivered by the same speaker to ten different audiences. The speech consisted of seventy statements, each one emphasized in a given manner. The effectiveness of these modes of emphasis was tested by examining the audiences to measure what they remembered from the speeches. The results, as Jersild summarized them, are as follows:

The most effective, though not the most economical, form of emphasis is repetition to the extent of three or more presentations. The benefit arising from repetition does not increase in proportion to the number of added repetitions.

Repetition is most effective when the several presentations are separated by intervals of time. One of the least effective forms of emphasis is to repeat an item immediately following its first presentation.

The most impressive point in a discourse is its opening statement. The first statements have a distinct advantage over those which come last. To surpass the effect of primacy it is necessary to resort to three or more repetitions or to introduce special verbal emphasis devices.

Of the more artificial forms of emphasis, the device of using verbal comments which direct attention to an item (such as, "Now get this") is most effective. Next in effectiveness comes the device of introducing a short pause; following this, that of raising the voice above the accustomed amplitude; gesticulation, by a gesture and banging with one's fist, comes next in order, and in general has a beneficial effect. The device of speaking very slowly not only stands lowest in effectiveness but has a decided negative effect.

Until further studies similar to Jersild's have been conducted, his conclusions must be considered relatively tentative. Meanwhile, they offer much better guidance than the *ex cathedra* advice which has been liberally sprinkled through treatises on speech. They suggest to the persuasive speaker that he would do well to state his most important appeals first, repeat them at intervals throughout his speech, "point up" his conclusion with such phrases as, "The one thing I most want you to remember is . . . ," and make a balanced use of the pause, of increased volume, and of emphatic gestures. His study also has a significant message for the speaker who labors for impressiveness by a low, measured, deliberate rate of articulation. The normal rate of one hundred and thirty-five words a minute would seem to be preferable to the "ministerial" rate of ninety words a minute.

The subject and the audience

In considering how to control the attention and interest of his audience, the speaker should always keep in mind that this is a question of *means,* not the *end* itself. His primary purpose is not to keep his audience attentive, but to concentrate the favorable attention of his listeners into channels that will induce acceptance of his purpose. With this basic factor in mind, it is evident that speakers will sometimes deliberately choose to talk about subjects in which their audience needs to have an interest aroused.

Teachers, for example, often have to teach required subjects (such as trigonometry, archeology, geology, or economics) which a portion of their classes considers to be as "dry as dust." Preachers and moralists may attempt to arouse in their audiences an awareness of spiritual and social evils which their listeners consider unimportant or outside the range of their own interests. A candidate for the local School Board may feel intensely the need to arouse the voters to an awareness of the inadequacy of school facilities; whereas, their own feelings go no further than a desire to keep down taxes. A student may wish to persuade his fellows that "school spirit" properly conceived means an ardor for education, rather than a noisy support of athletic teams. In all such instances, a chief problem of the speaker will be to find means of creating an interest in the subject that his audience does not initially possess.

When a subject possesses within itself deep and evident elements of interest (such as "How to Get Rich") the interest may be called *intrinsic*—that is, lying within the subject matter. When the speaker must devise means of bringing to his subject from some other source an interest not felt in it by his listeners, he must use what we call *extrinsic* interest, that is, an interest that is possessed by the audience, but that the speaker has to find special means of attaching to the subject. This process of linking one's subject with an extrinsic interest shared by the speaker and his audience is very like the procedure of striking up an acquaintance with a stranger through the discovery that you and he know the same people, or come from the same town. At one moment he is completely uninteresting to you—just one more in the continual stream of people whom you pass by with scarcely a thought. Then, by the chance mention of your home town or the name of a friend, he enters actively into your stream of consciousness and becomes a part of your circle of interests.

Intrinsic and extrinsic interests must be handled very differently by the persuasive speaker. If his subject possesses the former, he can throw himself into it with wholehearted enthusiasm. His role is somewhat like that of the cheer leader, stirring to a higher pitch feelings that already exist. His speech will have some of the characteristics of heated discussion of plate markings at a stamp collectors' club meeting. He can lose himself in his subject, with almost no cross references to anything else. But when the speaker must depend upon extrinsic interest, his entire handling of the subject is greatly affected. Too great an enthusiasm for it will serve only to emphasize the gulf between him and his noninterested auditors. If he loses himself in his subject, he is lost indeed, as far as that audience is concerned. His hearers will only be confirmed in their belief that he is an odd creature who has developed an eccentric attachment to something that most people rightly ignore.

Instead, the speaker should approach his topic obliquely. He should demonstrate a detached, almost a casual attitude toward it. He should prove by his words and manner that, no more than his audience, has he been swept off his feet by this (to them) strange type of interest. After a slight introduction to his field of interest, he should launch at once into a more animated discussion of the related topic through which he means to secure the concern of his auditors. Here his enthusiasm is matched by theirs and will be respected and reciprocated. As his speech progresses, he should take every opportunity to cement more and more strongly the bonds which unite his own interest with that which he has chosen to serve as an intermediary. On this bridge he gradually leads his audience over to an enthusiasm for his original subject.

The contrast in method between speeches using these two types of interest is of sufficient importance to merit illustration from the practice of skillful speakers. In the first passage that follows, the speaker is Jeremiah S. Black; the occasion, a speech to the Supreme Court of the United States, before which Black was defending the right of trial by jury. There was no slightest doubt of the intrinsic interest of the case: the whole duty of the judges was to pay the

closest attention to it. The speaker therefore properly commenced
with a stern emphasis on the importance of his theme:

> I am not afraid that you will underrate the importance of this case. It
> concerns the rights of the whole people. Such questions have generally
> been settled by arms; but since the beginning of the world no battle has
> ever been lost or won upon which the liberties of a nation were so dis-
> tinctly staked as they are on the result of this argument.

Because of its nature, the use of extrinsic interest cannot be illustrated so concisely. The speaker needs time to lead from one type of
interest into another. An unusually concise example, however, is
supplied by a speech which President Franklin D. Roosevelt delivered
on September 2, 1940, at the dedication of the Great Smoky Mountains National Park. His purpose was to arouse the American people
to a danger which they failed to understand and refused to admit.
Hence, he approached his real purpose by way of the ostensible
subject of his speech:

> Here in the Great Smokies, we meet today to dedicate these mountains,
> streams, and forests to the service of the American people. We are living
> under governments which are proving their devotion to national parks.
> The Governors of North Carolina and of Tennessee have greatly helped
> us, and the Secretary of the Interior has today ready for dedication two
> more parks—Kings Canyon in California and the Olympic National Park
> in the State of Washington—and soon, I hope, will have a third, the Big
> Bend Park in Texas.
> There are trees here that stood before our forefathers came to this
> continent; there are brooks that still run as clear as on the day the first
> pioneer cupped his hand and drank from them. In this park we shall
> conserve the pine, the redbud, the dogwood, the azalea, the rhododendron,
> the trout, and the thrush for the happiness of the American people.
> The old frontier, that put the hard fiber in the American spirit and the
> long muscles in the American back, lives and will live in these untamed
> mountains to give future generations a sense of the land from which their
> forefathers hewed their homes.
> The hewing was hard. The dangers were many. The rifle could never
> be far from the axe. The pioneers stood on their own feet, shot their own
> game, and fought off their own enemies. In time of accident or mis-
> fortune they helped each other. In time of Indian attack, they stood by
> each other.

Today we no longer face Indians, and hard and lonely struggles with nature—and also, we have grown soft in many ways. If we are to survive, we cannot be soft in a world in which there are dangers that threaten Americans—dangers far more deadly than those the frontiersmen had to face.

The earth has been so shrunk by the airplane and the radio that Europe is closer to America today than was one side of these mountains to the other when the pioneers toiled through the primeval forest. The arrow, the tomahawk, and the scalping-knife have been replaced by the airplane, the bomb, the tank, and the machine gun. Their threat is as close to us today as was the threat to the frontiersman when hostile Indians were lurking on the other side of the gap.

In these paragraphs President Roosevelt first indicated that he, as much as any of his listeners, preferred the idyllic peace of the forest to the frenzies of war; that he intended to continue the preparation in America of parks where a life of peace could be enjoyed. Then he reminded his hearers that these peaceful scenes had to be won by the hardships of war, and thus led into his theme, that they now might have to be defended in the same way. In other words, he tried to arouse an interest in defense by an appeal through the very contrary desire of his auditors for the ways of peace. This is the method of attaching to a speaker's subject an extrinsic interest.

Conclusion

The basic position of attention in the technique of persuasive speaking requires its most careful consideration. The speaker will want a clear understanding of what attention is, how it operates, how and why its operation is limited, what factors that create interest lie within objects and what within auditors, the specific methods that can be depended upon for inducing attention, the methods of implanting an impression so deeply in the mind that it will be remembered, the tested modes of emphasis, and the types of interest—related to the individual and to the subject, controlled by will or arising spontaneously—that may be appealed to. As he gains proficiency in the theory and mastery of controlling attention, he will be well prepared for the second phase of the technique of persuasion—the use of suggestion.

Exercises

1. Explain the significance of the statement: "The chief task of the persuasive speaker is to serve as a 'selector' of his audience's attention." Why is attention a vital factor in persuasive speaking?

2. What are the chief interests of your associates? Make a list of the chief topics that they discuss in conversational gatherings. Group together the interests that most of them have in common.

3. Considering this list of interests which you have just drawn up, make a list of five speech topics that are based directly upon the interests of your friends. How could you best develop these topics to take full advantage of their interests, without simply repeating facts already well known to them? Select one of your five topics and compose a short speech that will deal with several of your friends' interests, yet will have freshness, vitality, novelty, and the lure of the unfamiliar.

4. Make up another list of five speech topics, this time deliberately avoiding subjects in which your friends are interested. Select subjects in which they ought to be interested, but are not. Then plan how you can bridge the gap so as to connect these "dull" topics with interesting factors. Choose one of the topics for extensive development. In the introduction, be sure to start with your audience's point of view and see how you can best gradually swing over to your own. Every one of your main ideas should similarly have a point of attachment with your auditors' interests, but should point unfailingly toward the conclusion you want to reach. Your aim is so to present your unfamiliar material that it will seem to arise naturally and inevitably out of considerations that your audience fully accepts. When your speech has been prepared, look it over with this final caution in mind: it should be interesting, but interest is not its chief goal. Interest is only a means by which you hope to accomplish your end. Do not yield to the temptation to be *merely* interesting. Keep working steadily toward the proposal which it is your purpose to have the audience accept.

5. What relationship exists between ability and interest? Between personality and interest? Between our fundamental convictions, or "philosophy of life," and our interests? Between our social influence, prestige, and status, and our interests?

6. What is the real difference between "narrow" and "well-rounded" individuals? Which should make the better speakers? Why?

7. Is a specialist likely to have a broad range of interests? Can he have? Are specialists usually effective speakers to general audiences? Explain. What advice would you give to a specialist in railway economics to help him become an effective persuasive speaker?

8. Discuss the following questions:

   a. What is the relationship between attention and tension?
   b. How would you define attention in your own words?
   c. What is the relationship between attention and consciousness?
   d. How does attention operate?
   e. What are the limitations upon attention?
   f. What attention values may an object have?
   g. How may a speaker utilize these attention values?
   h. What subjective factors help to determine our interests?
   i. Through what sensory channels should a speaker seek to gain his audience's attention?
   j. What are the elements of interest? Explain how each one can be utilized in persuasive speaking.
   k. What has been experimentally established regarding the operation of memory?
   l. What are the five principles for impressing material on the memory of auditors?
   m. How did Jersild undertake to study the means of emphasis? What were his results? Of what importance is repetition as a means of emphasis? What is the relationship between emphasis and memory? Between emphasis and attention? Between memory and attention?
   n. By what types of interest can individuals be motivated?
   o. What is the essential distinction between intrinsic and extrinsic interests? By what differing techniques can each best be utilized in persuasive speaking?
   p. What is the relationship between interest and will power?

9. To broaden your knowledge of the nature and means of utilizing attention in persuasive discourses, the following readings are commended:

Floyd H. Allport, *Theories of Perception and the Concept of Structure* (New York: Wiley, 1955).

W. H. Bexton, W. Heron, and T. H. Scott, "Effects of Decreased Variation in Sensory Environment," *Canadian Journal of Psychology,* VIII (1954), 70-76.

Donald E. Broadbent, "Attention and the Perception of Speech," *Scientific American,* 206 (1962), 143-151.

————, *Perception and Communication* (London: Scientific Book Guild, 1961), particularly Chapters 2 and 9.

Arthur W. Combs and Donald Snygg, *Individual Behavior* (New York: Harper, 1959).

Laura Crowell, "Building the 'Four Freedoms' Speech," *Speech Monographs,* XXII (November, 1955), 266-283.

Ray Ehrensberger, "An Experimental Study of the Relative Effectiveness of Certain Forms of Emphasis in Public Speaking," *Speech Monographs,* XII (1945), 94-111.

D. W. Fisk and S. R. Maddi, *Function of Varied Experience* (Homewood, Ill.: Dorsey Press, 1961).

Wilma H. Grimes, "The Mirth Experience in Public Address," *Speech Monographs,* XXII (November, 1955), 243-255.

W. Heron, "The Pathology of Boredom," *Scientific American,* 196 (January, 1957), 52-56.

A. T. Jersild, "Modes of Emphasis in Public Speaking," *Journal of Applied Psychology,* XII (December, 1928), 611-612.

P. E. Lull, "The Effectiveness of Humor in Persuasive Speeches," *Speech Monographs,* VII (1940), 26-40.

Joseph Tiffin and Max D. Steer, "An Experimental Analysis of Emphasis," *Speech Monographs,* IV (1937), 69-74.

Suggestion

IN A SENSE EVERYONE KNOWS WHAT "SUGGESTION" means. We use the term frequently in everyday conversation. "My suggestion is that we all have lunch at the corner lunchroom." "I suggest that you take the political science course taught by Professor Zilch." The expression is used very freely, and usually very loosely. Sometimes all the speaker means is that he is proposing a topic worthy of discussion. More often, we use the word *suggestion* to mean, "This is just my own idea; I don't care whether or not you do it; in any event, I have no intention of arguing about it." A *proposal* we all regard as a point of view that is clearly defined, carefully considered, adequately supported, and worthy of defense. A *suggestion*, on the other hand, is likely to be offered at random, without much prior thought, without any detailed support; and it will probably be dropped without protest by its proposer in case it meets opposition. In fact, when a random idea proposed by one member of a group is objected to by another, the originator of the idea may shrug off any discussion of it by saying, "Oh well, it was just a suggestion." All of us are accustomed to this use of the term. But the strict meaning of suggestion, as used in this chapter, is more definitive.

The meaning of suggestion

Dr. Jon Eisenson, an expert in the psychology of speech, defines suggestion as "the uncritical acceptance of an opinion as the basis for belief or action." McDougall, proponent of dynamic psychology, defines suggestion as "a process of communication resulting in the acceptance with conviction of the communicated proposition independently of the subject's appreciation of any logically adequate grounds for its acceptance." As these two definitions indicate, the precise meaning of suggestion is somewhat more limited than its generalized use would imply. What suggestion means is that an idea is stated in such a manner that its acceptance is sought without analysis or consideration. What suggestion invites is not a process of judgment but an immediate acceptance.

In Chapter 5, Wendell Johnson was quoted as saying that the process of education is to lead individuals to delay their responses to any stimulus while they have time to weigh its significance. In this sense, suggestion is anti-educational. When we are under the influence of suggestion we do not canvass all possibilities of action, but quickly seize upon the dominant one. Should we later make the rueful discovery that we have acted unwisely, our only real defense is, "It seemed like a good idea at the time." To the extent that the suggestion was successful, it seemed the *only* idea at that time. This result may sometimes be achieved by hypnosis—but this lies beyond the province of persuasive speaking. A somewhat similar kind of compulsive suggestion is illustrated in the cohesive responsiveness of a lynch mob, but this, too, happily, lies well outside the ordinary uses of persuasive speech. However, lesser degrees of suggestiveness are often of considerable persuasive usefulness.

The Ideomotor Principle is one psychological description of suggestion. It is based upon the observation that ideas are not passive, but dynamic. Any idea that enters the mind tends to express itself in some form of action. Whether the action really fulfills the idea is dependent upon several factors: how clearly and definitely it was perceived, what emotional associations it has, and how strongly it is inhibited by alternative ideas. If a clearly formulated idea enters the mind, especially if it is "loaded" with emotion, and if it is not held in check by contrary ideas, it will be acted upon. Even when these favorable factors do not exist, there is still a tendency to accept any idea of which one becomes conscious. If you were told that the moon is made of green cheese, you would unhesitatingly believe the statement, except for a rush of inhibiting ideas, such as: That is an old joke, the reports of astronomers say nothing of cheese on the moon, and cheese would soon spoil. None of these objections occurs to a child, so he readily accepts the statement.

The ideomotor principle is easily illustrated. Think of an itching sensation on the end of your nose, and the chances are good that your nose will itch; or, if you succeed in inhibiting that response, an itching feeling will break out somewhere else. If you are driving a car up a narrow, winding mountain road, you may decide what to do in case another car should suddenly come toward you around a bend. Should the other car appear, your predetermined response would occur almost automatically. If you go to New York City with the idea that it is an exciting place, you will be thrilled by your visit there; if you go with the thought that it is dirty, noisy, unlovely, and crowded, your visit will be a nerve-racking experience. If the idea "pops into your mind" that you would like to go to a movie, you are apt to be restless and unhappy unless you can go.

If a speaker can implant in the minds of his auditors a clear idea, if he can make the idea emotionally attractive, and if he can direct their thinking away from contrary ideas, their acceptance of his proposal will follow as a matter of course. Almost inevitably the perception produces a response. When the response is only partially what the speaker desires, it is because the idea he implanted did not completely eject all alternative possibilities, but combined with some of them. When the response is completely disappointing, the speaker's idea has been overcome by others that proved more attractive.

The ethics of suggestion

As you think over the point of view expressed in Chapter 2, it will be clear that suggestion is scarcely an ethical mode of persuasion. Our reason for studying it is because experience proves that it does work. We need frequently to be on guard against its unethical uses. Adolf Hitler pointed out that if you tell a big enough lie and tell it often enough, many people will believe it. A great deal of the propaganda emanating from the communist dictatorships seems obviously based upon this same premise. We in the democracies may as well admit that much of our own advertising is also based upon this psychological fact that what is said often enough and positively enough will probably be believed, whether or not it is wholly true. It is for this reason that advertising campaigns tend to be built around easily grasped slogans, such as, "Watch the Buicks go by!" "Picture yourself behind the wheel of a Ford!" "Smoke Luckies!" "Buy now!" Suggestion is also a basis for the popular advertising method of quoting celebrities as advocates of particular brands of razors, cigarettes, liquor, automobiles. The seller does not desire to have the recipient of the ad stop to ponder the merits of the product. The strong suggestion simply is, "Buy!"

In an ideal society, suggestion would be denounced as a shoddy and dangerous substitute for thinking. Even in a less-than-ideal society, this same charge is quite proper. Nevertheless, the fact is that we are deluged on many sides by suggestive persuasion. It *must be analyzed* in order that we may properly defend ourselves against it. The question of whether a speaker may himself make ethical use of suggestion in a good cause is a problem in philosophy. Jon Eisenson concludes his discussion of suggestion by presenting a definition of persuasion that is clearly based on suggestive processes: "We may define persuasion," he says, "as a process of initiating certain action patterns in our listeners and of blocking off others which might interfere with our speech objective." We find ourselves in a quandary if we accept the principle that persuasion itself is justifiable—when the speaker knows what he is talking about and has a socially desirable objective—but that suggestion is a mode of persuasion that must be denied to ethical speakers. In order to avoid the educationally unsound position of reaching too quick a conclusion on so vital a question as this, we shall do well to delay a final judgment while we consider in more detail how suggestion operates. See Exercise 2 at the end of this chapter, which suggests that you join with the class in a discussion of the problem.

Types of suggestion

It is fruitless to evaluate suggestion without differentiating its types, for it operates in many different ways. Some of them may seem to you to be completely acceptable; others may merit consideration only in order that we may avoid being susceptible to them. The types of suggestion commonly distinguished are: direct, indirect, positive, negative, and counter.

A. DIRECT

Direct suggestion is explicit command. It is an order to be obeyed, such as: "Halt!" "Forward, march!" or "Shoulder arms!" The teacher says, "Copy the questions as I read them to you"; the parent says, "Pick up your toys"; the billboard says, "Buy American!"; the persuasive speaker says:

"Turn the rascals out!"
"Pay as you go!"
"Save America from foreign isms!"
"Let us strive on to finish the work we are in."

Direct suggestion also operates to secure belief as well as action. This is accomplished when a debatable proposition is so stated that it is accepted without proof. Examples of two such statements which are contradictory, but are both highly suggestive, are: "Haste makes waste" and "He who hesitates is lost." In persuasive speaking, examples of this type of suggestion abound. A few illustrations will indicate how it is used:

"The poison of politics is mixed with the bread of relief."—HERBERT C. HOOVER.
"Idealists may have been at the front door preaching social justice, but

party henchmen have been at the back door handing out jobs."—ALFRED A. LANDON.

"Nine mocking years with the golden calf and three long years of the scourge! Nine crazy years at the ticker and three long years in the bread line! Nine mad years of mirage and three long years of despair!"—A description of the years of Republican dominance, from 1920 to 1932, by FRANKLIN D. ROOSEVELT.

Direct suggestion operates by inhibiting the thought processes of the listeners. Instead of giving intellectual consideration to the point the speaker raises, the audience must be induced to give instant acceptance to it. The process has been called the use of the "short circuit" instead of the "long circuit"; that is, the neural impulse goes in the manner of a reflex directly from the receptor to the effector, rather than making the intermediate journey through the association areas of the brain, where the merits of the assertion could be weighed.

B. INDIRECT

Even more valuable and more widely used is indirect suggestion. It consists of implanting an idea in the mind of a listener without seeming to do so. The hearer appears to reach the conclusion himself; he thinks it is his own idea. Frequently, as one listens to a speech, his mind leaps on ahead to formulate a conclusion that is suggested but never phrased by the speaker. This is an ideal means of instilling a proposition in the mind of an auditor; for he then thinks of it as his own, prides himself upon it accordingly, may even feel superior to the speaker because he thought of it while the speaker apparently did not, and will consequently cling to the conclusion fondly and tenaciously.

Indirect suggestion works by the positive, emotionally attractive statement of an antecedent proposition in such a manner that the necessary conclusion will occur to the listener. It operates best when the subject's thinking is *dissociated;* that is, when his thought processes are so fully occupied with an irrelevant problem that the speaker's point can slip through without critical examination. The magician, for instance, attracts attention to the manipulation of his right hand, while his left performs the trick. On the verbal plane, indirect suggestion is illustrated by such statements as the following: "Fools rush in where angels fear to tread," meaning, "You had better abandon the plan you have in mind"; or, "An ounce of prevention is worth a pound of cure," meaning, "If I were you, I'd observe some precautionary measures before acting."

Bruce Barton used indirect suggestion very effectively in his speech, "Which Knew Not Joseph," in which he wished as inoffensively as possible to implant the idea in the minds of the utility executives who composed his audience that they would do well to engage the services of his advertising agency. The entire speech consists of anecdotes which would lead to that conclusion, and Mr. Barton ended with one more pointed analogy:

Asking an advertising man to talk about advertising at a convention like this is a good deal like asking a doctor to talk about health. I have listened to many such addresses, and they are all about the same. The eminent physician says, "Drink plenty of water. Stay outdoors as much as you can. Eat good food. Don't worry. Get eight hours of sleep. And if you have anything the matter with you, call a doctor."

Had Mr. Barton declared in so many words, "I'm an expert in advertising and you are not. You had better hire me to compose your ads," these self-sufficient executives might have replied with the colloquial sneer, "What have you got that we haven't got?" But when the speaker disarmed them with a liberal display of good fellowship and humor, when he dissociated their thought processes by getting them to think of medical advice, and when he led their minds to the very brink of a favorable decision by his carefully chosen analogy, it was both easy and pleasant for them to leap ahead to the conclusion which the speaker desired.

Guidance in the use of direct and indirect suggestion may be indicated by the following series of contrasts:

Direct suggestion	Indirect suggestion
Use when the audience is polarized.	Use when the audience is mentally alert.
Use when the audience feels itself inferior to the speaker intellectually or in other ways.	Use when the audience feels itself equal or superior to the speaker intellectually or in other ways.
Use when the speaker's prestige is high.	Use when the speaker's prestige is comparatively low.
Use when addressing youthful auditors.	Use when addressing adults.
Use when some immediate, definite, precise form of action is required.	Use when the aim is to create an attitude or a belief which may lead to future action.
Use when the speaker is completely master of the speech situation.	Use when the speaker is comparatively unskilled.

Not all of the factors in either column will apply for any given speech. More often some of them will favor the use of direct, and others of indirect suggestion. Both forms of suggestion, as a matter of fact, are often employed in the same speech. Thus, in the following passage, taken from the conclusion of Clarence Darrow's plea in defense of two murderers, Richard Leopold and Robert Loeb (or "Dickie" and "Babe," as he called them), the speaker suggested indirectly that contrary to appearances the judge would really gain in popularity by withholding the death penalty, and he suggested directly that in any event such was the judge's duty. The entire speech is a masterpiece of persuasive speaking, which might well serve as a de-detailed case study in the use of various forms of motivation. Several of them may be noted in this single paragraph. The plea was successful. Said Mr. Darrow:

Now, I must say a word more and then I will leave this with you where I should have left it long ago. None of us are unmindful of the public; courts are not, and juries are not. We placed our fate in the hands of a trained court, thinking that he would be more mindful and considerate than a jury. I cannot say how people feel. I have stood here for three months as one might stand at the ocean trying to sweep back the tide. I hope the seas are subsiding and the wind is falling, and I believe they are, but I wish to make no false pretense to this court. The easy thing and the popular thing to do is to hang my clients. I know it. Men and women who do not think will applaud. The cruel and thoughtless will approve. It will be easy today; but in Chicago, and reaching out over the length and breadth of the land, more and more fathers and mothers, the humane, the kind and the hopeful, who are gaining an understanding and asking questions not only about these poor boys, but about their own,—these will join in no acclaim at the death of my clients. These would ask that the shedding of blood be stopped, and that the normal feelings of man resume their sway. And as the days and the months and the years go on, they will ask it more and more. But, your Honor, what they shall ask may not count. I know the easy way. I know your Honor stands between the future and the past. I know the future is with me, and what I stand for here; not merely for the lives of these two unfortunate lads, but for all boys and all girls; for all of the young, and as far as possible, for all of the old. I am pleading for life, understanding, charity, kindness, and the infinite mercy that considers all. I am pleading that we overcome cruelty with kindness and hatred with love. I know the future is on my side. Your Honor stands between the past and the future. You may hang these boys; you may hang them by the neck until they are dead. But in doing it you will turn your all toward the past. In doing it you are making it harder for every other boy who in ignorance and darkness must grope his way through the mazes which only childhood knows. In doing it you will make it harder for unborn children. You may save them and make it easier for every child that some time may stand where these boys stand. You will make it easier for every human being with an aspiration and a vision and a hope and a fate. I am pleading for the future; I am pleading for a time when hatred and cruelty will not control the hearts of men. When we can learn by reason and judgment and understanding and faith that all life is worth saving, and that mercy is the highest attribute of man.

C. POSITIVE AND NEGATIVE FORMS

Positive suggestion is simply the phrasing of suggestion affirmatively. It is much preferable to the negative form, although the latter is frequently used. The parent who says to the small child, "Don't poke beans up your nose" is using negative suggestion. The *don't* is much less vivid than the mental image of pushing beans into the nostrils—and much less compelling! This is true of almost all negative suggestions. "Don't walk on the grass" is a reminder of the pleasure of doing just that. Negative suggestion is consequently apt to have the opposite of its intended effect. The vegetable hawker who says, "I suppose you don't want no fresh tomatoes today?" is almost certain to receive the response, "No, none today." The politician who says, "Don't vote for Jim Smith, my opponent" is unwittingly instilling in the minds of his hearers the suggestion: Vote for Jim Smith. Disadvantages of negative suggestion may be summarized as follows:

1. Its negative elements are much less vivid and compelling than the positive suggestion to which they are linked. Hence, if the audience is influenced at all, it is apt to be by the latter portion of the statement.

2. Negative suggestion usually implies uncertainty and indecision —as though the speaker did not dare to come out frankly and boldly with the program he wished to have followed: "Keep on the walk!" "Vote for me!" "Buy tomatoes!"

3. Negative suggestion may be assumed to be used to veil the lack of any definite program. Thus, criticism of the party in power is often turned aside with the comment, "The critics of the administration have no constructive program of their own to offer. They can find fault, but they cannot lead."

Positive suggestion, on the other hand, has all the advantages which the negative form lacks: it emphasizes the act to be done, or the proposition to be believed; it is decisive and confident; and it presents a definite program to be adopted. Were it not for such famous and influential examples as the Ten Commandments and Washington's phrase, "No entangling alliances," one might be tempted to say dogmatically: Never use negative suggestion. It may at least be said that *most* effective suggestion is in the positive form and that that form should be used unless the speaker has some special reason for preferring the negative statement.

Negative suggestion is most justified in reform campaigns, where what is opposed is readily described, but what is favored is much harder to put into words. For instance, the Prohibitionists could easily dramatize the evil effects of liquor, but to suggest directly a way of life without the influence of liquor is much harder. When the persuasive speaker has a problem of this sort, the use of positive suggestion becomes all but impossible, and he is forced into the negative form.

D. COUNTERSUGGESTION

When the speaker knows that his auditor is apt to be resentful of any advice, and is constitutionally inclined to disagree with what he is told, countersuggestion may be used. This form may be defined as negation used in the hope that it will be rejected. For those people who are said to be "contrasuggestible," it is the only effective mode. The "argumentative type" of individual is hard to convince and rebels against suggestion, but he may be easily led by a speaker who suggests the opposite of what he really desires. The wives of bullheaded husbands usually master the art of suggesting a trip to the seashore when they really want to go to the mountains. Lionel Crocker, in his book, *Public Speaking for College Students,* relates how a stubborn father was induced to permit his son to spend a year on the Floating University. After a direct appeal by the son had failed, a letter was dispatched to the father by one of the faculty members implying that it would be much better if the son were not permitted to go. The father resented the interference in his family affairs, and sent his son on the cruise as a form of protest.

The limitations and dangers of the use of countersuggestion are evident. If it fails, the speaker has himself brought about the opposite of what he desired. And even when it succeeds, there is apt to be a residue of resentful and belligerent feelings that tend to strain future relationships. The speaker who uses countersuggestion can hardly hope for continued prestige with his auditors; consequently, his future influence will be impaired. It is ordinarily used only as a last resort, when other measures have failed.

Factors affecting suggestion

The effectiveness of suggestion is dependent upon the source from which it comes, the circumstances under which it is used, the degree of suggestibility of the auditors, the duration of the suggestion, and the volume of the suggestion.

The value of prestige has been commented upon in two previous chapters. The term is almost synonymous with suggestive power. The possession of prestige means that what is said will be accepted without proof or hesitation. If Einstein says there is no such thing as a straight line, so be it. Our senses seem to contradict the statement, but there is no arguing with the world's foremost mathematician. The source from which a statement comes is frequently the decisive factor in determining whether it will be accepted. This is one reason why politicians spend so much time in trying to destroy one another's characters. Examples abound: For instance, the presidential election campaign of 1956 started on a "high plane," but soon degenerated into attacks upon the character and motives of the candidates, for this seemed necessary to win votes.

The sources of suggestion are numerous. They might be classified, in the order of increasing effectiveness, as commonplace, expert, and social. In the first category are the speakers who are unknown or undistinguished. Such a one may say, "South America is a land of opportunity." An audience would ordinarily respond by demanding proof or elaboration. If the same statement should be made by a noted writer on South America, or should come officially from such an organization as the Pan American Union, it would find much readier acceptance. And if the statement is heard on all sides as a generally accepted truism, it is a rare individual who would doubt it.

During the heat of a political campaign, in the softened light and symbolic surroundings of a church, or surrounded by a carefree crowd at a circus, we are much more suggestible than we would be normally. The circumstances in which suggestions are offered are important in determining their influence. When sister says, "Let's ask Dad for the car," brother is apt to reply, "Not now. He just received the blanks for his income tax report." Suggestion works best when (1) the audience is inclined to be favorable to the proposition; (2) the audience is in a generally agreeable emotional state; (3) the audience is polarized to such a degree that its judgment is inhibited.

C. SUGGESTIBILITY OF AUDITORS

Experiments to determine how susceptible people are to suggestion are common. One favorite device is to show the subjects a series of lines, of which the second is longer than the first, the third longer than the second, and the rest are of the same length. The subjects almost invariably will accept the implicit suggestion that each succeeding line is longer than the one before it. In another test, the experimenter shows his subjects several bottles which he says are full of perfume. He says he is testing their sense of smell and asks that after he removes the stoppers the subjects will raise their hands as soon as they can detect the odor. Invariably, hands are raised, although the bottles contain only water. A third type of experiment consists of showing a picture to a group for a few seconds, then asking a series of questions as to what was in it. Most of the questions concern the actual contents of the picture, but several refer to objects that were not in it. For instance, one question might be, "What color was the dog?" although no dog appeared in the picture. The spurious questions are often answered along with the others.

Conclusions which emerge from such studies include the following: (1) everyone is suggestible in some degree; (2) age is a distinct factor in suggestibility: children are more suggestible than college students, and college students more than adults; (3) women are measurably, although not much more suggestible than men; (4) the experience, general knowledge, and intelligence of the subjects are factors, although not as important as might be assumed; (5) social facilitation is an important factor; that is, in a group the more suggestible members respond first, and their response increases the tendency of the others to accept the suggestion.

Suggestion operates visually, too. We readily accept the suggestion that the figures in this drawing increase in size as they recede into the background.

D. DURATION

Suggestion is like water, the continual dropping of which will wear away stones. One of the most fundamental rules in the influencing of public opinion is to keep at it. Tell the audience again, and again, and again. The potently indirect suggestion of Ivory Soap's slogan, "It floats," appeared on billboards and in newsprint years ago, and it still appears regularly. Bruce Barton, in his speech on advertising, which has been previously quoted, declared that the most important rule is to "be persistent."

You can't expect to advertise in flush times and live on the memory of it when you are hard up. You can't expect to advertise when you are in trouble, or about to be in trouble, and expect to get anything in that direction. It is a day-by-day and hour-by-hour business. If the money that has been thrown away by people who advertised spasmodically was all gathered together, it would found and endow the most beautiful home in the world for aged advertising men and their widows. Don't throw any more of that money away. If advertising is worth doing at all, it is worth doing all the time.

The inexperienced young minister is apt to rack his brains trying to find new themes for his weekly sermons. But the older man knows that he must hammer away time and again on the few propositions which, in a lifetime of endeavor, he may get his congregations to accept. A new proposition must be heard over and over again, before it can settle down into the consciousness as an old friend and be at home there. When a new fashion appears it seems fantastic, then we begin to accept it, next to admire its attractive features, and, finally, any change from it to something else seems odd.

A third term was first mentioned for President Roosevelt only as a remote and terrifying possibility. Even ardent New Dealers opposed it. But as the months passed and the nominating convention drew nearer, the idea of a third term was made more and more familiar by constant repetition. The enemies of the plan helped it along as well as did its friends; for every mention of it, unfriendly or not, helped to imbed it in the public mind. By July, 1940, when the convention was held, the third-term specter had been worn so thin by repetition that it played no part in the convention and little in the election. Suggestion is not like a rubber band, which weakens as it is stretched; rather it is like a climbing vine, which gets sturdier as it grows.

E. VOLUME

This last aid to suggestion needs merely be mentioned, for its merits must be apparent from what has previously been said. The voice of one suggester is less effective than the combined voices of many. What *every*one believes, every*one* willingly accepts.

Methods of suggestion

In addition to the methods of suggestion which have been discussed in the preceding pages, the persuasive speaker will be aided by a consideration of the tentative laws of suggestion and by a description of some practical techniques.

A. LAWS

Hollingworth, in *The Psychology of the Audience,* formulated seven laws of suggestion which may briefly be paraphrased, and which together serve as a general summary for some of the principles that have been discussed:

1. With the kind of audiences speakers normally address, the strength of a suggestion is in proportion to its indirectness. The auditors will act most surely on what they take to be their own ideas.

2. A suggestion is more dynamic the more forcefully and vividly it is presented. President Franklin D. Roosevelt was an effective persuasive speaker, in part because he could compress a whole social philosophy into such brief compass as his statement of the "four freedoms" of which humanity must be assured: the freedom from fear, freedom from want, freedom of religion, and freedom of speech.

3. Suggestion is more effective in a positive than in a negative form.

4. The effectiveness of suggestion varies directly in proportion to the prestige of its source.

5. The effectiveness of suggestion varies directly in proportion to the favorableness of the attitude it encounters. It is obvious that if a suggestion points in the direction of a pre-existing desire, it is likely to be successful. Here the function of suggestion is not to "create" a response, but simply to "release" it.

6. Repetition, especially with variation in the phrasing, is an effective agent of suggestion.

7. To secure a response without thought, it is essential so to phrase the suggestion that it will not invite comparison with any rival idea.

B. STYLE

The persuasive effect of sheer stylistic excellence is tremendous. "Give me the right word," wrote Joseph Conrad, "and the right accent and I will move the world." This is scarcely an overstatement. Declared one close observer of the American scene, Edward A. Thurber, "The man of rhythms breaks in upon the council, and because he stands well and waves well and booms well, he is listened to, and his advice is assumed as good; nay the council leaps upon him, draws him to its bosom, and hails him mightily." This is consciously extravagant phrasing, but it agrees very well in sentiment with the soberer statement of Lloyd George, in his inaugural address as Rector of Edinburgh University, that "Parliamentary government means etymologically as well as in reality government by talk.... A programme is successful when a truth becomes a tag.... In the end we are governed by the winning tag." In these two statements we have tributes to the two kinds of oral style which have proved most effective: the grand and the epigrammatic.

The grand style is well illustrated by the rolling periods of Edmund Burke's denunciation of Warren Hastings. Fanny Burney, a good friend of Hastings, related that as she sat in the balcony of the parliamentary hall listening to the flood of Burke's eloquence pouring out, the blood pounded in her temples and she felt herself overwhelmed with a conviction of his guilt. Critics of our day frequently complain about the rhetorical splendor of the orations of Burke, of Webster, and of their oratorical peers, but persuasive speaking will suffer if the suggestive power of rhythm and phrase is forgotten. In brief illustration may be cited Webster's expression of a rather commonplace idea in a speech which he made to some New York businessmen.

Though individuals flourish and decay, states are immortal ... the individuals who compose them may change, as the atoms of our bodies change, but the political community still exists in its aggregate capacity, as our bodies still exist in their natural capacity; with this only difference, that we know that our natural frames must soon dissolve, and return to their original dust; but for our country, she yet lives, she ever dwells in our hearts, and it will, even at the last solemn moment, go up as our final aspiration to Heaven that she may be immortal.

Something of this same grand style is evident in the speeches of the wartime prime minister of Great Britain, Winston Churchill, who has proved his worth as a persuasive speaker to stand in the company of the truly great.

Epigrammatic speaking consists of the formation of "the winning tags" of which Lloyd George spoke. How much of our thinking is directed by slogans, proverbs, and bywords! In politics the presidential campaigns have been dominated by them: "Rum, Romanism, and Rebellion!"; "The Square Deal"; "He kept us out of war"; "Back to normalcy!"; "The full dinner pail!"; and "The forgotten man." In business there has been amply demonstrated the sales value of a good trade name, such as Frigidaire, Kodak, or Jello, and of good sales slogans, such as "I'd walk a mile for a Camel," "Milk from contented cows," "For economical transportation," and "Say it with flowers." Listen to the conversation of your associates and find how much of their conduct is justified by the quotation of apt proverbs: "The better the day, the better the deed"; "A penny saved is a penny earned"; "A bird in the hand is worth two in the bush"; and "History repeats itself."

The extensive use that a speaker may make of the epigrammatic style, as well as its considerable suggestive power, may be well illus-

trated with a paragraph chosen from a speech on "Democratic Aris-
tocracy," delivered by Henry Van Dyke, at the College of William and
Mary, on November 27, 1926. Said Dr. Van Dyke, as he drew near
his conclusion:

"Know thyself," was Solon's motto, inscribed on the Delphian Shrine.
But if knowledge is power, this means also the control of thyself. Keep
the body out of the sensual mire, and the mind above the body, and the
eternal laws of God above the mind. In two great points of goodness the
world is growing better—the sense of justice and the sentiment of mercy.
But in the third element of virtue, self-control, it seems to be standing
still or slipping back. The popular gospel of the day is self-expression,
which means let yourself go, follow your passions, gratify your appetites,
acknowledge no inhibitions. This is cynic doctrine, the doctrine of dogs
imperfectly house-broken. But the philosophy of manhood is nobler. It
calls us to

Move upward, working out the beast.

It bids us bring our passions and powers into subjection to reason and
conscience. Trust no outward agent to do this for you. No congress can
legislate you virtuous: no church can enchant you good. You must do it
yourself. By the grace of God above you and within you, you must possess
and captain your soul.

The power of the word is not to be disdained. Apart even from the
idea it contains, an effective phrase is a strong motivator of human
conduct. With rare insight, an early eighteenth-century English squire,
Andrew Fletcher, declared, "Give me the making of the songs of a
nation, and I care not who makes its laws." More effective, he knew,
than law courts and jails is the directive power of entrancing style.

C. STORIES

Parables, analogies, examples, illustrations, allegories, and anecdotes have always been effective instruments of suggestion. Aesop,
one of the first great moral teachers, impressed his truths indelibly
upon the minds of men by means of his fables. Jesus almost never
preached except through parables. The really persuasive speeches of

all ages are loaded with stories. These stories are suggestive in that the speakers relate how something happens in the narrative, and then they ask the audience to assume with them that the same thing will occur or has occurred in regard to their proposal.

The suggestive use of analogy is well illustrated in a striking instance of it which President Franklin D. Roosevelt employed during the 1936 campaign, to indicate how his severest critics had welcomed his program during the dark days of 1933.

> Some of these people really forget how sick they were. But I know how sick they were. I have their fever charts. I know how the knees of all of our rugged individualists were trembling four years ago and how their hearts fluttered. They came to Washington in great numbers. Washington did not look like a dangerous bureaucracy to them then. Oh, no! It looked like an emergency hospital. All of the distinguished patients wanted two things—a quick hypodermic to end the pain and a course of treatment to cure the disease. They wanted them in a hurry; we gave them both. And now most of the patients seem to be doing very nicely. Some of them are even well enough to throw their crutches at the doctor.

Abraham Lincoln never asked an argument to do what an illustration could achieve more easily. When, during the secessionist fever just prior to the Civil War, there were threats that New York City would secede from the Union and become a city-state, "I reckon," remarked Lincoln, "it will be some time before the Front Door sets up housekeeping on its own account." In his debates with Douglas, when the "Little Giant" defended slavery on the ground that the slaves themselves did not object to it, Lincoln replied thus: "I have heard it all my life," he declared, "and, as the boy said about skinning eels, it don't hurt 'em so very much; it has always been done, they're used to it." To weaken the effect of a long brief prepared by an opposing attorney, Lincoln said of it: "It's like the lazy preacher that used to write long sermons, and the explanation was, he got to writin' and was too lazy to stop." None of these analogies is logically sound, but all are persuasively effective. They *suggest* the speaker's conclusion more effectively than he would have been able to *prove* it.

D. PRESUMPTION

Suggestion operates when the speaker presumes that, of course, his audience agrees with him. This can be done in any one of several ways. One method is by assuming that the desired belief or conduct already exists. One very successful teacher of English literature is always graciously complimentary to his classes. Whenever he mentions any literary classic, it is always with the phrase, "As you will recall . . ." or "You have doubtless read. . . ." If his students are unfamiliar with the reading that has been assigned, he assumes that they have been spending all their available time in pursuing an independent reading program of their own. As a result, his students feel honor bound not to disappoint his expectation of them, and they do a great deal more than the normal quota of reading for his courses. This professor profits from the advice of Alexander Pope:

> Men must be taught as if you taught them not,
> And things unknown propos'd as things forgot.

A similar device is to impute to the audience the speaker's own ideas, as though he is but echoing what they already believe. The salesman uses this device when he tells the prospect that "We have created this product in response to strong public demand." A politician uses it when he represents himself as the people's own candidate (and what one does not!). In this vein Wendell Willkie presented his candidacy for the presidency: "I represent your power, the power of the people, to judge, to choose and to elect in a political campaign. This power you have not given away to Mr. Roosevelt. If you elect me as your President, you will never give it away to anybody."

A third common type of presumption consists of assuming the truth of the speaker's contention and reasoning on from there. The automobile advertisement, "Ask the man who owns one," assumes that, of course, any driver of that kind of car is pleased with it. The sales line, "Compare the values!" is of similar import. Former President Herbert Hoover, speaking at Oakland, California, on October 5, 1935, started his speech with two basic assumptions: namely, that the principles of the New Deal had "been forced upon us" and that these principles in operation were responsible for the continuance of the depression. With these two hypotheses accepted, it was easy to condemn the administration in detail. Huey Long, a master of persuasive speaking, used presumption of this sort during the 1932 campaign in Louisiana, when he said:

They'll tell you that what you've got to do is tear up Longism in this state. All right, my friends—get you a bomb or some dynamite and blow up that building yonder [pointing to the new Capitol]. That's a good place to start. Then go out and tear up the concrete roads I've built. Get your spades and your shovels and scrape the gravel off them roads we've graveled, and let a rain come on 'em. That'll put 'em back like they was before I come. Tear down the new buildings I've built at the University. Take the money away from the school boards that I've give 'em to run your schools. And when your child starts out to school tomorrow morning, call him back and snatch the free school books out of his hand that Huey Long gave him. Then you'll be rid of Longism in this state, my friends, and not till then.

E. QUESTIONS

Many a speaker has hammered home his point simply with a series of questions. The implication is that he would never ask them if the answers did not favor his cause. Much can be suggested in this fashion that could never be proved. Bruce Barton used this method in one of his speeches in the congressional campaign of 1938, when he declared, "The middle classes of this country are being liquidated," and proceeded to "prove" the contention as follows:

Is that too strong a statement? Test it from your own knowledge and acquaintanceship. [Method of presumption.] Do you know any small farmer who is as well off as he was a year ago? Do you know any small manufacturer who is as well off as he was a year ago? Do you know any merchant, any doctor, any country lawyer, any teacher, any white collar worker who feels as well off, as secure, as he or she did a year ago?

"Leading" questions are ruled out in the courtroom, for they suggest too strongly the desired answer. Alert lawyers nevertheless manage to include them in their cross-examination of witnesses. And persuasive speakers use them freely in their speeches. A few examples will illustrate the type:

"Did you see blood stains on Mr. X's hands?"

"Have you considered how your wife could get along after your death on so small an amount of insurance?"

"What would you do if your present car should break down during your trip?"

"Would a loan of $300 relieve the financial strain and help you better to enjoy your vacation?"

"Have you wondered how much training would be required to fit you for the foremanship of your department?"

Without argument, without even assertion—guilelessly and inoffensively—such questions as these carry into the auditor's mind the conclusion the speaker wishes him to accept.

Conclusion

Suggestion is of value to the persuasive speaker when he needs to secure a decision in a hurry, when his audience is incapable of following through a long and involved logical argument, when the audience is sufficiently predisposed toward the proposal so that it needs only direction—not proof—and when the speaker's prestige is so great that the audience wants to know only what he believes, not why he believes it. Unfortunately, much suggestion is used, too, by speakers who have proposals to advance which could not withstand logical analysis. Selling shoddy merchandise or presenting shoddy ideas, they have to depend upon slipping their proposition by the auditors' critical faculties without examination. On the other hand, speakers whose proposals are thoroughly sound often find suggestion a valuable persuasive tool. The fact that their method of presentation is nonlogical is of itself no proof that the speakers' ideas are bad.

Suggestion, in whatever form it is offered, is an attempt to secure the acceptance of a belief or course of action without logical consideration of it. It operates best when the thinking of the audience is inhibited or dissociated; when the audience is composed of unusually suggestible individuals; when the circumstances are particularly favorable to suggestion; when the suggestion is widespread and has been of long duration; and when the speaker's prestige is high. Like all methods of motivation, it has definite techniques and methods that the speaker can master and use. Also like other forms of motivation, it is not entirely understood, it is not foolproof, its results cannot be wholly predictable, and it operates best when employed by a speaker of ability and assurance. The speaker who is just trying to master the art of persuasive speaking can profit much from a thorough study of the principles of suggestion.

Exercises

1. Restate in your own words the nature of suggestion, as it is used in persuasive speaking.

2. Now that you have read the entire chapter, what do you think of the ethics of using suggestion? How should the ethical problem be dealt with? Why is the answer difficult?

3. In reading the persuasive speeches found printed in this book, what uses of suggestion do you find? Identify the various types and methods, and (so far as you can) the factors affecting the speakers' choice of suggestive materials. What do you think of the ethics of utilizing such suggestion as you find in these speeches?

4. Collect five advertisements containing positive, direct suggestion. Find at least three containing indirect suggestion. Can you find any with negative suggestion? If so, for what purpose was it used?

5. Discuss the nature, extent, effectiveness, and ethics of suggestion as you have observed it in teaching, politics, preaching, and selling.

6. How suggestible do you find your friends to be? Are there any striking differences among them in their susceptibility to suggestion? Are any of them definitely contrasuggestible? Select two of your friends who are very different in their susceptibility to suggestion, and plan an effective persuasive appeal to be directed to each of them.

7. Analyze yourself as objectively and as closely as you can to determine your own reactions to suggestion. What sources have particularly strong suggestive power over your thinking? To what, if any, sources of suggestion which influence most of your associates are you immune? Why? What types of suggestion are most influential in affecting your thinking? Can you illustrate with some specific instances?

8. Restate the ideomotor principle in your own words. Of what value is it in the persuasive process? Illustrate its operation from your own experience or observation.

9. Listen carefully for instances of suggestion in its various forms in some speech that you hear. Evaluate the speaker's success as a suggester. What criticisms could you offer to improve his technique?

10. What differences in suggestion would be proper for a speech supporting the proposal that "a year of military training should be compulsory in peacetime for all healthy boys upon reaching the age of eighteen," if it were to be presented successively to the following audiences:

    a. A troop of Boy Scouts.
    b. A group of mothers whose sons had been killed in battle.
    c. A group of young women.
    d. A group of veterans of the last war.
    e. A group of middle-aged businessmen.
    f. A group of high school boys.

11. Answer the following questions:

    a. What is hypnosis? How does it resemble milder degrees of suggestion?
    b. Explain each of the several types of suggestion. How can each be used in persuasive speech?
    c. What kinds of motivation do you find in the extract from Darrow's speech in defense of Leopold and Loeb?
    d. Under what circumstances is negative suggestion preferred?
    e. What are the factors that determine the effectiveness of suggestion? Explain each one in terms of the persuasive-speaking situation. Illustrate each from your own experience or observation.
    f. Explain the "laws" of suggestion.
    g. How is style a factor in suggestion?
    h. How are stories used as instruments of suggestion?
    i. What is the suggestive use of presumption? What forms may it take?
    j. How do questions function as suggestion devices?

12. For a further exploration of the meanings and uses of suggestion, the following readings will be helpful:

John Waite Bowers, "Language Intensity, Social Introversion, and Attitude Change," *Speech Monographs,* 30 (November, 1963), 345-352.

Donald E. Broadbent, *Perception and Communication* (London: Scientific Book Guild, 1961), particularly Chapter X, "The Selective Nature of Learning," pp. 244-267.

T. E. Coffin, "Suggestibility and Levels of Difficulty," in G. E. Swanson, T. M. Newcomb, and E. L. Hartley (eds.), *Readings in Social Psychology* (New York: Holt, 2nd ed., 1952), pp. 11-18.

Joseph F. Donceel, Benjamin S. Alimena, and Catherine M. Birch, "Influence of Prestige Suggestion on the Answers of a Personality Inventory," *Journal of Applied Psychology*, 33 (August, 1949), 352-355.

T. N. Ewing, "A Study of Certain Factors Involved in Changes in Opinion," *Journal of Social Psychology*, 16 (1942), 63-88.

C. R. Griffith, "A Comment upon the Psychology of the Audience," *Psychological Monographs*, 30 (1921), 36-47.

Clark L. Hull, *Hypnosis and Suggestibility* (New York: Appleton-Century, 1933).

Arthur Jenness, "Facilitation of Response to Suggestion by Response to Previous Suggestion of a Different Type," *Journal of Experimental Psychology*, 16 (1933), 55-82.

Irving Lorge, "Prestige, Suggestion, and Attitudes," *Journal of Abnormal and Social Psychology*, VII (November, 1936), 386-402.

T. S. Ludlum, "Effects of Certain Techniques of Credibility upon Audience Attitude," *Speech Monographs*, XXV (November, 1958), 278-284.

C. H. Marple, "The Comparative Suggestibility of Three Age Levels to the Suggestion of Group versus Expert Opinion," *Journal of Abnormal and Social Psychology*, IV (1933), 176-186.

John A. McNulty and Richard H. Walters, "Emotional Arousal, Conflict, and Susceptibility to Social Influence," *Canadian Journal of Psychology*, XVI (September, 1962), 211-220.

N. E. Miller and J. Dollard, *Social Learning and Imitation* (New Haven: Yale University Press, 1941).

John J. B. Morgan, "Effect of Non-Rational Factors on Inductive Reasoning," *Journal of Experimental Psychology*, 34 (February, 1944), 159-168.

Stanley F. Paulson, "The Effects of the Prestige of the Speaker and Acknowledgement of Opposing Arguments on Audience Retention and Shift of Opinion," *Speech Monographs*, XXI (November, 1954), 267-271.

L. S. Penrose, *On the Objective Study of Crowd Behavior* (London: H. K. Lewis, 1952).

W. A. Peterson and N. P. Gist, "Rumor and Public Opinion," *American Journal of Sociology*, 57 (1951), 159-167.

Leo Postman and Rheem F. Jarrett, "An Experimental Analysis of 'Learning Without Awareness,'" *American Journal of Psychology*, 65 (April, 1952), 244-255.

T. M. Sawyer, Jr., "Shift of Attitude Following Persuasion as Related to Estimate of Majority Attitude," *Speech Monographs*, XXII (March, 1955), 68-78.

Thomas M. Scheidel, "Sex and Persuasability," *Speech Monographs*, XXX (November, 1963), 353-358.

Rosalea Ann Schonbar, "Students' Attitudes toward Communists: I: The Relation between Intensity of Attitude and Amount of Information," *Journal of Psychology*, 27 (1949), 55-71.

R. Tagiuri and L. Petrullo (eds.), *Person Perception and Interpersonal Behavior* (Stanford: Stanford University Press, 1958).

D. L. Thistlethwaite, H. de Haan, and J. Kamenetsky, "The Effects of 'Directive' and 'Non-Directive' Communication Procedures on Attitudes," *Journal of Abnormal and Social Psychology*, 51 (1955), 3-12.

Gordon L. Thomas and David C. Ralph, "A Study of the Effect of Audience Proximity on Persuasion," *Speech Monographs*, XXVI (November, 1959), 300-307.

Philip K. Tomkins and Larry A. Samovar, "An Experimental Study of the Effects of Credibility on the Comprehension of Content," *Speech Monographs*, XXXI (June, 1964), 120-123.

W. Weiss, "Opinion Congruence with a Negative Source on One Issue as a Factor Influencing Agreement on Another Issue," *Journal of Abnormal and Social Psychology*, 54 (1957), 180-186.

A. Zander and A. R. Cohen, "Attributed Social Power and Group Acceptance: A Classroom Experimental Demonstration," *Journal of Abnormal and Social Psychology*, 51 (1955), 490-492.

✍ 8.

Identification

As has been pointed out earlier in several different contexts, persuasion is very different from argument. Argument means that two defined positions (an affirmative and a negative) are set up as opposites, and each side assumes a burden of proof to develop in attempting to destroy the basis for the other side. After the argument is ended, the spectators feel disappointed unless there is a decision rendered as to which side wins and which loses. Argument is a contest.

Persuasion, like argument, becomes needed when there are two differing points of view. The persuasive speaker seeks to change the attitudes, feelings, beliefs, or conduct of his listeners. But so long as he is being persuasive, he avoids any direct attack; he attempts to play the role of a guide, leading the audience out of its confusion of mistakes onto the clear highway to what the speaker thinks is the right decision. The persuasive speaker does not contest, denounce, berate, or insist; instead he beguiles, entices, invites, and induces agreement. And in order to do so he uses what is often called "common ground" —and what might more accurately be called "identification."

The meaning of identification

In a significant contribution to rhetoric, *A Rhetoric of Motives,* Kenneth Burke developed the concept of *identification* as the key to persuasion. "You persuade a man only in so far as you can talk his language by speech, gesture, tonality, order, image, attitude, idea, *identifying* your ways with his," wrote Burke. Identification consists of making clear the commonality, the similarity, the overlapping, the basic union of the point of view of the speaker with the varying points of view of his listeners.

It has been observed by Hayakawa, the editor of *Etc., A Review of General Semantics,* that "what we call society is a vast network of mutual agreements." Institutions—including marriage, an athletic team, a fraternity, a church, and a state—exist because the members feel that they have common needs, interests, and methods of working and living together. To be a social being means in large part the ability to see the other person's point of view, to unite for common purposes, and to speak and act in ways acceptable to the group. When we speak to one another we use a set of symbols that have become meaningful only through long centuries of mutual agreement. Our very civilization exists because mankind has made progressive efforts to eliminate or de-emphasize divisive differences and to cultivate and enhance a vast array of convictions and customs that we all share. We all feel very strongly the urge to "belong." In this sense of commonality lies that *identification* which makes persuasion possible.

As Kenneth Burke points out, "Identification is compensatory to division. If men were not apart from one another, there would be no need for the rhetorician to proclaim their unity." We all realize that a degree of division does exist. You want the same job someone else wants; you support the Republican Party, your associate supports the Democrats; you are majoring in Economics, your friend in Electrical Engineering; you like jazz and Hemingway, your brother prefers opera and Robert Louis Stevenson. Such differences multiply endlessly. Yet underlying them and interweaving with them are also multiple similarities: a common belief in the free enterprise system, in self-government, in education, in artistic excellence. What the persuasive speaker needs to learn is to look through and around the difference to the more fundamental and meaningful factors of identification.

Let us imagine a meeting of the local school board in which two members hold opposing views on the desirability of replacing the old gymnasium with a new one. Speaker *A,* who wants to scrap the old structure and build a modern one in its place, seeks to *identify* his point of view with ideas and feelings held by all members of the board. He speaks of the value of a good education, of the pride they naturally have in providing the best facilities they can afford for their own community, of the added safety features of a new building, which will protect the welfare of their children. Speaker *B,* opposing the replacement of the old gym, also (if he is wise) molds his persuasion upon identification with deep-seated attitudes, feelings, and beliefs of his audience. His persuasion consists of a reminder of exciting athletic contests that have been held in the old gym; he speaks of the values of simplicity and of educating students to the importance of living within their means; he notes the expense, the trouble, and the loss of valuable use of the gym during the interval while the old building is being dismantled and the new one erected. In both instances, the speaker tries not to "oppose" ideas held by others, but to *identify* his own cause with some of their fundamental feelings.

A fine example of the use of identification is found in the opening sentences of a sermon by Norman Vincent Peale, entitled, "The Secret of Power Over Your Weakness." "At luncheon," Peale begins, "I was seated beside the president of a small steel company. We talked about steel, people, and God. 'In a way, you and I are in the same business,' he said. 'I make steel; but you, as a minister, put steel into people.' " Here is an example of two men of widely different backgrounds who found a way of "speaking the same language" to discuss their different interests and responsibilities. The result was to emphasize their commonality of views.

Identification preferable to conflict

In a humanity composed of egocentric individuals, it perhaps should be wondered at that there is so much harmony, rather than that conflict does exist. With self-interest as the fundamental motivation of human conduct, it is remarkable that social organization, depending as it must upon co-operation and mutual consideration, could be developed. One reason why human beings are able much of the time to avoid conflict is that they can see its disadvantages. Even though our emotions frequently impel us to verbal or physical battle, we readily agree that such conflict is misdirected, wasteful, and achieves at best but temporary results.

Misdirected. Conflict increases tension, arouses the emotions, stirs up latent prejudices and dislikes, emphasizes differences rather than similarity and agreement, and makes progress in no other way as surely and as swiftly as it does in widening the breach between the disputants. What starts as a minor difference becomes, in the heat of argument, major. Disputants who commence their argument with feelings of mutual respect and liking find themselves rapidly drifting apart rather than together. Even if, in the end, one of them will admit that the other is right on the point at issue, the total effect of the conflict has been to leave them further apart and separated on more grounds than they were when the argument started. While the intellectual difference is being plowed out, seeds of emotional difference are being plowed in—and they are very apt to bear the fruits of resentment and antagonism.

Wasteful. Conflict is wasteful in that it destroys harmony while seeking to achieve it. Minds that have painfully been brought together at one point have been torn apart at others. The typical argument brings in irrelevant issues, encourages exaggeration and misrepresentation, leads frequently to stinging personal attacks, and altogether produces far more heat than light.

Temporary. Under the most favorable conditions, when conflict is reduced to a minimum or entirely eliminated, argument has but a temporary effect upon most auditors. When one disputant is forced into acquiescence by the superior argumentative ability of his opponent, the one thing certain is that he will tend to swing back to his former position. The writer has observed many political discussions during the course of a presidential campaign in which the same set of disputants always wins the arguments and secures grudging agreement with its views—but at the next gathering of the same people, the same arguments have to be repeated again. The mind seems to be like a pendulum, which can be moved forcibly from its position, but generally swings back to it. A permanent change can be accomplished only by shifting the base or fundamental point of attachment.

A typical example. A typical argument, with its generation of irrelevant emotional conflict and the consequent heightening of differences, has been described by William James in his book, *Pragmatism*. Like most arguments, it achieved nothing and could have been avoided if the final solution had been applied before it commenced. But having arisen, and swept on to the emotional plane, note that Professor James could say only that his solution *assuaged* ("allayed, mitigated, eased, or lessened") the dispute, and that the more emotional disputants refused to accept any conclusion except their own.

Some years ago [wrote James], being with a camping party in the mountains, I returned from a solitary ramble to find everyone engaged in a ferocious metaphysical dispute. The corpus of dispute was a squirrel— a live squirrel supposed to be clinging to one side of a tree-trunk; while over against the tree's opposite side a human being was imagined to stand. This human witness tries to get sight of the squirrel by moving rapidly around the tree, but no matter how fast he goes, the squirrel moves as fast in the opposite direction, and always keeps the tree between himself and the man, so that never a glimpse of him is caught. The resultant metaphysical problem now is this: Does the man go around the squirrel? In the unlimited leisure of the wilderness, discussion had been worn threadbare. Everyone had taken sides and was obstinate; and the numbers on both sides were even. Each side, when I appeared, therefore appealed to me to make it a majority. Mindful of the scholastic adage that whenever you meet a contradiction, you must make a distinction, I immediately sought and found one, as follows: "Which party is right," I said, "depends on what you practically mean by going around the squirrel. If you mean passing from the north of him to the east, then to the south, then to the west, and then to the north of him again, obviously the man does go around him, for he occupies these successive positions. But if, on the contrary, you mean being first in front of him, then on the right of him, then behind him, then on his left, and finally in front again, it is quite obvious that the man fails to go around him, for by the compensating movements the squirrel makes, he keeps his belly turned towards the man all the time, and his back turned away. Make the distinction and there is no occasion for any further dispute. You are both right and both wrong according as you conceive the verb 'to go around' in one practical fashion or the other."

Although one or two of the hotter disputants called my speech shuffling evasion, saying that they wanted no quibbling or scholastic hair-splitting, but meant just plain honest English "round," the majority seemed to think that the distinction had assuaged the dispute.

Adjusting disagreement

Despite the admitted disadvantages of conflict, disagreements do arise, and they must be adjusted somehow. Various methods may be described briefly and assessed.

Ascendance. The complete triumph and domination of one party to the dispute may be secured. If the "right side" wins, this should be a good solution, but it has two weaknesses: (1) scarcely ever in a dispute is the truth all on one side; (2) even if it were, the defeated disputant would have a residue of feelings of resentment which would militate against future harmony between "winner" and "loser." One successful labor conciliator explained his success by saying, "I always give the decision to one side and the language to the other." To prevent at least the appearance of ascendance, if not the fact, is vital to a satisfactory solution.

Submission. The corollary to ascendance, submission, is even more unsatisfactory. To lose a dispute completely is not only to surrender the point at issue, but to suffer a serious blow to the ego as well. It is the type of solution any normal disputant will avoid if he can.

Tolerance. When an individual agrees to permit the continuance of an action or the expression of a point of view which he does not like, he is said to be exercising tolerance. It is equivalent to saying, "I think you are wrong, but I am willing to permit your error to exist without disturbing it." Implicit in tolerance is a feeling of superiority and derogation which prevents any truly cordial relationship between the tolerator and the tolerated individuals. The latter is granted his position not as a matter of right, but as a charitable concession by the former. As a basis for normal, harmonious relationship, tolerance is better than ascendance or submission, but it is far short of a permanently satisfactory adjustment.

Compromise. A better method is for each party to the dispute to say: "I'll surrender part of my point, if you will do likewise, and we'll come to an agreement on a midposition which will contain parts of what we both believe." Often this is the best solution that can be found. If it is based upon an honest attempt at conciliation by both disputants, it may produce satisfactory results. But compromise can never be completely satisfactory, and it is often simply an armistice, rather than a final basis for peace. In the first place, both disputants have had to surrender part of what they believe to be right, so that each is partly dissatisfied with the solution. Each feels that if perfect justice were done, the other would have made all the concessions. Thus, if a prospective buyer and an automobile dealer are haggling over the trade-in value of the former's car, they may finally agree to "split the difference." But the dealer will feel that he paid too much and the buyer that he got too little. In the second place, to protect themselves against the effects of expected compromise, each disputant is likely to ask for more than he actually thinks he should receive. Thus the initial difference is enlarged, and any attempt to reach an agreement is discouraged. In the third place, if one disputant honestly states his basic position, he is apt to suspect the other of having deliberately taken an extreme view in order to be in a "good bargaining position." Thus, in labor disputes both employer and employee are prone to feel that their own demands are minimum and that the position of the other party has been made deliberately extreme. This attitude, of course, discourages any movement toward conciliation. Finally, no matter what compromise agreement is reached, each disputant is likely to feel that the other may have "outsmarted" him. Americans, for instance, are constantly complaining about the superior finesse of European diplomats; and the Europeans, in turn, accuse the Americans of driving hard bargains. "Don't let that slicker get the best of you" is the kind of advice one is apt to receive from his friends when he sets out to reach a compromise agreement. It is not a good augury for the achievement of lasting harmony.

Identification. Unquestionably, the best means of solving a dispute is to discover that none exists. If neither side triumphs, neither must surrender; if there is mutual respect, there is no need of tolerance; if both want the same thing, nothing must be given up. It is only out

The evolution of the means of solving disputes.

of this kind of situation that real harmony, based on complete satisfaction, can arise. Identification occurs when disputants see that
instead of standing apart, they stand together. This situation may be
created by external forces, as when two foes are brought together
by an attack upon them both by a third party. Thus, following World
War II, the democratic Allies were quickly reconciled with Germany
and Japan through common fear of the aggressive designs of Russia.

A quarreling couple may be brought together by an attack upon one or both of them by an outsider. Hartzell Spence, in *One Foot in Heaven,* describes how his father, a Methodist minister, united the quarreling factions in one of his parishes by deliberately making himself disagreeable. The church members forgot their jealousies in the necessity of uniting to oust the unpopular pastor. The Reverend Mr. Spence was moved on to another charge; and the church he left, strengthened with its new unity, turned in relief to a program of real co-operation with its new minister. This kind of external creation of common ground cannot be used by the persuasive speaker. He needs to learn how to find it or create it in the conditions that have given rise to the disagreement. There are various means by which this may be done.

Bases for establishing identification

A. COMMUNITY OF INTERESTS

Individuals are sufficiently similar so that any two of them have much in common. In some circumstances their community of interests is self-evident; at other times it is obscured by a temporary emphasis upon their differences. Quarreling individuals or nations appear to themselves to have little in common; they regard one another with suspicion, accumulating ill will and such eventual dislike that they come to resent any suggestion that they resemble one another at all. This tendency is most clearly seen among nations in times of international tension. Hence, it may be profitable to observe the technique of trained diplomats in attempting to pierce beneath this smoldering hostility to demonstrate the existence of a real community of interests upon which lasting harmony can be based. Three spokesmen of our United States Department of State may be cited, as they explain the purpose of their program of international conciliation.

Cordell Hull, when he was Secretary of State, phrased the purpose of his reciprocal-trade program in carefully chosen words, to accentuate the common ground upon which it was based:

What we are seeking to accomplish by means of reciprocal trade agreements is to create such a basis for international trade as will enable mutually beneficial commerce among nations to flow more and more into the channels of natural advantage.

What "natural advantage" is to be sought was explained more in detail by Francis B. Sayre, then Assistant Secretary of State:

Daily life in each great nation has come to depend upon commodities from almost every other country of the world. The important electrical industry, for instance, could not operate a day without basic materials which come from some seventeen separate countries. Drug stores daily call upon every continent of the world. The bakery and confectionery industries use more than a dozen materials, such as exotic nuts, spices, flavorings and fruits, from twenty-eight countries. It has been estimated that the materials necessary for making a radio travel an aggregate of some 250,000 miles. Even beauty shops use materials from seventeen countries.

Former Undersecretary of State Sumner Welles contributed to the discussion at a difficult point: to try to establish a real community of interest among the nations of the Western Hemisphere. They differ from one another in language, in race, in cultural backgrounds, and in their predominant religions. They are competitors in many areas of trade, and South America's commercial relationships were much stronger with Europe than with the United States. They are all joined together geographically, it is true, yet in other parts of the world it seems to be demonstrated that physical propinquity is a chief cause of mutual suspicion and wars. Mr. Welles faced as difficult a task in trying to establish a bond of common ground as any persuasive speaker is likely to. This is what he said:

Although our individual inheritance may differ, there is not an independent nation of this continent that has not achieved its independence and that has not maintained it save through the expenditure of the blood and of the treasure of its citizens. The love of individual liberty and of freedom is just as deeply ingrained in the national consciousness of our neighbors as it is in our own. The principles of democracy are instinct in every nation of the Americas. Because at times, by reason of the stress and strain of domestic vicissitudes, passing manifestations may appear to obscure these principles, that does not imply that those ideals upon which every nation of this continent has been founded are not still uppermost in the spirit of every American people.

What these statesmen were seeking to accomplish in international affairs is precisely what every persuasive speaker should attempt in furthering his aim of bringing an audience round to his point of view; namely, to demonstrate by every means in his power that both parties to the discussion have identical interests—that their bases of agreement are numerous and fundamental and that their apparent differences are accidental and readily brushed aside.

B. ACQUIRED OBJECTIVITY

In order to see that one has interests in common with others, it is necessary to see the other person's point of view. As has been amply illustrated in earlier pages, this is difficult to do. The tendency of our thinking is to concentrate upon our own viewpoint; but there are degrees of subjectivity. It is possible to be relatively objective. One of the most valuable mental traits a persuasive speaker can have is objectivity in examining the motives of his auditors. His own reasons for believing as he does are relatively unimportant; what he must know is what reasons govern their thinking. When he can see them, he doubtless will discover that they have many points in common with his own and he can approach the minds of his persuadees by that route.

How the mind works in shifting from a subjective to an objective viewpoint has been described by Julian S. Huxley, who saw just such a shift occur on a mass scale among the people of England during the first two years of the war against the Nazis. The social distinctions, which had been very important in English life, unexpectedly gave way before a growing sense of national unity that proved a veritable fountain of strength for the island's defenders. Huxley described the psychological phenomena of the change in the following terms: "first, the resistance to new modes of thinking, then the effort of intellect and imagination to grasp their meaning and their implications, then the intellectual satisfaction that came of their assimilation, and finally the sense of community of purpose when they had been widely accepted."

Something like this process will have to be followed by a persuasive speaker who wants to achieve the mental objectivity that will help him to overcome opposition: first, recognize clearly that the persuadee sees the problem very differently from the way you do; second, list as fully and as accurately as you can the reasons which probably motivate his thinking on the subject; third, try to *become,* intellectually and imaginatively, as fully as you can, the persuadee; fourth, from *his* point of view, as thoroughly as you have been able to achieve it, determine what seem to be the elements of common ground in your mutual consideration of the problem; fifth, formulate such an approach to your proposal as he himself might make, leading gradually, by way of the points upon which you both agree, to the necessary controversial points and thence to the conclusion.

Such a mental metamorphosis cannot be accomplished hastily or easily. It requires a careful and thorough preparation, with a full realization of the two cardinal difficulties: first, that it is hard to know what another person does think; second, that it is very hard to give up one's own manner of thinking, even imaginatively. When you think you have got your mind adjusted to seeing the persuadee's point of view, it would be well to make a careful self-examination to be sure that the supposed transfer has really occurred. The problem here is very like that of the farmer who, searching for his lost cows, first of all asked himself, "Where would I go if I were a cow?" So the salesman approaching a prospective customer should ask himself, "If I were in Mr. Blank's position, what would be my attitude toward an agent who suddenly appeared, out of nowhere, with the proposal that I buy these goods?" The result should be the formulation of an approach that would start the discussion somewhere near the point at which Mr. Blank's thinking was occupied when the interview commenced.

It is disconcerting to note how frequently people say of their opponents: "So-and-so is certainly narrow-minded"; or, "Did you ever hear a more peculiar point of view?"; or, "I don't see how any sensible person could believe what he does." This is the normal, almost the automatic reaction that our minds make to contrary opinions. The ability to think otherwise—to delve into the heart of opposing views and really to understand them—is rare and must be acquired. The persuasive speaker should make it one of his most persistent aims. As was pointed out in Chapter 5, it was chiefly by this means that Benjamin Franklin made himself a highly effective persuader.

Types of identification

The areas in which people find identification are not all intellectual convictions. Grant and Lee, when they met at Appomattox, had much in common, although they had fought on opposite sides. On a campaign trip through Emporia, Kansas, President Franklin D. Roosevelt greeted William Allen White with actual, zestful pleasure, although the Kansas editor was busily trying to secure his defeat. Salesmen representing rival firms meet together in convivial sales conventions. The Senate of the United States represents every shade of political, economic, and social theory, yet there is a strong bond of fellow feeling uniting the members of "The World's Most Exclusive Club." There are many ways in which divergent individuals are drawn together. The types of identification may be classified in the fourfold division: interests, feelings, beliefs, and methods.

A. INTERESTS

Mutual interests form a strong bond. A youth contemplating marriage is advised to seek a wife whose interests correspond to his own. It is not so important that they reach the same conclusions, as it is that they can talk about the same things. Without common interests they will scarcely be in a position to talk at all. This is the broadest plane upon which minds can meet. An Italian fish peddler, an English banker, a French peasant, a Swiss watchmaker, and a German chemist are worlds apart in most respects, but they are united in their common interest in the fate of Europe. At a baseball game in the Yankee

Stadium the stands will be crowded with "fans" from every walk of life—differing in vocation, in education, in politics, in race, in ability, in religion—but vociferously and enthusiastically united in a common interest in whether Mickey Mantle will get a safe hit and bring in the winning run for the Yankees.

Acquaintanceships are usually struck up on the basis of mutual interests. It is an interesting exercise to analyze what caused one's own friendships to develop and to continue. As one runs through the list, he may find himself saying: We met at a dance, or at a ball game, or at the photography-supply counter, or in the Museum of Fine Arts; or: We met on a train and discovered we were both interested in fishing, or reading, or collecting butterflies.

If this is the way individuals are drawn together, it is no less the way bonds may be cemented between a speaker and his audience. Norman Thomas drew large crowds wherever he spoke, not because so many people believed in socialism, but because he filled his talks with anecdotes and illustrations drawn from the active interests of his auditors. As Norman Thomas himself explained his own platform success: "One must not only believe in what one is saying but also that it matters, especially that it *matters to the people to whom one is speaking*. If not, why bother?" Here is the way William Stedman appealed to common interests in opening an intercollegiate debate, before a student audience: "We feel it a great privilege to be able to battle this evening with the forensic representative of Middlebury College. We are forced to add, the college which has hounded us in football and which also boasts an A-1 ski team. Already this year Williams has met Middlebury in the Dartmouth practice tournament on the isolation question; so that I feel that we meet on common ground."

The speeches are endless in which the speaker begins: "I want to talk to you tonight about ——, a subject in which I have long been interested." Unless the audience has an unusual interest in the speaker as a person, that biographical detail will only make it moan. Much better is the speech which commences: "You people have lately been showing a great deal of interest in ———. I have discovered some facts about that subject which I think you would like to hear." Or the speaker might simply plunge into his speech upon a topic in which he knows his audience is interested. Thus Robert H. Jackson started a commencement address by saying: "Perhaps you have heard about the college executives who were discussing what they wanted to do after retirement age. One hoped to run a prison or school of correction, so the alumni would never come back to visit. Another chose to manage an orphan asylum so he would not be plagued with advice from parents." Such material was certain to arouse interest in a college audience.

Out of the interests of his audience, the speaker can surely find a basis for identifying himself and his cause with them. It should form a bridge, over which his appeals can march. If this bridge of common interests is not formed in the introduction to the speech, the remainder is very likely to go unheard—or at least unconsidered.

B. FEELINGS

People are much more similar emotionally than they are intellectually. Imbeciles and geniuses alike feel fear, hatred, love, and disgust. Both conservatives and liberals are open to an appeal to their patriotism, loyalty, and sense of duty. Most persons respond readily to humor or to the thrill of exciting tales. When William Howard Taft faced one of the most difficult speaking situations a candidate could have, he saved the meeting from angry dissolution by the apt use of humor. During the 1912 campaign, when the Republicans were split by the third-party movement of Theodore Roosevelt, Taft spoke in New York City to a mixed crowd of resentful "regular" Republicans and Bull Moose insurgents. Early in his speech, several insurgents hurled cabbages at the speaker. At once Taft's supporters arose to do battle, and a riot was threatened which would not only break up that meeting, but, publicized in the morning's paper, would do irreparable harm to the party's cause in the campaign. Taft quieted the crowd and converted their incipient anger into a roar of good-humored laughter when he pointed to the cabbages at his feet and said, "Never mind, my friends. Our opponents are just losing their heads!"

Aside from the use of humor, appeals to loyalty and fear are great unifiers. In the speech just mentioned, Taft proceeded to appeal for support through his auditors' loyalty to their party and fear of a Democratic victory. By these combined appeals of loyalty and fear Winston Churchill welded the English people together in the discouraging days of 1940. Beneath the surface stirrings of discontent, a speaker can usually find a deeper loyalty or a more basic fear through which he can lead his audience to a common agreement and unity of purpose.

C. BELIEFS

Salesmen have proved the efficacy of the "yes" technique. They have discovered that if a prospect can be induced to say: "Yes," "Yes," "Yes" to a series of propositions, it is difficult for him to shift suddenly from the affirmative to the negative attitude and say "No" to the closing appeal to buy. The secret is simple: The salesman starts his canvass with a series of beliefs which he knows his prospective customer accepts—such as, "I suppose that, like most women, you want a radio that is beautiful, dependable, and easy to operate?" Yes. "You have heard of the New Century F-M, of course?" Yes. "You subscribe to several magazines, do you not?" Yes. "And you frequently see our full-page ads setting forth the advantages of the New Century F-M?" Yes. "Everybody regards the New Century F-M as one of the very best radios, you know." Yes. "A product sold as widely as ours has to be good. We couldn't afford to have our advertising offset by a lot of complaints. Do you happen to know anyone who owns a New Century F-M?" Yes. "Does it work well?" Yes, it does. "Is it satisfactory in every way?" Yes. "You know, we have various colors to fit every color scheme. You'd want a light brown for this room, I suppose?" Yes. "Let's see, would you place it over there by the window?" Yes. "Well, I don't want you to buy one without having you and your husband see for yourselves how well it works and how beautiful it is. If you say the word, I'll have the delivery truck bring over this cabinet model this afternoon, and you can keep it right here in your home, with no obligation whatsoever, until you decide whether or not you want to buy it. Is that all right?" Yes, I guess it is.

This presentation is, of course, more compact than a real sales talk would be. In the actual presentation, the salesman would spend more time in elaborating the details of his machine, would place booklets with illustrations in the prospect's hands, would get her to point out the models she liked best, would secure as many positive statements as possible regarding what qualities she liked in a radio. But the expanded talk would follow the same principles as the skeletal example: it would proceed upon a basis of common beliefs, without ever, if possible, getting onto controversial ground.

James Albert Winans, in his textbook, *Speech Making,* set forth the ideal very well in the form of a dialogue between two men who had a problem to iron out. Said the first, "Well, let's talk over our points of difference." "No," replied the other, "let's talk over our points of agreement." That is the proper subject matter for the persuasive speech.

D. METHODS

Disputants who have little else in common may get together on the common ground of method. We like the people who talk our language, who have our habits, who share our prejudices. Among the businessmen who go to South America, the ones who succeed best are those who learn the language of the country, who adopt the *siesta* custom, who accept tolerantly the leisurely, even the inefficient methods of the people with whom they dwell. "Let's do it your way" is a good mental approach for a persuasive speaker to carry to his audience. The professor-in-politics is a subject of frequent jest, because the typical academic manners of speech and thought are so different from those of the electorate. More professors might be elected to office if they would adjust their approach.

When in Rome you are to do as the Romans do: this is the method of identification.

S. J. Woolf used the method of identification to accomplish a journalistic triumph. Woolf, who was an artist and special interviewer for *The New York Times,* went to London to sketch and interview George Bernard Shaw for his newspaper. As had been expected, Shaw refused, declaring with his typical impishness that he had already been immortalized in a portrait bust by Rodin. Woolf met the problem, as he related in his autobiography, *Here Am I,* by using Shaw's own methods of impudent bravado. The Rodin portrait, Woolf declared in a note to the dramatist, might make you immortal in Europe, "but as for America, with true Shavian modesty, may I say that true immortality will not be yours until I have drawn you?" To this note Shaw replied that he had decided to permit the drawing—but that his charge for sitting for it would be $3,750 an hour. Woolf instantly agreed, with the proviso: "my price for drawing is the same amount." In fitting conclusion to this correspondence, they chose the Fourth of July for the sitting, so that two vital documents would have appeared on the same date.

When we dine out we must seat the ladies in their chairs, use the proper forks, and dip our fingers in the finger bowl, not drink from it. One who breaks these rules of etiquette is regarded as a dolt and loses caste. For etiquette is the common ground of accepted social usage upon which people meet. There is, similarly, an etiquette or accepted mode of procedure for most activities. A new member of a business firm, a new "pledge" to a fraternity, a new professor on a college faculty, a new member of Congress, would do well not to hasten forward with measures which he wishes his new colleagues to accept. He should first take careful note of the customary avenues for presenting new proposals: what type of measure is brought up in open discussion and what type is generally submitted first to the executive council or a special committee? Would the proposal he has in mind be more properly presented by a department head or some other administrative official? Such considerations as these are sometimes condemned as "playing politics." There is nothing unworthy about them; they merely consist of learning and playing according to the rules of the game. Every game has its rules, and every unruly player is considered a nuisance by the others.

Henry Ward Beecher, in his third lecture to the Yale divinity students, gave to these neophytes precisely this fruit of his long and successful preaching experience:

> Now, in order to reach and help all these varying phases of your congregation, you must take human nature as you find it, in its broad range. Understand this, that the same law that led the Apostle to make himself a Greek to the Greeks, and a Jew to the Jews, and to put himself under the law with those who were under the law; and that same everlasting good sense of conformity in these things, for the sake of taking hold of men where they can be reached, and lifting them up, requires you to study human nature as it is, and not as people tell you it ought to be. If a man can be saved by pure intellectual preaching, let him have it. If others require a predominance of emotion, provide that for them. If by others the truth is taken more easily through the imagination, give it to them in forms attractive to the imagination. If there are still others who demand it in the form of facts and rules, see that they have it in that form. Take men as it has pleased God to make them; and let your preaching, so far as it concerns the selection of material, and the mode and method by which you are presenting the truth, follow the wants of the persons themselves, and not simply the measure of your own minds.

Flexibility of this sort is a chief source of strength. In this manner does meekness inherit the earth.

Utilizing identification

In addition to the methods that have already been given for using the techniques of identification, six final suggestions may be offered for the consideration of the persuasive speaker.

1. *Always stress the obvious relations that the speaker has with his audience.* These relationships can be covered simply in such an opening statement as: I am always glad to speak to a group of fellow Masons, or Baptists, or Rotarians, or Pennsylvanians, or salesmen, or life-insurance policyholders; or: Speaking to a college audience such as this carries me back to my own school days; or: We have come

together for the common purpose of . . . ; or: Our common experiences together have given us a common basis of understanding. Through these obvious, noncontroversial, easily expressed and easily understood connections, an immediate (though probably weak) bond is established. This type of relationship serves much the same function as a casual introduction of two individuals by a third. In itself, the introduction is not a strong bond, but at least it initiates an acquaintance which otherwise might not ever have commenced. It is like a front porch—a good entryway, though not a place on which to linger.

2. *Always stress any basic relations that the speaker may have with his audience.* If the speaker has close ties of any sort with his auditors, they should always be made evident and their significance clarified. For instance, the elected representative of a constituency would do well to follow the example set by the opening paragraph of President Grover Cleveland's first inaugural address:

In the presence of this vast assemblage of my countrymen, I am about to supplement and seal by the oath which I shall take, the manifestation of the will of a great and free people. In the exercise of their power and right of self-government they have committed to one of their fellow citizens a supreme and sacred trust, and he here consecrates himself to their service.

3. *Always stress the agreement of the speaker and his audience upon fundamental aims and beliefs.* If there is not such fundamental agreement, there can be little hope of results from discussion. Disputants can get nowhere if they are arguing from fundamentally different hypotheses. But it often happens that there is an essential community of basic beliefs that is not evident. The speaker can go far toward winning agreement by demonstrating this essential agreement in his first remarks. An example of this technique is found in one of the greatest American legislative speeches: Carl Schurz's plea in the United States Senate, on January 30, 1872, for a complete restoration of civil rights to the citizens of the Southern states. The period was one of bitter animosity toward the "rebels," and Schurz faced an audience which had voted over and over again for heavy punishment of the South. The plea he made in this speech was never-

theless successful. The entire address is a masterpiece of persuasive appeal, but two sentences only will be quoted here to show his opening emphasis upon the fundamental agreement of the Senators regarding his basic point:

> Let me assume that, if we differ as to the means to be employed, we are agreed as to the supreme end and aim to be reached. That end and aim of our endeavors can be no other than to secure to all the States the blessings of good and free government, and the highest degree of prosperity and well-being they can attain, and to revive in all citizens of this republic that love for the Union and its institutions, and that inspiring consciousness of a common nationality, which, after all, must bind all Americans together.

4. *Strive to keep the auditor's attention directed away from the minor points of difference.* When opposing arguments are of minor import, it is often better to ignore them than to answer them, so that the speaker can keep the whole attention of the audience upon the vital matters that are above dispute. This method was used by Patrick Henry in what is generally considered the most eloquent speech in American history—his "Liberty or Death" challenge to the Virginia House of Burgesses. After debate had proceeded for some time, Henry arose to compliment "the patriotism, as well as abilities, of the worthy gentlemen" who had been speaking against Virginia's participating in the impending struggle. "But different men often see the same subject in different lights," Henry continued, and then, without refutation of their views or further indication of a difference of opinion, he proceeded to his powerful demonstration that "There is no retreat but in submission and slavery! Our chains are forged! Their clanking may be heard on the plains of Boston! The war is inevitable—and let it come! I repeat it, sir, let it come!" Wirt, Patrick Henry's biographer, declared that when the orator sat down there was no applause; the members sat for several moments as though entranced, then several started from their seats as "The cry *to arms!* seemed to quiver on every lip, and gleam from every eye." Surely no such result could have been attained had the speaker gone into a minute examination of the points in dispute.

5. *Work toward your own conclusion, but do it by means of the audience's line of reasoning.* What you conclude is all-important; it is your sole reason for speaking. But there is no reason why you should force your audience to proceed to that conclusion by the same route that you followed. They may be activated just as legitimately and much more easily by an entirely different line of thought. Woodrow Wilson fully appreciated this fact and applied it in his own speaking. When addressing a convention of the Daughters of the American Revolution, for instance, on October 11, 1915, he set out to win them from a program of sentimental reminiscence of the past to an active, liberal reshaping of the present. He wished to draw them from their reverence for the Washingtonian dictum of "No entangling alliances" to a responsible facing of the problems of a world-wide war. His method was to go at once to the premises they held dear and to develop his point with language that might have been drawn directly from one of their own reports:

There is a very great thrill [he said] to be had from the memories of the American Revolution, but the American Revolution was a beginning, not a consummation, and the duty laid upon us by that beginning is the duty of bringing the things then begun to a noble triumph of completion. For it seems to me that the peculiarity of patriotism in America is that it is not a mere sentiment. It is an active principle of conduct. It is something that was born into the world, not to please it, but to regenerate it. It is something that was born into the world to replace systems that had preceded it and to bring men out upon a new plane of privilege. The glory of the men whose memories you honor and perpetuate is that they saw this vision, and it was a vision of the future. It was a vision of great days to come when a little handful of three million people upon the borders of a single sea should have become a great multitude of free men and women spreading across a great continent, dominating the shores of two oceans, and sending West as well as East the influences of individual freedom.

6. *Avoid carefully any initial appearance of dogmatism in belief, words, or manner.* Any positive statement serves as a challenge. It invites attack. To start a speech by swinging challenges at the audi-

ence is like starting a boxing match by swinging blows at one's opponent. It is a good way to get knocked out. The practiced boxer knows that he must first "feel out" his opponent, then gradually step up the tempo of the match. So it is in a speech. The good speaker starts disarmingly; he parries, and pivots, and dances his way lightly into position for a knockout blow, *before* he begins hammering. After the audience has come to see the relationships which it has with the speaker, and to understand their fundamental agreement on all vital points; and after it has been "warmed up" by an emotional appreciation of the significance of his subject, then, and only then, has the time arrived when the speaker dare use the positive, direct suggestion of dogmatic certainty.

A good opening note is that struck by Alexander Hamilton Stephens in an address to the legislature of Georgia, on February 22, 1866. "You ask my views on the existing state of affairs," said Stephens; "our duties at the present, and the prospects of the future? This is a task from which, under other circumstances, I might very well shrink. He who ventures to speak, and to give counsel and advice in times of peril, or disaster, assumes no enviable position. Far be that rashness from me which sometimes prompts the forward to rush in where angels might fear to tread." From such a modest start he could go on with much better hope of success in his plea for a close cooperation with the victorious government at Washington than could have attended any assumption of superior judgment and dogmatic assurance. He met his audience, in other words, on the basis of identifying his and their mutual uncertainty as to the best solution for their problem, and from that point proceeded to unfold the best solution he could devise. His method merits imitation.

Persuasion through identification

Hartzell Spence, in his biography of his father, *One Foot in Heaven,* presents an excellent example of the use of the technique of identification. The Reverend William Spence was conducting an evangelistic campaign which consisted of personal visits to nonchurch members, combined with appeals for conversion during the regular Sunday services. The campaign proved unusually successful in gaining adherents to the church.

Father's greatest triumph was not the number reached, however, but one particular interview that did not even end in conversion.

For years Dr. Harlan Horrigan, an unusually skilled dentist, had been the town's outspoken sceptic. He prided himself in laughing at all religion, particularly Christianity. Wherever there was a revival meeting he would surely appear, not to worship but to scoff.

"It's better entertainment than the Kiwanis minstrels," he said.

Father's personal-visitation campaign intrigued Dr. Horrigan. Here was a new technique. He attended the first two Sunday services, sitting in the balcony. Several times during the week he entered the church to watch the "little meetings," during which the solicitors dropped in to report their progress and to fortify their faith for renewed efforts.

Father watched him. Twice Dr. Horrigan deliberately crossed his path at the church door, trying to provoke him, but father merely smiled.

The third week father acted. He sauntered into the dentist's office just at noon, when the receptionist was at lunch.

"It would appear," he remarked dryly, looking around the empty office, "that I have a larger practise than you have."

"Come in, come in," Dr. Horrigan invited. "I'm delighted to see you. I wondered when you'd get around to me."

"Oh, I'm not here professionally," father answered. "I was in Dr. Updegraf's office, and I saw you here alone. I just want to ask you a question."

"Shoot," Dr. Horrigan said suspiciously.

"Well, it's this. You have been watching revivals with an impartial eye for a good many years, I'm told."

"That's right. Best show on earth. Better than a circus. When people make monkeys of themselves, it's amusing."

"Indeed it is," father agreed. "As an expert sceptic and one not likely to be swayed emotionally, what do you think of my new method?"

"What do you mean?"

"Well, you and I will both agree, probably, that the old-time revival is through. People don't respond to it any more."

"That's right."

"Do you think personal visitation is any better?"

"Well—"

"Come, come," father coaxed. "I'm not trying to convert you. I'm serious about this. It's my job. I have to find a way to get under the hides of people in a very materialistic world. Am I on the right track?"

"I wouldn't be surprised. At least you are appealing to reason, not to the emotions. My chief argument against religion is that it is an emotional appeal. There's no intelligence in it."

"Perhaps you're right," father continued. "Christianity has been sold the wrong way. It's like getting a drunkard to sign the pledge without curing the thirst."

"Exactly."

"That's why I'm trying to sell Christianity on a business basis. My competitor is indifference or scepticism. I have to make the Christian way of life better in every way than scepticism, or it won't stay sold. Just as I'd be sure, if I were a shoe salesman, that my product was better than that of any of my competitors."

"I see your point," Dr. Horrigan admitted, "but I still don't think you have anything to sell."

"Why not?"

"Because basically you are peddling something there's no truth in. How do you know Christ was the Son of God? He was a teacher whose philosophy had a great impact on civilization. But so was Karl Marx. So was Confucius. Are they any less divine? The philosophy of Confucius was merely a practical code. Sensible men would think and act the same way if they had never heard of Confucius. Jesus came into a chaotic world and restored it to order merely by being practical. If anything, He was an opportunist. That doesn't prove He was divine or that there is any divinity. Science will catch up with you clerics one of these days and prove you wrong. Then what?"

"Then the world will be much the poorer," father answered. "Even if Christ were not divine, His teaching has survived, where the teaching of the Romans, the Greeks, the Egyptians, the Chinese, all have been rejected by the Western world. Christ's teaching was the one single force that released men from the dark age of ignorance and made possible this modern world. Without Christianity, there would be no enlightenment as we know it."

"Perhaps that's true," Dr. Horrigan conceded. "I'll admit the Christian philosophy made Western civilization possible. But I still say it was and is *only* a philosophy."

"Then you will admit that as a philosophy, if not as a religion, it is worth while?"

"As a philosophy, yes. As a religion, no."

"And you will concede that without this philosophy we would have no modern world at all?"

"Somebody else would have expressed the same ideas, because we needed them."

"All right, but the man who *did* express them was *Jesus,* and you ought to respect Him for it."

"As a philosopher, I do."

"Do you laugh at Confucius?"

"No."

"Then why do you laugh at Jesus?"

"I don't laugh at Jesus, I laugh at Christianity."

"Well," father chuckled, "at times it does seem funny, I'll admit. But it is the best thing we have. And it would be a lot better if these poor instruments God has to work with had more backbone. I feel better now that I know you are not making fun of Christ."

"I'm just laughing at all religion, that's all."

"I'm glad to know that," father said. "But why can't you leave the religious angle out of Christianity, and respect it merely as a good rule for living? You live the Christian life yourself, you just don't profess it."

"Well, I suppose maybe that's so."

"All right, then. When you laugh at Christianity you laugh at the very rules you live by. Do you laugh at Clyde Potter because he still drives a horse when everyone else is riding in an automobile?"

"No, of course not."

"You respect his belief in the infallibility of the horse."

"Of course."

"Then all I ask of you," father concluded, "is that you respect our belief in Christianity as a religion. You don't have to believe it, but you are just professing narrowness when you laugh at it. You respect Christ as a teacher, I'll respect Him as the Son of God, and we'll both be happy."

Father was surprised on the closing Sunday of the revival, to see Dr. Horrigan again in the audience. He had pondered long over their conversation and had built his final sermon not as a defense of Christianity, but as a great rule of conduct that all men should respect for what it had accomplished, whether or not they were Christians.

"But we, as Christians," he said, "are happier than those who practise Christianity without believing in it. For we have the courage of conviction. We have God the Father and Christ His Son to turn to when we need encouragement. When a man's wife dies a rule of conduct is little comfort. The hope of eternity is great and consoling, but it must be believed.

There are some things a man accepts on faith. The dentist does not have to be told, when he sees severe erosion in a tooth, that there is a cavity beneath. He knows and, seeking, he finds it. We Christians do not have to be told there is an eternal life. We know. And, seeking, we find it."

He looked directly at Dr. Horrigan then and quoted a verse of Scripture: "If any man will do the will of my Father in Heaven, he shall know whether the doctrine be of God or whether I speak it of myself."

Once again he offered the altar call. And this time Dr. Horrigan did not laugh.

In this passage there are represented various kinds of identification. The Reverend Mr. Spence first met Doctor Horrigan on the common ground of preference for the intellectual over emotional appeals. By asking his advice, he seemed to agree with Doctor Horrigan's belief that he was superior to the "revivalists." In the initial conversation, he "spoke the doctor's language," discussing religion in terms of business competition. He then found what element in Christianity (its rule of conduct) was respected by Doctor Horrigan, and subsequently directed all his attention to building upon this identification of agreement. In his concluding sermon, when he again noticed the doctor in his congregation, he inserted an analogy drawn from dentistry, to make one further appeal through the courtesy expressed in going to his opponent's profession for an illustration of their point of difference. Throughout the interview the Reverend Mr. Spence used the common ground of method. The Socratic technique which he employed, of asking questions through which the opponent is forced to confute himself, is very irritating and for that reason is usually an ineffective agency of persuasion. But since Doctor Horrigan prided himself above all on his hardheadedness, his respect was won for an opponent who could and did best him by using his own method of direct attack.

Conclusion

In summary the point of this chapter simply is: don't argue—agree. Be like the good salesman, who never tells his prospective customer, "You are wrong on that point." He always says, "Yes, but—," and the most progressive salesman is even apt to say, "Yes, and—." Conflict is misdirected, wasteful, and temporary. Of all the means of adjusting disagreements, reaching a basis of identification is best. The types of identification that the speaker should use include common interests, feelings, beliefs, and methods. He can find some real community of interests with his persuadees if he can cultivate objectivity in his thinking. In the example of the skillful persuader, the Reverend William Spence, there are good points upon which any speaker can profitably ponder.

Exercises

1. Make a list of five current community, national, and international conflicts. State briefly the nature of the dispute in each. What are the principal points of difference, issues, or claims of each side in these disputes? On what aspects of the disputes are they in agreement? What common ground do you find even on the points that are chiefly at issue? Restate the nature of each dispute in order to show (*a*) the large element of agreement, and (*b*) the relatively minor points of disagreement.

2. Selecting one of the disputes which you have analyzed in the preceding project, appoint yourself an attorney representing one of the disputants and prepare a speech that is designed not to crush or overwhelm the other disputant, but to win him over to the side you have espoused.

3. Have you disagreed, outwardly or inwardly, with anyone recently? For example, have you felt unjustly treated by a friend, a member of your family, a teacher, or an employer; or have you disagreed with the policy pursued by the national, state, or local officials—or with the actions of your minister, or the officers of an organization to which you belong? List two or three such instances of disagreement and analyze them to see what elements of common ground actually exist between you and the person or organization with which you disagreed. Are you both seeking the same ends? Are your interests, beliefs, feelings, or methods similar? Are the points of difference vital or are they simply of an irritating but relatively superficial type?

4. Upon the basis of the foregoing analysis, prepare a speech designed to win over to your point of view one of the individuals with whose course of action you disagreed.

5. Select some dispute that may exist between two of your friends, between two fraternities on the campus, between some of the students and the administration or faculty members, or between two off-campus groups, such as an employer-employee dispute. Appoint yourself a hypothetical conciliator for the dispute. Study it carefully to determine all the facts

available to you. Then work out the best solution you can, based upon the common-ground approach. Finally, plan how you would "sell" this solution to the two disputants, assuming that they are gathered together as a single audience to hear you.

6. Find in your own experience or observation a dispute that has been settled by each of the means of adjusting disagreement described in this chapter. What were the satisfactory and unsatisfactory elements of each solution? Upon the basis of your own experience, do you disagree with the hierarchy of means of adjusting disagreement suggested here?

7. Discuss the following questions:

   a. What is meant by "winning an argument"? What is left unwon?

   b. Are disputants always able to agree upon fundamentals? If not, what procedure would you recommend?

   c. What are the demerits of conflict? Does it have any compensating advantages?

   d. Discuss the advantages and disadvantages of tolerance. Of compromise.

   e. Of what value is objectivity to a disputant? How prevalent is objective thinking? How may it be cultivated? Recall Chapter 4 in this connection.

   f. Can you illustrate each of the types of identification with incidents from your own experience?

   g. What are the six suggestions for using the technique of identification?

   h. Could you suggest any improvement upon the identification technique as used by the Reverend Mr. Spence in his discussion with Doctor Horrigan?

8. Identification (with its correlates, institutionalization, the in-group, and acculturation) may be further explored through the following readings:

Floyd H. Allport, *Institutional Behavior* (Chapel Hill: University of North Carolina Press, 1933).

Victor Barnouw, *Culture and Personality* (Homewood, Ill.: Dorsey Press, 1963).

Ina Corinne Brown, *Understanding Other Cultures* (Englewood Cliffs, N.J.: Prentice-Hall, 1963).

R. L. Bruckberger, *Image of America* (New York: Viking Press, 1959).

Kenneth Burke, *A Rhetoric of Motives* (New York: Prentice-Hall, 1950).

Leopold Bellak, "On the Problems of the Concept of Projection: A Theory of Apperceptive Distortion," in Lawrence E. Abt and Leopold

Bellak (eds.), *Projective Psychology: Clinical Approaches to the Total Personality* (New York: Grove Press, 1959).

Jessie Bernard, "Sociological Mirror for Cultural Anthropologists," *American Anthropologist,* 51 (1949), 676ff.

John B. Carroll and Joseph B. Casagrande, "The Function of Language Classification in Behavior," in Eleanor E. Macoby, Theodore M. Newcomb, and Eugene L. Hartley (eds.), *Readings in Social Psychology,* 3rd ed. (New York: Holt, 1958), pp. 18-31.

J. T. Daniel and George L. Hinds, "An Introductory Study of Identification Reactions in Reading, Writing, Speaking and Listening," *Western Speech,* XI (February, 1947), 3-9.

Dennis G. Day, "Persuasion and the Concepts of Identification," *Quarterly Journal of Speech,* 66 (October, 1960), 270-273.

Lawrence K. Frank, "Psychology and Social Order," in Daniel Lerner (ed.), *The Human Meaning of the Social Sciences* (New York: Meridian Books, 1959), pp. 214-241.

Erving Goffman, *Encounters: Two Studies in the Sociology of Interaction* (Indianapolis: Bobbs-Merrill, 1961).

―――, *The Presentation of the Self in Everyday Life* (New York: Doubleday Anchor Books, 1959).

Douglas G. Haring (ed.), *Personal Character and Cultural Milieu,* 3rd ed. (Syracuse: Syracuse University Press, 1956).

Marie Hochmuth, "Kenneth Burke and the 'New Rhetoric,' " *Quarterly Journal of Speech,* 37 (April, 1952), 133-144.

Virginia Holland, "Rhetorical Criticism: A Burkean Method," *Quarterly Journal of Speech,* 39 (December, 1953), 444-450.

Ralph Linton, *The Cultural Background of Personality* (New York: Appleton-Century, 1945).

Robert K. Merton, *Social Theory and Social Structure* (New York: The Free Press of Glencoe, rev., 1957), particularly Chapter XII, "The Sociology of Knowledge," pp. 456-488.

―――, "The Role Set: Problems in Sociological Theory," *British Journal of Sociology,* VIII (1957), 106-120.

John Morley, *On Compromise* (New York: Macmillan, 1874).

Robert T. Oliver, *Culture and Communication* (Springfield, Ill.: Charles C Thomas, 1962.

Chaim Perelman and L. Obrechts-Tyteca, "Act and Person in Argument," trans., William Sacksteder, in Maurice Natanson and Henry W. Johnstone, Jr. (eds.), *Philosophy, Rhetoric, and Argumentation* (University Park: The Pennsylvania State University Press, 1965), pp. 102-125.

Paul E. Pfuetze, *Self, Society, Existence* (New York: Harper Torchbooks, 1961).

David Riesman, Nathan Glazer, and Reuel Denney, *The Lonely Crowd* (New York: Doubleday Anchor Books, 1954).

Charles Daniel Smith, "Other Available Means of Persuasion: From the Point of View of Literary Criticism," *Today's Speech,* III (November, 1955), 33-34.

T. V. Smith, "Compromise: Its Context and Limits," *Ethics,* 53 (October, 1942), 1-13.

Eleutherius Winance, *The Communist Persuasion: A Personal Experience of Brainwashing* (New York: P. J. Kenedy and Sons, 1959).

Kurt H. Wolff, "The Sociology of Knowledge: Emphasis on an Empirical Attitude," *Philosophy of Science,* X (1943), 104-123.

Modes of Appeal

This, then, will be the clue to our inquiry. We shall assume that what each man does is based not on direct and certain knowledge, but on pictures made by himself or given to him. . . . The way in which the world is imagined determines at any particular moment what men will do. . . .

Inevitably our opinions cover a bigger space, a longer reach of time, a greater number of things, than we can directly observe. . . . There is a connection between our vision and the facts, but it is often a strange connection. . . . It stamps itself upon the evidence in the very act of securing the evidence. . . . Certainly for the most part, the way we see things is a combination of what is there and what we expected to find. . . . Sometimes consciously, more often without knowing it, we are impressed by those facts which fit our philosophy.

—WALTER LIPPMANN, *Public Opinion*

✍ 9.

Evidence and Authority

KNOWLEDGE IS POWER. THIS IS A POINT OF VIEW AT least as old as Aristotle and Plato, and it is reinforced in our daily experience. The Arabians have an ancient proverb that is much to the point: "Blessed is the man who knows, and knows that he knows. He is a leader; follow him." In our contemporary society high status is accorded to the expert, whatever his field may be. Wide and exact knowledge insures an unmistakable and undeniable eminence. "He knows what he is talking about" is a statement that we rightly consider to be high praise.

On the other hand, mere glibness and assurance divorced from knowledge merit only suspicion and rejection. "An empty-mouthed babbler" is one of the worst forms of denunciation. Among your acquaintances are some who are careful never to express an opinion that is not backed up by genuine information; these you respect and trust. Others (who may have many likable qualities) are too likely to "run off at the mouth" on any subject that occurs to them, with little idea of what they are talking about. These you may like—but when they express a judgment, you are on your guard.

Obviously, solidarity of factual information is a valuable persuasive ingredient. We cannot, like the youthful Francis Bacon, "take all knowledge to be our province." But, when we make a persuasive speech on a specific subject, we have a moral as well as an intellectual responsibility to know what we are talking about. This we owe to ourselves; and this much all our associates have an absolute right to expect.

What we should like to believe is true, or what from certain points of view may be made to appear to be true, is very likely in the long run to be confuted by what actually *is* true. Sir Arthur Keith, in explaining the immense impact of Charles Darwin upon the intellectual currents of his age, pointed out, "However longingly his readers clung to age-long beliefs, Darwin compelled them to face facts and draw conclusions, often at enmity with their predilections." Abraham Lincoln once declared that his purpose in addressing his audiences was to "soak them with facts." In a letter to Salmon P. Chase, during the debate over the Fugitive Slave Law, Lincoln wrote, "My only object was to impress you with what I believe to be true." Facts alone cannot prevail in a specific situation without skillful presentation; but the most eloquent speaker who ignores or repudiates what is true will sacrifice both his cause and his reputation.

In presenting what is true, a speaker may sometimes rely largely upon his own direct experience, and tell his listeners, "This I know, because I was there and saw it myself." Many more times—say, in speaking about communist influence in India—he will succeed in influencing his audience only as he presents to them solidly factual evidence of an objective nature, buttressed by quotations from experts who will be accepted by the listeners as reliable authorities. These are the types of proof with which this chapter is concerned.

Permanent versus temporary influence

A common theme in business advertisements is the reminder, "We are an old, established firm, here to stay." Costly experience has taught us to beware of the fly-by-night salesman who makes but one appearance in the community, never to reappear. With nothing but immediate results to consider, there is danger that trickery and deceit may freely be employed. Many have learned what Lincoln pointed out. "You may fool all the people some of the time." Similarly, an impassioned speaker addressing a strange audience on an unfamiliar subject may be tempted to misrepresent facts and thereby win agreement with an unsound point of view. Hollywood motion picture producers have learned the trick of building cities of pasteboard, consisting only of false fronts, that stand long enough to be photographed. But such methods serve only when a merely temporary effect is desired. A lasting business reputation has to be built upon the satisfaction of customers over a long period of time. A city that can be lived in must be constructed of wood and stone. And persuasive effectiveness that is to grow and last must be based upon the discovery by audiences that the speaker customarily presents proposals that stand the test of experience.

As a persuasive speaker, one of your first considerations should be the long-term effectiveness of whatever you may say. Any pleasure in applause that might be earned by pretense or perversion of facts would soon turn to regret after your audience learned that it had been misled. A speech that clearly has been prepared with little cost of time and labor in determining the real facts of the question being discussed often turns out to be extremely costly in loss of trust and confidence as events indicate that the speaker has been wrong. Senator William E. Borah in a White House conference in the summer of 1939 created newspaper headlines when he asserted that he had information—superior to that of the President and Secretary of State—that indicated positively there was no immediate danger of war. But his influence over the public was blasted when the invasion of Poland by Germany shortly occurred.

An eloquent student speaker made a deep impression upon his student audience when he asserted that the inmates of the Northeastern Federal Penitentiary read more and better books than the students of Bucknell University. When, however, a factual report was later submitted—based upon statistics on the number and kinds of books withdrawn from the two libraries—which utterly repudiated the speaker's supposedly genuine assertions, his audience simply refused thenceforth to take him at his word. He had won what seemed like a cheap triumph by fabricating a contention based solely upon his own imagination, but the eventual effect was his loss of influence with all those who observed how wilfully he perverted the truth to support a false point.

Henry Clay's famous observation that he "would rather be right than be president" was rephrased perhaps more pertinently by Harry Truman, as "I'd rather be right and be president." The speaker who is right is the one who, in the long run, will tend to have success. Permanent influence can be based upon no other foundation. Audiences that have been misled can have no recourse but to consider the speaker either dishonest or incapable. In either event, he cannot be depended upon for wise counsel or leadership. Lasting influence can only be won through durable facts.

The use of factual evidence to insure a lasting influence over the judgment of an audience requires a careful consideration of what facts should be used and of how they may most effectively be employed. The first consideration in preparing a speech (and sometimes the most convincing way to introduce the topic to the audience) is analysis of the problem to be discussed. When the nature of the problem is clarified, the speaker's consideration shifts to available subject matter, to determine what among the facts he might use may actually serve in the minds of his audience as pertinent evidence. The facts finally to be used will consist of statistics, testimony, experience, or—in some instances—a significant lack of data that in itself constitutes negative evidence. With the facts selected, the final problem of the speaker is how to marshal them in a manner to carry conviction with his audience. The area from preliminary analysis to final organization of factual evidence is covered in this chapter, with the emphasis upon a kind of persuasive speaking that will secure permanent rather than merely temporary influence for the speaker as a person and for the proposal he advocates.

Analysis

Analysis is a process of looking closely at something to see what it really consists of. It is a determination of essentials, in their nature and in their relationships. Thus, a chemist analyzes a compound to find what elements compose it, and in what proportions. A mining engineer analyzes ore to find its richness; a doctor analyzes a patient to diagnose his illness. Any process of thought or investigation that is designed to reveal the integral nature of an object, situation, or event may be considered *analysis*. Analysis, then, is an attempt to understand the precise character of whatever is being observed. A child puzzling over a mechanical toy until he learns how to operate it is as truly engaged in analysis as is a scientist in the laboratory or a lawyer preparing a brief. The essentials are the same: each one looks hard at a complex subject matter that he does not understand very well in an effort to reduce it to relatively simple parts with an interrelationship that he can comprehend. This is what analysis is. Everyone engages in it daily. There is no mystery to it, though there may be some hard thinking required. The scientist, the child, and the speaker with a persuasive speech to prepare, all have problems very much alike. The process of analysis they should pursue goes through the following steps: observation, correlation, induction, verification, and application.

Observation. If the proposal you have decided upon for your persuasive speech is, *children should be given music lessons,* your constructive thinking on the subject should begin with observation of relevant facts. You assemble in your mind or on paper bits of data that you observe directly or recall from previous experience and reading. Your notes may include such facts as: (1) the most popular students you know are musical; (2) music enters into many pleasurable group activities; (3) the people you know who are most skilled musically started taking lessons when very young; (4) of six young children you can call readily to mind, two are taking music lessons and four are not; (5) methods of teaching music have changed greatly in recent years; (6) the standard comic-strip joke of youngsters conniving to escape their music lesson doesn't seem to apply to children you know. These and perhaps many more items constitute your observations on the topic you have chosen. They are unrelated and some may not be pertinent, but you are confident that each observation listed is in itself true. This is the first step in analysis of the subject matter. As has been indicated in earlier chapters, analysis of the audience has occurred before the topic is analyzed.

Correlation. A careful consideration of the above list indicates that certain relationships exist among the items. The popularity of musical students, for instance, is clearly related to the prevalence of music as a form of entertainment. The fact that the methods of teaching music have changed may account for the fact that children no longer object to taking lessons, as they once did. And, if it is true that music lessons are most effective when commenced early in life, it surely is significant that only one third of the children you know are studying music. By establishing these relationships among your miscellaneously assembled data, you have carried the process of analysis into a stage that begins to bring clarification. Already two factors of great helpfulness have been accomplished. First, by *observation* of your broad general topic, you have discerned certain significant elements within it; and second, by *correlating* those elements you have established apparent relationships among them.

Induction. As you think about the items you have listed, you begin very naturally to draw certain conclusions from them. Assuming that popularity is in itself worth while, and observing that musical students are popular, you readily conclude that musical training has value. Actually, you have engaged in what logicians call *syllogistic thinking,* with a major premise (popularity has value), minor premise (musical skill wins popularity), and conclusion (musical skill is worth attaining). You conclude also, on the basis of observed data, that youth is the best time to learn music and that far too few children are taking lessons. As you rearrange these data into logical sequence, you decide that there is a need for children to take music lessons because: (1) musical ability has value; (2) childhood is the best time to learn music; and (3) too few take advantage of the opportunity. In other words, there is a *need* for the proposal you wish to advance. The process of induction has carried your analysis to the point of drawing general conclusions from the assembled data.

Verification. Realizing the tendency to believe what we want to believe, with the concurrent danger that we may have assembled data that seem convincing to us but that may not convince an audience, we should next subject the tentative conclusions reached to careful verification. Such verification may consist in part in broadening the field of observation. Think of additional popular students to determine whether musical ability is always or even usually an element of popularity. Question several accomplished musicians to find at what age they began the study of music. Extend your original list of six children to half a dozen more, and find how many of them are taking music lessons. Such extension of your own observation may well be supported by reference to established authorities, either as you may read their conclusions in *Etude* and other music journals, or as you may interview them. Out of this process of verifiaction comes either support for your original inductions or the necessity for modifying them. The broader and more representative your inquiry is, the greater is the chance that your conclusions will seem reasonable to your audience.

Application. As the final step in your analysis, you decide upon a specific application of the ideas you have assembled. Perhaps your audience consists of parents of young children, whom you may advise to obtain music lessons for them. Perhaps your audience consists of college students, whom you will urge to study music now, even though it is late to begin, for musical skill is worth its cost in time and effort. Or your audience may be music teachers, whom you will show how to adapt their services to the wider need you envisage. Finally, if you are to speak to small children, you will have to apply the same conclusion in language and with illustrations that will be meaningful to them. In any event, the job of analysis has not been completed until you have determined how your data should be adapted to whatever specific audience you will address. In persuasive speaking this audience adaptation is often the most vital step of all.

The nature of evidence

As has been shown in the discussion of analysis, the task of the speaker is to look hard at his subject until he sees the elements in it that are significantly pertinent. Of all the facts one might assemble, some are of merely casual or incidental interest, whereas others are essential in forming a correct judgment. The task of the persuasive speaker is to select the facts concerning his proposal that will appear to his prospective audience to be sound and convincing evidence. Using again the proposal of music lessons for children as an example, it is apparent that different audiences will be influenced by different types of facts. Some, for instance, will recall their own childhood distaste for lessons that were forced upon them, and therefore will be persuaded most effectively by information showing: (1) that methods of teaching music have changed; and (2) that children now enjoy their music lessons. Other auditors will be particularly eager to find the means of making their children popular, and consequently will respond to the suggestions on the relation of popularity to musical ability. Still others may harbor strong objections to spending money for "frills" and will have to be shown facts indicating that music training is a profitable investment.

The essential consideration is that the facts which constitute evidence in a persuasive speech are true facts selected on a basis of audience predilections. The scientist in his laboratory, or the logician in his study, will search only to find what is true, whether the facts are palatable or not. But when that same scientist or logician becomes a persuasive speaker, he achieves success primarily in terms of his ability to look at the subject from the point of view of the audience, and to present the data that will be most impressive for the particular people whom he addresses.

From the standpoint of persuasion, evidence may be defined as *all facts that, in the opinion of the audience, have relevance in affecting judgment on the topic under consideration.* This differs from the philosopher's or scientist's or logician's definition of evidence by incorporating the effect upon the audience. It is precisely in this respect that persuasion differs from philosophy, science, and logic. The discovery of truth on the one hand, and the influencing of people to accept it, on the other, are two separate and distinct sciences. Whereas the logician may conclude his search for evidence after he has found all that bears pertinently upon the subject under examination, the persuasive speaker must continue his search to the next stage of determining how the assembled data can be made to affect his expected audiences. In the selection and presentation of evidence, the persuasive speaker must be not only a logician but a social psychologist as well. Otherwise he will have the experience of hearing his audiences retort, "What you say sounds logical enough, but I still disagree."

Facts as statistics

It is natural that statistics should play an increasingly large role in our thinking. People in our age are continually expanding the range of their thinking, and statistics are a primary means of compressing, summarizing, and simplifying the facts that must be taken into account. For example, because of communist imperialism and modern developments of transportation and communication we are now interested in the problems of peoples in every area of the earth. It is impossible, however, to have a detailed and specific knowledge of events and conditions in Korea, Siam, Bulgaria, and Venezuela. From sheer necessity we depend upon such generalization as percentages of illiteracy, mortality rates, living standards, and consumption and production levels in these and other countries. Similarly, within the past few years Americans have largely come to accept a sense of greater responsibility for the health and welfare of all classes of our own people. Here again the information upon which we must depend in assessing the needs of the aged, the unemployed, the diseased, and the impoverished is presented in statistical form. It is inevitable, for instance, that discussions of federal aid for education should contain references to average salary levels for teachers in different sections of the country, as well as many other summarized data in statistical form.

The essential fact about statistics is that they are simply generalizations derived from comparisons of individual instances. Thus, the Bureau of Labor Statistics issues a monthly "Cost of Living Index" based upon a statistical summary of the prices charged for certain key items in a number of representative cities. All over the country people conclude that the cost of living has risen or declined, based upon this statistical sampling, rather than upon the comparatively difficult analysis of their own bills for clothing, food, and other expenditures. Statistics of this nature have become so thoroughly integrated into our habits of thought that they have assumed a very considerable persuasive value. Audiences are so accustomed to depending upon statistical generalizations that often they will accept them as valid even when they are contradicted by their own direct experience and observation. A notable example is the general expectation of a Republican Party victory in the election of 1948, based upon the statistical sampling of several public opinion polls, even though, as the election showed, a majority of the voters actually preferred election of—and planned to vote for—the Democratic candidates.

Statistics influence many of our day-by-day activities and judgments. Thus, we pay insurance premiums based upon statistics on expected mortality rates. We postpone purchase of a new car or a television set because of statistical indications of a future decline in prices. We ask for a salary increase based upon the Cost of Living Index. Without the assistance of summarized information in statistical form we should be totally unable to exercise judgment on many of the complex and personally unfamiliar problems that daily confront us.

The dependence of our audiences upon statistics makes it imperative for the persuasive speaker to use them. The primary concern is to use them in a manner that will actually be persuasively effective. From this point of view, several considerations must be kept in mind.

1. *The source of the statistics must be acceptable to the audience.* With contradictory statistics on unemployment, cost of living, profits, and average wage scales presented by the National Association of Manufacturers, the American Federation of Labor, and various government agencies, the very first concern of the persuasive speaker should be to convince his audience that the statistics he is using are the ones that are most accurate. With alert audiences it is far from effective to say simply, "Figures show that. . . ." The barrage of statistics with which all newspaper readers are daily deluged has taught the necessity of caution in evaluating their source. Before any statistics are presented to an audience, the persuasive speaker should take care

to evaluate their source in terms that the audience will trust. In order to do this effectively, he must, of course, make a careful analysis himself of the various sources, in order to have a clear conception of their reliability and weakness.

2. *The reliability of statistics depends primarily upon the disinterestedness and technical ability of the agency that gathers and interprets them.* An organization seeking to increase either wages or profits might be suspected of selecting samples that would help to establish its own point of view. Life insurance companies might be inclined to present mortality data that justify a profitable level of premium charges. Thus, the first question concerning any source of statistics is whether the source has any direct interest in representing a particular kind of conclusion. Even when this factor has been examined, the source must also be examined in terms of its technical ability to select truly representative samples and to interpret them correctly. The election of 1948 showed how inadequate was the skill of the public-opinion sampling organizations. In statistics on the number of unemployed persons, reliability depends upon the definition of "unemployed," and upon the thoroughness of the survey. Any Cost of Living Index must depend upon accurate judgment of the areas and items upon which the survey is based. Like any other kind of generalization, statistics are no better than the judgment represented in compiling them.

3. *The presentation of the statistics should make them truly meaningful to the audience.* As previously indicated, the chief function of statistics is to summarize in comprehensible form wide ranges of information that are too complex or unfamiliar to be understood as individual items. But the very processes of lumping together numbers of specific facts into one broad generalized figure destroys much of the significance of the data being presented. To say that the average salary level of teachers in X state is 40 per cent lower than in Y state falls far short of conveying to an audience the actual meaning of the lower living standards, poorer training, and greater sacrifice involved in that fact. The statistic is useful and even indispensable. But to make it really persuasive, the speaker must help the audience to see beyond

the mere figure into the problems it represents for great numbers of individual teachers, students, and communities.

Generally speaking, statistics are ineffective in a persuasive speech unless the speaker takes time to show their significance. Statistics are a bare skeleton which must be clothed with illustrative examples, with interpretation, and by specific application to the audience. The number of statistics used should be reduced so far as possible without neglecting essential information. And each of the figures presented to the audience should be discussed in sufficient detail to make its nature and significance clear and impressive.

In summary, four points about statistics should be kept in mind: (*a*) they are a useful and perhaps indispensable method of presenting the kind of information audiences require; (b) they should be evaluated both in terms of audience acceptability, and (c) the trustworthiness and technical ability of their source; and (d) the richness of meaning concealed in them should be brought out and emphasized so that it will not be missed.

Facts as testimony

When a problem such as control of atomic power is being considered, it is natural for people to inquire, What does Lilienthal, or Oppenheimer, or Conant, or Vannevar Bush think of it? For on all subjects of importance lying outside one's personal experience, the natural inclination is to seek and follow the opinion of those whose business it is to know. Just so does one seek the professional opinion of a doctor or chemist or engineer on technical problems that fall within their provinces. In various studies it has been found that audiences incline to follow public opinion more than expert testimony. This is particularly true on questions of broad social or political policy, such as race relations and codes of ethics. But in many specific situations the expert is called in if he is available, and his judgment is sought if he himself can not be present.

Testimony sometimes constitutes part of a record of facts from which persuasive speeches are developed. In tracing, for instance, the gradual process by which the United States got into World War II, statements of Franklin Roosevelt, Wendell Willkie, and Cordell Hull would have to be cited as a part of the fabric of facts, correlated with such events as passage of the Neutrality Act and the later Lend-Lease program. The task of the persuasive speaker is to select the statements that: (1) fairly and accurately represent the point of view of the speaker; and (2) are relevant in indicating judgments about the speaker's proposal.

Testimony in persuasive speeches is normally used in support of a point the speaker is making. In effect the speaker tells his audience, "My analysis leads toward such-and-such a conclusion; so do the statistics I have cited; and, in addition, we find that this is also the view of the outstanding experts whom I am about to quote." Using testimony in this manner, several precautions should be observed:

1. Cite experts whose word will carry considerable weight with the audience you are addressing. Help develop the confidence of your audience by showing why the experts cited are qualified by special knowledge and experience to speak authoritatively.

2. Select the quotations with utmost care. They should be brief and precisely to the point, with irrelevant observations omitted. At the same time, both the selection and the cutting down of the quotation used should be done in such a fashion as to adhere strictly to the letter and spirit of what the authority meant to convey.

3. The significance of the testimony must be made clear to the audience. Often a speaker should spend considerable time in preparing his audience to understand the value of the testimony to be offered. The casual or hurried insertion of a quotation into a speech usually does no good, and may serve to confuse the hearers. The insertion of testimony in a speech is akin to calling a witness in a law court trial, and should be handled so as to make its effect fully felt.

4. On subjects concerning which there is a variance in expert opinion, it is well to explain to the audience why the experts disagree, and to make careful distinctions between their various points of view. Often it will be found that on basic essentials they are actually in agreement, however much they may appear to differ. On postwar conditions in China, for example, some "experts" considered Mao Tse-

tung and his followers as communist tools of Moscow, whereas others described them as merely "agrarian liberals." But amid all the confusion of views, there has been substantial agreement that actual communist control of China has proved to be a serious danger to the cause of democratic freedom.

Facts as personal experience

In a broad sense, all human knowledge is based upon experience. The experience that is most effective in influencing thought and actions is that which is most immediate, most vivid, and most vital. It is proverbial that "A burned child dreads the fire." A single or far-removed experience will have much less effect than a large number of related experiences, or than a recent one. In terms of the persuasive speech, an audience will be influenced most of all by its own experiences, and secondarily by those of the speaker, by others whom he may cite, by hypothetical instances, and by comparison and contrast.

1. The *experience of the audience* itself is of such primary value that a persuasive speaker should plan to make considerable use of it. The effective persuasive speech will be sprinkled with such phrases as, "You know from your own experience that . . ."; "You will recall what happened when . . ."; "All of you have frequently observed . . ."; and similar references to what the audience already knows.

2. The *personal experience of the speaker* himself may be cited with great persuasive effect. In discussing conditions in a foreign country, the speaker has a great advantage when he can say, "While I was there I saw. . . ." Normally a speaker will choose to discuss with an audience topics with which he has had personal contact. In most instances, his relation with the subject matter of the speech is much closer than any the audience has had. It is entirely natural, then, that the audience will be influenced by having the speaker tell them of experiences that help to make vivid and meaningful the other facts in his speech.

3. *Specific instances* describing the experience of other individuals or groups may have considerable persuasive value. In a speech on the value of honesty, for instance, the speaker may cite instances from the

lives of Washington, Lincoln, and many other noted individuals. He might describe disasters that have befallen nations because of broken treaties. He might tell of some businesses that flourished because of public confidence, and of others that failed because of sharp practices. The persuasive value of such experiences lies in the very fact that they have been shared by many persons under differing circumstances, but always with the same effects.

4. *Hypothetical instances* constitute anticipated or probable experience that would occur under certain conditions. Thus, the speaker might ask, "What would happen if we did adopt the proposal for higher school taxes? Isn't it true that we should be able to secure better trained teachers, build better school houses, and provide better equipment? Won't that, in the long run, have advantages for our children that are worth far more than the small extra cost each of us will have to pay?" Since persuasion is aimed at obtaining a change from existing conditions, it often is inevitable that the speaker will have to forecast probable results from his proposal, and support it by citing hypothetical instances of what will result from its adoption.

5. *Comparison and contrast* of varying experiences is another way of utilizing experience to support your persuasive proposal. This method was used to good effect by a student from the University of Montana, debating against a team from Kansas State College, in 1925, on the power of the Supreme Court to rule Acts of Congress unconstitutional. The debater described an old prospector, Bill Johnson, who bought an old, rattletrap Ford car, which served him very well to haul his supplies up to his mountain camp.

"But a week or two later when Bill started to town again, things didn't go quite so well. Going down grade he began to have trouble, as green drivers usually do have in the mountains. On the long down grades, the brakes on his car would heat pretty badly; they would bind and jerk and almost stop the car entirely." Disgusted with this difficulty, Bill stopped and, with the aid of a crowbar, "jerked those offending brakes right out of that old Ford car."

"A few days later, a sheepherder found the car smashed almost beyond recognition at the bottom of a deep ravine near a turn in the highway; and beneath the car was what was left of old Bill Johnson. He'd gotten rid of his brake trouble, all right; but he'd forgotten to play safe."

Then the speaker added: "Tonight, our friends from Kansas are asking us to do just about the same thing to our government that old Bill did to his secondhand Ford. They tell us that our government has some brakes on ill-advised action in the form of the check of the Supreme Court, and they are suggesting that to get rid of the occasional delays and checks that come from these brakes, we ought to yank them off entirely and go on down the grade unchecked. As you consider their arguments, I want you to remember the experience of old Bill Johnson." This is an example of a form of appeal to experience—through comparison, or analogy, which is often highly persuasive. Of course it is open to being countered by still another comparison, such as: "Old Bill would have done better if he had traded in his old Ford on a better car." Comparisons help to clarify reasoning, but seldom are able to stand wholly by themselves. They must be supported by all the other forms of factual evidence to give them real stability.

Negative evidence

It sometimes happens that the very absence of factual evidence is in itself convincing. Negative evidence consists of the significant lack of relevant data. A familiar example is the failure of a suspected criminal to establish an alibi for the period when a crime was committed. His inability to show where he was at the time establishes at least the possibility that he may have been at the scene of the crime. More positively, if he asserted that he was registered at a hotel in a distant city, negative evidence would be provided by absence of his name on the registration records of the hotel.

In advocating a change from existing conditions, the speaker may well utilize negative evidence. He may say, for instance, "Where are the benefits you expected to receive from the political party now in power? You cannot find them in higher wages, or in lower living costs, for no such benefits exist. You will not find them in improved international relations, for the tension and distrust are as great as before. You will not find them in more efficient government, for the fumbling and red tape are as pronounced as ever. The fact is, the more you look for the promised benefits, the more convinced you become that they simply do not exist."

In opposing a conflicting point of view, the speaker also may find negative evidence of value. Communist spokesmen, for instance, are positive in their claims of improved living conditions provided their system is adopted. One way of persuading an audience of the hollowness of such claims is to invite their attention to the fate of the peoples of North Korea, Eastern Germany, Poland, the Baltic States, Hungary, Rumania, Czechoslovakia, Red China, and other areas which have been taken over by the Communists since the end of World War II. The claims of the advantages of communism are still being made—but the evidence to support such claims simply cannot be found. One way of dramatizing its lack is to point out that the communist regimes still are unwilling to permit the holding of free elections, which would permit the captive peoples to express their own opinions of the "advantages" they are supposed to enjoy.

Likewise, in advocating his own proposal the speaker may advantageously use negative evidence. "My opponents," he may point out, "have charged that certain evils will be introduced by the adoption of what I propose. But look at my plan; examine it carefully from every point of view. In what nooks and crannies of it do you find any such weaknesses concealed? They simply are not there. The weaknesses charged against it are actually nothing but the frail ghosts of my opponents' fears. But we, who do not believe in ghosts, will not be deterred from a right action by purely chimerical objections." By such a line of reasoning, supported by specific references to the proposal advocated, a speaker may support a constructive argument by negative means. Using this method, a lawyer, for instance, may plead the innocence of his client by showing that the prosecution has failed to establish motive, opportunity, or actual proof of commission of the alleged crime. The significant absence of facts is sometimes as effective persuasively as facts themselves.

Expository persuasion

In many instances the most influential persuasive speaking is that which is almost entirely *expository*. As has been shown in studies on suggestion, there is a natural tendency to believe whatever is presented to the mind. Unless auditors have some pre-established reason for disagreeing with the speaker's proposal, a simple factual explanation of it, wholly divorced from argument, may be the best way of winning acceptance for it. Arguments are most easily won by being avoided. An argumentative approach impels opposition and raises doubts as to the validity of the proposal. On the other hand, when a speaker calmly assumes that the factual presentation he is making is, beyond question, simply a matter-of-fact analysis of the true situation, the probability is that many or most of his auditors will accede to his conclusions.

Whenever a speech critic sets about the selection of speeches with the purpose of classifying them according to the general speech purposes—to *inform,* to *entertain,* or to *persuade*—he is certain to experience great difficulty as between the first and the third purpose. Many speeches that appear at first to be *informative* turn out on closer examination to be *persuasive,* in that the information presented actually leads directly toward establishment of a particular point of view or specific proposal. It is an indication of good speech composition when the speaker is able to establish his proposal by a maximum of exposition and a minimum of argument.

A moral problem is involved if the speaker deliberately conceals or avoids information relevant to his subject in order to deceive an audience into believing that all the facts point inexorably toward one single conclusion. To do this is to invite suspicion and opposition, both from members of the audience who know better and from all auditors who may subsequently learn that they have been misled.

Expository persuasion, however, need not follow this unethical practice. The speaker's analysis may point out both weakness and strength in his proposal. We may assume that he himself would not favor a particular conclusion unless in the consideration of all points of view he felt it to be the best. It follows naturally, then, that both his analysis and his subsequent factual development will adduce the evidence that led him to form his own conclusion. This same factual presentation will often convince the audience precisely as it did him. Without concealment of opposing views, the weight of facts is shown to support the one conclusion that appears to the speaker as the normal and proper solution for the problem discussed.

An example of expository persuasion is found in a sermon delivered in the First Presbyterian Church of Peoria, Illinois, on September 17, 1950, by the Reverend Edward D. Gates. He said,

> From the year 1900 to 1950, this world of ours has witnessed warfare on a scale that has outslaughtered all previous history. Do you realize that if tonight every man, woman, and child within the continental limits of these United States were suddenly wiped off the earth, their number would be less than the number of human beings who have died in war, or by causes directly resulting from war, during the fifty years, 1900 to 1950? Recent studies by Professor Quincy Wright of the University of Chicago inform us that during the first thirty years of our century European nations alone fought seventy-four wars, the average war four years long, or wars lasting a total of two hundred ninety-seven years. From the eleventh to the twentieth century, during those nine hundred years, war casualties amounted to about eighteen million. But in the first thirty years only of this century, from 1900 to 1930, there were killed by warfare 33⅓ per cent more human beings than in all those previous nine hundred years! And this does not include five continents and World War II and its immediate prelude.

We might say that he was not persuading—he was merely stating a set of facts. But what listener could avoid concluding that in our day war has become so costly that, as President Eisenhower has phrased it, "There is no alternative to peace"?

For a more extended example, in which both the pros and cons of the speaker's contention are examined, we turn to an extract from a speech made to a public forum in Palm Springs, Florida, on February 5, 1951, by Mr. Pyo Wook Han, then First Secretary (now Minister) of the Korean Embassy in Washington:

> Now for our first question: could the outbreak of war in Korea have been prevented? This question, in turn, breaks down into several considerations.

Occasionally someone suggests that the government of the Republic of Korea has been not quite perfect, and that if it were better the Communists would not have attacked it. This, it seems to me, is reasoning from false facts to a conclusion that would not follow even if the facts were correct. If the Republic of Korea had been unsatisfactory, there might have been internal revolt and a break-down of the loyalty of the citizens. The fact is that although the Communists made every effort to arouse dissatisfaction and subversion, they failed. Korea was attacked from outside precisely because it proved too strong internally to be captured by subversion.

It has also been suggested in some quarters that an attack could have been prevented if the southern Korean leaders had been more "reasonable." It is true that the fighting would have been wholly unnecessary if south Korea had consented to surrender itself to Communist control. This could have been done when "coalition" was proposed back in 1946. It could have been done when the northern Communists protested United Nations intervention in 1948 and suggested instead a re-unification of Korea under their control. It could have been accomplished at any subsequent period by the mere surrender of all Korea to the Communist demands.

Instead, we tried to develop a sound democracy internally and to do our part to help hold back the Communist forces of aggression which threatened to over-run the entire Far East.

Could the attack on Korea have been prevented if American troops had not been withdrawn or if a positive pledge of American support had been given to us, similar to the Truman Doctrine for Greece and Turkey? Perhaps it could; but that is a matter for American policy-makers to decide. It surely is not for us Koreans to claim that American power should be wrapped around us as a permanent protection.

Could the attack have been prevented if the Republic of Korea had built up a large, well-trained and well-equipped army, instead of maintaining a mere security force of about 100,000 men? Perhaps so. At any rate our Government over and over again pleaded for the arms which would have been required to train and equip a large force. But we were repeatedly advised to keep our army small and geared merely to the requirement of dealing with possible internal problems. This advice, I am sure, was well meant. It was based upon the theory that our best defense was to be inoffensive; to be so weak that we could not constitute a threat to the Communist north.

Conclusion

In presenting his factual evidence, the speaker will do well to inter-mingle the various kinds. Statistics become more meaningful when related as closely as possible to the personal experience of the auditors. The testimony of authorities, likewise, should be related both to the various kinds of experience cited and to statistical evidence. By piling one type of evidence upon another a cumulative effect is achieved that often is very convincing. At one stage in the speech, auditors may think, "It is possible that what he says may be true." As additional facts are adduced, they add, "He is probably right." Finally, as facts are piled upon facts, they conclude, "He most certainly is right!" The speaker needs to watch his audience carefully to note when this third stage seems to be reached, for to continue after that is to court the danger of anticlimax and surfeit. As every salesman learns, to stop when the sale is made is one of the essentials of successful selling.

The emphasis in this chapter upon use of facts in persuasive speak-ing does not belie what has been said repeatedly concerning the need of keeping the attention primarily upon the audience. In the selection of his facts, as in his sociopsychological analysis of his auditors, the persuasive speaker must always be audience-minded. He analyzes his subject to determine its meaning in relation to his audience. He realizes that the very nature of evidence is the utilization of such facts as will influence the judgment of those to whom he is appealing. Con-sequently, the statistics, testimony, experience, and negative evidence he employs will be selected primarily from the consideration of prob-able audience effect. Like the parent who wishes to educate his chil-dren so that they can successfully overcome life's problems, the persuasive speaker chooses for his audience the kind of facts, and presents them in such a manner as he believes will do them the most good. He both forms and informs the opinions of his hearers at the same time. This is persuasive speaking upon a solid basis that will achieve both immediate effects and lasting influence. It is a type of persuasion for which every speaker will find wide use.

Exercises

1. Phrase a persuasive proposal that will invite a change of belief or feelings or the performance of some action by the audience and can be supported largely by factual exposition rather than by argument or appeals.

2. Make a selection of evidence bearing upon your proposal, including statistics, authoritative quotations, incidents from your own experience and other specific examples. Indicate how you may utilize negative evidence to support the proposal.

3. Prepare a five-minute speech in which you use at least two different types of factual evidence from the assortment you have accumulated. Use enough of each type of evidence to achieve the value of cumulation.

4. In presenting your speech to the audience, try to eliminate every appearance of argumentativeness. Make the speech as expository as you can, though making sure that the evidence presented actually leads toward acceptance of your proposal.

5. In subsequent class discussion of the speeches as delivered, evaluate the effectiveness of the nonargumentative, factual presentations. For each speech, members of the audience should phrase the speaker's proposal, to be sure it was clear and rightly understood. The class should assess the success of the speaker in changing audience attitudes toward the proposal through the selection of evidence he utilized.

6. As an exercise in factual analysis, choose one of the following proposals and analyze it successively through each of the steps of observation, correlation, induction, verification, and application:

   a. Racial discrimination cannot be ended by laws.
   b. The voting age should be lowered to eighteen years.
   c. Married college graduates should have larger families.
   d. Liberal arts education should precede professional training.
   e. Congressmen should be required to have a college education.
   f. The United Nations should have an international police force.

7. The entire class may join in a discussion analyzing one or several of the foregoing proposals, to make sure that all understand the process of factual analysis.

8. Read a printed speech representing *expository persuasion.* Phrase the speaker's proposal and show how he marshaled facts to support it.

9. Cite an example of a speaker you have known or read about whose influence gradually expanded because of his careful adherence to facts.

10. The following readings discuss problems in formulating sound judgments and methods of helping others to arrive at dependable conclusions:

Richard D. Altick, *The Scholar Adventurers* (New York: The Free Press, 1960).

J. Jeffrey Auer, *An Introduction to Research in Speech* (New York: Harper and Row, 1959).

Jacques Barzun and Henry F. Graff, *The Modern Researcher* (New York: Harcourt, Brace, 1957).

Samuel L. Becker, "Research on Emotional and Logical Proofs," *Southern Speech Journal,* 28 (Spring, 1963), 198-207.

David K. Berlo, "Problems in Communication Research," *Central States Speech Journal,* VII (Fall, 1955), 3-7.

J. Samuel Bois, *Explorations in Awareness* (New York: Harper and Row, 1957).

Ernest G. Bormann, *Theory and Research in the Communicative Arts* (New York: Holt, Rinehart and Winston, 1965).

Milton Dickens, "Laws of Experimental Research," *Western Speech,* XXIV (Autumn, 1960), 197-200.

Clyde W. Dow (ed.), *An Introduction to Graduate Study in Speech and Theatre* (East Lansing: Michigan State University Press, 1961).

Leon Festinger and Daniel Katz (eds.), *Research Methods in the Behavioral Sciences* (New York: Holt, Rinehart and Winston, 1953).

William L. Hays, *Statistics for Psychologists* (New York: Holt, Rinehart and Winston, 1963).

Henry Hazlitt, *Thinking as a Science* (New York: Dutton, 1916).

Darrell Huff, *How to Lie with Statistics* (New York: Norton, 1954).

Robert Oppenheimer, "Analogy in Science," *American Psychologist,* XI (March, 1956), 127-136.

Robert T. Oliver, *Becoming an Informed Citizen* (New York: Holt, Rinehart and Winston, 1964).

Charles R. Petrie, Jr., "Informative Speaking: A Summary and Bibliography of Related Research," *Speech Monographs,* XXX (June, 1963), 79-91.

Murray Sidman, *Tactics of Scientific Research: Evaluating Experimental Data in Psychology* (New York: Basic Books, 1960).

Josephine Tey, *The Daughter of Time* (New York: Berkley Medallion Books, 1951).

H. P. Weld and M. Roff, "A Study in the Formation of Opinions Based on Legal Evidence," *American Journal of Psychology,* 51 (1938), 609-628.

Harry L. Weinberg, *Levels of Knowing and Existence* (New York: Harpers, 1959).

Dynamic Logic

IN A BOOK CALLED *The Technique of Controversy,*
Boris Bogoslovsky called attention to two facts which he finds singu-
larly contradictory. The first fact is that psychologists and logicians
are accustomed to pointing out that we human beings are very illogical
in our thinking; and the second fact is that, especially in fairly recent
times, we illogical thinkers have made enormous advances in conquer-
ing nature through an acute ability to deduce and utilize the secrets
of chemistry, biology, physics, and other natural sciences. Even in the
realm of the less exact social sciences, much has been accomplished
to improve the quality of learning and to devise means of social adjustments of many types. As Bogoslovsky points out, this is a paradox: we
think badly—but effectively. What is the answer?

The answer which he (and others) proposes is that there is a need
for a re-examination of the old logic formulated by Aristotle. If you
have already had a course in formal logic, you have found it to consist
of a formidable array of "laws of exact thinking"—laws that prove
difficult to memorize, for they have little obvious relationship to the
way your mind seems to work in meeting the problems of daily living.
John Dewey also confronted this problem, and in 1910 wrote a book,
How We Think, in which he sought to describe how the mind really
does work in the process of arriving at a decision. His method has
been so widely used in speech texts that you have probably already
encountered it. Later in this chapter it will be discussed in terms of
persuasive speaking.

Relation of logic to persuasion

For a full generation, then, students of speech have been concerned with an active reconsideration of the relationship of logic to the processes of persuasion. What has become evident is that it is useful to distinguish two different functions of the reasoning process, namely: reasoning to ascertain what is true, and reasoning to secure the acceptance of this truth by listeners. These two procedures may be called *reasoning of analysis* and *reasoning of advocacy.* Rignano, in *The Psychology of Reasoning,* distinguishes them as "constructive" versus "intentional" reasoning. Both are necessary. They do not conflict; rather, they are supplementary. Reasoning of analysis is the discovery or demonstration of significant relationships among facts, which leads inexorably to an inescapable conclusion. Reasoning of advocacy is the presentation of such relationships in a way that will tend to win audience acceptance of the conclusion.

It follows, then, that formal or analytical logic is one thing, and dynamic or persuasive logic is another. There is as much difference between the two as there is difference between a mathematician's adding up a column of figures to get the right answer and a salesman's adding up a list of values in order to make a sale. There is the difference that exists between an objective scientist and a lawyer trying to win a case in court. For the persuasive speaker is a *retained attorney.* He already has arrived at his conclusion—which is to say, he has formulated his proposal. What he desires of reasoning is not to use it to arrive at a conclusion, but to use it to win agreement.

The persuasive speaker, then, and the logician have much in common in *reaching sound conclusions,* but the persuasive speaker must go on to get them accepted. Max Black, in his elementary logic textbook, *Critical Thinking,* defines logic as "the use of possible truths as evidence in support of other possible truths." Just so does a scientist in the laboratory try out possible experiments to determine the validity of a possibly true hypothesis. By the very act of having become a persuasive speaker, an individual places himself in a different category.

He is seeking to establish a proposition which he has himself already accepted as being true. The logic he wants to use is the logic of the advocate.

The logic required by the persuasive speaker must be utilitarian. It must serve the purpose of winning agreement under the perverse conditions of ignorance and prejudice with which the minds of many auditors are clouded. For the speaker there seldom can be achieved the rigorous conditions of exactitude taken for granted in treatises on formal logic. In much or most persuasion, the syllogism is of little help, for it is hard to expect of an audience that it will agree to the essential condition that A cannot be both A and not-A at the same time. An audience is too likely to think, "My attitudes are convictions; yours are prejudices." It will believe that a certain type of activity is "good" when performed by one political party and "bad" when performed by another. Again, the rules for inductive and deductive logic are of more help to the logician in his study than to the speaker in the auditorium, for the train of reasoning pursued by the latter is frequently derailed by the insertion of audience inattentiveness across the track or the will to believe something other than what the reasoning indicates.

John Stuart Mill once declared of so rigorous a logical science as geometry that "If mankind had found the theorems of geometry useless they would long ago have found them false." Similarly, J. M. Keynes wrote that President Woodrow Wilson (probably our most highly educated president) once ended an argument over policy by exclaiming, "Logic! Logic! I don't care a damn for logic. I am going to include pensions."

Mortimer J. Adler, in his treatise, *Dialectic,* stressed the lack of scientific objectivity involved in any persuasive situation. "Actual controversy," he wrote, "occurs when two minds are engaged in dispute. It is evident that such dispute could only occur because the two individuals in question are in some way partisan. They have taken sides; they are defending or attacking beliefs or propositions." The absolute rejection of logic by disputants is not infrequent, as when one may exclaim, "You seem to be right, but I still am not convinced!" For persuasive purposes, the kind of logic that is needed is the kind that will win the response, "I do believe."

Logic of the advocate

The persuasive speaker should seek for a logical basis which will permit him to *prove as little as possible and refute as little as possible.* An unwise debater eager only to display his argumentative skill might delight in holding an opponent up to ridicule before an audience by proving an entire case against him and by refuting every argument presented. For the persuasive speaker, however, the audience is the "opponent." It is the audience that is to be won over. To pulverize the audience with a slashing attack against its pet beliefs might be an impressive performance but would seldom win an agreeable response to the speaker's proposal. It is far better for the speaker to *minimize differences, stress agreements,* and *narrow the point at issue.*

Chapter 9 discussed analysis as a tool for discovering the essential facts in a general area of knowledge. Anaylsis may further be used as a tool of persuasive reasoning to show an audience that what may appear to be a sharp disagreement is really almost a meeting of minds. When analysis is not so used, needless controversy is created. For instance, a demand for a considerable wage increase by a labor union might be met by a refusal by management to grant any increase at all. Unskilled "arguers" for either side might pile up reasons to show the merit of one proposal as against the injustice of the other—thus widening the already existing breach. A skilled "persuader" would try, on the other hand, through use of persuasive analysis, to narrow the gap by pointing out that both sides seek the same thing: greater and more stable prosperity for the industry, for example. Both labor and management have been pursuing the same ends toward that goal: higher productivity per man-hour accompanied by ever-increased rewards to both workers and owners. These gains have been secured by an attempt on both sides to understand the problems of the other, so they can work together as a team, rather than fight one another to the detriment of both. These things could be said by proponents of either management or labor, and the probability would be that after they were said the opposition would be considerably relaxed. Then, in a spirit of mutual accord on the fundamental points of view, the specific (and relatively minor) difference over this particular wage request could be discussed.

Such an analysis as is illustrated demonstrates the method of "proving as little as possible." The wise persuasive speaker will seek to *reduce* his persuasive task by making it as evident as possible that his differences with the auditors he must persuade are minimal. And for the same reason, when he comes to reply to arguments against his proposal, he will use the same method. He will seek ardently for every possible way in which he can agree with what has been presented. If he is a labor representative, he will say,

Yes, as you say, wages have been increased steadily for years. Taxes on profits are higher. Replacement costs for machinery are also higher. Net profits have been reduced. We will not argue with any of these points, for you are right in presenting them. The only way in which we seem to differ at all is in consideration of whether the past necessarily sets a pattern for the future. I know you do not think so fundamentally. You are always exercising every ingenuity to bring out new models and improve upon what your customers are able to buy. And the point that goes right along with this is the fact that the past cannot set a pattern for the future of labor, either. We graduated from the ten-hour day—with serious opposition by some parts of management, but with benefit to the whole industry. We graduated some time ago from the philosophy that management alone can determine how the industry is run. Everyone recognizes now that labor has a stake in it too, and that this new feeling of partnership has given greater stability to our industry than it ever had before. This is a developing process that cannot and should not be stopped. Labor is asking now for greater benefits for itself. We ask this in full confidence that it will be true now, as it has been in the past, that every gain for labor has in the final outcome helped management as well. Labor and management are going to continue to march side by side as mutually respecting partners, each seeking the welfare of the other since neither can exist at all without the other. The profits of management under our system are far greater than the profits you as individuals could expect under a system of state control. We want the present system to persist and become ever stronger. But it can only do so as labor is assured of a fair share of the goods that are produced.

There may or may not be agreement with the line of reasoning presented in the hypothetical "rebuttal" just outlined, but at least it minimizes disagreement, is conciliatory in tone, and points, as well as the speaker can, toward a voluntary acceptance by the auditors of the speaker's proposal. It is logic as used not by the rigorous logician, but by the advocate who knows that his success depends basically upon proving as little as possible and refuting as little as possible. *Rather than to build up arguments, his task is to build up agreements.* This above all is the purpose of persuasive reasoning. This is the sole test to which it should be put: To what extent does it secure permanently desirable results?

Standards of judgment

In advocacy, as well as in pure logic, there is need to establish definite and accepted standards of judgment. In a great many persuasive situations it may be presumed that both sides desire equally to arrive at right conclusions—even though strong personal preferences may blind them to what is objectively true. At least, the basic desire to be right creates a willingness to test their points of view by definite standards of judgment, provided only that standards are established which each will accept as fair.

Hence, in undertaking to win agreement with his proposal, one of the primary needs of the persuasive speaker is to formulate a set of standards by which his proposal, and also all counterproposals that his audience may entertain, can and should be tested.

An instance of this approach to persuasion is found in a letter written by Abraham Lincoln to one of his more troublesome commanding generals. It is quoted in full, as illustrating the method and suggesting the value of using standards in persuasive discourse:

Executive Mansion, Washington
February 3, 1862

Major-General McClellan:
My dear Sir:—
You and I have distinct and different plans for a movement of the Army of the Potomac—yours to be down the Chesapeake, up the Rap-

pahanock to Urbana, and across land to the terminus of the railroad on
the York River; mine to move directly to a point on the railroad south-
west of Manassas.

If you will give me satisfactory answers to the following questions, I
shall gladly yield my plan to yours.

First. Does not your plan involve a greatly larger expenditure of time
and money than mine?

Second. Wherein is a victory more certain by your plan than mine?

Third. Wherein is a victory more valuable by your plan than mine?

Fourth. In fact, would it not be less valuable in this, that it would break
no great line of the enemy's communications, while mine would?

Fifth. In case of disaster, would not a retreat be more difficult by your
plan than mine?

Yours truly,
Abraham Lincoln

Lincoln's letter is persuasive advocacy rather than argument. He
stresses the basic agreement between himself and McClellan by the
simple assumption that of course they both wish to achieve the goals
indicated in the questions: a valuable and certain victory, at the least
possible cost, with provision for effective retreat in case of failure.
Far from accusing McClellan of pursuing false goals, then, Lincoln
clearly and simply establishes the unity of the two men on that score.
Despite this fundamental unity, however, there is a sharp issue between them on method, and since this is the point at which a decision
is demanded, Lincoln defines it clearly in his opening paragraph: in
effect, sets forth his own proposal, in contradistinction to McClellan's.
Next, before presenting his standards of judgment, Lincoln conciliates
his opponent by himself assuming all the risk. He does not say (except
by implication), "You must abandon your plan if it is wrong." Instead,
he says, "I shall gladly yield my plan to yours." After that, he sets up
the standards by which the two must be judged—standards presumably fully as acceptable to McClellan as to himself.

The standards of judgment which the persuasive speaker establishes should be clearly distinguished from arguments. They are not
arguments supporting his proposal, but tests to which both it and all
counterproposals should be submitted. The standards themselves
should be of such a nature that they appear uncontroversial to the

audience. They are like the scales on which a butcher weighs the meat: if the meat weighs a full pound, the customer will pay for a pound; if it weighs less, less will be paid.

One way to make sure that *standards* rather than *arguments* are being formulated is to ascertain that they apply with equal validity to all opposing proposals. When the labor union asks for an increase of 30¢ an hour, management offers nothing, and a fact-finding board recommends 15¢, standards have to be set up to facilitate a judgment as to which proposal is most acceptable. These may be in the form either of questions to be answered or of principles to be accepted. As examples, the following standards might be acceptable in the wage dispute:

1. Would the profits of the industry be more equitably distributed by one proposal than by either of the others? (Or, stated as a principle: the plan should be followed which will provide most equity in distribution of total income.)

2. According to which proposal will the stability of the industry be best assured? (Or: the plan should be followed which will best assure stability of the industry.)

3. Which proposal best protects the fundamental interests of both management and labor? (Or: the welfare of management and labor both should be protected.)

When a set of standards is proposed by a persuasive speaker, he should be sure: (1) that his suggested standards will be fully accepted by his auditors as tests of all opposing proposals; and (2) that all pertinent standards are included in his list. If he fails to win agreement with his standards, his audience will say, in effect, "That line of reasoning may be all right for you, but it doesn't impress us." And if his list of standards is incomplete, the audience may say, "You are right so far as you go, but you have failed to take into account such-and-so."

Establishment of proper standards for judgment on any proposal is a guarantee of orderliness in thinking about it, and an invitation (if not a guarantee) for an audience to follow the speaker along from his premises to his conclusion. There can be no positive guarantee, of course, that the auditors might not first accept the standards but end by concluding, "You seem to be right, but still we don't agree with you." When that point is reached, the function of logic in persuasion is ended and other forms of support (such as emotion or rationalization) are needed.

Thought processes

The speaker's proposal confronts the audience with a necessity for making a choice. What occurs in a persuasive speech, then, is a leading of the minds of the audience toward a decision. Analysts of thought processes are inclined to agree that in all thinking toward a decision there is a relatively similar process, whatever the subject matter may be. That is, the mind follows the same pattern whether deciding to buy a house, to scratch the left ear, or to eat mince instead of apple pie. Obviously, if there is any such universal pattern governing human decision-making, the persuasive speaker should know it, for it will tremendously simplify his problem of organizing his appeals.

John Dewey, in *How We Think* (1910), as we have previously noted, presented an analysis which has been widely accepted. Dewey said that all thinking toward a decision involves five steps. *First,* there is a "felt difficulty," an awareness that something is wrong, a sense of need for a change. *Second,* there is analysis of the cause of the difficulty and a definition of the need. *Third,* there is a survey of possible ways of satisfying the need. *Fourth,* there is evaluation of the ways, leading to one being selected as the best—at least under the circumstances. *Fifth,* the preferred solution is acted upon. To illustrate these five steps with the simplest example cited above, you may (1) become aware of an uncomfortable feeling in your left ear; (2) you decide it itches; (3) you wonder whether to ignore it, to scratch it, to hunch your shoulder up against it, or to make some excuse for leaving the room to scratch it in private; (4) considering all the possibilities, to scratch it seems best; so (5) you do. The individual who says, "Nonsense, my mind doesn't go through all those processes at all," may be misinterpreting the speed with which his mind operates. The last four steps may be telescoped together, but Dewey, at least, insists that they occur.

In group discussion it is often useful to carry the thinking of the audience through each of the five steps: (1) is the present situation unsatisfactory; (2) if so, why and how; (3) what can be done about it; (4) what should be done about it; (5) what steps do we take to accomplish the agreed-upon solution? Similarly, in a persuasive speech it often may be wise to follow just this procedure. The chief advantages are that: (1) you start where the audience is, with a recognition of a problem confronting them—rather than where the speaker is, with a solution which he has worked out; (2) your method of presentation is logical without being argumentative; (3) the audience is invited to think along with the speaker, considering each process as it logically unfolds, and thus coming to have a personal commitment to the line of reasoning that is leading toward the speaker's proposal; (4) the specific proposal of the speaker is presented to the auditors only after they have been led to understand in detail how and why it was formulated; and (5) having agreed with the parts of the speech leading up to the proposal, it is easier to agree than to disagree with the proposal itself.

When the audience is confronted with a clear-cut and definite choice between the speaker's proposal and one contrasting possibility, the process is essentially the same. As an example you may be in your room for an evening of hard study when a friend bursts in to invite you to go to a movie. You have to choose between two contrasting alternatives. Your *first* reaction may be an awareness of a difficulty in deciding. *Second,* you define the difficulty as the fact that a test will be given in the morning, and you must study for it. *Third,* analyzing possibilities, you consider going to the movie and studying afterward, going to the movie and then getting a good sleep, or staying home to study. *Fourth,* you decide to stay home. *Fifth,* you say so positively enough to send your friend off without you. In the example cited, you have been the audience, rather than the speaker. If you are the speaker in a similar situation, you tell the audience, (1) "I know my proposal presents several difficulties"; (2) "You have to decide what course of action will be best for you"; (3) "Naturally, there are a number of things (the standards of judgment) that will help you decide which course is best"; (4) "Examining these, we find my proposal is the better of the two alternatives"; (5) "Therefore, let us join now in taking the action I have proposed."

It will be noticed that where the audience is confronted with two clear-cut alternatives (as was the case in Lincoln's letter to McClellan and in the invitation to a movie) the speaker's proposal is not and cannot be concealed from the audience until the end of the speech. Even so, however, the speaker still "starts where the audience is" by analyzing the difficulty that exists in deciding between the two. As the third step in the process, the speaker cannot present a list of possible alternative actions, for there are only two and these two are presented in Step one. In such instances, the third step consists of the enumeration of the various standards of reasoning which should be applied in reaching a decision.

To the extent that the Dewey five-fold process really represents how minds naturally operate in thinking toward a decision, it obviously presents a sound method of developing a persuasive speech. It should not be concluded, however, that it is the only method, nor in all instances necessarily the best. Another widely used means of reasoning toward a decision is through use of what are called "stock issues."

Stock issues

The stock issues are so called because they represent questions that anyone will naturally want answered when considering whether to adopt a given proposal. They may be enumerated as follows: (1) Is there a need for a change? (2) Will the proposal prove practical? (3) Will the proposal prove beneficial? (4) Will the proposal introduce new difficulties or bad effects? This series of tests for any proposal is another form of reasoning which persuasive speakers will often find of value. These stock issues are always of value to the speaker in guiding his own analysis of the subject matter, and on occasion they are useful as the outline for his speech.

Need. Chapter 8 discussed an example of a speech designed to arouse support for increased taxes to build a new gymnasium. The speaker could not expect audience support until after he had convincingly demonstrated a need for the additional building. He would have to cite statistics and specific instances of overcrowding, and perhaps compare and contrast the situation with facilities in other communities. In other words, he would need to present such factual evidence as was analyzed in Chapter 9 to prove that a need exists.

Practicality. As a second step, he would need to demonstrate that his proposal for higher taxes is practical. He should indicate how much money would be required and how it would be raised. He might suggest the precise forms of taxation needed, showing how the added burden would be distributed equitably without working undue hardship on any groups or individuals. He might further support his contention of practicality by citing methods of construction that could be used to provide cheaper or better school buildings.

Benefits. To arouse the positive interest and desire that will induce active support for his proposal, the speaker should show the benefits that will flow from it. He would demonstrate that the community would profit in various ways: by having its children better educated, by being more desirable to prospective newcomers, by becoming more attractive, and by increasing property values. The better his analysis of his audience has been, the more able he will be to picture the particular benefits that will motivate this particular group of listeners.

No Bad Effects. A sensible caution teaches us not to accept any proposal without considering what its bad effects might be. Thus Lincoln, writing to McClellan, included a consideration of the results of a possible defeat. Similarly, the speaker advocating higher taxes for school buildings might expect his audience to worry about possible evils that might flow from his proposal. They might fear that graft would be involved in letting the building contract; or that new residents attracted to the town might be of an undesirable type; or that other public services (the police, or fire department, or town officials) might demand new buildings to match those erected for the schools. This part of the speech is actually *rebuttal.* Often it is unwise for a speaker even to suggest the possibility of such ill effects by mentioning them. At other times, the awareness of possible evils might be evident enough so that refuting them will be a major part of the persuasive task. Under any circumstances, it at least is wise for the speaker himself to have considered possible bad effects and how they might be avoided—both to be sure that his proposal is sound, and to be able to answer questions or challenges that might arise.

The stock issues have become almost standardized as the form around which debates are organized. They have an undeniable value in discussing any issue that is solidly and clearly set forth before the persuasive speech commences. If an audience knows that the speaker is appearing as an advocate for a certain proposal, it often is best for him to proceed right through the series of stock issues, clarifying the reasons for supporting his proposal, and combatting contrary views as he does so. This is argument, however, not persuasion, and the differences between the two should not be minimized.

Inductive and deductive reasoning

In a strict sense all the reasoning that we do is either inductive or deductive, or a combination of the two. *Induction* means to reason from a specific example, or from a cluster of examples, to a generalized conclusion. *Deduction* means to start with an accepted generalization (such as, that all men are created equal) and to judge of a specific instance in terms of that conclusion. The Dewey Thought Process is largely inductive; the Stock Issues lead chiefly to deductive reasoning. In these and other examples, however, we tend in practice to combine the two forms.

An example of inductive reasoning for persuasive effect is found in a speech delivered by Frederick Osborn, on January 8, 1951, to the Economic Club in Detroit. He set out to pile up specific instances with which to demonstrate that the United States is in a gravely dangerous situation:

Now, as long as the world is constituted as it is—I say the "world" meaning all the world's peoples—that makes for a dreadfully dangerous situation, because the world is in an extraordinary shape. A little group of people—originally only sixty million Europeans—started about four hundred years ago and made this extraordinary advance, which we call civilization. I suppose it is. It has extended the life of man to an average expectancy of seventy years. It has given us a security such as mankind has never known before; physical well-being and health; material things in great quantity; medicine; education for the masses; and all these other things which we enjoy. That advance is still solely limited to this little group of originally sixty million Europeans, and now some four hundred million people of European descent. And the advance hasn't touched the rest of the world's people. They are still on the margin of starvation. They are still wholly without possessions. Now, I'm talking about the great mass of the other billion six or eight hundred million people: the Indians of South America, the Africans of Africa, the mass of the people of India, the mass of the people of China, and so on. They are wholly without education. Most of them are on the verge of being without food. They have only the clothes they wear on their backs. And in this world are this group of people of European descent who are wealthy beyond the imagining of the rest of the world; and the American and Canadian groups, who are twice as wealthy as those still living in Western Europe. Naturally, the peoples of the world are jealous of us, and naturally that jealousy can easily be turned into hatred by an aggressive group of dictators. That is just the situation we have today. The men in the Kremlin are spending all their energies, with a cunning and a thoroughness beyond our conception, to teach these people to hate us—and they already control not very far from half the people of the world, who are not allowed to hear anything else. So, it is a plenty dangerous world for us. . . .

From the foregoing example it is evident that reasoning from induction is very little different from accumulation of specific evidence to "prove a point." Deductive reasoning differs in this essential respect—that when we reason deductively, the "point" is a truism that may be taken for granted without proof. There may also be presented a set of specific data, but if so it is to illustrate, rather than to "prove." In deductive reasoning, the speaker starts with a proposition that the audience already accepts—such as, that the people in Asia live under conditions that we would consider highly undesirable. Then, specific instances are cited to illuminate the point and make it real. Often, out of this citation of specific instances there will emerge a definite conclusion as to something that needs to be done to remedy the conditions. In other words, the speaker interprets the

general principle in a way that makes clear its application in support
of the specific proposal he has to present. A condensed example of this
kind of speaking is found in a speech by Dean Acheson, then U. S.
Secretary of State, delivered at the University of California on March
16, 1950:

> The free society values the individual as an end in himself. It requires
> of him only that self-discipline and self-restraint which make the rights of
> each individual compatible with the rights of every other individual.
> Individual freedom, therefore, implies individual responsibility not to
> exercise freedom in ways inconsistent with the freedom of other indi-
> viduals, and responsibility positively to make constructive use of freedom
> in the building of a just society.

In both inductive and deductive reasoning the speaker tries to
proceed nonargumentatively, assuming agreement as he proceeds
toward his conclusion. In the first instance he can do this because
he is citing specific instances, which will be recognized as true, and
from them "inevitably" emerges the natural conclusion of their cumulative meaning. This, of course, only results if the instances are
genuinely representative and if there are enough of them to suggest
to the listeners that the speaker has an adequate number of legitimate
samples. In deductive reasoning, on the other hand, the audience
agrees with what is said because the very meaning of this form of
reasoning is that it does start with a generally accepted truism. It is
his responsibility, thereafter, to make sure that the specific conclusion
he reaches does, indeed, rise inevitably out of the stated premise.

The logical form of deductive reasoning is the *syllogism*. In syllogistic reasoning, the truism is called the "major premise." The specific
instance (or instances) cited constitute the "minor premise." And
from the relationship of the two emerges the "conclusion." Thus: All
men are mortal. Socrates is a man. Therefore, Socrates is mortal.

Actually, there are three kinds of syllogisms, which means that
there are three forms of deductive reasoning. The one just cited is
called *categorical*. A second form is called the *disjunctive syllogism,*
which means that the major premise provides a choice between two
alternatives. For example, "An international organization is either a

government or a consultative body. The United Nations is certainly
not a government. Therefore, it is a consultative organization." And
the third type of syllogism is called *hypothetical*. This means that the
real question is whether or not the major premise describes a true
state of affairs. It is stated in the following form: "If the Communists
keep agreements, it is useful to negotiate agreements with them.
Actually, the record shows that they do not keep agreements. Hence,
it is useless to negotiate with them."

In inductive reasoning, the main precaution is to make sure that
the examples point dependably to an inescapable conclusion. In deductive (or syllogistic) reasoning, the main precaution is to be sure
that the major and minor premises are accepted without reservation
by the audience. Since this is essential, most speakers avoid the bare
statement of syllogisms and spend time enough to establish first the
major and then the minor premise firmly and acceptably in the minds
of the listeners. The speaker first fixes the skeletal form of the syllogism in his mind, then enlarges and elaborates it. The audience does
not identify the syllogism, in many cases, but nevertheless is won
by the logic of the reasoning process.

The rhetorical syllogism

In addition to the three standard forms of the syllogism included
in the field of logic, Aristotle noted a fourth, which he called the
enthymeme, and which modern writers often call the "rhetorical syllogism." Aristotle insisted that few audiences can be expected to follow
through the strictly logical processes of the syllogism, but that they
may much more readily be influenced by the enthymeme. There
are two significant differences between the formal syllogism and the
rhetorical syllogism.

First, the enthymeme or rhetorical syllogism is *abbreviated*. It
assumes audience acceptance of the major premise and does not
complicate the thinking processes of the listeners by mentioning it.
Hence, the speaker might say, "Since the Russians can't be trusted to
keep an agreement, why bother to negotiate with them?" This form
is fully as logical as the formal syllogism, but if you seek to diagram

the reasoning, it is necessary to supply the missing major premise, "negotiations are useful only if the agreements will be honored."

Second, the rhetorical syllogism may deal with probabilities rather than with certainties. When this is the case, the syllogism ceases to be logical and becomes merely psychological. The major premise is not *known* to be true, but experience or common sense or general opinion leads us to believe it probably is true. For example, "Being a *grind* will get you nothing but a Phi Beta Kappa key." This rhetorical syllogism could be outlined fully as follows:

> *Major premise:* Academic scholarship is impractical and useless.
> *Minor premise:* Phi Beta Kappa honors only academic scholarship.
> *Conclusion:* There is little real value in earning a Phi Beta Kappa key.

Obviously, in addition to being abbreviated, the example cited is also based upon presumptions which are untested and not clearly defined. Nevertheless, as Aristotle and many after him have insisted, this form of "reasoning" is often more persuasively effective than formal syllogisms.

Audience-centered versus subject-centered

Chapter 1, and every subsequent chapter, has emphasized the fact that persuasion is a process of leading auditors voluntarily toward a decision they will make willingly. Argument is a method of driving an audience toward a conclusion which facts and logic make it difficult for them to reject. Persuasion consists of finding the reasons that will appeal especially to the auditors being addressed, so that it is properly considered to be *audience-centered*. Argument consists of drawing from the subject matter the reasons that might logically have to be considered by anyone who thinks of the proposal objectively; hence argument is to a larger degree *subject-centered*.

Argumentation has a place of its own and should not be neglected. In a courtroom, for instance, argument is required to demonstrate the factual and logical basis for a sound decision. In any speech addressed to a wide and diverse audience (as when the speech is delivered over the radio or printed in the papers), the reasoning must be sound enough to withstand the attacks and to influence the thinking of auditors who approach the subject in very different ways. And in any sustained campaign, extending over months or years, the basically logical and factual soundness of the arguments is of much more importance than the transitory appeal that might be made to a particular audience in any specific situation.

In the beginning of this chapter a distinction was made between *reasoning* and *reasoning for persuasion*. Argument depends upon the former. It is the undisguised presentation to an audience of "significant relationships among facts," leading inevitably toward a conclusion dictated by the facts. Obviously there are times and places when speaking of this kind is required. And obviously, too, it is impossible unless and until the audience will grant that the facts are actually as represented, and that the relationships among them that the speaker demonstrates are inevitable. As we have seen earlier in this chapter, this particular set of conditions is rather difficult to find in an ordinary audience-situation. When minds are inflamed, when passions are aroused, when personal interests are involved, it is evident that differing individuals do not see the facts alike and that the inductions they draw from them often vary widely.

The speaker in search of a guide will find his own judgment of the audience-situation the final arbiter that he must accept. But, as a general rule, it might be suggested to use *persuasion* when speaking to a specific and homogeneous audience, to obtain an immediate decision, and especially so when the proposal involves strong personal feelings; and to use *argument* when addressing a wide variety of auditors, for a decision that will either be delayed or that will involve many different groups, and when the proposal is relatively far removed from identifiable effects on the listeners.

Forms of reasoning

There are many different ways of classifying the forms of reasoning. Any good textbook on logic will list and analyze many of them. Most of them, however, have but a dim and hazy relationship to the process of actual persuasion. As Mortimer J. Adler declares in his

Dialectic, ". . . it is clear that no actual argument or controversy ever resembles in entirety, or even in large measure, the abstract form of dialectic." What he says of argument is even more true of persuasion. The rigorously objective thinking required by the various types of the syllogism and other forms of logic is as far from the hurly-burly of ordinary human conflict as Plato's conception of the ideal is from the world as we know it. It is well for the persuasive speaker, and for everyone else, to know how to think logically in formulating conclusions. In persuasion, in any event, the forms of reasoning must be geared to the kinds of audience reactions the speaker will expect to find.

Forms of reasoning useful in persuasion include *causes, consequences,* and *consistency.*

Causes. "From such-and-such a cause, certain effects may be expected." This is a kind of reasoning that is deeply rooted in our everyday experience. If you put your hand on a hot kettle, it will be burned; if you elect an incompetent man, the duties of the office will be neglected; if a nation violates its treaty obligations, it may expect other nations to resent and resist its actions. These and many similar examples of reasoning from cause to probable results may readily be adduced from daily experience. Such causal deductions frequently may be very persuasive. Yet they may get an audience response of "Yes, but . . . ," or "Not so" if they seem to contain any of the following fallacies:

1. Falsely assumed connection between cause and effect (as, "If a Republican President is elected, farmers will have better crops.")
2. Citation of coincidental occurrence as a cause (as, "Having left my rabbit foot at home, I was struck by a car.")
3. Ascription to a cause of a result beyond its power to achieve (as, "Early to bed, early to rise, makes a man healthy, wealthy, and wise.")

Of course, every one of the examples cited is a persuasive appeal that has been used with effect (even the first one!) so, as might well be asserted, even such fallacies have persuasive power in some situations. Nevertheless, since they are fallacies, the persuasive speaker will consider them both dangerous and distasteful to use.

Consequences. "I told you so" is one of the terms we least like to hear. It is an appeal to consequences in a particularly obnoxious form. Yet it often constitutes a powerful deterrent to further action of the kind referred to. "Well, now you've smashed the fenders perhaps you *will* take driving lessons" is another example of persuasion based on consequences. "Let's look at the record," a popular campaign term of Al Smith's, is another form of turning audience attention to consequences in order to influence their future actions. "Do you suffer from insomnia? Drink Postum" is another instance of consequential reasoning. Reasoning from consequences is a way of saying to the audience, "You don't like what happened to you when you didn't follow my advice; now let's try it my way and see if things don't turn out better." The auditors may well agree, unless they find you guilty of such fallacies as:

1. Assigning false causes to the consequences you cite (as, the lady whose husband pointed to the smashed fenders might reply bitingly, "The accident wasn't my fault. You'd better have the other driver take lessons").

2. Drawing improper inferences between the consequences you cite and the plan of action you suggest (as, intimating that if "the record" of the party in power is bad, all political ills will automatically be remedied if candidates of your own party are elected).

3. Presuming that undesirable consequences will necessarily be repeated (for, the auditors may well reply, "True, we failed this time, but we'll try the same thing again and hope to do it better").

4. Ignoring changes in circumstances which will produce different future consequences from the same actions (as, now that federal bank-deposit insurance is in effect, a general depression ought not to result in the loss of depositors' money even if many banks should fail).

Consistency. To show that your reasoning is consistent, while that of your opponents is inconsistent, is often of great persuasive weight. The whole train of a speaker's reasoning, through the Dewey thought-formula's five steps, or through the four stock issues, should be so carefully integrated that the audience will never doubt the consistency of what he is saying. In addition to this care for self-consistency within the framework of any one persuasive appeal, strong persuasive effect is often achieved by pointing out the inconsistencies of opposing speakers. Lincoln, for example, in his series of debates with Douglas, made frequent use of this method of rebuttal. One instance occurred in the last debate of the series, at Alton, Illinois, before an audience of six thousand when Lincoln said to Douglas:

You say slavery is wrong; but don't you constantly argue that this is not the right place to oppose it? You say it must not be opposed in the free states, because slavery is not there; it must not be opposed in the slave states, because it is there; it must not be opposed in politics, because that will make a fuss; it must not be opposed in the pulpit, because it is not religion. Then where is the place to oppose it? There is no suitable place to oppose it.

Inconsistencies constitute fallacies that weaken the persuasive effectiveness of a speech if they are noted by an audience, or the inconsistencies of opposition to the speaker's proposal may be pointed out by him with telling effect. The following types should be studied, both so that you may avoid them yourself and so you may point them out when used by the opposition:

1. Shifting the ground of argument (as, "A moment ago you were saying that no professor should be elected to public office; now you say that no professor should be elected unless he has had experience in community service").

2. Self-contradiction (as, "I am opposed to government spending, but I favor unemployment insurance, public works, federal aid to education, and all other programs for the good of the public").

3. Assumptions without logical coherence (an instance of use in rebuttal, as, in Lincoln's speech at Alton: "Judge Douglas will have it that I want a Negro wife. He never can be brought to understand that there is any middle ground on this subject. I have lived until my fiftieth year, and have never had a Negro woman either for a slave or a wife, and I think I can live fifty centuries, for that matter, without having had one for either").

Conclusion

Reasoning is a rigorous process of sifting wheat from chaff, truth from error, and establishing essential conclusions from consideration of all relevant data. The reasoning of the logician or the scientist is directed to discovering what, under certain assumed or controlled conditions, is true. The reasoning of the advocate is designed for a different purpose: to win audience agreement to the speaker's proposal. To ignore this distinction and to try to force the logician's processes into a persuasive pattern is to risk the dangers of artificiality and misdirection of effort. In minimizing disagreement, the persuasive speaker will often do best to try to prove as little as possible and refute as little as possible, by narrowing the grounds of dispute and emphasizing the commonality of goals. When the essential points at issue are defined, the speaker should establish a just and equitable set of standards of reasoning by which the audience will be willing to have the speaker's proposal and its opposition tested.

The reasoning process through which the speaker may lead his auditors' mind toward his conclusion may be the Dewey fivefold thought process, the four stock issues, or (less formally) the methods of reasoning from causes, from consequences, or through any consistently maintained processes. In any of these methods, the essential consideration is to "meet the audience where it is," to "get it loaded aboard the speaker's train of reasoning," and to "keep it on the train until the destination is reached."

Exercises

1. Compare the statement from Chapter 9, "... what from certain points of view may be made to appear to be true, is very likely in the long run to be confuted by what actually *is* true," with the following assertion from this chapter: "*Reasoning* is one thing and *reasoning for persuasion* is another." Is there a basic inconsistency between these two conclusions? Are *facts* and *relationships between facts* similarly subject to objective *validation?* The class may be divided into two groups, one to argue that both propositions are true; the other that one or both is false, with specific illustrations adduced by the class members in support of their points of view.

2. Differentiate clearly between "standards" and "arguments." Write out a specific persuasive proposal and (*a*) the standards to be used in judging it, and (*b*) the arguments with which you would support it.

3. Phrase a specific persuasive proposal and support it with (*a*) reasoning based on the Dewey thought process, and (*b*) the stock issues.

4. Phrase a specific proposal and support it with reasoning derived from (*a*) causes; (*b*) consequences; and (*c*) demonstration of consistency of judgment.

5. Select the ideational development from the 2nd, 3rd, or 4th exercise and prepare a persuasive speech in accordance with it. Preferably, different class members should select different types of development, so that all will be represented. Following the speeches there may be class discussion as to which method seems most effective for the particular speeches delivered to the group.

6. From one of the following collections, select a persuasive speech, analyze its structure of reasoning, and evaluate the speaker's use of logic as a means toward attainment of his purpose: Carroll C. Arnold, Douglas Ehninger, and John C. Gerber, *The Speaker's Resource Book* (Chicago: Scott, Foresman, 1966); Goodwin F. Berquist, Jr., *Speeches for Illustration and Example* (Chicago: Scott, Foresman, 1965); Robert T. Oliver and Eugene E. White, *Selected Speeches from American History* (Boston: Allyn and Bacon, 1966).

7. For consideration in depth of the persuasive uses of reasoning, the following readings will be useful:

S. F. Barker, *Induction and Hypothesis* (Ithaca: Cornell University Press, 1957).

Monroe C. Beardsley, *Thinking Straight,* 2nd ed. (Englewood Cliffs, N.J.: Prentice-Hall, 1956).

Max Black, *Critical Thinking* (New York: Prentice-Hall, 1952).

Barry E. Collins and Harold Guetzkow, *A Social Psychology of Group Processes for Decision-Making* (New York: Wiley, 1964).

Gary Lynn Cronkhite, "Logic, Emotion, and the Paradigm of Persuasion," *Quarterly Journal of Speech,* 50 (February, 1964), 13-18.

John Dewey, *How We Think* (Boston: Heath, 1910).

E. R. Emmett, *The Use of Reason* (London: Longmans, 1960).

F. Ward Fearnside and William B. Holther, *Fallacy: The Counterfeit of Argument* (Englewood Cliffs, N.J.: Prentice-Hall, 1959).

William V. Haney, *Communication: Patterns and Incidents* (Homewood, Ill.: Richard D. Irwin, 1960).

E. F. Heidbreder, "Reasons Used in Solving Problems," *Journal of Experimental Psychology,* 10 (October, 1927), 397-414.

Robert B. Huber, *Influencing Through Argument* (New York: McKay, 1963).

William Hummel and Keith Huntress, *The Analysis of Propaganda* (New York: William Sloan, 1949).

Irving L. Janis and F. Frick, "The Relationship between Attitudes toward Conclusions and Errors in Judging Logical Validity of Syllogisms," *Journal of Experimental Psychology*, 33 (July, 1943), 73-77.

Henry W. Johnstone, Jr., *Philosophy and Argument* (University Park: The Pennsylvania State University Press, 1959).

Arthur N. Kruger, *Modern Debate: Its Logic and Strategy* (New York: McGraw-Hill, 1960).

Harold L. Larrabee, *Reliable Knowledge* (Boston: Houghton, Mifflin, 1945).

John J. B. Morgan, "Effects of Non-Rational Factors on Inductive Reasoning," *Journal of Experimental Psychology*, 34 (February, 1944), 159-168.

————, "The Distortion of Syllogistic Reasoning Produced by Personal Convictions," *Journal of Social Psychology*, 20 (1944), 35-59.

Robert T. Oliver and Dominick A. Barbara, *The Healthy Mind in Communion and Communication* (Springfield, Ill.: Charles C Thomas, 1962).

J. Peterson, "The Functioning of Ideas in Social Groups," *Psychological Review*, 25 (1918), 214-226.

Michael Polanyi, *Personal Power* (Chicago: University of Chicago Press, 1958).

Francis F. Powers, "The Influence of Intelligence and Personality Traits upon False Beliefs," *Journal of Social Psychology*, 2 (November, 1931), 490-493.

Lionel Ruby, *The Art of Making Sense* (Philadelphia: Lippincott, 1954).

Thomas C. Schelling, *The Strategy of Conflict* (Cambridge: Harvard University Press, 1960).

Emotion

WE ALL TEND TO BE SOMEWHAT SUSPICIOUS OF "EMO-
tional speaking." What we object to, however, is an attempt to "sway
our emotions" to a conclusion that reason would reject. We know
that emotional appeals are influential; yet we fear that somehow they
are intellectually unworthy; and as a matter of fact, we only partially
understand what emotional appeals really are. For all these reasons,
students of persuasive speech may be expected to approach the topic
of emotion somewhat hesitantly. In this chapter we shall attempt to
clarify what emotional appeals are, what their function is, and how
they may be utilized.

The importance of emotions

Emotion has always been considered to play a vital role in persuasive speaking. Aristotle pointed out that "persuasion may come
through the hearers, when the speech stirs their emotions. Our judgments when we are pleased and friendly are not the same as when
we are pained and hostile. It is toward producing these effects, as we
maintain, that present-day writers on rhetoric direct the whole of their
efforts." Three hundred years later Cicero wrote that "all the emotions of the mind, which nature has given to man, must be intimately
known; for all the force and art of speaking must be employed in
allaying or exciting the feelings of those who listen." The opinions
of these ancient rhetoricians are well supported by the psychologists
and by the practice of skilled speakers of today.

As Woodrow Wilson phrased it, "We speak of this as an age in which mind is monarch, but I take it for granted that, if that is true, mind is one of those modern monarchs who reign but do not govern. As a matter of fact, the world is governed in every generation by a great House of Commons made up of the passions; and we can only be careful to see to it that the handsome passions are in a majority." To give predominant influence to the emotions that uplift and improve our fellows is one of the great challenges we face as students of persuasive speech.

Most of what really seems important to us is deeply involved in emotion: our friendships, our ambitions, our hopes, our fears, our likes and dislikes, our interests. Even the ideas that we cherish are important to us because we do *cherish* them, which is to say, because we have an emotional attachment to them. When we are emotional it is because we are concerned, we feel deeply about the subject, we have a sense of personal involvement in it, we care what happens in relation to it—it has become a part of ourselves. To be emotional is to personalize. We think of the objective individual as one who stands aside from a situation as a mere spectator or judge, rather than as a participant. The emotional person is one who enters into the situation and becomes a part of it. It is needless to argue whether it is better to do one or the other. In point of fact, most normal persons find that if a situation is important to them they do respond emotionally to it. Whether or not they should do so is merely an academic question.

Try the experiment of attending one football game in which you are emotionally involved as a strong partisan of one of the teams, and another in which you know and care little or nothing about either team. Even if the play in the latter game is much superior to that in the former, it will inevitably be the former that means more to you and that (even if your favored team loses) you enjoy more. Unless we are emotionally involved, most of us find that indifference or at best a forced attentiveness is our normal response.

If it is intelligence that defines what a situation means, it is emotion that determines what it means to us. When an individual is taking a predominantly intellectual interest in a subject, we say he is being "objective" rather than "subjective." We may further describe him as being "detached" or "disinterested" or "uncommitted"—or "unemotional." We readily recognize that emotionality implies a sense of personal connection. Emotion is a basic factor in loyalty, responsibility, trustworthiness, patriotism, religion, love, determination, ambition, and practically every other quality we might admire in human conduct—as well as their opposites. To consider emotion unworthy is to derogate most of the characteristics that distinguish man from an electric calculating machine.

Dean Ralph Dennis of Northwestern University once wrote that if an individual could imagine himself as a stranger from another planet, flying through interplanetary space, and seeing earth off in the distance for the first time, he would view conditions on this globe far differently from the way any of us now do. This is one way of dramatically emphasizing to what extremes we have to go to separate ourselves from emotional involvement in the life we live. Since none of us can meet Dean Dennis' condition, none can expect to be freed from emotionality.

For the persuasive speaker it is axiomatic that if people are motivated to a large degree by emotions, persuasive speech must, to have a motivating effect, be emotional. In any event, there can be no question whether a speech will or will not contain emotional elements. The only way to avoid it would be to speak in completely colorless scientific symbols—in algebraic formulas, for instance—and to do so in a flatly monotonous and depersonalized voice. Even if that were done, it would still be likely that the content of what was communicated would have an emotional effect. Imagine, for instance, the emotional reaction of physicists to Einstein's theory, simply stated in the formula, $E = mc^2$. If it must be presumed, then, that persuasive speakers will be emotional, our task is to analyze what is involved in the process and to improve our skill in utilizing emotion for the easier, quicker, and fuller achievement of our persuasive goals.

Emotion defined

The speaker was short, sturdy, heavy-set; his voice was solemn and vibrant with terrible earnestness. His words fell with heavy emphasis upon rows of silent men, intent to catch every inflection, every expression of his face. "Long, dark months of trials and tribulations lie before us," intoned the speaker. "Not only great dangers, but many more misfortunes, many shortcomings, many mistakes, many disappointments will surely be our lot. Death and sorrow will be the companions of our journey; hardship our garment; constancy and valor our only shield. We must be united, we must be undaunted, we must be inflexible. Our qualities and deeds must burn and glow through the gloom of Europe until they become the veritable beacon of its salvation." As the speaker sat down, a thunder of applause rolled through the House of Commons. Winston Churchill, one of the greatest speakers in the long tradition of English oratory, had just finished his fourth report on the war situation, with an emotional conclusion. His speech had dealt with the destruction of English cities by German bombs, with the failure of English armies in the field, with the addition of Japan to the Axis powers. He minced no words in asserting these facts, yet left his hearers stirred with animation and hope. He gave them the power of a great emotion to spur them on. Of what did the emotion consist?

Emotion is the affective or "feeling" response we make to any situation. Our minds say, "It means such and such." Our emotions say, "It means such and such *to us.*" The operation of the mind is discriminative, but an emotional response is total; it involves the whole body. We feel it in the pit of the stomach, in the increased rate of breathing and the quickening of the pulse, in the flush of color to the face or the sudden blanch of pallor, in the trembling of the muscles and the tingling of the roots of the hair.

Emotion may be defined objectively as *a state of bodily tension accompanied by an intellectual concept of what the tension means.* In one situation when the body is "trembling with emotion," the mind says, "I am angry"; in another, "I am afraid"; in another, "I am sorry"; in still another, "I am in love." The body behaves in much the same way whether it perceives a bear in the woods, a fist raised to strike, a truck run over a child, or a lover returning from a journey. The individual in all these instances is stirred by emotion. The intelligence, interpreting the situation, informs the individual whether he is weeping from fear, from anger, or from joy.

An emotional state is interpreted according to four fundamental feeling tones, which are pleasantness, unpleasantness, excitement, or depression. Every sensation that an individual experiences is to some extent pleasant or unpleasant, and has a tendency to elevate or depress his spirits. But it is characteristic of an emotional sensation to be *distinctly* pleasant or unpleasant, exciting or depressing. Disgust, for instance, is unpleasant and depressing; anger is unpleasant and exciting; relief is pleasant and depressing; joy is pleasant and exciting. For every emotion, one of these four combinations of feeling tones is present in greater or less degree. It is one of the crucial means of identifying an emotional experience.

An emotion is present whenever "a group of perceptions or ideas is swamped by feeling." In an emotional state, the feeling tone is more important than the idea that accompanies it. We emotionalize less with the head, and more with the heart. For this reason, we do not always understand our own emotional states. Frequently, it is difficult to give an accurate description of our emotional reactions or even say just what has caused them. We may feel somewhat ashamed after an emotional outburst, for our reason tells us that the emotional reaction was out of proportion to the stimulating situation or that it was inappropriate in the social circumstances. But when the emotion occurs, it truly "swamps" our intellectual processes so that our emotion tends to control us, rather than we it.

Individuals, of course, vary in the extent to which they yield to their emotions, and circumstances are also exceedingly potent in determining the degree of emotional dominance over the mind. In a speech situation these circumstances are determined in great part by the skill and technique of the speaker. If he is a master of emotional appeals he may sweep his auditors along with him. If not, they may sit coldly aloof, offended by his clumsy attempts to smother their reason beneath waves of emotion.

Emotional behavior

Certain principles regarding the behavior of emotion should be kept in mind by the speaker.

First, *emotions come suddenly, but die away slowly.* They tend to persist as a *mood.* An unpleasant emotion may leave an individual in a melancholy or irritable mood for hours. A speaker may have to deal with an emotion aroused by a previous speech, or by an occurrence that preceded the meeting. A salesman's presentation, for instance, may be affected greatly in its results by good or bad news that his auditor received hours before.

Second, *once an emotion has been aroused it tends to fasten itself upon contiguous objects.* Thus, an angry man may kick a stone. An audience, angered by some community situation, may vent its displeasure upon the speaker—or may be directed by the speaker to express its emotion in an energetic support of his proposal.

Third, *every emotion tends to express itself in action.* When people are emotionally aroused, they want to *do* something. The very term e-*motion* indicates its active nature. If an audience is emotionally aroused, and then the speaker takes time to present an analysis of his proposal, the emotional support that he might have had dissolves. When the emotion is at its height, the audience will be ready to buy, to vote, to give, to applaud, to take a stand.

Fourth, *emotional reactions tend to be similar among all individuals who share common experiences in a given situation.* It has long been observed that people are more alike emotionally than intellectually. Nevertheless, the persuasive speaker should be aware that in many situations the individuals present may not be sharing a common experience. Thus, in a church service of worship there may be some skeptics who have come to scoff. In a group frightened by a stuffed alligator, far different emotions will be experienced by the practical joker who plotted the fright. In an audience aroused against the democratic administration there may be some Democrats whose feelings are indeed aroused, but far differently from those of the majority of listeners.

Emotional drives

Any general definition of emotion is unsatisfactory, for there are many emotions, each very different from the others. Love, disgust, jealousy, hatred, fear, and pity may all be lumped together as affective or emotional states, but this is a beginning rather than a stopping point in the task of definition. Ever since Aristotle's pioneer effort in the *Rhetoric,* an unsolved problem has been to work out a satisfactory classification of the emotions.

An attempt to bring some order out of the chaos was made by Frederic Wickert, who examined the lists of goal values (emotional drives, or impelling motives) devised by seventy-three representative psychologists. Out of their combined judgment he formulated a statement of nine basic desires, urges, or goal values (as he calls them) which seem to represent as much agreement as can be found regarding the emotional drives. These are not the expressions of emotion, such as we have been discussing, but the *affective states* which give rise to them. They are the emotional sources of motivation to which the persuasive speaker should direct his appeal. According to this composite judgment of the psychologists, the emotional drives to which people are most subject are desires for:

1. *Freedom* for themselves—from restraints, routine duties, and external domination. "Life, liberty, and the pursuit of happiness" are appropriately joined in the Declaration of Independence.
2. *Helpfulness*—working for the welfare of others. Through Red Cross membership, purchase of tuberculosis seals, and in all manner of other charitable enterprises we seek to serve.
3. *New experience*—finding the novelty and variety in life. Fads and fashions appear in quick succession as we quest eagerly for that variety which adds spice to living.
4. *Power* and influence—controlling others. In the competitive struggle of life, we all seek to win such personal triumphs as we can.

5. *Recognition*—social acceptance, admiration, fame. To be treated with deference and respect is pleasant; to be at least accepted socially is essential to balanced living.

6. *Response*—enjoying friendship, fellowship, and intimate personal contacts. The sharing of our inmost feelings in comradeship is at once the impelling force and the goal of much of our social activity.

7. *Security* and stability—doing what is safe and conservative. Despite the thrill of the new, we tend to cling hardest to the safety of the old.

8. *Submission*—following along with the crowd. It is frequently a relief to escape from personal responsibility and effort by riding the band wagon of majority opinion.

9. *Workmanship*—doing things well and making them right the first time. There is a satisfaction in competency, a thrill in achievement, a deep-seated desire to make one's life worth while.

These are the kinds of emotional satisfaction which the speaker should make his auditors feel that they can achieve through acceptance of his proposal. The automobile salesman, for instance, may dwell upon the freedom offered by owning a car, the satisfaction of being able to take friends for rides in the country, the thrill of new experiences in travel, the increased prestige that ownership will bring, the value of an automobile in making it easier to visit friends and relatives, the fact that "everyone" owns a car these days, and that this particular model is especially popular, and, finally, that there is a real satisfaction in climbing in behind the wheel of this miracle of modern engineering science, with the certainty that its powerful engine will operate with perfect ease and dependability. So, too, should the preacher, the politician, the reformer, the lawyer examine whatever proposal he has to present and plan in detail how he can best make use of some or all of these emotional drives in winning support for his plea.

Note how, in the following paragraph, which is quoted from a baccalaureate address by Arnaud C. Marts, then president of Bucknell University, delivered on June 7, 1936, at least seven of these emotional drives are woven together into a moving plea for loyalty to the Church. Doctor Marts does not, of course, label his pleas or state them baldly, but so phrases them that, to borrow his own words, the emotional power of his message "silently and subconsciously infiltrates into the minds and thoughts of those who attend."

But with all its imperfections, the Church is the Community at its very best. There, if anywhere, may be found the fine-grained persons of the land, the persons whose eyes have looked beyond the moment into the unseen and eternal values. And though the voice of the minister may, at times, seem uninspired and uninspiring, we often hear the overtones of another voice, the voice of humanity and righteousness, speaking its silent message to the souls of those who can hear. The music may not always be the finest, but now and then a divine melody sings its way into the hearts of youths as they sit in the humble church pews and, like a siren, lures them out to do valiant battle for civilization. The Kingdom of Heaven is like unto a leaven. The leaven silently and subconsciously infiltrates into the minds and wills of those who attend church, uplifts them and motivates them to serve and bless the world.

Functions of emotional appeals

In persuasive speaking, there are three distinct functions that may be served by emotional appeals. The first is *to disarm the audience,* to remove its barriers of suspicion and possible hostility, to make it willing to listen. The most familiar means of doing this is by the use of humor. Laughter is a gentle and effective means of shaking an audience into a receptive attitude. It creates a bridge of good fellowship over which the later persuasive appeals may march. Similarly disarming may be a frank request for fair consideration, such as Henry Ward Beecher addressed to his hostile auditors at Liverpool; a veiled appeal for sympathy, such as was used by Fisher Ames when he told his Congressional colleagues that he had come from a sickbed, against his doctor's orders, to address them; or by a statement that the speaker's proposal is really against his own best interests and is presented only from a sense of duty and a desire to serve. By these four means speakers from time immemorial have sought to disarm audiences and render them susceptible to persuasion.

The second function of emotion is *to create a general mood* that will provide a proper atmosphere for the speaker's plea. If the speaker proposes to win his audience's support for a drive to aid the community's unemployed, and he finds his auditors in a mood of frivolous hilarity, his first endeavor must be to win them over to a mood of tender solicitude and sympathy. In order to accomplish this, he will first have to enter into their spirit, establish a bond of common feeling, and then, after they have been disarmed, relate some instances that show the need of human sympathy.

The third function of emotion is *to energize the audience's support* of the speaker's proposal by linking it with the emotional drives that have been discussed. A purely intellectual argument may make the audience say, "Yes, that is true"; but the addition of an emotional plea is needed to make the listeners add, "And let's do something about it!"

Emotional effects on judgment

Emotional appeals have always been somewhat suspect because of the quite proper assumption that they befuddle the hearer's judgment. The effects of emotional excitement upon mental processes are readily observed. Kellogg experimented with a group of subjects by exposing them to such severe emotional shock as suddenly slicing a live mouse in two before them and subsequently testing their muscular steadiness, which he found to be very much affected. Landis, in an elaborate series of tests, submitted twenty-five subjects to a great variety of emotional shocks, including reading descriptions of hideous skin diseases, reading pornographic material, putting their hands in a covered pail filled with ice water and frogs, administering an electric shock, and having a firecracker unexpectedly explode under their chairs. Meanwhile, the subjects took a true-false test and did mental arithmetic. Such tests as these confirm the observation that anyone can readily make of himself and his associates; namely, that our judgment when angry, or disturbed, or anxious is not good. Love is blind—and so are the other emotions. Effective speakers know this—and some profit by it.

Extreme emotionality is the mark of the demagogue, the irresponsible type of evangelist, the high-pressure salesman, the shyster lawyer. The speaker who calls names, exaggerates, and generalizes; who shouts and waves his arms; who perspires and pontificates is doubtless trying to mislead his auditors' minds. They would do well to remember the admission of the Reverend Lyman Beecher: "The less I have to say, the louder I shout." There is truth in the satiric commentary of a newspaper columnist that when a practiced public speaker says, "Beyond the shadow of a doubt—" he is indulging in pure bluff. Empty emotionality is of as little value as emptiness of any other sort.

But without some emotional support, the judgment never acts at all. The only completely emotionless acts we perform are ones that habit has made automatic. William James pointed out that belief is compounded of three factors:

1. The presence of an idea in the mind.
2. Freedom of the mind from inhibiting ideas.
3. Emotional intensity of the idea.

The speaker who wishes to win belief for his proposal must be responsible for establishing each of these factors. The first two are predominately intellectual; the third provides the emotional charge necessary to secure action. It is noteworthy that the great speeches which have endured, the "orations" effective in their own day and cited as models in ours, have a solid body of facts and logic through which the judgment of the auditors is led to the right decision, and it is in the conclusion that the speaker concentrated his emotional plea. The judgment is first pointed in the right direction, then it is propelled and energized emotionally. It is in this type of speech that the mind and the emotions work together as allies.

Humor as an emotional appeal

Humor and the laughter response associated with it clearly are included among the emotions. Humor deserves special note as a type of emotional appeal because of its very considerable utility in persuasive (as well as in entertaining) speaking. The successful persuasive speaker knows how to get his audiences to laugh with him in full-bodied approval of his mood, attitude, or point of view; and to join him in laughing at some object, person, or point of view toward which he wishes to direct scorn.

Humor has been defined in many different ways, probably because it takes varying forms and serves various functions. The persuasive speaker should learn to use it to perform the following basic functions:

To disarm opposition. When the audience thinks the speaker is overly serious, or inclined to be pompous or pretentious, or that he is an "outsider" not yet accepted fully into the group, a judicious use of humor turned against himself may serve the speaker well. It is hard to dislike a man who laughs at his own foibles. Thus a speaker might say, "Your chairman has just described me as an expert. I wish my wife could have been here to hear him pour it on! Now you and I know very well that an expert is only a little squirt a long way from home. It's true I did write a book on this subject once, and I've been plagued ever since by serious-minded people who keep asking me to explain parts of it I can't remember. But what I shall talk to you about tonight might be an additional chapter in it, if I had it to write all over again." In such an example, the speaker succeeds in laughing at himself without surrendering his proper claim to prestige, and the resulting laughter is not accompanied by any loss of respect. But there is likely to be an increase in good will.

Similarly, if the audience is opposed to the proposal, the speaker may well open his talk with humor directed against his own subject. During the period of Harding-Coolidge-and-Hoover occupancy of the White House, for instance, Will Rogers alternated his appeals on behalf of the Democrats with quips about their being "hungry," "forlorn," and "eager to get their own noses in the public trough." Once again, it is hard to feel strong antagonism against a proposal while you are bubbling with friendly laughter about it.

To develop antagonism. Many a persuasive speech is designed to build up audience opposition toward intolerance or selfishness or a particular program such as communist aggression in Asia. Humor has a role to play in this respect, too. As J. C. Gregory has said in his book, *The Nature of Laughter,* "The triumphant laugh of aggressive or satirical wit has an echo of war, and scorn or contempt or superiority may tinge laughter." Thus a speaker defending the free enterprise system may direct a laugh against his opponents by saying, "We all despise tainted money. But my observation is that most people who despise it loudest do so because it taint theirs!" From Aristophanes through Cervantes and Swift to Thurber and E. B. White, writers have used satiric laughter to attack what they regard as evils. Lincoln's whiplash scorn of Douglas for declaring he could not oppose slavery without favoring interracial marriage has previously been quoted. In one of his 1944 campaign speeches, President Roosevelt laughed the Republicans to scorn for their insinuations against his dog Fala. In both the 1952 and 1956 presidential campaigns, Adlai Stevenson effectively used humor as a persuasive weapon with which to attack his opponents.

To develop group unity. Humor is essentially *social.* When we hear a joke, we immediately want to tell it to others. When we enjoy a joke in an audience situation, we tend to turn to our fellows and share our enjoyment with them. Humor unites an audience and creates a warm bond of good-fellowship. Laughing together has a pronounced unifying influence. Once again to cite Lincoln, it was one of his common practices to relieve the tension created by disharmony in his cabinet meetings by telling jokes. Harry Truman's surprising victory in the presidential campaign of 1948 was preceded by a "whistle-stop" tour of the country, where from auditorium platforms and on the rear end of the train he joked and quipped, sometimes gently and often bitingly, about his relations with "the worst Congress in American history." By his personalized, wise-cracking campaign, the dispirited, divided, and hopeless Democratic majority was once more welded into a victoriously united party.

To energize support. Many a serious speech is remembered primarily for its few humorous stories. If the speaker is wise, these stories carry within themselves the main point he wishes to establish. And the mere fact of their being *remembered* keeps the point in the audience's minds and thus increases the likelihood that it will have a lasting influence. This is one way in which humor *energizes* support. Another way is through the resulting increase in audience unity, with the tendency for the audience to go from the meeting ready to *work together* for the speaker's proposal. Likewise, if humor has developed antagonism toward the speaker's opponents, a direct result is the consequent increase of support for the speaker and his cause.

Franklin Roosevelt used humor to energize support when he addressed the Young Democrats at Baltimore in the campaign of 1936. "Flaming youth has become a flaming question," he told them, and went on:

> Many older people seem to take unmerited pride in the mere fact that they are adults. When youth comes crashing in on them with enthusiasm and ideals, they put on their most patronizing smiles, and pat the young man or young woman on the shoulder, and in a worldly wise sort of way send them out with what they call their blessing. But—as every young person knows—that is not a blessing; it is a cold shower.

With the spirit of camaraderie created through such "folksy" talk, Roosevelt was able to whip up the kind of enthusiastic support that carried him back into the White House (to borrow one of his expressions) again, and again, and again. Humor rightly used becomes fuel to stoke the flames of ardor and to insure unity and vigor in carrying on a fight.

Polarizing the audience

When individuals are crowded together, as they are in a large audience, each one becomes relatively anonymous and insignificant. He loses something of the sense of his own identity and willingly feels himself a part of a huge organism. His inhibitions are weakened, as he yields his responsibility to the crowd. He is sensitive to the reactions of his fellows and willingly joins in with them. As a consequence, crowds tend to act as units, to go to extremes in their emotional expressions, to subordinate their judgments even more readily than do individuals to their emotions. They become childlike as they find a common denominator in their basic emotions, rather than in their higher mental processes. As Emerson wisely observed, "Our minds descend to meet." Crowds are less discriminative than individuals, more impatient, freer in their expressions of favor and disfavor, more amenable to command and leadership.

A crowd has been defined as "a mass of individuals with their intellects turned off." Such an audience may be found at a national political convention. It will cheer or boo its speakers, but will not remain indifferent to them. It demands of its speakers that they surrender their discrimination, their balanced judgment, their tolerance, their logical analyses; it demands humor, satire, an opponent to be attacked, dogmatism, and highly flavored emotionalism. Given this, it in turn will surrender its judgment to the speaker and roar for his proposal.

An audience may be said to be "polarized" when it is subject to a high degree to a unified emotional response. Every audience can be classified on a scale of polarization (as was done in Chapter 4), and it is extremely useful for a persuasive speaker to evaluate his audiences on this scale. The degree and kind of polarization of his audience are strong indications to the persuasive speaker of where and how his task of persuasion must begin and of the methods he should employ. The following factors should be considered:

1. Is the audience already polarized (i.e., emotionally unified) or are the feelings of the audience unaroused, unrelated to one another, and unorganized in relation to the subject to be discussed? A lynch mob dragging some wretch out to be hanged is highly polarized; casual passers-by on a street corner where a speaker is trying to attract their attention are unpolarized. Normal audiences vary in a wide range between these extremes. If an audience gathers with a relatively clear sense of purpose, if it is homogeneous, and if it is organized in relation to the topic (such as a church group gathered for a religious service, or a political convention gathered to nominate a candidate), the degree of polarization will be relatively high. If an audience is composed of individuals who have been required to attend (as for a compulsory high school assembly); is relatively unhomogeneous (as in a community meeting of rabid partisans representing widely different views on the problem that brought them together—such as Negroes and white people, old and young, educated and uneducated, native Americans and recent immigrants, all meeting together to decide on what kind of recreational program should be adopted), and is unorganized, the polarization will be nonexistent or very small.

2. Is the polarization directed toward or away from the speaker's proposal? Can the speaker expect to ride upon the crest of a wave of pre-existing feeling, or must he attempt to oppose the flood?

Considering these same factors from a somewhat different point of view, the speaker may ask himself the following questions about a prospective audience:

1. Will the group have any definite feelings of any kind about my proposal?
2. Will the feelings be strong or weak?
3. Will the audience all feel similarly, or will there be wide differences?
4. Will the feelings be favorable toward the proposal or unfavorable?

When the speaker confronts an audience that has little feeling of any kind toward his proposal, when the feelings may be strong but are of wide variations, or when there is a tide of feeling against what he represents, he will himself have to: (1) exhibit little emotion of any kind in the beginning; or (2) find an emotional basis (such as humor or antagonism against some common foe or enthusiasm for some common loyalty) in which all the auditors can and readily will join.

Methods of inducing polarization that the speaker may utilize include the following:

1. Have the auditors sit close together, thus enhancing the feeling of commonality;
2. Get the audience to engage in uninhibited overt activity, such as laughing, standing, cheering, or applauding together;
3. Ask the audience to join in a common ritual, such as singing, pledging allegiance to the flag, or repeating a prayer;
4. Display freely such unifying symbols as the flag, pictures of a revered leader, the cross, the elephant, or the donkey;
5. Stress the uniformity of feeling among the auditors with such terms as, "Everyone here is aware...," "I am sure we all know...," etc.; and
6. Heighten these feelings by appeals to common ground and assertions that will secure a "yes response."

Types of emotional appeals

Within the boundaries of these considerations, the following types of emotional appeals may be recommended as generally helpful in persuasive speeches:

1. Appeals to feelings, attitudes, and beliefs that represent majority opinion. Many studies have demonstrated that, on matters of general conduct, individuals tend to be more strongly influenced by prevailing public opinion than by expert testimony or logical reasoning. "What everybody believes must be so" is a widespread feeling.

2. Appeals to traditional, long-established teachings. Even when the current of public opinion is running strong, it can often be countered successfully by urgent reminders that the teachings of religion, or the experience of the nation, is to a contrary effect. Thus, "everyone may believe" that a particular set of beliefs should be outlawed—but an audience may be persuaded to contrary judgment by a reminder that our nation has grown on a philosophy of tolerance, and that evil has always resulted when this principle was forgotten.

3. Appeals to self-interest and to unselfish brotherhood—either separately or, much better, in combination. "Our property values will be increased and this will be a better community for all who live in it" is often a potent kind of appeal. It may be that people act according to the first appeal, but like to think they act according to the second; and it may be that the desire to be helpful is also fundamental enough to be a real motive to action. In any event, when the two are combined, they unquestionably are very strong.

4. Appeals to popularity and unity with the group. The tendency of millions of people (men as well as women) to change their clothing to conform to changing styles is one evidence of the strength of this appeal. Conformity is praised as meaning loyalty and co-operativeness, and it is rewarded with group approval and the security that comes from being one of the crowd. The persuasive speaker gains a reservoir of emotional strength for his proposal when he represents it as being, in effect, what most of the group really wants.

In each of these types of emotional appeals, it should be re-emphasized, the speaker must take care to phrase his speech in terms of the prevailing situation in which he appears. Failure to do this will weaken persuasiveness regardless of how solidly the appeals seem to rest upon "basic and universal drives."

Using emotional appeals

Several indications already have been given of how emotional appeals should be used. It is perhaps only necessary to add that unless they are a sincere expression of the speaker's own feelings, they will not ring true. Emotion is, remember, as much physiological as mental. It expresses itself not only through carefully chosen words and a planned use of ritual and group action, but also through the posture and movements of the speaker's body, through the tension of his muscles, through the vibrant quality of his voice. A speaker cannot "use" emotion in the same sense in which he can use statistics or an illustrative story. He must himself feel before he can get an audience to feel. For every speech there must be an emotional as well as an intellectual preparation.

The eminent Chautauqua lecturer, George W. Bain, declared that if he were to speak on poverty, he would take care to approach the meeting place by way of the slums, so that his heart as well as his mind would be prepared. The speaker must not only know his facts; he must live them. His statistics should not be figures, but human instances. If he speaks of a battlefield, he should sense its blood, and filth, and suffering; if he speaks of the "dawn of a new day," he should see its security, freedom, and peace. Facts may be drawn from any almanac, but we can never speak emotionally except from the depths of our own sympathetic insight.

No speaker can "use" emotion in the sense that he might use statistics or an authoritative quotation. Emotion is part and parcel of his personality, his choice of materials, his language, his bearing, his voice, and his relations with the group. Each of these factors should be considered.

Personality. Individuals who are "overcome by their emotions" may have a kind of limited effectiveness. Auditors may respond deeply to the extreme grief of a mother who has just seen her son killed in an automobile accident. But such individuals have little opportunity to control or direct the responses of the audience. A persuasive speaker should feel what he is transmitting and that fact should be evident to his audience; but his feelings should be under full control. The persuasive effect of understatement is well known. If, however, the "control" seems to be actually a lack of feeling, the audience will more likely react against the speaker than with or for his proposal. As Emerson wisely said, "What you are stands over you and thunders so loud I cannot hear what you say." We react to speakers perhaps even more than we do to their messages.

Choice of materials. Personalized instances generally have a more emotional effect upon audiences than depersonalized statistics or objective facts. In all our discussion of emotion we have stressed the element of personal involvement. We respond to a situation emotionally not in terms of what it means, but in terms of what it means to us. This being true, the persuasive speaker should choose his materials to illustrate ways in which the audience is related to the subject, either directly or through the audience's own beliefs and ideals.

Language. De Quincey pointed out that there is a "literature of knowledge" and a "literature of power." There is language that simply conveys information—such as the statement that "This room is twelve feet square," and there is language that suggests reactions—such as "This room is just the right size for concentrated work." Stylists have pointed to the utility of "loaded words" in arousing emotion: such terms as gluttonous, bestial, peaceful, self-sacrificing—and all others that *both convey a concept and suggest an attitude toward it.* As was pointed out in a preceding chapter, Churchill's phrase, "blood, toil, tears and sweat," had a persuasive effect simply through the language used. Overemphasis upon a conversational, colloquial style is destructive to this deep-seated source of persuasive power. Triteness and flatulence in style may well ruin a speech that contains other ingredients of high persuasive effectiveness.

Bearing. The relation of posture and gesture to emotional appeal has been well illustrated by psychologists who present pictures of individuals to groups and ask for responses based wholly on the pictures. Strong and relatively uniform emotional reactions are secured to pictures of individuals frowning, leering, smiling, yawning, etc. A speaker who shuffles onto the platform, picks nervously at his clothing, scratches his nose, and looks vacantly out the window will convey an impression difficult to correlate with his claim to leadership in establishing his proposal. Confidence and ease convey one type of emotionalism; controlled tension and deep feeling another. If a speaker has learned and mastered ordinary platform behavior and then feels deeply what he is trying to convey, his bearing should ordinarily help in conveying it.

Comparative effects of emotion and logic

In view of the importance of determining what kinds of persuasion are of greatest effectiveness, it is not surprising that various attempts have been made to discover experimental evidence on the question. Four such studies are worthy of note, both because of their results and to provide descriptions of their methodology.

1. COLLINS

The first study was made by G. Rowland Collins in 1924. He wrote four speeches urging the advantages of the "Open Shop" as an industrial policy, and had the speeches read to an audience of 277 students in a class in Marketing at New York University. Neither the reader nor the audience knew the nature of the experiment. The first speech consisted entirely of emotional appeals. The second speech consisted entirely of logical argument. Speech number three consisted of brief emotional appeals intermingled with logical arguments. Speech number four consisted of a logical argument capped with an extended emotional conclusion. Following the readings, the auditors were asked to vote as to which speech had been most influential in affecting their opinion of the "Open Shop." The third speech was preferred by 118 auditors, the first by 99, the fourth by 32, and the second by 28. This was a victory for the intermingled emotional and reasoning appeals, with the completely emotional speech a close second in audience favor.

2. MENEFEE AND GRANNEBERG

In 1940, a similar study was conducted at the University of Washington by Seldon C. Menefee and Audrey G. Granneberg. They prepared four speeches, two of which were strictly emotional and two strictly logical. One emotional and one logical speech were in favor of an isolationist policy for the United States, the others for a policy of collective security. The speeches were submitted to the judgments of ten faculty members, who agreed that they represented both the viewpoint and the type of appeal described for each one. Audiences were secured by dividing 331 students of introductory sociology into four groups, ranging in number from 78 to 86 persons. To group *A* was presented the emotional appeal for isolation; to group *B* the logical appeal for isolation; to group *C* the emotional appeal for collective security; and to group *D* the logical appeal for collective security. A subsequent questionnaire study of the groups of auditors revealed that, in the opinion of the experimenters, "Emotional propaganda was much more effective in changing student opinion regarding our foreign policy than was logical argumentation." So conclusive were the results that "the probability of getting a difference as large or larger than this by pure chance would be only 17 in 10,000."

3. MILLSON

An experiment conducted by Howard Millson in 1932 offers some evidence concerning the relative effectiveness of logic and emotion, although it was not designed specifically to differentiate the two. Millson worked with four debaters, composing affirmative and negative teams, who debated the question of compulsory unemployment insurance before a total of twenty audiences comprising 937 auditors, including college students and members of the Pythian Lodge. In all the debates the negative team used the typical conversational mode of presentation, which Millson described as offering a "nice adjustment of Argument and Persuasion"; that is, an intermingling of logic and emotion. The affirmative team prepared and memorized three different types of speeches. One, the conversational mode, it used once; another, the academic mode, which was primarily logical, it used twice; and the third, the exhibitory mode, which was predominantly emotional, it used twice. Audiences were questioned as to their attitudes toward compulsory unemployment insurance both before and after the debates, to determine to what extent their opinions were influenced by the speeches. Millson found that when the affirmative used either the conversational or the academic mode the shift of audience opinion was distinctly toward the negative, but that when the affirmative used the exhibitory (that is, the emotional) speeches, the shift of audience opinion was in the affirmative direction. Hence, this study substantiates the other two in indicating the superior influence of emotional speaking.

4. KNOWER

The remaining study, conducted by Franklin H. Knower, was the most carefully controlled of them all, and the results are less decisive. Knower sought experimental answers to eight questions, of which the one that bears most directly upon the problem of this chapter he stated thus: "Is an attitude more markedly changed by an argument which is predominantly factual and logical or one which is predominantly emotional?" To secure the answer, he chose as an issue the prohibition question, which at the time of his study (in 1931-32) was a very live problem. He took material from actual speeches, magazine articles, pamphlets, and books that had been written by wet and dry enthusiasts, and from this material he prepared four speeches, of which there was one emotional and one logical speech on each side of the question. He submitted the speeches to ten university teachers of speech, who confirmed his judgment that they actually represented the point of view and type of appeal described. Eight speech students, four men and four women, were selected to memorize and deliver the speeches. The audiences comprised a total of 607 speech students, who were divided into wet and dry groups as the result of their records on the Smith and Thurstone "Attitude toward Prohibition" test. Half of each group was then given an emotional speech and the other half a logical speech in an attempt to change their views. Following the speeches, each group was immediately retested on the Smith and Thurstone scale; and again, after an interval of from two to six weeks, they were once more given the test to see if the appeals had a lasting effect. A control group of 300 students was given the tests, but did not hear the speeches, in order to check on the chance changes of opinion.

Knower discovered that persuasive speaking does indeed have an effect. "About 25 per cent of the members of the experimental groups made a significant change in the direction of the argument," he found, "whereas the change in the control group was significant in less than 5 per cent of the cases." As for the comparative effects of logic and emotion, he concluded that "Although these college students would no doubt have denied that they could be swayed by an emotional appeal, the data show that on the whole approximately as many were swayed by one type of argument as by the other."

Conclusion

Emotion is a powerful and pervasive component of human living. We *feel* perhaps more than we *think,* though it is difficult and artificial to make the distinction, since the two reactions are commonly closely interwoven. In persuasive speeches, where a speaker is attempting to change the feelings, beliefs, or action of his audience, carefully directed emotional appeals are indispensable to success.

In this chapter the nature of emotions, their effects, and the ways in which they occur have been considered. It has been noted that a speaker cannot address a group without expressing emotion. There is no choice as to whether or not to be emotional as speakers; there is only the necessity of controlling and guiding our own emotions as speakers and appealing with insight to those emotions of the auditors that may help to win support for our proposals. It has been seen: (1) that emotion is a basic factor in human beings; (2) that emotion consists of perception of a situation, resulting in bodily stimulation, that may be interpreted as pleasant or unpleasant; (3) that emotions are always personalized, tend to persist, extend to contiguous objects, tend to express themselves in action, and are relatively similar among all normal individuals; (4) that the degree and depth of emotional unity, or "polarization," of the audience is a vital factor in persuasive speaking; (5) that emotional appeals must be based upon the common feelings existing in the particular speech situation; (6) that emotional effects are produced through the speaker's personality, choice of materials, language, bearing, voice, and relations with his audience; (7) that emotion serves the twofold function of energizing support and disarming opposition; and (8) that humor is one of the types of emotional appeals having a widespread and genuine persuasive utility.

None of this constitutes a precise formula for "using" emotion, but the speaker should profit from realizing the pervasive emotional effects in his whole pattern of dealing with the people to whom he talks.

Exercises

1. Try to list five important decisions you must make concerning which you can be wholly unemotional. Is it difficult—or impossible? Do you find yourself more emotionally aroused about a problem the more you are personally implicated in it? What does this suggest about the desirability of utilizing emotion in persuasive speech?

2. Think of two individuals—friends, acquaintances, or prominent public figures—whom you admire very much, one of whom seems very emotional, the other almost wholly unemotional. As you analyze the latter, do you find that he, too, is actually deeply emotional, though in a more restrained manner? Can you readily think of anyone who has qualities that arouse admiration who is not also prone to some type of emotionality? What does this line of consideration suggest about the nature of the persuasive speaker?

3. List two proposals concerning which you feel deeply, and two others of importance to you and your classroom audience about which you might be less emotional. In reality, if the latter two proposals also are important, can you (or should you) discuss them without emotion? What does this suggest concerning the emotional substance of the persuasive speech?

4. Cite instances from speeches that you hear of the three functions of emotion.

5. Discuss from your own experience and observation the effects of emotion upon the judgment.

6. Discuss the value of polarization, the means of effecting it, and the degree desired for each of the following speeches:

    a. A classroom lecture.

    b. A political speech to an unorganized body of voters.

    c. An appeal for contributions to the Red Cross addressed to a Kiwanis club.

    d. A pep talk to a school rally preceding a football game.

    e. An out-of-doors auction of household goods.

    7. How would you employ emotions in a talk to a housewife, trying to sell her a new radio?

    8. Prepare a five-minute persuasive speech that will permit you to make use of two sharply contrasting types of emotional appeal—such as humor and pathos; or repugnance and pleasure; or regret and satisfaction; or dislike and pity. Prepare and deliver the speech, practicing the interweaving or juxtaposition of your two selected emotional appeals.

    9. Prepare and deliver a five-minute persuasive speech in which you seek to build up one dominant emotional pattern, polarizing the audience as fully as you are able to in the brief time.

    10. Prepare and deliver a five-minute speech in which you concentrate your effort on disarming opposition to your proposal through use of humor, demonstration of your own unselfishness, and appeal to the self-interest and philanthropic sentiments of the audience.

    11. For further considerations of the persuasive effects of emotional appeals, the following readings may be consulted:

Aristotle, *Rhetoric,* trans. and ed., Lane Cooper (New York: Appleton, 1932), particularly Book 2.

Walter Coutu, "An Operational Definition of Meaning," *Quarterly Journal of Speech,* 48 (February, 1962), 59-64.

Ernest Dichter, *The Strategy of Desire* (New York: Doubleday, 1960).

Thomas Edward Fingeld, reported by Joseph A. DeVito, Richard Murphy, and Charles E. Osgood, "The Ability to Select Words to Convey Intended Meanings," *Quarterly Journal of Speech,* 52 (October, 1966), 255-258.

W. H. Grimes, "The Mirth Experience in Public Address," *Speech Monographs,* 22 (1955), 243-255.

E. H. Henrikson, "The Relation among Knowing a Person, Liking a Person, and Judging Him as a Speaker," *Speech Monographs,* 7 (1940), 22-25.

E. Katz and P. F. Lazarsfeld, *Personal Influence* (Glencoe, Ill.: The Free Press, 1955).

Franklin H. Knower, "Experimental Studies of Changes of Attitudes," *Journal of Social Psychology,* 6 (August, 1935), 315-345.

————, "The Use of Behavioral and Tonal Symbols as Tests of Speaking Achievement," *Journal of Applied Psychology,* 29 (1945), 229-235.

Irving J. Lee, "Some Conceptions of Emotional Appeal in Rhetorical Theory," *Speech Monographs,* 6 (1939), 66-86.

P. E. Lull, "The Effectiveness of Humor in Persuasive Speeches," *Speech Monographs,* 7 (1940), 26-40.

F. H. Lund, "The Psychology of Belief," *Journal of Abnormal and Social Psychology,* 20 (1925), 63-112 and 174-224.

Gerald R. Miller and Murray A. Hewgill, "Some Recent Research on Fear-Arousing Message Appeals," *Speech Monographs,* 33 (November, 1966), 377-391.

O. L. Penee, "Emotionally Loaded Arguments: Its Effectiveness in Stimulating Recall," *Quarterly Journal of Speech,* 40 (October, 1954), 272-276.

M. L. Reymert (ed.), *Feelings and Emotions* (New York: McGraw-Hill, 1950).

R. C. Ruechelle, "An Experimental Study of Audience Recognition of Emotional and Intellectual Appeals in Persuasion," *Speech Monographs,* 25 (1958), 49-58.

S. Schacter, "Deviation, Rejection, and Communication," *Journal of Abnormal and Social Psychology,* 46 (1951), 190-207.

Maurice R. Stein, Arthur J. Vidich, and David Manning White (eds.), *Identity and Anxiety* (Glencoe, Ill.: The Free Press, 1960).

Lester Thonssen and A. Craig Baird, "Emotion in Speech," in *Speech Criticism* (New York: Ronald Press, 1948), pp. 357-382.

Carl H. Weaver, "Measuring Point of View as a Barrier to Communication," *Journal of Communication,* 7 (Spring, 1957), 5-14.

Edward Weismiller, "Fact and Fancy," *Atlantic Monthly* (October, 1963), pp. 93-95.

Frederic Wickert, "A Test for Personal Goal Values," *Journal of Social Psychology,* 11 (May, 1940), 259-274.

Charles Henry Woolbert, "Persuasion: Principles and Methods," *Quarterly Journal of Speech Education,* V (January, March, May, 1919), 12-25, 110-119, and 211-238.

G. K. Zipf, *Human Behavior and the Principle of Least Effort* (Reading, Mass.: Addison-Wesley, 1949).

Rationalization

EVIDENCE, AUTHORITY, LOGIC, AND EMOTION ARE ALL somewhat more familiar terms than *rationalization,* though it, too, is coming into common usage. Like emotion, rationalization is regarded with suspicion, is not clearly definable, and the methods of utilizing it in persuasive speech are less clear-cut than are the uses of facts and logic. Nevertheless, there is no doubt whatsoever of its great importance in the thinking process. And since a great many of our decisions actually are reached by rationalization, no study of persuasive speech can ignore this type of mental process. We are always in need of being on guard against it; and there may be occasions on which it should be used.

The extent of rationalization

Is this type of thinking done very often? Henshaw Ward, in *Builders of Delusion,* expressed his opinion that "The great body of logical thought has been a passionate defense of opinions that were thoroughly believed before any thinking was done." Dashiell, a representative objective psychologist, found that "strict logic, thoroughly logical reasoning, is exceptional in human life." The philosopher Pareto, in *Mind and Society,* concluded that we act actually because of the needs and mechanisms of behavior, and that one of these needs is to justify our actions with pseudological reasons. There is no question but that rationalization is a widespread habit.

Nor are intelligence and education any bars to it. In fact, the more an individual has learned to respect reason, the more he is apt to invent "reasons" for what he does. Ask a child why he has done something, and the answer is likely to be simply, "Because." But the more sophisticated a person becomes, the less this kind of answer satisfies him. He must go on to concoct an explanation that will sound reasonable. Interesting results have been secured in the study of rationalization by means of hypnosis. A subject under hypnosis will be commanded to perform a given act upon some stated signal. For instance, he will be asked to walk across the room and offer a match to someone when he observes him wiping his glasses. After he has come out of the hypnotic trance and the group is engaged in quiet conversation, the glasses are wiped and the subject immediately jumps up to offer a match. Then, feeling exceedingly foolish, he will hasten to explain that he thought the man with the glasses was reaching for a cigarette.

Reasons for rationalization

The primary function of rationalization is to serve as a defense for our egos. It is used to prevent censure by ourselves or by our associates. A very successful automobile salesman declares that he never sells cars. He simply permits a prospect to buy—and then he gives him some good reasons to justify his purchase in the eyes of his wife, his mother-in-law, and his banker. The salesman realizes that everyone would like to have a new automobile. There is no need of persuading a prospect to do what he already wants to do. But there is need of assuring him of some means of escaping unpleasant consequences for his act. Much practical persuasive speaking actually is pointed squarely toward this purpose: to show the audience that it will be praised rather than blamed for doing what the speaker proposes.

Without rationalization, our egos would be sadly bruised. Every failure would then have to be faced as such. Our shortcomings and inefficiencies would have to be admitted. With rationalization, we live in a world largely of our own contriving. The basketball player who misses a crucial shot at the basket may limp slightly as he walks away from the foul line to suggest that he turned his ankle as he tried for the shot. The man who is ousted from his position may "discover" that his boss has an incurable antipathy to employees with blue eyes. To the student who fails in an examination, the questions were "unfair." To the bridge player who makes an error, the noise of the car that passed by was "distracting." Whatever is done wrong is always due to some factor beyond the individual's control. Without this cushion for our egos to recline upon, life would be far harsher than it is.

Rationalization defined

Rationalization is a device of respectability by which we human beings protect and pamper our egos. It is a process of reasoning designed not to discover or to defend what may be true, but to discover and defend what we should like to represent as true. It is the colored glasses through which we look at reality. It is a preference for "good" reasons instead of "real" reasons for explaining what we have done or failed to do. It is a process of justifying ourselves, our groups, and our beliefs.

In the paragraph above, rationalization was described as "respectable"—because it adopts the form of logical reasoning. Far from flouting reason or denying it, rationalization pays to reasoning the sincere tribute of imitation. As H. L. Hollingworth explained in *The Psychology of the Audience,* "It is not quite true that the average man reasons scarcely at all. On the contrary, he has a passion for argument, and prides himself in it; but he reasons stupidly. He mistakes coincidence for proof, correlation for causality, confidence for necessity, publicity for expertness, and appearance for reality. Habit, suggestion, and imitation constitute his instruments of thinking, as distinguished from his emotional reactions, and his inadequate background of knowledge, coupled with the urgency of his needs, makes him the ready prey of the fakir and the charlatan." As Hollingworth has so specifically indicated, the processes of rationalization parallel those of reason. To most of us in most situations *they appear to be reason.* Since man prides himself upon being a reasoning creature, rationalization could not achieve its primary purpose (the preservation of self-pride) unless it did assume the respectable aspect of seeming to be reasonable. One of the commonest uses of rationalization is denial that it is being used. It can only fulfill its function of *protecting and pampering* the ego when the ego blinds itself to the fact that it is rationalizing.

Dr. Eric Berne, in *The Mind in Action,* gives a psychiatric explanation of what rationalization is:

Conscious decisions are regulated, we like to think, by the Reality Principle and the conscious conscience. Unconscious decisions may be simplified and energy saved by means of habit in the case of actions which have little emotional significance. In most emotional situations, decisions depend on the result of the conflict between the unconscious forces of the Super-ego and the Id. Once the decision has been made without the individual being aware of the real forces behind it, he takes upon himself the task of finding justifications for it and convincing himself and others that it has been made in accordance with the realities of the situation. This is called "rationalization."

In another passage Berne declares, "The problem of a human being is the same as the problem of any energy system, namely to 'find' the path of least resistance for the discharge of tension." This process of finding the path of least resistance or of most comfortable release (rationalization) is vastly different from finding the path of reality (along which the individual might be projected directly away from his own concept of his own well-being). Psychiatrically, then, rationalization consists of "finding justifications" for the "discharge of tension" that has been built up by the discovery of the individual that what he is thinking or doing is in conflict with what is socially approved. In such an instance the individual hastily concocts an "explanation" that will gloss over his real motivation in socially respectable terms. It is by precisely this process, psychiatrists declare, that our sexual and homicidal desires, which assert themselves freely during sleep, are masked in conventionally acceptable dream symbols.

Kimball Young, in *Personality and Problems of Adjustment,* offers a sociopsychological explanation of rationalization.

. . . In social interaction . . . , people soon learn to make excuses or justify their acts to others and to themselves. We call this habitual pattern *rationalization.* It is a means of keeping peace with ourselves and our fellows when our actual but often unconscious desires and their expression, were they fully known, would make us ridiculous, disliked, or even the subject of punishment by those in power. We all seek to justify our behavior. Most of the "reasons" we give ourselves and others are not the genuine causes of our conduct but are the excuses which we imagine will be acceptable to others and, incidentally, to ourselves. The real or genuine reasons are often hidden from us.

It is evident that there is no real conflict of views between the psychiatric and sociopsychological views of rationalization. The former lays great stress upon the "unconscious conflicts" within the individual and the consequent need for self-justification. The latter stresses the need to avoid social conflicts and thinks the "good reasons" are concocted primarily for others and only incidentally for ourselves. But both agree on the protective function of rationalization and on the forms it takes.

Restated, rationalization is self-justification. It is a defensive or protective explanation, clothed in a form sufficiently resembling reasoning to appear respectable. Its whole aim, in fact, is to be "acceptable." It deals with appearances rather than with realities, with what will look good rather than with what is true. Rationalizations are alibis and excuses—often elaborate in form. We are rationalizing when we hide undesirable realities behind a screen of favorable interpretation. "Did you forget the appointment?" "Umm, not exactly, but just before the hour for it I received a very important long-distance telephone call that shifted everything else out of my mind." That is an example of rationalization.

Characteristics of rationalization

How can we know when rationalization occurs—either in our own thinking or in that of others? It may not be possible to tell in each specific instance, but there are certain characteristics of rationalization that help identify it.

1. Rationalization puts a favorable interpretation upon what the speaker or his group does, feels, or believes. We rationalize when we say:

Oh, it's not prejudice! My dislike of women drivers is based on experience!

Of course I always vote a straight ticket. One must be loyal to his party.

Maybe it did cost too much. But then, I got the money easily.

Why, I believe that because it's the only thing decent people can believe.

2. Rationalization is ex post facto thinking or finding reasons to justify an act after it has been performed or a decision after it has been made. The following examples illustrate this tendency:

During your freshman year you "went along with the crowd," took in all the sports and social events, and ended the year on probation. You explained to your parents: "College is a lot different from high school. The professors don't give you any help. The subjects are all new. Classes were too large to permit any discussion. Besides, nobody likes a 'grind' and the social advantages are more important than grades. Grades are artificial, anyway."

A professor who knows nothing about automobiles does know a friendly dealer and buys a car from him. Then he learns about its power brakes, power steering, added safety features, and high trade-in value— so he can explain to his friends why he decided on this particular car.

3. Rationalization is passionate; it is argument with heat. Instead of trying to find *correct* answers, it tries to find answers that *satisfy the needs* of the speaker. Hence, there is an urgent desire to win approval for the precise point of view advocated. We should suspect rationalization (in ourselves or others) in such expressions as:

Of course it's true! No one who knows anything about the subject could doubt it for a minute!

Of all the dumb ideas! Anyone who believes that must go around with his eyes blindfolded!

But I've done it for years. Surely experience means something!

4. Rationalization deals in irrelevancies. Facts, statistics, illustrations, authoritative quotations, and logic may abound, but the "proof" doesn't bear directly upon the proposal. The more skillful the rationalizer is, however, the harder it will be for listeners to detect the lack of logical connection. For instance:

It's easy to see why we have so much divorce in this country. Americans are individualists. Jack Z. Sprat, the well-known marriage counselor, has written, "Divorce is a canker eating away the base of the American home." Statistics show that this generation marries an average of three years later than the previous generation did. I know a couple that married at the age of eighteen and lived together happily for thirty-three years. What we need is more religion, better education, and a higher level of morality. No wonder the American divorce rate is so high!

5. Rationalization imposes stereotyped patterns upon individual events or conditions. This is another use of what Walter Lippmann has called "the pictures in our heads." We look upon each fresh experience through the colored glasses of our own past experience, and through the derived experience of our culture. As Gardner Murphy phrases it, "The actual stuff of which most thinking is made is social stuff." In other words, we see what, in accordance with our education and social customs, we are *supposed to see*. The Southern white man sees the Negro not alone as an individual, but also as an individual who has already been catalogued and labeled by several generations of social judgment. Similarly, most people have a stereotyped "picture in their heads" of politicians, Communists, artists, farmers; and of such experiences as failure, love, war, travel, competition. The stereotype often imposes itself upon the actual perception and dominates it.

6. Rationalization also is self-reinforcing, and hence it tends to perpetuate itself. In the words of Vernon Rank, "Once we have rationalized in a situation, we tend to reinforce the arguments we have used by adding particulars and further embellishment, as if to assure ourselves that what we did was correct, or the only possible and reasonable thing to do." This reinforcement serves as "a justification of the original rationalization, supplying additional selected and corroborating details, the total of which merely makes us more certain that we can fully justify our behavior."

As the foregoing characteristics indicate, rationalization exists because our potentialities far outrun our abilities. It is a bridge linking our primitive past with our ideally intellectual future. Our animalistic residues cause actions which are unacceptable to our humanistic intellect. We can neither forgo the actions nor reconcile ourselves to them. Hence, we find *explanations* that will make these actions seem other than they are. This process of spreading a protective veil of verbalization over the naked fabric of elemental fact is what we mean by rationalization.

Functions of rationalization

A great proportion of education is designed to develop "straight instead of crooked thinking." Granted that individuals find it extremely difficult to think except in terms of self-justification, is it not all the more important to insist as well as we can upon rigorously objective reasoning? Does rationalization have any proper functions that should be recommended? However we might decide such a question ideally, the fact is that a great proportion of our thinking-toward-a-decision is rationalizing (some estimates run as high as 80 and 90 per cent). Obviously such thinking must serve functions that prove useful or it could not persist in such proportion. Some of these useful functions of interest to persuasive speakers are:

1. Rationalization builds morale by protecting bruised or endangered egos. After an organization has experienced a disastrous failure, perhaps through the fault of its members, its continued existence may depend upon masking the extent and cause of the failure. Many a football coach, for instance, has found that he must fabricate excuses for his players if they have lost a series of games, in order to build up their spirits so they can face the rest of their schedule with courage and determination. Hence, he will explain to them that their schedule is unusually tough, that they have been plagued with injuries, that they have had a lot of "tough breaks," and that by the "law of compensation" they can expect better luck in the future. Similarly, supervisors have learned that inexperienced employees need special encouragement till they have mastered their jobs. Teachers have discovered that praise is often a better motivator for their students than blame. Many such devices of rationalization are indispensable if the spirit of "try, try again" is to be stimulated.

2. Rationalization may be necessary with a particular audience if it is to be motivated at all. As Walter Dill Scott, student of persua-

sive techniques and long-time president of Northwestern University, wrote: "The orator who has welded his audience into a homogeneous crowd should never be guilty of attempting to reason with them, for by the very process of forming them into a crowd, he has deprived them of the power of critical thinking. He should affirm reasonable things and affirm conclusions which he has come to by processes of reasoning, but he should not presume to conduct the crowd through such a process." If it be argued that a speaker should not reduce his auditors to an "unthinking crowd," we can only remind ourselves that many experts insist "strict logic . . . is exceptional in human life" even under the calmest and most favorable of circumstances. If in many situations it is simply true that audiences *cannot* follow logical reasoning—and may be too sophisticated or alert to yield to emotional pleas— then the speaker has but one of two choices: (1) to attempt to achieve his desired result (which may, of course, be a thoroughly admirable one) by rationalization, or else (2) abandon his purpose as hopeless.

In time of crisis, such as war, a severe depression, or a dangerous epidemic, there may be only two alternatives: either to surrender to the danger with consequent destruction of the existing society, or for some leaders who know how to deal with the threat to organize society to oppose it by the kinds of specious reasoning that will produce the desired effect. Of course there is ethical danger in such a conclusion, but the remedy seems to be to find the means of rendering human beings more logical, rather than to condemn or proscribe the means by which united action may be secured.

3. Rationalization saves much suffering, conflict, and unpleasantness by masking selfish or unsavory motives. The hallowed term *love,* for instance, confers eminent respectability upon sexual urges that would be distasteful if discussed in other more "scientific" terms. It might be argued that no individual ever acts unselfishly; yet even those who so believe, and who consequently must label such terms as *neighborliness, charity, generosity, courage,* and *helpfulness* as rationalizations must see a great social usefulness in the employment of these labels. If human motives are basically self-centered, there nevertheless is a value in attempting to direct them toward socially desirable ends

by justifying them with whatever rationalization may prove beneficial. To cite an example, if a banker is determined to foreclose the mortgages on a group of farms, it might be highly desirable to help him rationalize a belief that his own business would benefit, and his standing in the community be preserved, if the foreclosures could be avoided by agreeing to easier terms of payment, which, of course, he would do "to help the tenants."

4. Rationalization makes it possible to think in broad terms and to deal with a complicated world. It is impossible for any individual to know a fraction of the facts that are necessary in dealing with our civilization. We have to think in stereotypes, labeling one nation as aggressive, one political party as conservative, one set of dogmas as progressive, one religion as satisfying, and so forth. To attempt to go through a single day performing no acts or thinking no thoughts except upon the basis of full information and rigorously logical thinking is utterly impossible. We accept and act upon broad generalizations that (so far as we know) have no validity except that "everyone" believes them or some newspaper reports them. Whether or not the United States should aid financially in the industrialization of Southern Asia is a complicated question with almost infinite facts to be correlated before a "true" answer could emerge. Many of these facts cannot be known till some future date when any action would be too late. Even the presently existing facts are so diverse that not even the experts can consider them all. Hence, we have to make some kind of decision upon the basis of a "calculated risk," and then pursue it even though we may not understand very clearly to what result it may lead. On a more limited and personal plane, each individual has to reach many decisions (such as what vocation to pursue) involving a great many unknown and unknowable factors. In such a world, we can act with confidence—if, indeed, we can act at all—only as we indulge in a rationalistic process of lulling ourselves into the delusion that we really do know what we are doing and why.

Detecting rationalization

One of the reasons for studying persuasion, of course, is to improve your ability to defend your own judgment against persuasive appeals that are not logically and factually sound. In this era of international propaganda and of domestic "high pressure" salesmanship and political demagoguery, it is well to understand that many logical fallacies are presented to entrap the unwary. They include irrelevant analogies, illustrations, facts, or arguments; name calling, ridicule, and sarcasm; the citation of unreliable authorities; and obscurity parading as profound thinking. Other familiar forms include the argument that a contention is true because everyone believes it, or because it is old, or because it is new, or because it is scientific, or because no one can prove it to be false, or because it would be unpleasant not to think it true, or because it is associated with contentions that are true, or because the speaker believes it to be true.

It is not always easy to identify rationalization when it is used, for it presents itself in the form of reasoned argument. It may consist of evidence which is sound enough (but irrelevant) and of chains of inferences which are false only in their major premise. Hence, rationalization may appear to be good sound reasoning unless examined against the full background of facts. Generally, however, it gives itself away by revealing its inherent characteristics of intellectual form added to passionate, defensive, and *post hoc* content. In the following brief extract from a speech by a United States representative, delivered on May 1, 1936, see how many kinds of rationalization you can identify:

Under the "brain trust" policy of promoting scarcity in a hungry land, our bread lines have lengthened, our relief rolls have expanded, and the unemployed wearily walking our city streets have increased to the terrifying total of over 12,600,000.

Is it any wonder that you are today so heavily burdened with taxes, is it surprising that the prices for the necessities of life are so high, when, for instance, millions of your American dollars are spent to provide seed for farmers, and then you are taxed to provide funds to pay the farmer for not sowing all of it? Next you are taxed to pay the farmer for plowing under his planted crops, thus wasting whatever money was used for seed, and then you are compelled to pay extravagant prices for food because your money helped the farmer to create a shortage. Finally, you are taxed to buy imported foodstuffs—simply because our own farmers have not been permitted to produce sufficient for our needs.

That is what is known as "brain trust" intelligence. That is planned economy substituted by the Democratic administration at Washington for the economy of nature and the plan of Nature's God. It somehow never seems to occur to the New Dealers that the attempt to alleviate hunger by the destruction of crops is tantamount to the folly of seeking to fatten a calf by reducing its food supply.

Now add to this the morally and politically indefensible policy which, on the one hand, takes millions from you in taxes to pay for making land less fruitful, and, on the other, squanders additional millions for irrigation projects intended to make the land more productive and you have a fairly vivid panorama of the antics of the Democratic New Dealers in their endeavor to arrogate to themselves the functions of divinity.

Uses of rationalization in persuasion

Out of the consideration of the nature, characteristics, and functions of rationalization there emerge some indications of the uses of rationalization in persuasive speaking. These may be enumerated as follows:

1. To secure unity and coherence in a group by providing a set of stereotypes, goals, or motivations that all or most will accept.

2. To undermine or refute opposing doctrines that the audience may not clearly understand and so can only be led to oppose by rationalistic reasoning that will have, for them, the appearance of reality and justification.

3. To enhance the morale and determination of a group by presenting their motives, goals, and ideals in a favorable light.

4. To secure acceptance for a speaker's proposal by picturing it in terms of the kind of motivation that actually appeals to his audience under whatever circumstances exist when he speaks to them.

5. To explain the failure of a program in a manner that will win support for another effort to carry it to completion.

6. To justify a decision or an action in order to organize support behind it.

7. To minimize disagreement within the group by pointing out that while everyone has the right to his own opinion, loyalty to the common purpose demands the sacrifice of individual preferences for the good of the whole.

Methods of rationalization in persuasion

The following catalogue of methods of rationalization has a dual usefulness. It may aid the persuasive speaker to rationalize effectively when he has to. And it serves as a partial checklist by which as listeners we can detect more surely when rationalization is being used upon us. Such a list cannot possibly be complete, for the methods of rationalization are almost endless. Descartes, a close disciple of rigorous reasoning, decided that every single hypothesis upon which he might try to erect a structure of valid logic must itself be *assumed* rather than proved (and thus lead inevitably to rationalization) except one: *cogito, ergo sum*—"I think, therefore [as a thinking organism] I exist." The history of science is a series of discoveries that previous reasoning has been based on false premises: thus Aristotelian physics yielded to Newtonian physics, and that in turn to the Einsteinian hypotheses. Science considered the world flat for more of our historic era than it has been considered round. Thus it has been in every field of man's endeavor. The truth we have today is considered true because it is what we do have today—but tomorrow it, too, may be cast aside. "All is vanity," sighed the ancient author of Ecclesiastes. "What is truth?" inquired Pilate, and none may say for sure. Some have attempted to answer, "Truth is what works," but burning witches "worked" for many years, and so did the belief in the flatness of the world. To attempt a complete catalogue of devices of rationalization might require a long book. But some of the more obvious methods may be cited.[1]

1. *Affirming the consequent.* If anyone declared, "*X* is true because *X* is true," nobody would accept his statement as being logical. But when he says, "If *Y* is true, *X* is true. *Y* is true. Therefore, *X* is

[1] This same list appeared in my first book, *Training for Effective Speech*, 1939, and is repeated in *The New Training for Effective Speech*, 1946, rev. 1950.

true," it sounds sufficiently logical to be widely accepted. "If you win money at the race track, your rabbit's foot must be lucky. You do win money at the race track. Therefore, your rabbit's foot is lucky!"

2. *Argument based on sympathy.* This consists of an appeal to sympathy, thinly veiled as argument. "I could not get my assignment because I was sick. Therefore, I should not be given a low grade." "Think of the unemployed men, the hopeless women, the under-nourished children, the families without homes. The industrial system responsible for these conditions must be destroyed."

3. *Argument by applying labels.* President Harry Truman, in a speech on September 4, 1949, said: "Last November the people gave the selfish interests the surprise of their lives. The people just didn't believe that programs designed to assure them decent housing, adequate wages, improved medical care and better education were 'socialism' or 'regimentation.' So the selfish interests retired to a back room with their high-priced advertising experts and thought things over. They decided that the old set of scare words had become a little mildewed. Maybe it was time for a change. So they came up with a new set of scare words. Now they're talking about 'collectivism,' 'statism,' and the 'welfare state.' " President Truman's cogent remarks explain well what is meant by "argument by applying labels"—but perhaps he should note that "selfish interests" and "high-priced advertising experts" belong in the same category. Rationalization is hard to avoid!

4. *Argument from antiquity.* This is an appeal to age. "The old-time religion (or economic or political systems) is good enough for me." "Our ancestors got along under this system and I guess we can, too." "We've always done it that way!"

5. *Argument from ignorance.* This is an assertion that your argument is proved by the fact that it cannot be refuted. "No one can successfully disprove the possibility of communicating with the spirits of the dead. There is not an iota of direct evidence that such communication is impossible. Who, then, dares to challenge my claim that it can be done!"

6. *Argument from novelty.* This is an appeal to recency or newness. "The latest theory, you know, shows a different point of view." "Your idea is old-fashioned; it goes back to the horse and buggy days. Mine is in accord with the newest theories."

7. *Argument from popularity.* "Fifty million Frenchmen can't be wrong!" "Buy the car that leads the field!" "More people smoke Cuties than any other cigarette."

8. *Argumentum ad hominem.* This is a transference of the argument from principles to personalities. "So, he is advocating a new road building program? That sounds like the kind of plan he would come out with! He has proved to be the most spendthrift Governor the state ever had." "How can the 'Prisoner of Chillon' be a good poem? Everyone knows how Byron lived!"

9. *Being sufficiently obscure to sound convincing.* H. L. Hollingworth calls this "depending upon the impressiveness of words." Glittering rhetoric has often proved an effective substitute for sound argument. Thus T. V. Smith, then a leading Congressman, said in August, 1937 (probably with his tongue in his cheek): "Democratic freedom means the general agreement to stay out of each other's light by respecting privacy for the sake of perfection and to humanize power by compounding that of each into the mutual catharsis furnished by compromise of interests. Here is the only social pathway to individuality." Who could deny the contention of a speaker who is so colloquially simple in the beginning and conclusion of his statement, and so nearly incomprehensible in its middle!

10. *Presentation of popularity as expertness.* This method is used not only in advertisements citing the opinions of movie stars, baseball players, and mountain climbers about tobacco, automobiles, and whiskey, but also in speeches citing the authority of Abraham Lincoln, Thomas Jefferson, and Andrew Jackson concerning industrial, social, and international problems of our time.

11. *Confusion of correlation with proof.* Because two things happen together or in immediate succession, it is assumed that one is the cause and the other the effect. "He has never lost a game while wearing his mother's wedding ring. It brings him luck." To say that "He

went to college and became a radical" does not demonstrate any causal relationship between the two facts; yet much rationalization of this sort passes muster as proof.

12. *Explanation intended to confuse or mislead.* This is the device of spreading a film of words over a situation to avoid the embarrassment of making a direct answer. Thus, in *The Confidence Man,* Herman Melville represents a character in the days just before the Civil War, concealing while seeming to explain his views on slavery:

> "If by abolitionist you mean a zealot," said the herb-doctor, "I am none; but if you mean a man, who, being a man, feels for all men, slaves included, and by any lawful act, opposed to nobody's interest, and therefore rousing nobody's enmity, would willingly abolish suffering (supposing it, in its degree, to exist) from among mankind, irrespective of color, then am I what you say."

13. *Use of irrelevant analogies, illustrations, facts, or arguments.* A speech may sometimes be very convincing because of the great quantity of specific examples, facts, and closely knit arguments that are used, when, as a matter of fact, they are irrelevant to the point that is being made. Notice, for instance, how one speaker "refuted" the contention that the sale of loss-leaders by chain stores was harmful to small retailers: ". . . the Census tells the essential truth. In 1929, there were 96,900 stores in Illinois; in 1933, shortly after the bottom of the worst depression in modern history, they numbered 98,870; and in 1935 they totalled 95,528." These figures, of course, do not reveal the vital information on the number of failures, replaced by new owners; nor do they show the effects on sales and profits of competition against the loss-leader method. Or note how the illustration-used-as-an-argument in the following advertisement neatly side-steps a discussion of whether *you* will profit from the course: "Enroll in our short story writing course and earn big money! Last week one of our students sold a short story for $100. Signing your name on our enrollment blank is like signing a blank check. You can fill in the figures yourself!"

14. *Use of ridicule and sarcasm.* Belittling an opponent's argument is often easier than refuting it. An example is found in Burke's com-

ments on the king's ministers, in his speech on American Taxation: "They never had any kind of system, right or wrong; but only invented occasionally some miserable tale for the day, in order meanly to sneak out of difficulties, into which they had proudly strutted." Roosevelt in 1932 helped win a first term in the White House by denouncing the Republican plank on prohibition as "high and dry on one end and moisterous on the other"—not good argument, but apparently effective rationalization.

These fourteen types of specious reasoning are far from a complete catalogue of the devices of rationalization. But they do illustrate the variety of forms it may take. Whenever you find such rationalizations in the speeches of others (or in your own), note whether it is the cause of truth or of self-interest that is being served. Yet, however we must condemn them as logicians or moralists, human limitations being what they are, such devices continue to have a considerable persuasive effect.

Rationalization and fallacies in reasoning

Since the fourteen types of rationalization that have been listed are all forms of logical fallacies, the question may arise whether rationalization actually exists as a separate form of motivation, or whether it is not merely a failure to use the forms of reasoning properly. The answer is that all rationalization is fallacious logic, but not all fallacious logic is rationalization. There may well be honest failures in reasoning when the reasoner is making every effort to pursue a clear trail of rigorous logic. Rationalization occurs only when the intent of the speaker (whether or not he may consciously realize it) is justification of the belief, feelings, or action of himself or his group.

Generations of physicists reasoned wrongly (but without rationalization) simply because they lacked the guidance of Planck's quantum theory. Even more generations of geographers were led into contorted reasoning about the world by the false belief that it was flat. Lack of evidence, wrong interpretation of the evidence, ignorance of logic, or lack of skill in reasoning may, singly or in combination, lead to false conclusions. When such objective causes are responsible for the result, the blame may properly be placed upon fallacious reasoning; for sound reasoning is defined as correct interpretation of all relevant data.

It is obvious, however, that much of what passes for reasoning fails of soundness for a very different reason. It fails because of a purposive twisting of the evidence or of the interpretation of it in order to support a conclusion favored by the speaker. The process of reasoning in such instances is necessarily fallacious, but it is directed and purposive. Often the speaker may be quite innocent in the sense that his rationalization is so spontaneous and natural that he is himself unaware that self-justification is his real purpose. Consequently, there may be strenuous differences of opinion as to whether a specific deviation from logic is a mere fallacy or is in fact rationalization. The motive, known or unknown, is always the test.

Emotion, reason, and rationalization compared

In a study published in 1936, the author undertook to present a cross-sectional analysis of emotion, reason, and rationalization to make clear their essential differences. In this classification, "reason" included both logic and factual exposition. The cross-sectional analysis is presented here to assist you in making a final summary of your own conclusions arising from your study of Chapters 9-12.

In general, as you survey the nature of these motive appeals, it may be said that in the use of emotion the attention of the auditors is diffused to include a general field of more or less closely related interests; the will to believe rather than the intelligence is appealed to; and there is no detailed attempt to progress from premise to conclusion. When reason is used, the auditors' intelligence is appealed to, the attention is closely centered upon pertinent facts, and there is a careful and visible progress from premise to conclusion. In rationalization, which falls midway between the other two avenues, a pretense is made of concentrating the attention; but in reality it is diverted to contiguous but irrelevant facts, and although both premise and conclusion are stated, their relationship is assumed rather than proved.

Specific differences in the three avenues are indicated in the following analysis.

A CROSS-SECTIONAL ANALYSIS

Emotion	Reason	Rationalization
1. Attempts to diffuse the attention, to include within its range a variety of ideas and attitudes.	1. Attempts to center attention upon immediate facts or contentions.	1. Attempts to focus the attention upon facts or concepts more or less irrelevant (but seeming to be immediately relevant) to the facts or contentions under discussion.
2. Deals with general attitudes and concepts.	2. Deals with specific ideas or concepts.	2. Deals with ideas definitely differentiated, but vaguely outlined.
3. Consists of subjective consideration of data, definitely linked up with hidden inferences and wishes.	3. Consists of objective consideration of data, attempting to weed out hidden inferences and the "will to believe."	3. Consists of subjective consideration masked in objective form.
4. Avoids securing an orderly sequence of thought responses, and keeps the attention centered on the end rather than on the means.	4. Consists of orderly thinking, with the steps by which conclusions are reached definitely traced.	4. Is orderly thinking without critical examination; tries to tie up the specific proposition with a suggested hypothesis, without permitting careful consideration of the relationships between them.
5. Fails to differentiate quality or strength of reasons, but appeals chiefly to the "good" ones.	5. Is an attempt to separate "real" from "good" reasons, and to give priority to the former.	5. Deals with a mixture of "real" and "good" reasons, all being presented as "real."
6. Consists of suggestion, thus trying to gain immediate decisions without the delay incident to deliberation.	6. Consists of deliberation, resulting in a delayed response.	6. Consists largely of suggestion, although the auditors believe they are using deliberation.
7. Attempts the widespread diffusion of neuronic impulses, to arouse a general state of bodily excitement, which demands outlet in immediate action.	7. Attempts the selective transmission of neuronic impulses along pathways "chosen" for this particular occasion.	7. Attempts selective transmission of neuronic impulses according to strong stimuli provided by the speaker, rather than by voluntary control of the auditor.

Emotion	Reason	Rationalization
8. Is concerned primarily with the motive power needed to accomplish actions.	8. Is concerned primarily with the direction or guidance of action.	8. Is concerned primarily with direction of action, though the elements of suggestion result in strengthening of the motive power.
9. Tries to tie up the specific proposition with established habit patterns.	9. Tries to rule out all personal factors.	9. Pretends to rule out all personal factors, but actually relates the problem to stereotypes, habit patterns, and the will-to-believe.

Conclusion

Rationalization, a form of reasoning from false premises or by illogical means, accounts for perhaps as much as 80 per cent or more of our thinking-toward-a-decision. As such, it is a major type of persuasive discourse. Appealing to self-interest, reasoning backward from results to socially acceptable causes, marked by emotionalism, and supported by irrelevancies, rationalization is far more concerned with appearances than with reality. It serves (1) to build morale by protecting bruised egos; (2) to appeal to audiences that reject emotionalism and are unable to follow strict reasoning; (3) to mask unpleasant or unsavory motives; and (4) to provide a basis for dealing with problems that lie outside our field of knowledge or beyond the power of our thinking capacity. All four of these functions are useful, if not indeed essential, in our complicated society.

The various indicated uses of rationalization in persuasion may be accomplished by a wide variety of means, of which fourteen representative devices are identified. These two catalogues of uses and methods should serve for identifying rationalization when used by others as well as indicating how a speaker may use it himself to accomplish his own persuasive goals.

Rationalization is not being defended in this chapter, but analyzed and evaluated for its persuasive effects.

Exercises

1. The class may be divided into two groups to participate in an informal debate, one group pointing out the values and utility of rationalization, the other its dangers and abuses.

2. For a fine analysis of rationalization in public address, read Herman Broch's "Adolf Hitler's Farewell Address," *Saturday Review of Literature,* October 21, 1944. Discuss the article in terms of the principles and methods described in this chapter.

3. Select a strongly partisan political speech and analyze it for rationalization. Explain why what seems like rationalization to some critics will appear as sober reason to others. What tests will you apply?

4. List five examples of rationalization that you have observed in either your own thinking or in the thinking of your associates. Identify the types of rationalization.

5. Prepare and deliver a five-minute speech utilizing rationalization, designed to build morale or preserve the prestige of your own school, fraternity, or some other group to which you belong. Make your speech a persuasive explanation of why some seeming failure actually contains within itself elements of success. (A familiar example is the old saw that a losing football team is building character.)

6. For further study of rationalization as a factor in persuasion, the following readings may be consulted:

Aristotle, "On Sophistical Refutations," from the *Organon,* trans., W. A. Pickard-Cambridge, in Richard McKean (ed.), *The Basic Works of Aristotle* (New York: Random House, 1941).

Edmund Bergler, *The Psychology of Gambling* (New York: Hill and Wang, 1957), particularly Chapter II, "The Gambler's Conscious Motivations," pp. 8-14.

Eric Berne, *The Mind in Action* (New York: Simon and Schuster, 1947).

Eduoard Claparède, "L'Autojustification," *Archives de Psychologie,* 20 (1927), 265-298.

W. Ward Fearnside and William B. Holther, *Fallacy: The Counterpart of Argument* (Englewood Cliffs, N.J.: Prentice-Hall, 1959).

S. I. Hayakawa with Basil H. Pillard, *Language in Thought and Action* (New York: Harcourt, Brace, 1949), particularly "A Semantic Parable," pp. 1-7, and Chapter X, "How We Know What We Know," pp. 165-185.

Ernest Jones, "Rationalization in Everyday Life," *Journal of Abnormal and Social Psychology,* III (August-September, 1908).

Walter Lippmann, *Public Opinion* (New York: Penguin Books, 1946), particularly Chapters I, VIII, and XI-XV.

Robert T. Oliver, "Human Motivation: Intellectuality, Emotionality, and Rationalization," *Quarterly Journal of Speech,* 22 (February, 1936), 67-77.

Chaim Perelman, "The Role of Decision in the Theory of Knowledge," in *The Idea of Justice and the Problem of Argument* (New York: Humanities Press, 1963), pp. 88-97.

Charles Sanders Pierce, "The Fixation of Belief," in *Philosophical Writings of Pierce,* ed., Justus Buchler (New York: Dover Publications, 1955).

Michael Polanyi, *Personal Knowledge* (Chicago: University of Chicago Press, 1958), particularly Part III: "The Justification of Personal Knowledge," pp. 249-324.

Vernon Rank, "Rationalization as a Factor in Communication," *Today's Speech,* IV (April, 1956), 10-21.

Angus Sinclair, *The Conditions of Knowing* (New York: Harcourt, Brace, 1951).

W. S. Taylor, "Rationalization and Its Social Significance," *Journal of Abnormal and Social Psychology,* 17 (1922-23), 410-418.

Hans Vaihinger, *The Philosophy of 'As If'* (New York: Harcourt, Brace, 1925).

Harry L. Weinberg, *Levels of Knowing and Existence* (New York: Harper, 1959).

E. Eugene Williams, "A Study in the Treatment of Rationalization in Four Selected Persuasive Speech Textbooks Published Since 1950," unpublished M.A. thesis (East Lansing: Michigan State University, 1961).

PART IV

===

The Speaking Process

... when there is communication without need for communication, merely so that someone may earn the social and intellectual prestige of becoming a priest of communication, the quality and communicative value of the message drop like a plummet.

—NORBERT WIENER, *The Human Use of Human Beings*

You persuade a man only in so far as you can talk his language by speech, gesture, tonality, order, image, attitude, idea, *identifying* your ways with his.

—KENNETH BURKE, *A Rhetoric of Motives*

The Platform Speech

THE PRECEDING TWELVE CHAPTERS TREAT OF THE persuasive process in broad terms. Much persuasion is accomplished in conversation, in casual discussion, and in more formal interviews. Persuasion may also be achieved in writing, including newspaper editorials, personal letters, magazine articles, and printed advertisements. Our chief concern, however, is with oral persuasion—and especially with that sought through public speeches.

When preparing a persuasive speech, you should be fortified by a thorough knowledge of the problems of motivation and adaptation to your specific audience that are discussed in the five chapters of Part I. You will also want to make use of the principles of persuasion presented in the three chapters of Part II and of the modes of persuasive appeal analyzed in the four chapters of Part III. Since this is a course in the *practice of persuasion,* you doubtless have given a number of speeches before you have had a chance to study and thoroughly digest all the content of those chapters. By the time you have proceeded far enough to begin rounding out your persuasive speeches in complete form, however, every speech should demonstrate mastery of these foregoing elements. Finally, you will seek practice in presentation of the several specific types of persuasion represented in the five chapters of Part V. The processes of persuasion, as you are learning, are exceedingly complex. There is no easy road to persuasive effectiveness. But one by one the elements of influence can be assimilated and improved. This is a goal worthy of hard work.

Common elements of persuasive speeches

In a very real sense, every persuasive speech is a unique problem and must be solved upon its own terms. To follow a set of generalized rules blindly is to ignore every individualized aspect of the particular persuasive problem which the speaker confronts. The classification of speeches is almost as fruitless as the classification of poets. It is very much to be doubted that the appreciation of Shelley is enhanced by calling him a "Romantic." The temptation is to look toward the label instead of toward the object itself. Let this warning, then, be posted for all persuasive speakers to read:

NOTICE!

Rules are of value only as summary statements of practices that previous speakers have found to be generally valuable.

Never follow a rule because it is a rule; always look at your own persuasive problem and then use your own best judgment as to whether the general practice that has been formalized into a rule will offer you the best solution.

Your general knowledge of human motivation,

— *plus* your specific analysis of the particular speech situation,

— *plus* your own alert judgment are worth far more than all the stereotyped rules that have ever been devised.

With this warning fresh in our minds, let us turn to an examination of some of the elements that persuasive speeches do have in common —the elements that justify setting off persuasion as an individual science, capable of being treated apart from other kinds of speaking.

A. GOALS

The definition of persuasion that appeared in Chapter 1 was formulated wholly in terms of the speaker's purpose: *the art of motivation, or of instilling, activating, or directing in another individual or other individuals a belief or a type of conduct recommended by the speaker.* This is appropriate, for it has always been customary to judge persuasive speaking in terms of its results. The speaker's purpose is to achieve a specific definite change in his auditor's way of thinking or acting. The most legitimate test of a persuasive speech is to ask whether or not it succeeded in its aim. Its method is much less easily determined than its function.

There is difficulty whenever an attempt is made to differentiate persuasion from other forms of discourse on the basis of the kinds of material incorporated in it. The entertaining speech is largely humorous—but humor may also be persuasive. The informative speech is expository—but exposition is essential to much of persuasion. Narration and description not only are modes of discourse in themselves, but frequently are also used for persuasive effect. It is not *what* the speaker says, but what he says it *for* that sets off persuasion as a separate form of speaking. Every truly persuasive speech is designed to achieve one or more of the following goals:

1. *To instill* a new belief or mode of conduct in the auditors.
2. *To stimulate* an existing but latent belief or mode of conduct.
3. *To direct* the specific nature of the auditors' incipient responses.

To Instill. In the first instance, the speaker faces his most difficult task; for he usually can instill a new idea only by driving out the old one, and this requires a derangement of old beliefs and of set habits of thought and action. The speaker should take care to emphasize the conservative elements in his proposal, to stress its connection with the old, and to minimize its new aspects. The speaker who announces a "brand new idea" or a "revolutionary theory" is but courting trouble. Much better was the method of Jesus, who, in advancing his new religious principles, soothed the advocates of the old Judaism by declaring, "Think not that I am come to destroy the law, or the prophets: I am not come to destroy, but to fulfil." And all through His ministry, whenever He preached to the people, He supported His teachings from two major sources: (1) from the common, everyday experiences of His hearers, which formed the substance of His parables; (2) from the sayings of the old Hebrew prophets, which He quoted and interpreted freely. Both these forms of support gave to His new message an atmosphere of familiarity which made easier its explicit acceptance. If "new wine" is not to be served in "old bottles," it should at least be proffered with old labels. Only by such methods is the instillation of a new proposal likely to succeed.

To Stimulate. Much persuasive speaking aims simply to activate existing but latent attitudes. A car salesman, for instance, finds his prospective customers already wanting new models; he has simply to stimulate their desires to make them predominate over the other latent desires which make alternative demands for their money. We all have latent patriotic, religious, and charitable feelings, so that these need not be instilled by the Fourth of July orators, the preachers, and the social workers, but merely intensified.

To Direct. The third phase of persuasive speaking is not argumentative, but pointedly interpretive. The speaker assumes that his audience is in full agreement with him, and that it is simply necessary to direct their thinking from fully accepted premises to the presumably inevitable conclusion. The tone of such speeches is authoritative and expository. The best persuasive technique, when the audience's frame of mind will permit it, is to avoid special persuasion and advance toward the desired conclusion wholly on the basis of assumption. The speaker who does this, however, should be wary lest he advance alone and leave his audience behind. An instructive example of this method is found in a speech by Alfred P. Sloan, Jr., on May 22, 1940, in which the speaker sought to establish by simple presumption a defense of the current industrial practices. Said Mr. Sloan:

American enterprise comprises thrift and skill; in other words, capital and management. Our democratic traditions gave equality of opportunity and equality of responsibility, placed no handicaps upon success, encouraged every individual to seek as high a place in business, the professions, or in politics as his ability would justify; and honored him for his accomplishments. That has contributed markedly to the outstanding success of American enterprise. In consequence, our industrial population earns more in purchasing power and enjoys a higher standard of living than any similar group anywhere. America with 7 per cent of the world's population enjoys more than 50 per cent of the world's wealth. That is the result of our system of enterprise.

Any speech that is designed to accomplish any of the three persuasive goals is truly a persuasive speech. And conversely, any speaker who sets out to persuade an audience should clearly determine which of these goals he is attempting to accomplish and should direct his efforts with single-minded concentration to that specific end. The speaker should first phrase his proposal, then analyze his audience, and then rephrase his proposal in terms of the precise persuasive task that his analysis reveals. Only after that step has been taken is he ready to commence the actual composition of his speech.

B. CHARACTERISTICS

As all persuasive speeches are bound together by their similarity of goal, so are they all marked by certain common characteristics. One of these is *progression*. A persuasive speech moves; it is going somewhere. It fails if it is static. The speech follows very much the same kind of course as a short-story plot. It may be diagramed as follows:

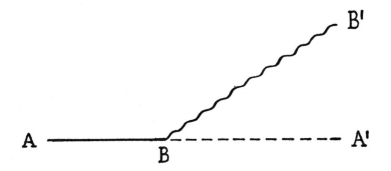

The audience's thinking on the subject under discussion was progressing along the course marked *A* to *A'*, but it is interrupted at the point marked *B* by the speaker's alternative proposal, much as the orderly course of the hero's life in a short story is deflected by the inciting incident. From that point there is a steadily rising action to the climax at *B'*, when the speaker's proposal is mentally accepted by the audience. If the speaker continues to talk after that point is reached, the result is just as destructive to persuasion as it would be to literature if the author should go wandering on beyond his denouement.

Another illustration from the plotting of a short story may be used to indicate the second characteristic of persuasive speaking, which is *conflict*. There is said to be only one short-story plot, which is: *A* wants *B*, but to get it he must struggle against the obstacles *C*. The plot is diagramed thus:

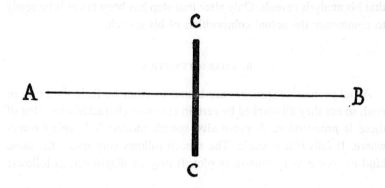

Similarly, the persuasive speaker *A* wants the agreement of the audience *B*, and to get it must struggle to overcome the obstacles *C*, which consist of all the reasons why the audience may be reluctant to accept his proposal. The speaker should, of course, make every effort to discover what the obstacles are, so that he will not be struggling in the dark. A salesman, for instance, desires nothing more than to have his prospective customer raise objection to his product, for that makes his selling task much easier by informing him what obstacles he has to overcome. Any disputant who does not encourage the fullest expression of his opponent's view is simply condemning himself to the necessity of struggling blindly against unknown forces. When these objections are unveiled, the effort should be to win the conflict by diplomacy, without the necessity of resorting to the warfare of argumentative pressure.

A third characteristic of persuasive speaking is that it invariably aims at the acceptance of a *proposal*. The proper phrasing of the proposal is, therefore, a matter of supreme importance. Normally it should be stated in terms of audience response. That is, the proposal may read, "I want my audience to...." This form is designed to insure that the thinking of the speaker will be audience-centered, and that his aim is directed toward the goal of audience reaction.

The concluding portion of the proposal should be absolutely precise in terms of what the speaker actually expects to accomplish in that particular speech. "I want my audience to agree that Red China ought not to be admitted to the United Nations under existing circumstances"; or "I want my audience to be stimulated to an intensified conviction that peoples now held under communist rule should be liberated"; or "I want my audience to believe that international problems are of concern to them as individuals." Emerson regretted in his time that education was deficient in teaching students the "art of putting things"—that is, in stating precisely the questions confronting them. Such precision in formulation of the proposal is a necessity for good persuasive speaking.

C. METHOD

Not all persuasive speeches proceed in the same fashion, but they do have a community of method by which they are marked. Inasmuch as this method has formed most of the substance of the preceding pages, a bare summary will suffice here as a checklist for the speaker in preparing his speeches:

1. Win attention to and interest in the proposal.
2. Show the audience how the proposal is in accord with:
    a. Its own best interests;
    b. Its standards of ethics and its ideals;
    c. The opinion of the majority;
    d. The judgment of experts.
3. Suggest directly or indirectly the value of the speaker's proposal.
4. Present the proposal not as an attack upon the audience's beliefs, but as a common goal sought by speaker and audience alike.
5. Align the proposal with both the conscious and the only partially realized desires and needs of the auditors.
6. State the proposal in words that fit into the accepted stereotypes and mental habits of the audience.

7. Present the proposal, if possible, under conditions that are physically and psychologically favorable to its acceptance.

8. Appeal through the avenues of motivation that are most open for these particular auditors.

    a. Remember that their action depends upon the energizing power of aroused feelings.

    b. Remember that they are not apt to act without having good reasons with which to justify the act to themselves and with which they can later justify it to their friends.

    c. Remember that the most capable and influential auditors are apt to reject a proposal that is not solidly supported by adequate facts and sound logic.

9. When the motive appeals have been selected, they must be adapted to fit the mood, attitudes, and degree of polarization of the audience.

Types of persuasive speeches

Having examined the points of resemblance among persuasive speeches, we shall now reverse the procedure and look at the points of difference. For they not only form a common *genus,* but they also divide into a number of *species.* An understanding of these differences should help the speaker to guide his preparation for a specific speech.

A. BASES FOR CLASSIFICATION

Any single basis for classifying persuasive speeches must be inadequate, for it cannot possibly account for all the essential factors involved. But when several bases are used, the speaker must realize that every speech needs to be placed in not one but all the categories that are established. The chief danger in classifying anything as diverse as persuasive speeches is that of oversimplifying the problem which they present. This danger may be avoided if the speaker will evaluate each speech situation in terms of the differences in the proposal, in the response desired, in the attitude of the audience, and in its degree of polarization. It should be remembered, too, that the speaker himself fits into a specific classification, as was pointed out in Chapter 4. How he will be able to utilize the factors represented in the four bases depends in part on whether he is:

1. Representing himself   *or* a group.
2. A temporary advocate   *or* a permanent advocate.
3. Seeking his own best   *or* supporting a community ideal.
   interests
4. Comparatively unknown *or* a recognized authority.

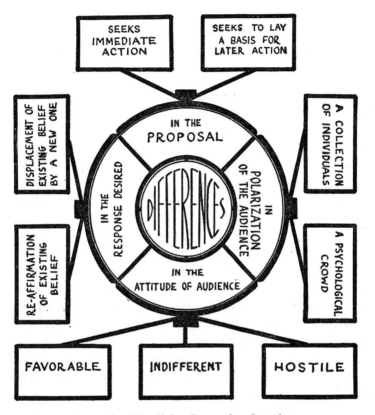

Bases for Classifying Persuasive Speeches

Arising from the differences listed in the previous paragraph, a large number of categories emerge. For instance, one speech might be classified as seeking immediate action in the reaffirmation of an existing belief by a nonpolarized audience that is indifferent to the proposal. Another speech might seek to lay the basis for later action in displacing an existing belief with a new one in a hostile "psychological crowd." Each of these factors should receive the speaker's careful consideration, and they occur in any sort of combination. The individual characteristics of each separate basis of classification should be studied carefully.

B. DIFFERENCES IN THE PROPOSAL

There is a far different persuasive task confronting the speaker who says, "Do it now!" from that before one who says, "Doesn't this sound like the reasonable thing to do when the opportunity arises?" The first speech is rigidly tested by its immediate results. It visibly succeeds or fails, almost in the moment of utterance. The element of delay in the second type of speech is a saving factor for the speaker's prestige and ego. If the desired action is never performed, the failure can be blamed upon innumerable circumstances that occur between the time the speech was delivered and the time when the opportunity for action arose. For this reason, speakers who seek a delayed response are likely to have a better reputation than they deserve. If their speeches are sprightly, entertaining, forceful, logical, or impressive—if they "sound good"—the presumption is all in favor of the speech's having been a success, even though "intervening factors" nullify the effect it ought to achieve. But for the speech aiming at an immediate action there is no such excuse possible. The audience responds or it doesn't; the speaker achieves his goal or he fails. This is so hard a test for speakers to face that it is no wonder most of them prefer to give the other type of speech.

A good example of these contrasting types is offered by the sales talk on one hand and the good will speech on the other. The aim of the first is to make a sale *now;* the aim of the second is to create in the audience a favorable attitude that will make *future* sales easier. There is almost no method of telling precisely how effective the latter speeches may be. But the former receives an absolute test every time it is used. This is the big advantage of the speech for immediate action.

It is a constant and inescapable education for the speaker. It forces him to forgo the elements of speaking which are merely "pretty," which win compliments, and which parade his erudition or skill; it keeps him precisely and completely concentrated upon the task of securing the acceptance of his proposal. It compels him to use motive appeals that work, not those that he thinks ought to influence people. It is distinctly empirical, not theoretical. The speaker who cannot secure immediate results should beware of preening himself upon his skill in creating good will, his value as an advance agent, or his ability in a general campaign address. He may be less successful even in these speeches than he imagines.

C. DIFFERENCES IN RESPONSE

When the speaker is trying to reanimate a latent belief of his auditors, his first thought should be: Why has this once-active belief fallen into disuse? Have circumstances changed or have the auditors changed? Is it advisable to reinterpret the belief in terms of new conditions; or should the audience have its old emotions, old attitudes, old loyalties aroused? What alternative beliefs may have driven this one to cover, or what obstacles may have arisen with power sufficient to block its expression?

During the 1930's, for instance, many Americans were saying that democracy was outworn, inefficient, incapable of meeting the economic problems of the twentieth century, and that dictatorship had proved itself to have many advantages. Underlying this kind of thought, of course, was a deep-seated attachment to democracy, which was in danger of being submerged, but was far from dead. One thinker, Will Durant, met this frame of mind with a direct challenge: "We must guard against loose thinking. . . ." He went on to specify in detail ten respects in which our way of life had greatly succeeded. And he ended with encouragement and a plea:

We need not worry, then, about the future. We are weary with too much war, and in our lassitude of mind we listen readily to a Spengler announcing the downfall of the Western World. . . . [But] never was our heritage of civilization and culture so secure, and never was it half so rich. Let us do our little share to preserve it, augment it, and pass it on, confident that time will wear away chiefly the dross of it, and that what is finally fair and noble in it will escape mortality, to illuminate and gladden many generations.

Whenever a once-vital point of view has weakened, there is a reason. The reason may be good, or bad, or even ridiculous; but whatever it is, it has manifested its ability to influence the thinking of the audience. The speaker's task, then, is to find that particular reason operative with his hearers, and to counterbalance it with new considerations or with an appealing reaffirmation of the old. When people have fallen into a cynical disregard for what they have long professed, they may be ashamed to reaffirm faith in it themselves, but feel relieved and pleased to have someone else do it for them. They become homesick for old ideas, just as they do for old scenes. Therein is a source of strength for the persuasive speaker who would turn his auditors back to what they formerly believed.

On the other hand, when an existing belief is to be displaced by a new one, the speaker should seek to determine what needs the present belief cares for, what satisfactions it offers, and, conversely, what its weaknesses and disadvantages are. Then the speaker can be more assured, more dogmatic, more absolute in his statements and more stringent in his demands. The audience that is indifferent may be favorably inclined toward the speaker's proposal once its interest has been aroused. It has been demonstrated by numerous studies of the "shift of opinion," which occurs in an audience as a result of hearing persuasive speeches, that there is apt to be a large shift from the neutral, undecided, or indifferent position toward whichever conclusion is most ably stated by the speakers. Millson, for instance, in an experiment to determine the effect upon the judgment of 122 college students of speeches favoring four separate solutions to a problem, found that 30 per cent of the entire group changed their opinions as a result of the discussion, but that *two thirds* of those who were originally *undecided* shifted toward one solution or another. Indifference and indecision seem to be relatively unstable. The individual who has nothing tangible to cling to, no point of view of his own to defend, is relatively open to conviction.

A hostile attitude is, of course, the most difficult for a speaker to confront. His chief endeavor should be to minimize the conflict, to prevent any expression of hostility by the auditors (so that their attitude will not crystallize into a positively formulated opinion), and to keep their attention centered upon the common ground that exists between them and the speaker. It is generally true, too, that hostility yields only by degrees. When possible, the speaker should attempt to overcome it by degrees, rather than all at once. His first speech might be aimed simply to *disarm* opposition by the use of humor, good fellowship, and a demonstration of disinterestedness. Later, he can suggest the disadvantages of the accepted solution and the converse advantages of his own. If haste ever makes waste, it is in flying directly into the teeth of avowed opposition. The longest way around may be not only the shortest, but the only, way home.

D. DIFFERENCES IN POLARIZATION

As was indicated in Chapter 11, the polarization of the audience is as significant a factor as its attitude. In the discussion of emotion, some methods were suggested for polarizing an audience, and the comparative advantages and disadvantages were explained. When the members of an audience are coolly and calmly self-possessed, the speaker should depend more upon facts and logic in supporting his proposal and less upon emotion. He will have to appeal more to individual differences than to common characteristics. This results in a slow tempo for the speech, as it turns now toward one group of hearers, now toward another. The danger is that what most appeals to some will alienate others, or at best leave them unmoved. Usually, when the audience is neither polarized nor favorable to the proposal, the speaker can hardly expect complete success. His best plan may well be to aim at laying a basis upon which future action may be secured.

The polarized audience, on the other hand, will respond much more easily and much more completely. For it, with its thought processes subordinated to its emotional reactions, the speaker must take care to phrase his desired response simply, concretely, and dramatically. He should call for immediate action, while his audience is eager to act. If he is asking for funds, he should actually take up a collection, or at least have the auditors sign pledge cards that will commit them to give. If he is making a sale, he should get the name on the dotted line. If he permits the auditors to "go home and think it over," his persuasive work will largely have to be done again. The most distinctive aspect of the polarized-audience situation is its urgent immediacy. There is little time for thought and no time for delay.

Basic preparation for the persuasive speech

In the preparation of each specific speech, every speaker will have his own personal method of procedure. There is no one best way that should be followed by everyone. However, there is one caution that should be written large for every inexperienced speaker to read. Framed, it should make a good motto to hang over the desk:

> SPEECH PREPARATION REQUIRES LONG, HARD WORK

The single fact that most distinguishes the practiced from the unpracticed speaker is that the former has learned from experience that the longer he works upon a speech, the better it is likely to be. Chauncey Depew epitomized this fact very well when he said, "A good speaker requires several weeks' notice for the preparation of a speech; an average speaker can do with a week; and a poor speaker will offer his remarks with no notice whatsoever." The same point was made, in effect, by President Franklin D. Roosevelt. When he was told in 1942 that what the country needed to stimulate it to increased efforts in the defense program was a "fireside chat" from him every week, he replied that he would gladly undertake to make the speeches if someone else would take over all the other duties of the presidency.

A. METHODS OF EXPERIENCED SPEAKERS

It is instructive to note the type of preparation practiced by the most experienced speakers. Dr. Stephen S. Wise, who delivered several speeches a week for years, always outlined every speech completely. Furthermore, his secretary writes, "He sometimes dictated 1,000 or 2,000, sometimes as much as 3,000 words." For the first ten years of his rabbinate he wrote out his sermons in full and memorized them—truly a strenuous apprenticeship. Harold L. Ickes, former Secretary of the Interior, who made frequent political addresses, wrote, "I dictate the first draft of my speeches and then I work them over until they suit me. Sometimes it is the sixth or seventh edition that is finally delivered."

President Franklin D. Roosevelt is generally considered one of the best speakers in recent times—and he is among those who worked hardest in the preparation of his speeches. When he had an important address to make, dispatches from Washington indicated a practical cessation of his other work for several days as he devoted his time to the speech. Many of his talks were revised from fifteen to twenty times before their final draft. This is one of the principal reasons why they sounded so natural, easy, and unaffected. The natural expression was found through hours of laborious search. One of his speeches, for instance, the Victory Dinner speech delivered to a group of his supporters gathered in Washington on March 4, 1937, and broadcast to the nation, was rewritten twenty-two times. An examination of the successive manuscript copies, which are kept at the Hyde Park library, reveals the purpose and results of these revisions. The general framework of the speech varies but little—the essential ideas remain as they were first formulated. But in paragraph after paragraph, sentence after sentence, general ideas are supplanted by concrete illustrations, negative suggestion is changed to positive, and the ideas are couched in increasingly personalized form. The speech took on more and more of President Roosevelt's typical manner of thought and expression as it was turned over in his mind.

B. ADVICE FOR BEGINNING SPEAKERS

One method of preparation for a persuasive speech that may be recommended is as follows:

1. The first step is to phrase carefully the exact purpose the speech is to accomplish. This should be written out in complete sentence form and considered thoughtfully, to make sure that it states precisely what the speaker wishes to accomplish.

2. Next, the speaker should make a thorough analysis of his audience—for which he can use the form presented in Chapter 4.

3. After this has been done, he should (taking into account his relationship with his auditors and their attitude toward him) ask himself, "What can I say that will have the greatest effect in moving this particular audience to accept the proposal that is to be presented in this speech?"

4. Taking a large sheet of paper, he should write down all the ideas he can think of that offer a possible answer to that question. His paper will doubtless be filled with a miscellaneous, disorderly jumble of thoughts good and bad.

5. Out of this hodgepodge he should cull and organize those ideas which, upon examination and consideration, seem to be best suited to his purpose. Some of the items on the first piece of paper will have to be discarded, others will be rephrased, and most of them will be subordinated to two or three cardinal points that carry the burden of his plea.

6. With the arrangement of these ideas in outline form, the speaker readily can see where the strengths and weaknesses of his speech lie. He can garner new material to support the points that need it and can prune and eliminate the redundant portions.

7. A careful recheck of the speech should now be made to see how closely it is directed to the achievement of the purpose formulated for it, and how well its appeals are suited to move its audience.

8. In the final construction, a good attention-compelling title, an interest-building introduction, and an action-inspiring conclusion should be prepared.

9. At last the speaker is ready to master his speech through study and practice in delivery, so that his intellectual preparation will be complete. There should be no fumbling for words or ideas as the speech is delivered.

10. The emotional preparation, insuring that the speaker will commence his speech with a depth of sincerity and a reservoir of earnest feeling, should be completed in the interval just preceding delivery of the speech. The last moments before the audience is addressed should be spent in a sympathetic comprehension of the full significance of the importance of the speech's goal.

With such a preparation, the speaker may confidently hope for success. Without it, he should be reconciled to the fate that is liable to overtake anyone who approaches casually and thoughtlessly any difficult and intricate task.

Conclusion

The platform speech is a difficult test of persuasive effectiveness. Since it is presented to many auditors, the problem of audience analysis is more difficult than when (as in conversation) there may be but one listener. Because the speaker values his reputation and relationships in the community more than any immediate result he hopes for from the speech, he must keep in mind the long-range as well as the immediate effects. In trying to formulate his precise goal for the speech, he must take into account factors of community feeling, the nature of the audience itself, the character of the occasion, and the relationship he has with the listeners—all of this underlying and intermingled with the conviction he has regarding what should be felt, or believed, or done about the subject he is discussing.

This chapter has sought to present an over-all consideration for preparing the persuasive platform speech—just as Chapter 5 attempted to re-create a concrete example of such speaking. Earlier chapters have presented considerable detail on methods of audience analysis and on the types of materials that may be utilized for specific effects. Still later chapters are concerned with several elements noted in this chapter, in order to provide more detailed guidance. And out of all these considerations there arises again and again the inescapable conclusion that persuasive speaking is an extremely demanding form of intellectual social endeavor. People can and are influenced (often greatly) by persuasive speaking; but the process is usually uncertain and always difficult. The good persuasive speaker must be an acute analyst—of himself, his audience, his subject matter, his purpose, and his methodology. This is why in the whole history of mankind only a few score persuasive speakers stand out as indubitably great. But every conscientious student can properly hope to improve his own effectiveness to a degree.

Exercises

1. Prepare and deliver a ten-minute speech designed to induce your audience of classmates (which may be assumed to be friendly toward you, but indifferent or hostile to your proposal) to take immediate action of some sort. Since you know your audience fairly well, take especial care to select your appeals on the basis of their probable influence upon the motives that will lead to the desired action.

2. Prepare and deliver a ten-minute speech designed to win agreement with a proposal that will not require immediate action. Take care to use the kind of material that will have a lasting effect, so that the speech will bear fruit in the course of time.

3. Make a preliminary estimate of the precise degree of success you expect to have for each of the foregoing speeches. By what means can you increase the degree of success? What factors in the situation that are beyond your control will influence the response of the audience? In view of these factors, would it be well to modify your proposal in any way?

4. After each of the foregoing speeches has been delivered, write an estimate of the degree of success which you think it achieved. How well does this correlate with your anticipation? Why? What did you learn about motivation through these speeches which you can utilize with advantage in later speeches?

5. Criticize each speech delivered by your classmates, using the following criteria:

   a. Were the proposal and the desired response made perfectly clear?
   b. Was the speaker aided by polarization of his audience or handicapped by its lack?

c. Did he make a close and continuing adaptation to the audience?
d. Was his presentation so tactful as to win over, rather than further antagonize, those auditors who disagreed with him?
e. In your judgment, did the speech appeal to the actual motives influencing the audience?
f. Evaluate the speech in terms of your own response to it.
g. What suggestions could you give to the speaker to help him improve his persuasive effectiveness?

6. The following persuasive speech, by Bruce Barton, has been reprinted many times and has become a classic example of workaday persuasive methods. It is unlikely to win a place in the anthologies of great oratory, for its purpose is the commonplace one of helping the speaker gain more customers and thereby make more money. The style and the moral tone are not elevated but keenly practical. The speech will not serve as a model for a national statesman who wishes to arouse his countrymen to sacrificial endeavor. But this speech has become very widely known because it is practically unequaled as an example of persuasion used with effect to achieve just such a result as most persuasive speakers are aiming to attain. It "meets the auditors where they are." It skillfully utilizes suggestion, identification, humor, and a swift series of specific illustrations that hold attention and focus it gradually and imperceptibly toward the conclusion without a trace of argumentativeness. Confronting an audience of men whose profession it is to compose their own advertisements, Mr. Barton led them without any challenge of their own abilities to what eventually emerged as the natural (if not inevitable) conclusion that they should engage the services of an outside advertising agency: presumably his own. The speech merits careful analysis, for it illustrates in some degree concepts from every chapter in this book.

WHICH KNEW NOT JOSEPH
by Bruce Barton

As president of the then Barton, Durstine, and Osborn Advertising Company, Mr. Barton delivered this speech to the public relations counsels of the electric utilities, at a meeting of the National Electric Light Association, in 1923.

There are two stories—and neither of them is new—which I desire to tell you, because they have a direct application to everyone's business. The first concerns a member of my profession, an advertising man, who was in the employ of a circus. It was his function to precede the circus into various communities, distribute tickets to the editor, put up on the barns pictures of the bearded lady and the man-eating snakes, and finally to get in touch with the proprietor of some store and persuade him to purchase the space on either side of the elephant for his advertisement in the parade.

Coming one day to a crossroads town, our friend found that there was only one store. The proprietor did not receive him enthusiastically. "Why should I advertise?" he demanded. "I have been here for twenty years. There isn't a man, woman, or child around these parts that doesn't know where I am and what I sell." The advertising man answered very promptly (because in our business if we hesitate we are lost), and he said to the proprietor, pointing across the street, "What is that building over there?" The proprietor answered, "That is the Methodist Episcopal Church." The advertising man said, "How long has that been there?" The proprietor said, "Oh, I don't know; seventy-five years probably." "And yet," exclaimed the advertising man, "they ring the church bell every Sunday morning."

My second story has also a religious flavor. It relates to a gentleman named Joseph, who is now deceased.

Those of you who were brought up on the Bible may have found there some account of his very remarkable business career. Those of you who have not read that book may have heard of Joseph through the works of Rudyard Kipling.

Said Mr. Kipling:

> Who shall doubt "the secret hid
> Under Cheops' pyramid"
> Was that the contractor did
> Cheops out of several millions?
> Or that Joseph's sudden rise
> To Comptroller of Supplies
> Was a fraud of monstrous size
> On King Pharaoh's swart Civilians?

The account of Joseph in the Old Testament is much more complete and to his credit. It tells how he left his country under difficulties and, coming into a strange country, he arose, through his diligence, to become the principal person in the state, second only to the King. Now, gentlemen, the Biblical narrative brings us to that point—the point where Joseph had public relations with all the other ancient nations, while his private relations held all the best-paying jobs—it brings us up to the climax of his career and then it hands us an awful jolt. Without any words of preparation or explanation, it says bluntly:

"And Joseph died, and there arose a new king in Egypt which knew not Joseph."

I submit, gentlemen, that this is one of the most staggering lines which has ever been written in a business biography. Here was a man so famous that everybody knew him and presto, a few people die, a few new ones are born, and nobody knows him. The tide of human life has moved on; the king who exalted the friends of Joseph is followed by a king who makes them slaves; all the advertising that the name "Joseph" had enjoyed in one generation is futile and of no avail, because that generation has gone.

Now, what has all that to do with you? Very much indeed. When we gathered in this room this afternoon, there were in this country, in bed, sick, several thousand old men. It perhaps is indelicate for me to refer to that fact, but it is a fact, and we are grown up and we have to face these things. On those old men you gentlemen collectively have spent a considerable amount of time and a considerable amount of money. It is to be supposed that you have made some impression upon them regarding your service and your purposes and your necessities. But in this interval, while we have been sitting here, those old men have died and all your time and all your money and whatever you have built up in the way of good will in their minds—all your labor and investment have passed out with them.

In the same brief interval, there have been born in this country several thousand lusty boys and girls to whom you gentlemen mean no more than the Einstein theory. They do not know the difference between a Mazda Lamp and a stick of Wrigley's chewing gum. Nobody has ever told them that Ivory Soap floats or that children cry for Castoria, or what sort of soap you ought to use if you want to have skin that people would like to touch. The whole job of giving them the information they are going to need in order to form an intelligent public opinion and to exercise an intelligent influence in the community has to be started from the beginning and done over again.

So the first very simple thing that I would say to you (and it is so simple that it seems to me it ought to be said at every convention of this kind) is that this business of public relations is a very constant business, that the fact that you told your story yesterday should not lead you into the delusion of supposing that you have ever told it. There is probably no fact in the United States that is easier to impress upon people's minds than that Ivory Soap floats, and yet the manufacturers of Ivory Soap think it is not inconsistent or wasteful to spend more than a million dollars a year in repeating that truth over and over again.

Cultivating good will is a day-by-day and hour-by-hour business, gentlemen. Every day and every hour the "king" dies and there arises a new "king" to whom you and all your works mean absolutely nothing.

Now, the second very simple thing which I might say to you is that in your dealings with the public, in what you write and say, you must be genuine.

When I came to New York a great many years ago I had a lot of trouble with banks. It was very hard to find any bank that would be willing to accept the very paltry weekly deposit that I wanted to make. Finally I discovered one which was not as closely guarded as the others, and I succeeded for a period of three years in being insulted by the teller every Saturday. At the end of three years when I came to draw out my money I had an audience with the vice-president who wanted personally to insult me. I said to myself, if I live and grow old in this town, some day I think I would like to take a crack at this situation.

And so as the years passed (as they have the habit of doing), and I lived and grew old, one day a bank official came in to us and said he would like to have us do some advertising for him. I said to this banker, "Now you go back to your office and shave off all the side-whiskers that there are in your bank and you take all the high hats and carry them out into the back yard of the bank and put them in a pile and light a match to the pile and burn them up, because I am going to advertise to people that you're human, and it may be a shock to have them come in and find you as you are."

So he went back to his bank and I wrote an advertisement which said:

> There is a young man in this town who is looking for a friendly bank; a bank where the officers will remember his name and where some interest will be shown when he comes in, etc.

It was very successful. It was too successful. It was so successful that we could not control it, and all over the country there broke out a perfect epidemic, a kind of measles, of "friendly banks." Bankers who had not smiled since infancy and who never had had or needed an electric fan in their offices suddenly sat up and said, "Why, we are friendly."

Well, our bank dropped out. The competition was too keen. But it culminated, I think, in a letter which I saw and which was mailed by the president of a really very important bank in a large city. I won't attempt to quote it verbatim, but it was to this effect:

> Dear Customer: As I sit here all alone in my office on Christmas Eve thinking of you and how much we love you, I really wish that you and every other customer could come in here personally so I could give you a good sound kiss.

Well, that is a trifle exaggerated, but the fact is this—if you don't feel these things you can't make other people feel them. Emerson said, as you will remember, "What you are thunders so loud I cannot hear what you say." Unless there is back of this desire for better public relations as a real conviction, a real genuine feeling that you are in business as a matter of service, not merely as a matter of advertising service—unless there is that, then it is very dangerous, indeed, to attempt to talk to the public. For as sure as you live the public will find you out.

The third very simple thing, and the last thing that I suggest, is this: In dealing with the public the great thing is to deal with them simply, briefly, and in language that they can understand.

Two men delivered speeches about sixty years ago at Gettysburg. One man was the greatest orator of his day, and he spoke for two hours and a half, and probably nobody in the room can remember a single word that he said. The other man spoke for considerably less than five minutes, and every school child has at some time learned Lincoln's Gettysburg Address, and remembers it more or less all his life. Many prayers have been uttered in the world—many long, fine-sounding prayers—but the only prayer that any large majority of people have ever learned is the Lord's Prayer, and it is less than two hundred words long. The same thing is true of the twenty-third Psalm, and there is hardly a Latin word in it. They are short, simple, easily understood words.

You electric light people have one difficulty. I was in Europe this spring, and I rode a great deal in taxicabs. In England I sat in a taxicab and watched the little clock go around in terms of shillings. Then I flew over to Amsterdam and watched it go around in terms of guilders. Then I went down to Brussels and it went around in terms of francs. Then I went to France and it went around in terms of francs of a different value.

I would sit there trying to divide fifteen into one hundred and multiply it by seven, and wonder just where I was getting off, and I have no doubt now that really I was transported in Europe at a very reasonable cost, but because those meters talked to me in terms that were unfamiliar I never stepped out of a taxicab without having a haunting suspicion that probably I had been "gypped."

In a degree you suffer like those taxicab men. You come to Mrs. Barton and you say, "Buy this washing machine and it will do your washing for just a few cents an hour." She says, "Isn't that wonderful!" She buys it, and at the end of the month she sits with your bill in her hands and she says, "We have run this five hours, and that will probably be so and so." Then she opens the bill and finds that she has not run it five hours; that she has run it 41 kw. and 11 amp. and 32 volts, and that the amount is not so-and-so but it is $2.67.

Well, that is a matter that I suppose you will eventually straighten out.

Asking an advertising man to talk about advertising in a convention like this is a good deal like asking a doctor to talk about health. I have listened to many such addresses and they are all about the same. The eminent physician says, "Drink plenty of water. Stay outdoors as much as you can. Eat good food. Don't worry. Get eight hours' sleep. And if you have anything the matter with you, call a doctor."

So I say to you that there is a certain technique about this matter of dealing with the public, and if you have anything seriously the matter with you—whether it be a big advertising problem or merely a bad letterhead (and some of you have wretched letterheads)—there probably is some advertising doctor in your town who has made a business of the thing, and it may be worth your while to call him in. But in the meantime, and in this very informal and necessarily general talk, I say to you, "Be genuine, be simple, be brief; talk to people in language that they understand; and finally, and most of all, be persistent." You can't expect to advertise in flush times and live on the memory of it when you are hard up. You can't expect to advertise when you are in trouble, or about to be in trouble, and expect to get anything in that direction. It is a day-by-day and hour-by-hour business. If the money that has been thrown away by people who advertised spasmodically was all gathered together it would found and endow the most wonderful home in the world for aged advertising men and their widows. Don't throw any more of that money away. If advertising is worth doing at all, it is worth doing all the time. For every day, gentlemen, the "king" dies, and there arises a new "king" who knows not Joseph.

Suggested Readings

Gary Lynn Cronkhite, "Logic, Emotion, and the Paradigm of Persuasion," *Quarterly Journal of Speech,* 50 (February, 1964), 13-18.

Herbert W. Hildebrandt and Walter W. Stevens, "Manuscript and Extemporaneous Delivery in Communicating Information," *Speech Monographs,* 30 (November, 1963), 369-372.

Edward Rogge and James C. Ching, *Advanced Public Speaking* (New York: Holt, Rinehart and Winston, 1966).

Wayne N. Thompson (ed.), "Quantitative Studies in Speech," *Speech Monographs,* 32 (June, 1965), 91-197.

✍ 14.

The Persuasive Goal

THE STARTING POINT IN THE PREPARATION OF THE persuasive speech is the formulation of the *general* and *specific purposes* to be achieved by it. It may be that the *subject* will be chosen either before or after the specific purpose is decided upon, but in either case no real preparation can commence except in terms of the goal the speech is intended to achieve. And just as the preparation starts with the specific purpose, so does all the work the speaker devotes to his speech center around that one central core. It is the purpose that dictates what kinds of main ideas are chosen, what supporting materials are used, and how the whole is knit together into a unified structure. Likewise, while the speech is being delivered, from the introduction through the conclusion, it is the specific purpose that remains at the heart of the speaker's thinking and determines the kind of last-minute adaptations he may make. It is highly important, then, as the study of persuasive speaking commences, to make sure that the nature and function of the speech purpose are clearly understood.

Purpose and subject matter

As has been indicated, the subject itself may be chosen either before or after the purpose is decided upon. A minister with a weekly sermon to deliver might clearly have in mind the purpose he wishes to achieve —and then he casts about to select an appropriate type of subject through which the purpose may be vitalized. Similarly, a candidate nominated for a high office knows that the purpose of his speeches will be to win votes, and for each speech he tries to select a subject that will help him win that particular audience to do as he wishes. As the annual Red Cross or Community Chest drive approaches, the speakers who make the appeals start considering what subject matter may best be used to accomplish their predetermined purpose of raising funds. A company employee invited to speak at the firm's annual dinner knows that his purpose is to win a promotion, and he tries to find a suitable topic to serve as a vehicle for achieving that end. In these and many another situation, the purpose is established first, and the search for a topic follows.

In many other instances the topic is selected before the purpose emerges. For the centennial celebration of an institution, the invited speaker knows what he must talk about but has to decide the purpose he will try to accomplish through his commemorative remarks. When a senior major in architecture is invited to talk to the local Association of Realtors, his topic is dictated by the circumstances, but the precise purpose remains to be formulated. An American who has studied conditions on a field trip through the Far East will be asked by various groups to talk about what he observed, and will need to select the purpose he wants to accomplish with each. In general, an expert in any field is invited to talk about the subject he knows best, and through which his reputation has been established, but the choice of his precise goal in each speech is necessarily his own.

At other times, it may well happen that the purpose and subject matter are selected practically simultaneously. Speech invitations often are completely "open" as to topic and purpose. A Women's Club, Grange, High School, Men's Service Club, or other community organization issues an invitation for a twenty-minute address. The speaker then begins to think of subjects he may discuss, or of purposes he wishes to accomplish, often intermingling the two in his mind. He may reject one subject because he doesn't see in it an opportunity to "do anything constructive" with the audience. He may reject one purpose because he can't quite see how he can utilize the necessary type of subject matter with that particular group of auditors. Eventually he makes a joint selection of topic and purpose—perhaps concluding, "I'll talk on rose gardens, because (1) I know something about rose culture; (2) the audience of home owners will be interested; and (3) the residential area of town is not very attractive and I may be able to stimulate the audience to help beautify it." In this and in many other instances the choice of subject and purpose is made practically simultaneously.

Primacy of the purpose

The particular order in which subject and purpose are selected is of no great importance. What is paramount is that no preparation for a persuasive speech can proceed until the purpose is clearly and definitely formulated. Since the purpose of persuasion is to *change* the beliefs, feelings, or actions of the audience, the speaker is helpless to select his speech materials until he knows for what they are to be used. As well ask a building contractor to buy materials for a building without informing him whether it will be a small family bungalow or a department store, as to prepare a speech without a purpose.

This warning about the starting point of preparation for a persuasive speech is needed, for it often happens that inexperienced speakers will make the basic error of collecting a body of information and anecdotes about their chosen subjects, and afterwards decide upon a purpose. Then they try to devise means of using the information assembled and jumble it all together into some sort of order, mildly touching from time to time upon the purpose as though it is enough to remind the audience now and then where all the talking is supposed to lead. When such a method is pursued, it is no wonder that so many persuasive speeches fail to achieve their goal.

The relationship between subject matter and purpose for the persuasive speech should be clearly understood and emphatically present in the speaker's mind. The materials of the speech (facts, logic, anecdotes, appeals) are there for one and only one purpose: *to help lead the audience to the desired conclusion.* When persuasion is the speaker's aim, there is absolutely no excuse whatever for anything being in the speech except to serve that precise end. If this rigid test is observed, persuasive speeches will be tightly and carefully organized, with every step in the preparation wholly dominated by the demands of the specific purpose.

The specific purpose as a proposal

There should never be any doubt in the mind of an audience, when a persuasive speech ends, as to precisely what the speaker intends them to think, feel, or do. As will be seen in the chapters grouped in Parts II and III, it may often be inadvisable for the audience to be clearly informed of the purpose until near the end of the speech. But it is inexcusably shoddy for the speaker himself to be unaware of his goal for an instant during the entire preparation and delivery of the speech.

The specific purpose of a persuasive speech is to rouse the audience to some very definite and clearly understood response. The audience, then, must know what is required of it. And the requirement should be one that the audience *can* make, can be induced to *want* to make, and in all probability *will* make. A purpose phrased to accomplish these three requirements is termed in this book a *proposal*. The proposal is a precise formulation of what the speaker wants to achieve with his audience.

William James, in "The Will to Believe," set forth three reasonable and suggestive requirements which a proposal (or "option," as he called it) should have, in order to increase its attractiveness for an audience. "Options may be of several kinds," he pointed out. "They may be (1) living or dead; (2) forced or avoidable; (3) momentous or trivial; and for our purposes we may call an option a genuine option when it is of the forced, living, and momentous kind."

Following James's advice, the persuasive speaker in formulating his proposal should consider, first of all, whether he is presenting the audience a proposition that is "living or dead." Does he ask them to deal with a problem that is at hand, that is within their reach, that is available for their participation? In other words, after he has aroused their feelings on the matter, can they really do something about it?

There may occasionally be a real reason for trying to persuade an audience that Alexander Pope would have been a finer poet if he had abjured the heroic couplet; or that the farmers in some distant section of the country are using the wrong type of seed for their winter wheat. But assuredly such proposals are "dead" in the sense that the audience can do little or nothing beyond agreeing or disagreeing with the speaker's conclusion. A "live" proposal is of such a nature that the audience will say (should it agree with the speaker), "All right, we shall feel or believe differently about this matter hereafter"; or, in many instances, "After hearing you, we are going to start right in doing what you have proposed." In formulating any persuasive proposal, the speaker should test it by asking, "Just what difference will it make whether the audience agrees with me or not?"

Secondly, the speaker should consider whether his proposal is "forced or avoidable." If it is forced, it is a question or challenge the audience cannot avoid. It is presented directly to them on a basis of "take it or leave it." The audience cannot shrug it off by declaring that after all it is no real concern of theirs. An "avoidable" proposal, on the other hand, is just what the name indicates. The audience may listen attentively and apparently sympathetically to what the speaker presents, and then leave the hall with the feeling that their whole duty in regard to the matter has been fulfilled in listening to the speech. It is to be feared that many persuasive speeches (however good they may seem to be) lead to no more dynamic result than this. To cite William James once again, he wrote that the test of one's religion is the way one confronts a social need. Some will say, "Some one must do it, but why should I?" The speaker's proposal is avoidable if the audience feels able to comment on it in the "why should I" spirit. And it is a forced proposal if the listeners are unable to put it off without admitting, "why not I?"

Thirdly, the proposal may be either "momentous or trivial." Obviously not all persuasive speeches are or should be on momentous subjects. A great deal of persuasive speaking is also required to settle differences over trivialities. But when there actually is a depth of real significance in the problem the speaker is discussing, he should take care to formulate his proposal in such a manner that the significance will not be missed.

The proposal and the audience

If the speaker is genuinely "audience-centered" in his preparation, he will naturally try to formulate his proposal in terms of precisely the kind of reaction he wants his listeners to make. This is done, however, far less often than might be supposed. It is easy for the speaker to think he is being audience-centered when actually he is trying to develop a well-rounded and "logical" treatment of his theme. Far different speech composition results from asking oneself, "Exactly what should my audience do as a result of my talk?" from one that will grow out of such a question as, "What is the best way to develop this topic?" Perhaps the latter question will yield a more logically organized composition, but strict adherence to the former will yield more effective persuasion.

An actual speech. This point may be illustrated by sketching the development of the construction of an actual speech. In the fall of 1942, the Victory Speakers' Bureau of the Office of Civilian Defense in Washington undertook to organize a nationwide organization of volunteer speakers who would mobilize community effort for wartime programs. One of the problems that arose was a campaign to counteract the rubber shortage by asking every citizen who owned more than five tires to sell his extra ones to the government. The aim was decidedly not to produce a "good speech," but to write an effective appeal that could be delivered by seventy-five thousand local speakers with the effect of bringing in the needed tires.

Analysis of a nationwide audience is doubtless impossible in general, but when a specific problem is used as the standard, helpful results may be obtained. It was decided that extra tires might be owned by the following groups:

1. Those who just happened to have them—because they kept their old tires when they bought new ones, or because they got extra tires at a bargain price, or for some other reason;

2. Those whose businesses depended upon keeping their cars running and who, consequently, had purchased extra tires as a prudent insurance against loss of their livelihood;

3. "Smart people," who prided themselves upon their alertness and who purchased extra tires while they were still being sold, as much to prove their own superior judgment as to have the tires;

4. "Hoarders," who recognized there would not be enough tires to go around and were determined to have more than their share.

The problem was to shape a brief speech that could be delivered by all kinds of speakers to all kinds of groups in every section of the country. The proposal was decidedly "live," "forced," and (considering the war needs) "momentous." It was: "Bring in your extra tires!" Upon analysis of the four presumed types of auditors in terms of the proposal, it was decided to limit the appeal to groups two and three. Group one was not considered to need any special persuasive pressure. As soon as it was announced that the government wanted to buy their tires to ensure a fair distribution of available supplies, it was assumed that they would hasten to co-operate. The members of group four probably could not be appealed to on any basis other than a threat of punishment if they did not yield their extra tires; and that was a method of force rather than persuasion to be consummated by policemen rather than speakers. Groups two and three probably were open to persuasion—but how?

The businessmen who depended upon tires for a livelihood would need to be convincingly reassured that tires would be available for their actual needs. Hence, as one main point in the speech the phrasing was devised, "The government is asking you to sell your extra tires not to take your car off the road but to keep it on the road." This point could be supported with facts on the number of tires and cars in the country, and with information on the development of synthetic rubber plants—both sets of facts designed to show that there were tires enough available if they were properly distributed.

The "smart" buyers had already enjoyed one principal fruit of their purchase of extra tires: their judgment had been demonstrated to be good. Now they could be asked to enjoy another: to accept the role of patriotic saviors of their less thoughtful neighbors by sharing their tires. To make this point, figures were assembled showing the number of cars that would have to cease operation (they were being put into storage daily at a tremendous rate) if the tires were not redistributed.

If such appeals really created a readiness to co-operate, the question of most vital import was precisely what action would be required of the auditors in order for them to act upon the speech's proposal. The purpose was not merely to convince the auditors that the country was confronted by a serious rubber shortage that could only be alleviated by the fair sharing of all available tires. In that case, the auditors might conclude that they should hold fast to all the tires they had or could get. No, the point was for each auditor to go home, pick up his telephone receiver, call the Railway Express Agency, and say, "I have an extra tire to sell to the government. Come and get it." Hence, a large portion of the speech was given over to an explanation of this process: no labeling or wrapping necessary—just call the Railway Express Agency. And the conclusion of the speech was designed to combine a patriotic appeal with a reminder to make the call.

A hypothetical example. The student who is seeking increased skill in persuasion would do well to follow some such process as is illustrated by the speech on tires. If his subject is "Structural Engineering," and his purpose is to persuade his fellow students to seek jobs in steel mills upon graduation, he should conduct his preparation of the speech through several stages. First, how should his audience of students be classified in relation to his purpose? To what different kinds of groups might he appeal with some hope of success?

To those who would gladly accept any kind of job?

To those having an interest in steel mills through their study of structural engineering?

To those who would regard working in a steel mill as a new and adventurous experience?

All these are possible audiences, and all different, even though they might sit tightly packed together in the same room. When the analysis of the audience is completed, the speaker should consider what kinds of material will prove most effective with each segment of his audience.

The question would arise as to whether these various kinds of appeals could be woven together into one speech. If not, which ones could most properly be omitted? Finally, as the crux of the matter, what specific action is desired of the students? To take jobs in a steel mill— yes. But unless the speaker is an employment agent for the mills, that goal is not specific enough. What should the audience do to lead to that action?

Should they go to the United States Employment Service office and register?

Should they band together and go in a body to a nearby steel mill to apply in person?

Should they sign an invitation for an employment agent of the mills to come to the campus to interview them?

Should they appoint the speaker (or someone else) as their representative to find out specifically what the employment opportunities might be?

Whatever precise action the audience would need to take ought to be clearly set forth, and an appeal for exactly that action should form the conclusion of the speech. The resultant talk might have flaws of one form or another, but at least it should be functional and directed squarely toward a "live" and "forced" proposal.

The individuality of the crowd

In the preceding section the assumption is that a single response is sought: one action to be performed individually by members of the audience. A factor to keep in mind is that even though the speech is addressed to all the auditors together, they must respond one by one. They may be interstimulated by one another's reactions, in a process called "social facilitation"—each member of the audience finding it easier to do what the great mass of them are doing than resisting and reacting in some different fashion. Yet the fact is that they sit one by one, they think one by one, and after the speech is ended they must act (or refrain from acting) on the speaker's proposal one by one. Persuasion is likely to be more effective if the speaker does not forget the individuality of the crowd.

This fact is readily illustrated from the practice of truly effective speakers. For instance, Varina Howell Davis, in *Jefferson Davis,* her biography of her husband, wrote:

> No speech was ever written for delivery. Dates and names were jotted down on two or three inches of paper, and these sufficed. Mr. Davis' speeches never read as they were delivered; he spoke fast, and thoughts crowded one another closely; a certain magnetism of manner and the excellent beauty and charm of his voice moved the multitude, and there were apparently no inattentive or indifferent listeners. He had one power that I have never seen excelled; while speaking he took in the individualty of the crowd, and seeing doubt or lack of coincidence with him in their faces, he answered the mental dissonance with arguments addressed to the ease of their minds. He was never tiresome because, as he said, he gave close attention to the necessity of stopping when he was done.

This summary by Mrs. Davis is practically a whole course in speech training. Don't write the speech. Use few notes. Speak fluently and cultivate a voice that will carry the mood of the speech. Be filled with thoughts that crowd upon one another. Speak with a certain magnetism. Stop when done. This is all good advice for any speaker.

It is her excellent phrase, "the individuality of the crowd," however, for which the passage has been particularly selected. Like other truly effective speakers, Jefferson Davis knew he was talking to people, to folks—and not to that nebulous abstraction, that nonexistent label, called an "audience." He realized as all persuasive speakers must that the persuasive proposal must be formulated, supported, and driven home for individual listeners rather than being aimed broadside at a general mass.

Booker T. Washington was praised especially for his ability to make every person in the hall—even those sitting behind pillars in the third balcony—feel that the speaker was talking in some special way directly to him. Carl Sandburg, attempting to explain the secret of Lincoln's power as a speaker, said he made every listener feel as though he and the speaker were seated side by side in a buckboard rolling across the prairie and engaged in a private conversation. The master propagandist Adolf Hitler, in *Mein Kampf* (a book still very much worth reading for its insights into persuasive methods, however evilly the writer may have been motivated) explained why he used speech rather than writing to build the Nazi Party: "An orator receives continuous guidance from his audience, enabling him to correct his lecture, since he can measure all the time on the countenance of his hearers the extent to which they are successful in following his arguments intelligently, and whether his words are producing the effect he desires."

Another great speaker of recent times was also a master of the *intimate touch*—remembering that he must address his proposal to persons, not to audiences. His talks were interlarded with such phrases as "My friends," "You and I know," "I have studied the map of your state as carefully as any one of you," and "I know your problems and they have become my problems as well." It was this quality of direct intimacy that won his nationwide broadcasts their description as "fireside chats." It was this *personalization*—this emphasis on the close relationship of speaker and individual listeners—that resulted in the common conclusion: "The New Deal was Franklin D. Roosevelt, neither more nor less."

Speakers must gauge the success or failure of their persuasiveness by the reactions of the individuals who compose the audiences. Even when we talk to people in the mass, they have to respond (with votes, with purchases, with changed lives) one by one. A flurry of questions from the floor may be better evidence of the effectiveness of a speech than a burst of applause. Harry Emerson Fosdick, the former great preacher of Riverside Church, has said that he knows a sermon has been a success only when some member of the congregation stops after church to say, "I think you will understand my problem. May I have a private conference with you?" One of the plainly marked routes to success in persuasion is to phrase and develop the proposal in accordance with Varina Howell Davis' penetrating phrase, "the individuality of the crowd."

Mechanics of the proposal

One of the chief causes of ineffective persuasion is failure to phrase the proposal specifically in terms of what the speaker wants the members of the audience actually to do. Let us assume that the subject matter is selected (The Need for New Community School Buildings, for example). The specific persuasive purpose is to induce the taxpaying auditors to support a plan for increased taxes with which to erect one or more new buildings. Facts, arguments, illustrations, and emotional appeals are assembled, all tending to show the need to help the children by relieving them from present overcrowded conditions. But the speaker must not make the mistake of being "subject-centered" as he prepares the speech. Whatever the facts derived from the subject may be, they will fail of the intended effect unless they are inserted as motives into the individual thinking of the various auditors who will hear (and read) the speech.

The speaker is getting seriously down to work on the persuasive problem when he begins to analyze his audience to discover into what categories it will fall in relation to his proposal. Some, with children in school, will be directly concerned; others, who have no school-age children, will not be. Of those who have children in school, some will feel that present facilities are good enough; some will feel that bad management by the school board and school administration is failing to take advantage of existing opportunities; some will have their attitude toward the schools distorted by imagined or real grievances about the way their own children are treated; some will suspect political or personal motives in any movement to spend more school funds; some will be enthusiastic for any plan to expand school facilities; and many will be so indifferent that when election day comes they will not even trouble to vote.

The actual time devoted to delivery of the speech may be only twenty minutes. But its eventual success or failure may well depend upon how many hours of intelligent analysis are devoted to considering how many voters are in each of the categories, in determining which of the segments must be appealed to, and in planning just how it can best be done.

The precise formulation of the proposal should result not from looking at the subject, but from looking at the audience-in-relation-to-the-subject.

Careful consideration should be given to the broad community *tinsit* (tendency-in-situation)—to the tendencies within the community in regard to education, to increasing taxes, to existing political conditions. And additional attention should be directed to the particular *tinsit* that will emerge when the meeting is held at which the speech is to be delivered—to determine what categories of voters will be present, how they will react toward one another, what they will think of the chairman and of the group that sponsors the meeting, what they will feel is the speaker's relation to the subject and to them as tax-payers.

Arising from such analyses, the speaker may formulate a proposal along *any one* of the following lines, or in any other specific way that seems to promise to achieve the maximum effect:

To induce belief that the actual per capita cost, spread over a period of years will be too small to be burdensome.

To create a general feeling of strong dissatisfaction with present conditions (leaving for later speeches the more explicit determination of what action to take).

To arouse a competitive desire to have schools that will give their children opportunities equal to those in rival communities.

To persuade members of the audience to organize into teams for house-to-house canvassing of the wards, to carry the message to individual voters.

To persuade each member present to go to the polls on election day.

These, of course, are but sample formulations of the proposal. To decide precisely what it should be is impossible except in terms of the audience analysis that has been recommended. The point the persuasive speaker should keep in mind is that he is not engaged in "persuasion in general," but in a limited and defined attempt to secure some specific response from the particular people to whom he is appealing under the special conditions existing at the time of the speech. Only as the persuasive goal is selected and refined in this manner can the speaker hope for genuine persuasive success.

Conclusion

This chapter has been written in the conviction that a great many persuasive speeches fail because the speaker is not sufficiently "audience-centered" as he prepares his speech. The proposal must be kept in mind as the end-all and be-all of the persuasive process. And the proposal is a "live," "forced," and "momentous" proposition only as it is realistically addressed to the specific auditors who will receive it under the particular conditions existing at the time of the speech. It should never leave any doubt in the minds of the audience that each individual in it is being asked to do some specific thing that will lead directly to a desirable result.

Exercises

1. Phrase five subjects on which you might give persuasive speeches.
2. For each subject, phrase one definite proposal.
3. Select one proposal and show how it is definitely correlated with the action-possibilities of the audience to which the speech might be addressed.
4. Considering the audience as a collection of individuals, show what specific action might be taken by each individual auditor in response to your proposal.
5. Analyze your audience into segments, based upon their probable initial reaction toward your proposal.
6. Prepare and deliver a five-minute persuasive speech supporting the proposal you selected for Exercise 3.
7. The following readings may be consulted:

William Norwood Brigance, "What Is a Successful Speech?" in Haig A. Bosmajian (ed.), *Readings in Speech* (New York: Harper and Row, 1965), pp. 14-19.

Walter Coutu, *Emergent Human Nature* (New York: Knopf, 1949), particularly Chapter VIII, "Human Needs Are Meanings," pp. 255-280.

William James, "The Will to Believe," in *The Will to Believe and Other Essays in Popular Philosophy* (New York: Longmans, Green, 1921), pp. 1-31.

Robert T. Oliver and Dominick A. Barbara, *The Healthy Mind in Communion and Communication* (Springfield, Ill.: Charles C Thomas, 1962).

Ivan Preston, "Inconsistency: A Persuasive Device," in James H. Campbell and Hal W. Hepler (eds.), *Dimensions in Communication* (Belmont, Cal.: Wadsworth, 1965), pp. 95-102.

✍ 15.

Organizing the Persuasive Speech

EVERY SPEECH SHOULD HAVE A BEGINNING, A MIDDLE, and an end. This elementary principle of composition would seem to be too obvious to require statement. But it is only necessary to read or to listen to a succession of speeches to realize that it is a truth that many speakers must consider to have only academic significance: something for textbooks to discuss, but not for practical speakers to use. As a matter of fact, there is no more practical consideration for the speaker to keep in mind than the necessity of this threefold process: (1) to get the audience started thinking along the line he wishes to pursue; (2) to secure the audience's willing acceptance of his point of view; (3) to clinch that acceptance with the positive affirmation or action his proposal requires. In briefest compass, these are the functions of the introduction, the discussion, and the conclusion of a persuasive speech.

Governing principles of organization

The persuasive speech should be so organized that it will tend to lead the auditors from where they are when the speaker begins to where he wants them to be.

The persuasive speech is unified around its proposal.

The coherence of the persuasive speech is provided by its persistent adherence to the task of motivation of the audience being addressed.

The developmental stages of the persuasive speech are determined by anticipated acceptance-responses of the audience.

The outline of the persuasive speech should represent vital stages in the link between the audience and the speaker's proposal.

1. *Introduction.* The introduction should always start where the audience is, not where the speaker is. If the audience is as well informed on the subject or as interested in it as the speaker, then there is no need for the speech. But when the audience needs to be aroused, the speaker must deliberately devise a method for securing its interest. This he may do with any of the attention devices discussed in Chapter 6. But he must always keep firmly in mind the various interweaving factors that enter into the speech: the audience, the speaker, the subject, and the occasion. A good question for the speaker to ask himself to aid in his search for the right type of introductory material is: *Why should this audience, on this occasion, care to hear me, with my particular status and background, discuss this proposal?* In the answer to this quadrilateral question lie the best cues as to what his introduction should contain.

2. *Discussion.* The discussion or body of the speech is subdivided in turn into two, or three, or four parts, depending on the amount of time the speaker will have. Each part is devoted to the development of one of the *main ideas* that the speaker has selected as the principal supports for his proposal. Each main idea should be chosen for its maximum motivational effect. For instance, a recent speech that the writer heard urging the local Kiwanis members to attend a regional meeting was built around the following ideas:

    I. The meeting will provide excitement, fun, and a dash of adventure.
    II. It will be socially advantageous to meet Kiwanians from the entire district.
    III. It is the duty of the members to support the club's activities.

In this instance, the speaker deduced that his auditors might be led to act upon the basis of the first two main ideas, *provided* he could give them, in the third, a means of salving their consciences, by making it appear that they were acting on a basis of obligation rather than out of regard for self-interest.

In any persuasive speech the first question regarding the main ideas should be: Are they adequate to achieve the purpose? If the auditors do accept these ideas without question, will they therefore be led to the conclusion which the speaker wants them to accept? Second: Are the ideas stated so clearly and emphasized so effectively that they will be understood and remembered? Third: Are the ideas supported sufficiently and in such a manner that the audience will want to accept them? Fourth: Does the speech contain more than enough to achieve the purpose? A speech not only can lead *to* agreement, but can just as surely lead *away from* it. A salesman, for instance, can talk himself out of a sale, as well as into one. Knowing when to stop is an essential attribute of a good speaker. To avoid the weakening effects of discursiveness, the speaker should always take care to have no more main ideas and no more development of each one than is essential for the achievement of the first three requirements that the main ideas must meet.

3. *Conclusion.* A persuasive speech fails if the speaker comes right up to the point of asking for acceptance of his proposal—successfully —but then stops. It is necessary not only to lay the basis for agreement, but actually to win it. The conclusion is the "sign on the dotted line" portion of the speech. The introduction has sown the seeds, the discussion has cultivated the crop, and the function of the conclusion is to reap the harvest. Generally the conclusion of a persuasive speech takes the form of an appeal for action. But this should be so phrased that the action will be almost taken for granted. It should be presented as the most natural thing to do. The speaker should make it easy for the audience to agree with him and hard to disagree. Having carried the auditors through the various stages of the discussion, he should not so much *ask* them *if* they will now accept his conclusion, but should agree with them that as a result of the foregoing factors, such-and-such is what they all want to do. Sometimes the conclusion assumes agreement and deals primarily with the means of putting it into effect. An appeal for funds, for instance, may conclude with the distribution of cards upon which every member can write his pledge, or the passing of a plate into which the money can be dropped. Whatever the speaker

wishes to accomplish by means of the speech should definitely be brought to a head and consummated in the concluding remarks.

Start with the audience

In every type of speaking it is advisable for the speaker to begin his talk with an effort to seize upon the existing interest of the audience. As an obvious illustration, when you see a friend in a crowd on a busy street, you must attract his attention before you can start talking to him. If you should arise to speak from the floor in the midst of an animated discussion, it is likewise apparent that your first requirement is to base your own remarks upon the topics and points of view that are already before the group for consideration. When you are the featured speaker, the chairman who introduces you does a part of the task of building a bridge between you as a person and your subject on the one hand, and the audience on the other. In all such instances, it might be asserted metaphorically that you can't transport the minds of the audience on your own train of ideas until after you have induced them to board the train. If you start talking without engaging attention to what you are saying, and interest in it, you may very likely proceed along your own course while leaving the audience behind.

Such considerations are already familiar to all who have made an initial study of public speaking. It is well known that a fundamental purpose of the introduction is to arouse interest in the subject, and that all through the speech the successful speaker must be *audience-centered* rather than *self-centered* or *subject-centered* in his thinking. However true this may be for all types of speaking, it is the very life and breath of persuasive speech.

Since persuasive speech seeks to induce the audience to change its own beliefs, feelings, or action, it follows as a matter of course that the subject must be developed from the audience's points of view. Earlier chapters, particularly Chapter 3, have reiterated this view and have shown how it needs to be woven into the very fabric of the speech. This requirement goes far beyond such methods as may readily be recommended to the speaker (though it also includes them):

1. Make liberal use of such personal pronouns as "we," "you," "you and I," and of such terms as "You know," "we all realize," "your problems," etc.

2. Make free use of questions as a means of drawing the audience into an active consideration of the subject, using:

    a. *Rhetorical questions,* or questions that answer themselves, such as "Can we ignore the very elements in our community that may ruin the lives of our own children?" "Would you enter into any business arrangement that was certain to fail?"

    b. *Questions of fact,* designed to emphasize your evidence, such as "How many families in the United States have an income of less than $3,000 a year? How do they live? What effects do their low income have on the rest of us? Let us examine these questions and see where they may lead."

    c. *Questions of opinion,* designed to suggest attitudes favoring the speaker's proposal, such as "How can these conditions best be remedied? Will it be done by electing a new political party to office? Will it require a basic change in our economic system? Or are there other remedies as yet untried?"

    d. *Test questions,* intended to establish standards for judging issues, such as "How, then, shall we decide these questions? Will the proposals that have been made prove practical? Will they achieve the desired results? Will they lead to new problems, perhaps worse than those now plaguing us?"

    e. *Suggestive questions,* that really embody arguments in question form, such as "Isn't it true that a war may be caused by the very effort to avoid it at all costs—by retreating, and submitting, and appeasing until all chance of equitable and honest negotiation has been lost?"

    f. *Definitive questions,* used to pin down the thinking of the audience to the precise points the speaker wishes to consider, such as "Just what, then, does religion mean to us as individuals? Is it a means of escaping from personal responsibility or is it a method of making sure that our real responsibilities will be understood and met?"

    g. *Personalized questions,* designed to bring the subject to bear directly upon every individual in the audience, such as "Can we avoid consideration of such a problem as this? If we don't try to solve it, what will happen to us? Is there any way out for such individuals as you and I?"

3. Adapt your introductory remarks to the immediate circumstances of the meeting—to the purpose for which it was called, to the remarks of other speakers, to any business that may have been conducted, or to any special features of the occasion (such as the fact that it may have been called by a petition, or that it meets on the Fourth of July, or that it is sponsored by the Mayor's Committee on Better Business).

4. Utilize special attention-getting devices, such as humorous stories, or challenges to the audience, or sensational facts, or dramatic references to current events.

5. Polarize the audience or unify its feelings by methods described in Chapter 11.

6. Present a "common ground" on which you and the audience are united in your broad view of the subject, whatever may be the differences on details.

All these devices are useful for establishing a direct relationship between the audience and the speaker's proposal. Their usefulness, however, is severely limited so long as they remain simply *devices.* They will not greatly assist any speaker who prepares his speech according to his own views or according to what the subject matter itself may seem to require, and *afterward inserts such devices in an attempt to relate his speech to his audience.* From its very inception, the persuasive speech should be audience-centered. The speaker should phrase his proposal, select his subject, gather his evidence, formulate his reasoning and other means of support, shape his illustrations, and decide on his specific phrasing all in terms of the key consideration, "What is the audience point of view that must be taken into account if my proposal is to win acceptance?" From such a point of view, the speaker will genuinely utilize the kinds of approach that have been outlined, so that they cease to be superficial devices and become an integral part of the fabric of his thinking.

Unify the persuasive speech around its proposal

The ancient world was unified in the fact that "All roads led to Rome." A persuasive speech is unified when all parts of it point toward the acceptance of its proposal. Persuasion occurs for the precise purpose of establishing proposals. The only unifying principle that applies, then, is the unity derived from this purpose. This principle is violated if the speaker introduces stories merely because they are interesting, or cites facts simply to display his information, or formulates arguments to demonstrate his skill in logic, or phrases his ideas as an exercise in stylistic display. In order to insure persuasive unity, the speaker should proceed through the following steps:

1. The proposal should be stated simply and directly in terms of the desired audience response.

2. The audience should be analyzed in terms of its relation to and probable attitudes toward the proposal.

3. The subject should be analyzed to determine what can be said about it to advance the thinking of the auditors of varying sorts toward the desired conclusion.

4. After such analysis, the speaker should decide upon several key ideas that he must implant in the audience's minds in order to dispose them favorably toward his proposal.

5. Each of these key ideas should be phrased in terms of greatest acceptability to the audience.

6. These key ideas should be arranged in an order that promises to be most effective in leading the audience by easy stages toward acceptance of the proposal. This order may be from the *most readily acceptable* to the *hardest to accept,* thus securing an early "yes response" from the audience and predisposing it to acquiesce in the more debatable points that follow. Sometimes the speaker may wish to start with the *least familiar* arguments, on the theory that their *novelty* may attract the audience, and their unfamiliarity may lead the audience to accept the facts the speaker knows far better than they do themselves. For some subjects the speaker may start with *appeals to self-interest,* so the audience will see what it has to gain by agreeing with him, and conclude with *demonstrations of public welfare* to be achieved by his proposal, so the audience will have good socially acceptable reasons for agreeing with him. The *Dewey thought formula* and *stock issues* methods of organizing the main ideas have been described in Chap-

ter 10. Whatever order of presentation is decided upon should be determined from the single consideration of what will most effectively lead the audience from where its thinking commences to a final acceptance of the proposal.

7. The supporting facts, reasoning, emotional appeals, and rationalization (whether embodied in examples, anecdotes, comparisons, statistics, quotations, or any other forms of support) should also be selected from the standpoint of audience motivation. An authority who may be quoted, for instance, is no more persuasive than the audience may think him to be. If he is unknown to the audience, the speaker should either not quote him or should be sure to build up an audience respect for his views.

8. Through internal summaries and a final conclusion, all the evidence should be drawn together and pointed directly toward audience acceptance of the proposal. Evidence that is not worth "nailing down" is scarcely worth introducing into the speech.

9. Frequent reference should be made through the speech to points previously discussed, so that the audience is never in doubt as to how the entire speech is knit together around the single purpose which the speaker hopes to achieve.

Achieve persuasive coherence through motivation

Coherence is the quality of *binding together*. A speech coheres when the audience sees a direct and ready relationship between the sentences and between the various points, ideas, or appeals. The fundamental source of all coherence is the basic unity of the speech. A speech that is truly unified is so inevitably one compact whole that the relations of the parts to one another are organic. One part grows out of another, and all grow together around the central core, which is the proposal.

As guides to persuasive coherence, the following tests should be kept in mind:

1. Are sentences and paragraphs united by *transitional* terms? Such words and phrases as *also, on the other hand, consequently, as I have said, in view of this fact,* and a multitude of similar terms help

to tie together the successive sentences. The speaker should remember that such transitions are far more essential in speaking than in writing, since spoken words once uttered are gone and the audience cannot retrace in their minds to seek a relationship that is not instantly apparent.

2. Are key words repeated? Note how Winston Churchill used this device to insure coherence in the following paragraph from his speech before the House of Commons on December 6, 1939: "The convoy system is now in full operation. Very few ships have been attacked in convoy; less than one in 750 has been sunk. Nevertheless, we must remember that convoy involves a certain definite loss of carrying power, since the ships have to wait during the assembly of the convoy, and the convoy must travel at the rate of the slowest ship. This loss is being steadily reduced by the institution of slow and fast convoys, and by other appropriate measures; but a certain delay must always remain, a certain diminution, that is to say, in the actual fertility of our convoys."

3. Is there an actual and apparent interrelationship of the ideas? The audience should always be aware of a definite progression from one stage to another; of the fact that one idea grows out of or is the natural outcome of those which precede it; and of the further fact that each idea also points ahead to what is to come.

4. Are the relationships of main and subordinate statements properly clarified? Sentences joined together by *and* conceal or deny this relationship. When *and* is used frequently, it is probable that the speaker himself does not see the real relationship of his ideas, and certainly his method of phrasing makes it more difficult for the audience. Consider the contrast between the following two paragraphs:

a. China in recent years has had a difficult history and was subjected to continuous warfare ever since 1937 and this is a much longer time than any other nation has had to fight and we blame the Chinese for falling into disunity and for other faults and we forget that war is a strain upon any nation and it would be much fairer for us to help rather than criticize.

The Psychology of Persuasive Speech

How much more coherent the ideas become when proper relationships are indicated between the main and subordinate ideas, as in the following:

> *b.* China in recent years has had a difficult history. We need only remember that she has been at war continuously ever since 1937, a much longer time than any other nation has had to fight. Instead of blaming the Chinese for falling into disunity and for other faults, we should recall that war is a considerable strain upon any nation. It would be much fairer for us to help rather than to criticize.

5. Is the audience shown clearly how each part of the speech relates to audience interests, needs, and motives? In a persuasive speech it is far more forgivable to permit a looseness of relationship among the ideas than it is to permit a looseness of relationship of any single part to the audience itself. The printed text of even a superior persuasive speech may read somewhat incoherently, provided the relationship of each part to the audience itself is clear. This may be one of the elements the great English debater and statesman, Charles James Fox, had in mind when he asked, "Did the speech read well? Then it was a poor speech." If there is a basic difference between written and oral composition, it lies in the fact that writing more often concentrates upon a proper development of the subject matter, whereas the speech concentrates upon influencing the audience in relation to the proposal. The writer makes sure that all sentences are tied together. The speaker makes sure that all sentences are tied to the audience. This particular characteristic may be illustrated by another brief quotation from Winston Churchill, this time from his speech of July 4, 1940:

> A large proportion of the French Fleet has, therefore, passed into our hands or has been put out of action or otherwise withheld from Germany by yesterday's events. The House will not expect me to say anything about other French ships which are at large except that it is our inflexible resolve to do everything that is possible in order to prevent them falling into the German grip. I leave the judgment of our action, with confidence, to Parliament. I leave it to the nation, and I leave it to the United States. I leave it to the world and history.

In all these five methods of securing coherence, the speaker is chiefly concerned to insure that the audience sees clearly how all the successive parts of the speech build together to lead directly toward acceptance of the proposal. The parts cohere fundamentally because they supplement one another in a common devotion to this single aim. In this sense, a persuasive speech is coherent precisely as is a football team. The players gear their efforts into shifting patterns of play, but all are designed to "establish the proposal" (i.e., make touchdowns) for their team and to "destroy the proposal" (i.e., prevent touchdowns) of the opposition. The relationship of one play to another, or even of the parts of a single play, on the football field are significant primarily in terms of the purpose to be achieved. Just so is it in a persuasive speech.

Develop through anticipated acceptance-responses

In organizing any speech, the theme, specific purpose, or proposal is first introduced to the audience, then supported by a series of main ideas, and finally concluded. We are here concerned with what *main ideas* should be formulated in the persuasive speech and how they should be developed. As in all our other reasoning about persuasion, the primary requirement is to manage the main ideas in such a manner as to predispose the audience to accept the proposal.

It is useful to think of the main ideas as constituting successive stages of audience acceptance of the proposal. Since the precise audience response cannot, of course, be known in advance, these responses can only be anticipated. One of the fundamental purposes of audience analysis is to predetermine:

1. What the audience will have to accept, if it is to agree to the proposal;
2. What the audience is likely to accept willingly; and
3. What must be done to win acceptance of essential considerations that may be resisted.

This kind of audience analysis has already been described and illustrated, in terms of the Victory Speakers speech to obtain surplus tires and a hypothetical speech to students who might be induced to apply for jobs with a steel company.

Restated, the process that the persuasive speaker should follow in selecting, phrasing, ordering, and supporting his main ideas is as follows:

1. Follow the process of insuring unity of the speech, as outlined earlier in this chapter.

2. Prepare a flexible body of supporting material for each main idea, so that the presentation of support for it may be either expanded or contracted as the response of the audience may seem to require. This means that the speaker in preparing his speech should utilize the "iceberg technique." As we know, some seven eighths of the iceberg is below the surface of the water, and only one eighth is seen. Similarly, a speaker should prepare many more supporting data than he thinks he probably will need for each of his main ideas. As he delivers his speech, he has the comfortable assurance that what he is telling the audience is only a fraction of what he could tell them in support of his assertions. This fact gives him a fullness of confidence that is inevitably reflected in his voice and bearing and thus becomes of itself a persuasive factor.

3. The speech should be so well prepared that the speaker can "forget" his material and give closest attention to audience responsiveness. When he sees that his audience is agreeing with his point, he should conclude what he is saying about it and proceed to the next stage—regardless of whether he has "covered" what he had planned to say. As all good salesmen know, many a sale is lost by saying too much after the prospect is already convinced. On the other hand, it may well prove true that you may say what you had planned for a particular point and the audience still remains unconvinced. On such occasions, it would be useless to "proceed" to another point. What would actually happen would be that you as the speaker might "proceed" but the audience would remain unmoved, thus nullifying your persuasive effort. What is clearly required in such an instance is that more persuasive ammunition is required to break through a resistance

area that has proved more stubborn than was anticipated when the speech was prepared.

Nothing is more fatal to effective persuasive speaking than the point of view that a speech is to be prepared and then delivered as a preordained whole. Persuasion is a form of force applied to overcome the resistance represented by audience reluctance, indifference, or opposition to the proposal. The speaker can no more be certain in advance of precisely how much force he will need to apply than can an artillery officer know for certain how much fire power will be required to break down enemy fortifications. The two rules to be kept in mind are: (1) have plenty of ammunition of the right kinds, and (2) keep using it until the objective is accomplished.

Once again we may profit from the insight of the effective persuader, Adolf Hitler, as he explained in *Mein Kampf* why he built up the Nazi Party through spoken rather than written propaganda:

An orator receives continuous guidance from his audience, enabling him to correct his lecture, since he can measure all the time on the countenances of his hearers the extent to which they are successful in following his arguments intelligently and whether his words are producing the effect he desires, whereas the writer has no acquaintance with his readers. Hence he is unable to prepare his sentences with a view to addressing a definite crowd of people, sitting in front of his eyes, but he is obliged to argue in general terms.

Supposing that an orator observes that his hearers do not understand him, he will make his explanation so elementary and clear that every single one must take it in; if he feels that they are incapable of following him, he will build up his ideas carefully and slowly until the weakest member has caught up; again, once he senses that they seem not to be convinced that he is correct in his arguments, he will repeat them over and over again with fresh illustrations and himself state their unspoken objections; he will continue thus until the last group of the opposition show him by their behavior and play of expression that they have capitulated to his demonstration of the case.

Outlining the body of a persuasive speech

Since an outline is a working guide to what the speaker intends to do while delivering his speech, it is obvious that an outline of a persuasive speech should have sufficient flexibility to make possible a close responsiveness of the speaker to his audience. The brief has already been described as a means of outlining or organizing the speech material for purposes of analyzing and testing its probable effectiveness. The brief is intended primarily as an aid to the speaker in his task of preparation. The outline can be completed only after the preliminary spadework has been done. As a guide to what the speaker will present to the audience, the following process is suggested:

First, phrase a *title.* The title should ordinarily be short and vivid. Often it is well to phrase a title that piques curiosity (like "The Forgotten Woman") or that will be remembered in retrospect as embodying the proposal (like "Look to the East").

Second, as has consistently been emphasized, phrase the proposal.

Third, determine upon and phrase the main ideas (based upon anticipated acceptance responses) that will serve as broad steps leading directly to audience agreement with the proposal. Each main idea should be designed to draw the audience closer to final agreement, and as the ideas are phrased with this purpose in mind, their interrelationships and order of presentation are generally dictated by their successive functions. To arrive at his main ideas, the speaker asks himself, "What will my audience have to believe before they can and will wish to accept my proposal?" The things they must believe become, then, the main ideas the speaker must establish.

Fourth, in support of each main idea, jot down the examples, statistics, testimony, personal experiences, reasoning, and so forth, that seem to promise the best results in winning agreement with the idea.

Fifth, formulate first an introduction and then a conclusion for the speech.

Sixth, put the material thus selected into outline form, so that (1) you may look at it in its essence to judge of its probable effectiveness as a whole; (2) you may get a clear idea of the functional plan

you are adopting and thus aid your memory in remembering it; and
(3) you may use it for review as the time for the speech approaches.

A brief sample outline for a persuasive speech might appear as
follows:

"Look to the East"

Proposal: This audience should agree that America's own best interests
will be served by helping to prevent the extension or continuance of
any communist government in Asia outside the borders of the Soviet
Union.

Introduction

I. Past experience teaches us that all events have beginnings, some of
which may be relatively remote.
   A. Our own present interest in world affairs was caused or at least
   heightened by such "foreign" affairs as Mussolini's invasion of
   Ethiopia, Hitler's seizure of Czechoslovakia, and Japan's annexa-
   tion of Manchuria.
   B. Neither Germany's attack on Poland nor Japan's bombing of
   Pearl Harbor happened without a prior series of events, which
   we can now see led directly to those outcomes.

II. We may safely assume that occurrences today are also building
toward some future eventuality that may be good or bad, depending
largely on what is now being done about them.

Body

I. *Seek audience acceptance for the idea that:* Establishment of a communist government in any area is equivalent to control of that area
by the Soviet Union.
   A. Cite testimony by communist leaders of various nationalities and
   by Soviet spokesmen, showing the dependence of worldwide
   communism upon Cominform and Kremlin leadership.
   B. Cite examples of specific Soviet domination of various countries
   with communist governments.

II. *Seek audience acceptance for the idea that:* Communist control of
Asia already extends over an area larger than that seized by Japan
prior to American demands presented in 1941 that Japan must re-
linquish at least part of her gains.
   A. Remind the audience, perhaps with aid of maps, of the comparative extent of prewar Japanese and postwar communist advances in Asia.

    B. Cite passages from Cordell Hull's *Memoirs,* Robert Sherwood's *Roosevelt and Hopkins,* and other sources to show how the United States regarded the Japanese advances as endangering American security.

    C. Ask your audience whether communism doesn't constitute at least as much of a menace to the United States as did Japanese imperialism.

III. *Seek audience acceptance for the idea that:* We should avoid the mistake of postponing opposition to conquest of Asia now, as we did postpone opposition prior to Pearl Harbor.

    A. Remind the audience of our sales of military supplies to Japan and of our various "isolationist" withdrawals from responsibility for Asian affairs.

    B. Remind the audience that Italy, Germany, and Japan all became more ambitious for conquest, the more their various military adventures succeeded.

    C. Draw the conclusion that as we permit communism to succeed in seizing new areas, Russia's ambition and military strength will both increase.

Conclusion

  I. We cannot escape the conclusion that events of the future—the out-break of war or the safeguarding of peace—depend upon present occurrences.

 II. We owe it to our own safety and to the preservation of democracy and freedom to take a strong national stand against the continued expansion or even the continued existence of communist governments in Asia beyond the boundaries of the Soviet Union.

It will be seen that an outline of this type has two characteristics. First, it is a rather definite plan for the course the persuasive speech should pursue. Second, based as it is upon a clear recognition of the need of securing audience acceptance of each succeeding main idea, it provides for a wide latitude of flexibility in determining just how much time and what kind and amount of supporting data should be devoted to the establishment of each idea. This combination of definiteness and flexibility is precisely the kind of outline needed for effective persuasive speaking.

Conclusion

The philosophy of persuasion presented in this book stresses the necessity of close consideration of the audience in the preparation and presentation of every persuasive speech. It has been emphasized throughout that the speaker should not only draw his persuasive appeals from himself and from the subject, but also from his audience; and that he should consider his audience not in the abstract but in direct relationship to its moods, feelings, attitudes, and circumstances at the time the speech is presented. The purpose of this chapter is to show that such a philosophy does not deny the need for careful advance preparation. Rather, the need for preparation is all the greater, as the primacy of the audience is understood.

In successive stages of preparation, suggestions have been presented for preparing and organizing a speech based upon anticipated audience responsiveness to the main ideas needed to support the speaker's proposal. A method of outlining has been suggested that encourages the utmost care in preparation, the freedom of the speaker to vary, modify, and adapt his speech as it progresses, with maximum latitude, and yet provides a precise plan of attack based upon careful predetermination of what must be accomplished to win acceptance of the proposal.

As the persuasive speaker conforms to the governing principles set forth at the beginning of this chapter, and elaborated in succeeding sections, he surely should gain increasing aptitude for speaking with flexible and sensitive reaction to the audience, yet utilizing the maximum advantages of careful preparation. For it cannot be reiterated too often that concentration upon the reaction of the audience is, first of all, an absolute necessity for successful persuasion, and, secondly, that such concentration is wholly consonant with and dependent upon a thorough mastery of the subject matter of the speech and systematic organization of its mode of presentation.

The goal of the persuasive speaker should be system without rigidity, and an alert adaptation to the needs of the immediate situation growing out of a thoughtful and orderly preparation. The more you know about your subject and the more clearly you see the general course your persuasion must follow, the greater freedom you can attain to vary and modify your specific mode of attack as the speech unfolds.

Exercises

1. Every persuasive speech prepared and delivered is in itself an exercise in persuasive outlining. All should be tested by the governing principles listed at the beginning of this chapter.

2. The class may discuss the question of the extent to which a persuasive speech outline should be modified during delivery of the speech, in accord with the perceived acceptance-responses of the audience.

3. As time permits, each of the speeches delivered in class should be analyzed and evaluated in class discussion, with particular attention to its organization.

4. After you have delivered a persuasive speech, write an evaluation of it in terms of the audience responsiveness to its successive stages. Indicate what changes in its organization you feel, in retrospect, would have improved its effectiveness.

5. Special studies of organization include the following:

E. P. Bettinghaus, "The Operation of Congruity in an Oral Communication Situation," *Speech Monographs,* 28 (August, 1961), 131-142.

R. S. Cathcart, "An Experimental Study of Four Methods of Presenting Evidence," *Speech Monographs,* 22 (August, 1955), 227-233.

H. Gilkinson, S. F. Paulson, and D. E. Sikkink, "Effects of Order and Authority in an Argumentative Speech," *Quarterly Journal of Speech,* 40 (April, 1954), 183-192.

C. I. Hovland (ed.), *The Order of Presentation in Persuasion* (New Haven: Yale University Press, 1957).

Gilbert Stillman McVaugh, "Structural Analysis of the Sermons of Harry Emerson Fosdick," *Quarterly Journal of Speech,* 18 (November, 1932), 531-546.

D. E. Sikkink, "An Experimental Study of the Effects on the Listener of Anticlimax Order and Authority in an Argumentative Speech," *Southern Speech Journal,* 22 (Winter, 1956), 73-78.

R. G. Smith, "An Experimental Study of the Effects of Speech Organization upon Attitudes of College Students," *Speech Monographs,* 18 (November, 1951), 292-301.

Eugene E. White and Clair R. Henderlider, "What Harry S Truman Told Us about His Speaking," *Quarterly Journal of Speech,* 40 (February, 1954), 37-42.

✍ 16.

Analyzing Evidence: The Brief

THE MORE YOU KNOW, HERBERT SPENCER ONCE wrote, the more confused your thinking will be until you get your knowledge and ideas organized. The brief is the standardized logical form of organizing arguments and their supporting evidence to determine whether they prove a specific proposal. The brief is precise and definite, offering little opportunity for individuality or experimentation or for specific adaptation to particular audiences. The brief is subject-centered and rigid in its requirements. For these very reasons it has real value for students who are learning how to assemble, organize, and evaluate their persuasive materials. The brief is a kind of specialized filing cabinet, with drawers labeled and waiting for the right subject matter to be placed in them. Thus it is easy to tell when essential materials are missing, and with a little practice it is also easy to tell when items are being incorrectly classified or wrongly used. The brief is a demanding but helpful taskmaster, and as such is a good device for guiding analysis of the subject matter and for helping to learn the principles of logical organization.

Uses of the brief

Lawyers use the brief as a means of presenting the evidence and arguments that they assemble for study by judges of appellate courts. For them it is an ideal vehicle, permitting them to organize their evidence in a fashion that is clear and readily studied by a dispassionate judge who makes every effort to eliminate from his thinking all considerations except the precise evidence and the laws by which it should be judged. Persuasive speakers, however, addressing audiences whose thinking is less rigorously controlled, have few or no occasions to use the brief as an actual outline from which their speeches are to be delivered. Since the brief is subject-centered, whereas persuasive speech is audience-centered, the brief would seem to be antithetical to the requirements of the persuasive speaking situation. If this is the case, of what value is a study of the brief to persuasive speakers?

To learn organization. The now seldom-used method of studying grammar by diagramming sentences had at least the value of requiring the student to understand the organization of the sentence into its several parts. The brief performs a similar function with respect to assembled facts and arguments relating to a proposal. Students who "do not know how to organize" (and their name seems to be legion) can scarcely fail to learn the principles of systematic relationship of materials as they work on formulating a brief. This value alone is sufficient to justify its study.

To determine the adequacy of materials. As speakers gather facts and ideas for support of their chosen proposals, it is often very difficult to tell when "enough" information and arguments have been gathered to establish the speaker's case. The best way to judge of their adequacy is to organize them into a brief, where it can be seen at a glance whether each essential point is fully developed and "proved." (It should be re-emphasized, however, that "adequacy" is used here in relation to subject matter rather than audience. What might be adequate to an impartial judge might be either too much or too little for an ordinary untrained and partial audience. Nevertheless, it obviously is advantageous for the persuasive speaker to know whether in an objective sense he has gathered the data necessary to establish his proposal logically.)

To arrange materials systematically. Facts, arguments, and appeals that are heaped together miscellaneously are of little value. When the same materials are systematically arranged in a brief, the speaker can see at a glance what they are. what their functions are, and how they may be used. With the brief serving thus as a "filing system" it is easy to use it as a point of departure in reorganizing the materials in an audience-centered persuasive outline.

To utilize the materials for debate. Debating is excellent practice in logical organization, logical argument, critical thinking, and development of intellectual quickness in detecting the strong and weak points in argument. Typically, the debate is developed according to the brief, for this method is a useful guide to orderly and adequate reasoning about the proposal. Students of persuasive speech may well proceed through practice in debating to strengthen their awareness of the methods of proof and rebuttal. The good debater is not necessarily a *persuasive* speaker, but persuasion surely may be aided by a background of training in debate.

Requirements of the brief

The brief is a logical organization of facts and arguments designed to prove the validity of a specific proposal. Its specific requirements arise out of this function.

First, the proposal has to be phrased in definite, unambiguous, precise terms. The most popular method is the form used in debate, "Resolved, that. . . ." A brief could not be drawn up to prove "federal aid to education." There is no assertion or proposal here to be proved. A brief could, however, be drawn to support the proposal, "Resolved, that the federal government should make grants to the several states for use in promoting public education, such grants to be equal to the sums raised by taxation within each state." Any doubtful terms in the proposal should be clearly defined.

Second, the brief should indicate what is and what is not to be proved. In other words, the brief contains an analytical section differentiating what has to be proved from what is: (1) irrelevant, or (2) admitted to be true. This analytical section identifies the issues, or points in dispute, which must be established with facts and reasoning.

Third, the brief should indicate the standards of reasoning by which the truth or falsity of the arguments can be gauged. Thus, it establishes the tests by which judgment on the evidence will be based. In some debate questions, for instance, the phrase "constitutionality waived" is inserted, meaning that whether or not the proposal is constitutional will not be considered as a standard of reasoning concerning its merits. As was indicated in the last chapter, these standards of reasoning should be equally applicable to all competing proposals, and thus equally acceptable to all the disputants.

Fourth, the brief should organize in logical form the arguments by which the proposal is supported (for an affirmative brief) or opposed (for a negative brief).

Fifth, the brief should assemble such evidence as is required to prove the arguments.

Sixth, the brief should conclude with a summation of the arguments, showing how they do, in effect, prove (or disprove) the proposal.

Form of the brief

The brief is organized into three parts, like other speech outlines: the introduction, body, and conclusion. The introduction should: (1) define any ambiguous terms; (2) state agreed-upon or admitted factors, which are therefore not in dispute; (3) state the issues or points of controversy that must be proved; and (4) establish the standards of reasoning by which the issues must be judged. In addition, the introduction *may* include such considerations as: (1) why the proposal is living, forced, and momentous—i.e., why it should be discussed; and (2) what its historical background has been. Whatever the material in the introduction may be, it should be noncontroversial. That is to say, the material in the introduction of an affirmative brief and a negative brief could be, and often is, identical. In any event, the introduction should exclude all materials that might be objected to by any of the disputants. The purpose of the introduction is to lay a basis of agreement on basic principles by which debate on the issues is possible. Argument could not proceed, for instance, on the proposal, Smith is guilty of murder, unless both prosecutor and defense attorney were agreed as to the nature of the law regarding murder and the nature of evidence required for conviction. The body presents the arguments (often the stock issues described in Chapter 10) together with their supporting evidence. And the conclusion summarizes the arguments and draws the conclusion that the proposal should (or should not) be accepted.

Within each of these three parts, the material is organized to show its logical connections. The brief is a series of assertions, followed by proof. Connecting terms are used between the assertions and the proof, and between various parts of the proof, to indicate their logical relationship. Thus the brief is interlarded with such words as *for, since, and, but,* and *therefore.*

Standardized symbols are utilized to indicate at a glance the relative functions of various elements in the brief, thus making easier the determination of whether a logical pattern has been achieved, and to mark the position of every item of proof. The main arguments are indicated by Roman numerals (I, II, III, etc.); the chief supporting assertions by capital letters (A, B, C, etc.); the evidence for the assertions by Arabic numerals (1, 2, 3, etc.); and the illustrative materials by which the evidence is developed by small letters (a, b, c, etc.) on the first level, and subsequently by parenthetical numbers—(1), (2), (3), etc., and, if necessary, by parenthetical small letters—(a), (b), (c), etc. Each of these symbols should unfailingly be attached to materials in the proof having the specific function reserved for such symbolic enumeration, so that there will never be any doubt as to the function of an item labelled A, or 1, or a, or (1), or (a). To further insure logical development, all items in the brief symbolized by one type of identification should be parallel in grammatical form. Thus all elements symbolized by A, B, C, etc., should be grammatically and logically parallel, as should those headed (1), (2), (3), etc. The conclusion of each issue may be symbolized by the prime order of the Roman numeral identifying it (I', II', III', etc.).

As a further requirement to insure logical coherence, all materials in the brief should be in the form of complete sentences. By definition a sentence is a complete thought, and it is only through such complete-

ness of expression that the function and meaning of the assertions and
evidence can be surely understood.

Specimen brief

The structure of the brief is essentially simple, for it is merely a
logical outline supporting a stated proposal. Nevertheless, it may be
difficult to understand how a brief is constructed, and why it necessarily takes the form it does, until an actual brief is analyzed in detail.
For this reason, the following brief is presented for individual study
and class discussions. In studying it, you should identify the various
parts of the brief, such as proposal, standards of reasoning, assertions,
authority, statistics, specific examples, and so forth, indicating the
kinds of materials described in Chapter 5, 6, and 7 that are contained
in the brief. In class discussion or in comparison of your identifications
with those of other students, you can determine whether or not you
have learned properly to identify the elements of factual evidence and
reasoning that go into a brief. In this sense, the following brief serves
as both a review and a partial test over the three chapters comprising
this unit.

Federal Aid to Education

Resolved, that the federal government should subsidize public education through annual grants to the several states, to a degree and in a
manner to be determined by law.

Introduction

I. This proposal shall be interpreted to mean that:
   A. Only public schools, excluding both secular and religious private
      schools, shall receive federal aid; and
   B. The states themselves, rather than local school districts, shall
      receive and disburse the aid funds; and
   C. Public education shall be interpreted as meaning public ele-
      mentary and secondary schools, excluding colleges and junior
      colleges.

II. This proposal shall be considered to comprise only the principle of
    federal aid to education on a basis presumed to be equitable, leaving
    the precise formulation of how much the states will receive, and
    upon what basis, to Congressional enactment.

III. The proposal is assumed to rest upon the following accepted facts, not in dispute, of discrepancies in education, as reported in the Statistical Abstract of the United States for 1954:

  A. Of the total population 25 years old and over, only 27 per cent have completed an 8th grade education, with extremes varying between:

    1. Louisiana and South Carolina, where less than 8 per cent have had 8 years of schooling; and

    2. New York and Oregon, where about 20 per cent have had 8 years of schooling; and

  B. State expenditures for public education averaged $224, with extremes varying from:

    1. New York, at $328 per pupil; to

    2. Mississippi, at $93 per pupil.

IV. The proposal should be decided in accordance with the following basic issues:

  A. Is there need for a change from the present system of state and local support?

  B. Would federal aid be practical?

  C. Would federal aid prove beneficial?

  D. Would federal aid introduce new evils?

V. These issues should be determined in accordance with the following considerations:

  A. The principle of local control over standards, goals, and methods of education should be maintained; and

  B. The value of providing reasonable facilities for twelve years of education to all normal persons of school age is recognized; and

  C. Freedom of thought and educational philosophy, subject only to such minimal instructional standards as the states may decree, should be guaranteed.

Affirmative Arguments

I. The present system of state and local support of education has proved inadequate and unjust, for:

  A. There are sharp discrepancies among the states in the amount of money spent per pupil, and in the number of years of education secured by school-age persons, for:

    1. This is shown in the census figures previously cited; and

    2. During World War II Selective Service rejected less than one man per 100 for mental and educational deficiencies in some states, and more than 13 per 100 in others; and

B. There are similar discrepancies in the quality of education provided in various states, for:
   1. Eight states require only one year of college for an elementary school teaching certificate; and
   2. Fifteen states require four years of college for any type of teaching certificate; and
   3. Four states require five years of college for a high school certificate; and
C. There are unjust discrepancies in the financial burdens borne by taxpayers in the several states, for:
   1. In thinly populated New Mexico and South Dakota, over 4 per cent of the total income is required to provide educational facilities; whereas
   2. In thickly populated and industrial states such as Maryland and Delaware better educational facilities are provided at a cost of approximately 2 per cent of total state income; therefore,

I'. The present system of state and local support proves to be:
A. Inadequate to insure the welfare of both the citizens and the nation; and
B. Unjust to both the pupils who get less education than they are entitled to and to those states which have to pay unduly large proportions of their income for substandard education; and
II. The proposal for federal subsidies for education is practical, for:
A. It is similar to federal subsidization of the postal system, in that:
   1. Similar types of service are rendered in all states; yet
   2. The cost of such services varies greatly among the states; and
   3. No one questions that the federal government should pay the difference in cost between carrying a letter 20 miles from one Texas ranch to another and 20 feet from one New York apartment to another; and
B. It is consistent with the philosophy of the graduated income tax, according to which:
   1. Taxes are paid according to ability; but
   2. Governmental services are rendered equally to all, regardless of taxes paid; and similarly
C. The whole executive, judicial, and legislative structure of the federal government is operated on the principle of graduated taxation but equality of service to all citizens, regardless of the state in which they live; and, furthermore,

D. The practicality of federal subsidization of education without disturbing local control of educational policies and methods has already been demonstrated: for

    1. Federal aid without federal control has been extended to the land-grant colleges for many years; and

    2. Federal aid for vocational schools under local jurisdiction has become an established practice; and

    3. The original leader in the fight for federal aid to education, Senator Robert A. Taft of Ohio, was well known as a determined opponent of extending federal control; therefore,

II'. The practicality of federal aid to education is proved by:

A. Comparison with federal aid in other fields; and

B. Experience with federal aid in some educational areas; and

C. Support for federal aid by an outstanding opponent of federal control; and

III. Federal aid to education would prove beneficial; for

A. Such aid would tend to eliminate the economic and social inequalities existing among various sections of our nation; for

    1. A 1947 survey by the U. S. Chamber of Commerce shows the lowest quality of markets (with an index of 59) in the Southeastern states and New Mexico, where educational opportunities are restricted; and the highest quality of markets (with an index of 128) in the Far West and Northeastern states, which provide the best educational opportunities; and

    2. The entire nation benefits from leadership, regardless of the state from which it comes, and suffers from crime, regardless of the state of its origin; and

B. The proportion of mental deficiency varies from 1 per cent or less in states having the best educational facilities to 12 per cent and more in states having the poorest educational facilities; and

C. The general principle that individuals and the nation benefit from improvement of educational facilities has been held consistently throughout our history; therefore,

III'. The beneficial results of federal aid to education are proved by:

A. The desirability of eliminating existing economic and social variations among different sections of the nation; and

B. The proved relationship between mental deficiency and lack of educational opportunity; and

C. The unquestioned principle of the value of education; and

IV. No new evils would be introduced by extending federal aid to education; for
  A. The provision that aid would be extended to public schools would neither encourage nor interfere with such private schools as may be maintained by religious or secular bodies; and
  B. Extension of aid to poorer states at the expense of taxpayers in wealthier states is neither new nor an evil, but a long-established practice in many fields; THEREFORE,

Conclusion

 I. Because there is definite need for a change from the unjust and inadequate educational system of the present; and

 II. Because the plan of federal aid is thoroughly practical; and

 III. Because federal aid would provide many benefits; and

 IV. Because the benefits would not be counteracted by new evils; BE IT RESOLVED THAT:
This house should go on record in favor of the resolution that the federal government should subsidize public education through annual grants to the several states, to a degree and in a manner to be determined by law.

Exercises

1. For the brief presented in this chapter, point out each of the major parts described among the "Requirements of the Brief."

2. Brief in detail, utilizing the proper form and supplying the pertinent evidence, an answer to *one* of the arguments presented in this brief.

3. Analyze the introduction to the brief on federal aid to education from the standpoint of one who opposes such aid. Is there anything in the introduction to which you might object? What else might you include?

4. Prepare a brief setting forth the negative view of the question of federal aid to education.

5. With a classmate, select a current controversial issue; one of you should prepare an affirmative, the other a negative brief on the subject. In a preliminary conference you should agree on the standards of judgment to be used as described in Chapter 10.

6. Show how the brief might have usefulness in presenting the campaign issues of a political party, in organizing a sales campaign, in mustering evidence for a proposal to be made to the board of an industrial concern.

7. Differentiate clearly between a brief and a speech plan or outline.

8. For further study of the nature, uses, and values of the brief, the following readings are recommended:

Dean C. Barnlund, "The Reflective Mind in the Making," *Speech Teacher,* I (March, 1952), 86-94.

Douglas Ehninger and Wayne Brockreide, *Decision by Debate* (New York: Dodd, Mead, 1963).

Robert B. Huber, *Influencing Through Argument* (New York: David McKay, 1963).

I. L. Janis and R. L. Feierabend, "Effects of Alternative Ways of Ordering Pro and Con Arguments in Persuasive Communications," in C. I. Hovland (ed.), *Yale Studies in Attitude Communication* (New Haven: Yale University Press, 1957), pp. 115-128.

Arthur N. Kruger, *Modern Debate: Its Logic and Strategy* (New York: McGraw-Hill, 1960).

Charles R. Petrie, Jr., "Informative Speaking: A Summary and Bibliography of Related Research," *Speech Monographs,* 30 (June, 1963), 79-91.

Stephen Toulmin, *Uses of Argument* (Cambridge: Cambridge University Press, 1958).

Herbert A. Wichelns, "Analysis and Synthesis in Argumentation," *Quarterly Journal of Speech Education,* XI (June, 1925), 266-272.

17

Delivering the Persuasive Speech

IN STUDYING THE DELIVERY OF PERSUASIVE SPEECHES
it is well to consider the problem as embracing all the effects that the
speaker as a person may have upon his audience while he is actually
before their attention—before, during, and after the presentation of
the speech. The impression the speaker makes will be affected by his
personal appearance, behavior, manner while speaking, voice, diction,
and the general impact of his personality upon the listeners. All these
factors are involved in the delivery of the speech. In our discussion we
shall proceed from the general to the particular, considering first the
personality factors in persuasive speech, the speaker-audience relationships, the attitudes conducive to persuasion, the visual impact of
the speaker on the hearers, and the effects of his voice, diction, and
phrasing of ideas. Each of these factors must be considered not according to some imagined general standard of "excellence," but in
terms of the particular situation in which the speech is delivered.

Personality and persuasion

As we all recognize, persuasion is to a considerable degree dependent upon personality. To the extent that an individual is regarded
as a leader in any given situation, he already has achieved a large part
of the persuasive process. For the very fact that others are ready to
follow him means that they are predisposed to adopt his methods in
moving toward his goals. This means that the study of personality in
relation to persuasion is largely a study of the factors of leadership.

The leader (or persuader) does not, as is sometimes indicated, "hold his following (or audience) in the hollow of his hand." Only through force, expressed or implied, can there be actual domination of a group by an individual. In a free society, the leader is a part of the group, and therefore is partly dominated by it. As Paul Pigors, in his rigorous study of the leader, *Leadership or Domination,* points out, "The leader is a stimulus, but he is also a response." He directs the group, but he directs it in accordance with the basic nature of the group itself. As Pigors also says, "Followers respect their leader's superiority in certain traits, his aspirations and judgments, because they recognize these traits as their own." It is precisely because the power of leadership (or persuasion) is drawn from the group that almost every chapter has stressed the fact that the persuasive speaker must draw his motivating power from the nature of the audience he is to address.

Just as we have stressed the fact that persuasion is always *situational*—drawing much of its effectiveness from the precise situation in which it occurs—so does Pigors insist that leadership cannot occur aside from given circumstances. "It is nonsense," he writes, "to talk of leadership in the abstract since no one can 'just lead' without having a goal. Leadership is always *in* some sphere of interest and *toward* some objective goal seen by leader and follower." In the same sense, it is nonsense to think of "persuasion" aside from specific persuasive situations, or to believe that there could be any "persuasive qualities" distinct from the circumstances under which they must operate. Thus the whole concept of delivery of the persuasive speech—including the nature of the speaker's personality—must be considered wholly in terms of the nature of the occasion in which the persuasion takes place.

"Personality," according to Gordon Allport, "is a factor of the situation, as well as the individual." This is a widely but not universally held theory. Kimball Young, in his *Social Psychology,* declares flatly that "we cannot escape the fact that there are universal and basic drives." Individuals have wants, needs, urges, characteristics, and abilities, Young and many other students of human nature believe, which are always to some degree or other operative, whatever the circumstances may be. Walter Coutu, author of *Emergent Human Nature,* renounces this view and holds that we "are" only what we "do" in any social context we may wish to select as a sample.

One reason why there is so wide a divergence of views as to whether personality factors are "innate" or are products of the situation is that in any given society it is almost impossible to tell the difference. Young may argue that we act as we do because of our inherent nature; Coutu would reply, "Not so, we act as we do because of what the situation means to us." In either instance, since all human beings have much the same innate inheritance, and since twentieth-century Americans are all subjected to very similar cultural surroundings, either school of thought can readily find evidence to support its own theory.

As students of persuasive speech, we cannot avoid being active participants in such theorizing. If man does possess innate "drives," it naturally behooves us to find what those drives are and to seek to formulate motivational appeals in terms of them. Thus, if we find that normal individuals crave "social recognition," we show them how to obtain such recognition by adhering to the goal we present in our speech. On the other hand, if such innate qualities are unimportant, we turn our attention away from the internal drives of persons and center it upon the cultural influences exercised in situations.

It may be that no "true" answer to this bewildering question will ever be found. We do, nevertheless, have a fairly reliable guide for our thinking about how persuasion may be accomplished. Whether it be because of innate tendencies or because of social pressures, it is nonetheless true that various "expectations" are current as to how individuals should behave. Each of us does have in mind certain characteristics of behavior that we admire, and others that we dislike. And, normally, the same qualities tend to be liked or disliked by most people in most situations. Thus, the persuasive speaker who is seeking to develop an effective personality can safely seek the admired qualities and avoid the others.

Even this, however, we must do "situationally." It is readily observed that a type of behavior that might be admired in a night club would be condemned in church. A manner of speaking that is persuasive in a poolroom might be repellent in an auditorium. The kind of persuasion used by a child to get his mother's consent to going to the movies might well receive a very negative response if used on strangers. Such cautionary examples as these should be kept in mind whenever the dangerous tendency develops to present "standards" of effective persuasive behavior—whether involving language, voice, bodily actions, or the whole broad impression-of-the-person which we term personality.

A frequently safe guide (though far from being a categorical formula) for the persuasive speaker is the general principle that *any personality will prove most effectively persuasive when it most clearly adheres to the audience's "pattern of expectation for leadership" in that particular type of situation.* When the audience consists of the speaker's superiors, and sometimes of his equals, the effective persuasive personality must exhibit the qualities required by the speaker's status. He must be a good follower, or a co-operating and participating member of the group. In these particular situations, it is co-operation rather than leadership that is "expected." However, generally when an individual is invited to speak, the opportunity for leadership is implied.

Each cultural group has its own "pattern of expectation for leadership." Thus, labor union members have a leadership pattern, manufacturers have another, and so do such other groups as uneducated share-crop farmers, college professors, insurance salesmen, and any and all other distinct groupings. Since all of us belong simultaneously to many different types of groups, we have different concepts of what leaders are and how they should act. We will expect one type of leadership in our own business, another from political figures, another in various kinds of social life, and so forth. The individual who attempts to carry one pattern of leadership from his business into his bridge club will meet with vigorous resistance.

There are, of course, certain broad and general expectations that most of us have for all kinds of social gatherings. We expect, for instance, that all adults with whom we will associate should be polite, should be reasonably clean, should generally refrain from obscene language, should speak distinctly enough to be heard and understood. It is impossible, however, to refine any such listing closely enough to make it possible to present a meaningful list of "rules" governing the personality that will prove persuasively effective. The best advice the student of persuasion should look for is to observe the qualities that are successful (that come to be expected) in various situations, and to be governed accordingly.

Speaker-audience relationships

Chapter 4 dealt in some detail with the speaker's function as one of the basic factors in persuasion: whether he represents himself alone or identifies himself with a major group; whether he is inexpert or a recognized authority; whether he seeks personal advantage or serves a public cause; whether he is a temporary or a permanent advocate; and whether he expresses uncertainty or confidence. Such facts are also of direct importance in considering the delivery of the speech. For the status of the speaker in the group he addresses, the degree of authority with which he may speak, the opportunity he may have for moral motivation, the continuity of his influence, and the poise with which he speaks are all clearly important determinants of the effectiveness of his speech.

In normal persuasive situations, the influence the speaker exerts while he is speaking is small in comparison with that he exerts during his lifetime of association in the community. His persuasive effectiveness is in part determined by his relationship with his audience: (1) before his speech; (2) at the time of his speech; and (3) after the speech.

Relationship before the speech. A speaker who is known to his audience as a friend, associate, or fellow townsman has, to a significant degree, either succeeded or failed in his persuasive effort even before his speech begins. The audience has formed an opinion of him as a person—of his integrity, intelligence, motives, and conscientiousness —and inevitably brings this opinion heavily to bear in judging what he may say. And even when a speaker is not known personally to his audience, they will almost certainly know enough of his background and status to give them rather definite preconceptions concerning him. Whatever a speaker may say in a five- to forty-five-minute speech seldom can be impressive enough to reverse judgments about him that are based upon all the audience knows of his past life and present status. Partly, the beginning of persuasion is effective social living.

Relationship at time of speech. Status may be defined as the degree of respect accorded an individual by others, or their estimate of his total worth in relation to themselves. It is not so easy, however, to discover precisely how status is determined. A speaker appearing before an audience he wishes to persuade will naturally benefit hugely by attaining the highest status he can. The weight accorded him as a person will significantly affect the reception given to his proposal. It is of sharp importance, then, for the speaker to take account of all the factors, many of them intangible, which will increase his status within the group. His appearance, behavior, and the way he is treated by others are all significant.

Such a minor thing as a dab of egg yolk on the speaker's chin might well be enough to destroy his persuasive effectiveness. Just so keenly do auditors react to small cues concerning personality elements. A speaker who shambles or scuffles onto the platform; whose shirt is dirty or wrinkled; who has failed to shave recently; who wears green socks with a tuxedo; or who in any way typifies himself to the audience as awkward, uncouth, or below the standards of expected social standing is doing as much to undermine his own effectiveness as might be done by rebuttal of his arguments. Similarly, a speaker who sits on the platform waiting to be introduced should be keenly aware that he is undergoing a scrutiny by the audience that will predetermine a large part of the total response to his persuasive appeal. They will note signs in his posture, facial expressions, and general behavior that indicate whether or not he feels adequate to the situation. In his reaction to the chairman and to other speakers, they will decide whether he is worthy of liking and respect. Good platform etiquette is worthy of serious attention as constituting part of the methodology of persuasion.

Since we draw a large portion of our own reactions to strangers from the treatment accorded them by people who appear to know them, it is surprising that no more attention is devoted to the way a speaker is treated by the chairman and other officials in charge of a meeting. When, for instance, an unknown speaker is invited to address a Rotary Club, the members begin to react to him partly in terms of how he may be greeted by the President, Secretary, and Program Chairman. Yet it often happens that these three are primarily concerned with their own interests and give only the most cursory notice to the individual they have invited as their guest speaker. The next and perhaps most important treatment of the speaker is the introduction accorded him. Mark Twain, who took his professional lecturing very seriously, found the introductions he received were so ineffective that he finally refused to be introduced and simply presented himself directly to the audience. A speaker who really desires to be persuasively effective should take some pains to see that the chairman who will introduce him is properly informed concerning what facts about his background should be presented to the audience. Unskilled chairmen often need rather precise coaching as to what to say and how to say it. If the speaker is unwilling to tell the chairman directly what to say, he may pass on this information through the program chairman or some other appropriate club officer. Whatever the means that may be selected, the important consideration is that proper efforts should be made to establish for the speaker a helpful status with the group he is addressing.

Relationship after the speech. In discussing speech-making, the attention of the students is naturally directed to the introduction, body, and conclusion of the speeches they are to make. It should not be thought, however, that the speech process ends even when the conclusion has been completed. The speaker is seeking to achieve an effect that will last at least long enough to get the audience to do what he wants them to do. Many a time an audience will be deeply impressed while a speech is in progress, but even while they are dispersing, other interests take precedence and a few moments after their hearty burst of applause has died away their minds are diverted far from the proposal that appeared to have won their support.

In "real life situations" (surely the only ones that count) effective persuasive speakers take great pains to see that there is an adequate "follow up" to their talks. Appropriate committees are appointed, with their membership carefully selected. Motions are adopted that formalize what the group is willing to do and provide the machinery for doing it. Persuasion to be effective often needs to consist not only of stimulation but also of organization. The word needs to be followed by the act. If the persuasive process is terminated too soon, it may almost as well never have begun. Once again, as was pointed out in Chapter 14 in connection with the speech on surplus tires, the speaker needs to determine precisely what the audience should do, and take the required steps to facilitate their doing it.

Attitudes conducive to persuasion

An attitude is a generalized evaluative response. The nature of this generalized response is a basic ingredient of persuasion. Leonard Doob's latest revision of his *Propaganda and Public Opinion* devotes more space to attitudes than to any other single persuasive element. Whether the generalized audience reaction toward the speaker's personality and proposal is friendly or unfriendly, favorable or unfavorable, a sense of urgency or of indifference, a feeling of personal responsibility or of mere objective interest, will be a vital determinant of what results from the speech. To a large degree the audience attitudes are predetermined by their prior knowledge of the speaker and by the character of public opinion in the community, but (as the preceding section indicates) attitudes are also created or modified by the behavior and appearance of the speaker at the time of his speech.

Attitudes vary in their *definitiveness, magnitude,* and *duration.* It is a key part of the persuasive speaker's task to bring the generalized attitude of his audience into sharp focus upon his specific proposal; to magnify or heighten the degree to which the attitude is felt; and to shore it up with facts and feelings that will last at least long enough to get his proposal put into effect. Much of this must be accomplished by the content of his speech; but much also must be done by the manner of delivery.

Audiences shape their attitudes in large degree by such factors as the sincerity of the speaker and the personalization of his proposal in terms of themselves. The better the speaker can convey to his listeners a sense of his own urgency that what he recommends be done, and can make them respond with feelings of personal responsibility for doing it, the better persuader he will be. And it is largely through voice, physical bearing, and manner of phrasing that these effects are achieved. Creation of helpful attitudes is a problem of delivery as well as of subject matter.

Perhaps the simplest generalization that can be made about attitudes conducive to persuasion is that the speaker's manner should radiate *self-respect and respect for the audience.* The two must go together. Without the first, no audience will consider the speaker a true leader; and without the second, no audience will willingly be led. "Trust thyself," wrote Ralph Waldo Emerson. "Every heart vibrates to that iron string." And, it should be added, trust and respect your audience, or the vibration will be one of withdrawal and resentment.

Impact of the speaker

The speaker's manner should reflect a carefully predetermined relationship between himself and the audience. If he is a noted expert coming from a distance, with considerable prestige and little or no personal acquaintance with the audience, there will normally be a relatively high degree of formality and a maintenance of "social distance" that tend to enhance the established prestige. On the other hand, if he is intimately known in the community, there must be more informality and good fellowship in his manner—a disarming demonstration that he is not seeking to impose his own judgment upon theirs, but is serving as a medium through which the facts can speak for themselves. Other differences in bearing and mode of presentation will depend upon whether the speaker is a recognized leader in the community, or holds a subordinate position: whether his status is high or low.

Two concepts of special value in relation to the visual impact the speaker should seek to make on his audience are: (1) the special circumstances that may affect the speech; and (2) the pattern of normal expectancy established in the minds of the audience.

The audience-situation may differ widely from what the speaker expects to find. Other speakers on the program, such extrinsic events as a fire breaking out in the vicinity of the meeting, or a failure on the part of the speaker accurately to anticipate the mood or attitudes of the audience may necessitate last-minute changes in his bearing and mode of presentation. A speaker who has predetermined upon a pattern of urgent and earnest exhortation may find himself confronted with a situation demanding relaxed, amiable, and jocular discussion of the proposal. It cannot be overemphasized that the persuasive speaker must be keenly alert to indications as to the manner of speech he must use to "meet the auditors where they are."

If the audience reactions were always as unpredictable as the preceding paragraph might seem to suggest, speakers would be hard put to it to make any specific preparation of their speeches. It is not true, however, that society is disorganized and unpredictable. For most speeches there is a pre-established "pattern of expectation" into which the speaker should fit. It behooves him to discover in advance what this pattern will be. On subjects in which the community feels a vital concern, they expect the speaker's manner to reflect an equal concern. For football rallies, political conventions, Kiwanis dinner meetings, high school commencements, church services, and many another speech situation, the proper manner befitting a speaker is largely dictated by social convention. Only careless or particularly unperceptive speakers will fail to note this expectation or fail to try, at least, to meet it.

The advice commonly given about the speaker's physical activity on the platform is based upon this rather stable pattern of expectation. Audiences expect their speakers to stand erect, to demonstrate ease and poise, to look at them while speaking, and to use relaxed and natural gestures and facial expressions. Notable violations of such expectations actually cause auditors to experience physical discomfort, and thereby to react against the speaker's personality and proposal. What is generally considered to be "good delivery" actually *is* good delivery—perhaps not for any reasons of logic, but simply because the pattern of expectation is a dictator in the social scene. Within the broad pattern there is ample room for individuality, but to violate the pattern itself is to invite failure.

Effects of the speaker's voice

Edward Sapir presented in *The American Journal of Sociology* (1926) a suggestive point of view about the persuasive use of voice. Voice, more than most other personality elements, declared Sapir, identifies the social group to which an individual belongs. Anyone who may doubt this should only consider the vocal differences among such diverse social groups as New Englanders, Midwesterners, Southerners, Londoners, and so forth. Although less consciously realized, differences among social groups in any one locality are also identified and often unconsciously interpreted. "We cannot draw up an absolute psychological scale for voice, intonation, rhythm, speech or pronunciation of vowels or consonants," Sapir wrote, "without ascertaining the social background of speech habits." Two conclusions emerge from the point of view that accepted voice patterns depend upon the social group to which the speaker and audience belong.

The first is that it is artificial and misleading to establish any one set of standards for the "good" voice. Whatever standard is established will prove ineffective in a great many social groupings.

The second conclusion is that what is important about a speaker's voice is its degree and kind of variation from the norm of the group. It is by no means always necessary or even desirable that the speaker's voice conform exactly to the patterns of his audience. It is, of course, necessary that he speak in such a manner that he can be understood. Aside from that requirement, the degree to which his voice should conform depends upon the nature of his relationships to the audience.

It is well known that a foreign visitor may draw part of his charm and effectiveness from the very strangeness of his intonations and other vocal elements. Even mispronunciation and misuse of idioms may be factors in aiding his communication. Since he is registered in the auditors' minds as *foreign,* the flavor of foreignness is accepted and expected. To the extent, of course, that he wishes to be accepted as "one of the group," and not regarded merely as an interesting outsider, he should seek for greater conformity. It is also well known that a local individual who goes to another section of the country to be educated and then returns with "strange" vocal patterns (such as a native of Arizona who returns home with a "Harvard accent") will be regarded with some resentment; the suspicion of the auditors is that this person whom they have considered one of themselves has become "affected" and "pretentious." Perhaps we may not so readily think of it, but it also is true that the vocal patterns effective for any individual are those which conform to his status in the group. We "expect" (and therefore fully accept) a more dominating tone from acknowledged superiors than from those we consider inferior. As a corollary, it follows that an individual seeking to change his status in the group should assist that desire by gradual and not too obtrusive changes of his speech patterns.

Considering voice in terms of status—and thinking always of the pattern of audience expectation—it is evident that serious harm is done by trying to be a "good fellow" through the medium of slovenly speech. If one desires a relatively high status, he simply must develop and utilize voice patterns that conform to the expectation of the audience concerning leadership qualities in the voice.

Since the persuasive speaker's voice should meet the requirements of the group, the principal suggestion to be made concerning it is to *seek such variations from the norm as are associated in the audience's minds with the status the speaker hopes to achieve.* "Correctness" in voice means adhering to the pattern of expectation concerning pitch range, rate, volume or force, and quality. And as a spur to attentiveness in attaining to this expectation pattern, we might meditate upon the accuracy of T. H. Pear's observation, in *Voice and Personality,* that: "Speech being a delicate, subtle and powerful form of behaviour, the way in which a thing is said is often as important as the message."

Persuasive diction

What has been written of voice applies with equal force to diction. Again to quote Pear: "The choice of words by any person in a position to speak freely tells us much. One is momentarily startled if a speaker by using an unexpected word or phrase, suddenly presents himself as a member of a quite different section of society. I remember a medical man, in a lecture, suddenly using a folk-name instead of an anatomical term. I was shocked, in more ways than one." Pear does not detail the ways in which the shock operated, but we may presume that he was first surprised, then curious as to why it was done, and finally suspicious that the doctor was not as expert as at first he had seemed. In any event, it is evident that the auditor's attention was diverted from what the speaker was saying to concern over a term he had used in saying it.

Aside from the principle of "variation within conformity"—which applies in regard to diction precisely as it does for voice—there is also the question of selecting the right words to convey the speaker's meaning. It is no easier here than in regard to voice to establish a "standard" to which speakers must conform. We are accustomed to receiving advice to use *simple* rather than *polysyllabic* words; and to speak *concretely* rather than *abstractly*. Doubtless this advice is often, and perhaps usually, good. Nevertheless, we have just quoted from Pear an example of "shock" at hearing a simple rather than a technical term. And we have the warning Dr. Samuel Johnson gave Boswell, that "He who thinks in larger terms will require larger words to express his meaning."

Similarly, while concreteness is normally desirable when exact understanding is desired, it sometimes happens that a speaker wishes to be *suggestive* rather than *prescriptive*. It is accounted an excellence in Shakespeare that one can reread his plays a dozen times, finding new and hitherto unsuspected meaning each time. It may also be true that a speaker will wish on occasion to implant in his audience's minds a mere suggestion of some potential reward or punishment that will be brooded upon and take form in terms of each auditor's own individual situation. "The consequences are going to be pretty bad" is quite conceivably a more effective warning under some circumstances than an explicit statement such as, "You will be fined five dollars," or "The mortgage will be foreclosed."

It is not suggested that there are no standards for persuasive diction. It is suggested, on the other hand, that the standards derive from the group rather than from formalized rules which, however intelligently drawn up, can never adhere to or keep up with the constantly shifting language patterns peculiar to every clearly defined social group. This point of view does not lead to chaos or to unregulated individual preference. On the contrary, the norms of each group are demanding. Consider, for instance, what an outsider a high school student is, if he is not up to date on current high school slang! As Marckwardt and Walcott observed in their monograph, *Facts about Current English Usage,* "A usage may be established; it may be popular; it may be regional; it may be upper or lower class; but strictly speaking, it cannot be disputable." It cannot be disputable in the sense that either it does or does not exist as the norm of expression; this is a matter of fact simply to be accepted or rejected upon the basis of observation.

The speaker's status and relations with the audience are guides to diction as well as to bodily bearing and voice. *Conformity is not always the ideal;* rather, the speaker should depart from the established pattern in the ways that will help to define, or even to achieve, the status he desires within the group. Abraham Lincoln, to cite an example, grew up in a rude pioneering society, but he gradually developed a diction that set him off from his fellows, helped win him the presidency, and established him as one of the best masters of American prose. There need be no slavish dependence upon group standards; there need only be a clear recognition that they are the norm *within which* and *from which* the speaker's own individual mode of expression develops.

Persuasive phrasing of ideas

Style, in a larger sense than usually is implied by diction, is of prime importance to the persuasive speaker. One example, on perhaps a crude plane, is the value of the slogan in national advertising. "My goodness, it's Guinness!" has doubtless done much for the popularity of England's best-selling ale. Such verbal coinages as "The Forgotten Man," "The war to end war," and "Remember the Alamo" are also acute reminders of the persuasive power of potent word combinations. Who can doubt the persuasive effectiveness of the phrasing in Winston Churchill's wartime speeches? Not only the ideas, not only the existing facts, but the very tenor of the words themselves were powerful incitements to action in such passages as:

> I cannot forecast to you the action of Russia. It is a riddle wrapped in a mystery inside an enigma. . . .
> I have nothing to offer but blood, toil, tears and sweat.
> We shall go on to the end, we shall fight in France, we shall fight on the seas and oceans, we shall fight with growing confidence and strength in the air, we shall defend our Island, whatever the cost may be, we shall fight on the beaches, we shall fight on the landing grounds, we shall fight in the fields and in the streets, we shall fight in the hills; we shall never surrender, and even if, which I do not for a moment believe, this Island or a large part of it were subjugated and starving, then our Empire beyond the seas, armed and guarded by the British Fleet, would carry on the struggle, until, in God's good time, the New World, with all its power and might, steps forth to the rescue and the liberation of the old.

There is little question but that such phrasing as this evolves from the two characteristics of leadership that were discussed in Chapter 4: from conformity to the crowd and ascendance above it. Churchill drew his stylistic strength from the fact that he was "Mr. England"; his roots were solidly entrenched in the deep soil of hallowed English tradition; he knew what Englishmen thought and felt because he was bone of their bone and flesh of their flesh—and from that depth of conformance he was enabled by superior ability to transcend the rest and to utter better than they could themselves their own best feelings and thoughts. Just so was Abraham Lincoln both a man "of the people" and "above the people." In his moving conclusion to the Second Inaugural Address he drew deep from the best elements in the American tradition to formulate a goal toward which all could aspire: "With malice toward none; with charity for all; with firmness in the right as God gives us to see the right, let us strive on to finish the work we are in; to bind up the nation's wounds; to care for him who shall have borne the battle, and for his widow, and his orphan—to do all which may achieve and cherish a just and lasting peace among ourselves, and with all nations."

There is probably no way of "teaching" ability to achieve style such as that of Churchill or Lincoln. Reference is easily made to many textbooks which contain lists of grammatical qualities to be sought and of stylistic faults to be avoided. Beyond what those books will convey, the chief need here is to reiterate the importance to the persuasive speaker of concentrating effort not only upon what he will say but upon the phrasing with which he says it. Our proper emphasis upon "extemporaneous" speech should not lead to any conclusion that the final phrasing of ideas is an unimportant element to be left purely to chance. As part of the preparation of the extemporaneous speech, the persuasive speaker should try to originate a number of key phrases or sentences, memorable and incisive in style, through which his significant ideas are expressed. Roosevelt did not wait for last-minute inspiration to provide "The New Deal." Last-minute inspiration is usually inadequate for the task.

Conclusion

As developed in this chapter, delivery is not a matter of mechanics but of adaptation to and purposeful variations from the standards of the audience to which a speech may be presented. The personality of the speaker as exemplified in his delivery of a speech should usually adhere to the "expectation for leadership" in that situation. The relationships of the speaker to his audience are seen to be significant not only while he is before the group, but also both before his appearance and after his speech is concluded. The key element in the relationship is found to be the status of the speaker within the group he addresses. A significant part of this relationship depends upon the attitudes the speaker seeks to engender or modify.

The bodily activity and appearance of the speaker should reflect a carefully predetermined relationship between himself and the audience, plus a sensitivity to such changes as an unexpectedly developed situation may require. Voice and diction, also, draw their effectiveness persuasively from calculated variations from the group norm, or, when a stranger is the speaker, from his conformance to the general concept of "strangeness" that the audience holds in regard to him. Style, as the final culmination or fitting together of all the aspects of expression, is neither easily understood nor amenable to prescriptive teaching. Nevertheless, far from being a mysterious and mystical "something," it appears to be a verbal aspect of the dual qualities of leadership: conformance to and transcendence of the group. So important is style persuasively that it is recommended the student bring the best fruits of his stylistic thinking into even extemporaneous speeches.

Exercises

1. Discuss Pigors' statement, "The leader is a stimulus but he is also a response." Illustrate your discussion with specific reference to various leaders.

2. Write an analysis of your own qualities of leadership as illustrated by the relationships you have established in your class in persuasive speech. Compare and contrast your own leadership experiences in class with those of other members of the group.

3. Discuss the relationship of the speaker's appearance, behavior while speaking, and voice to the specific circumstances in which he speaks.

4. To what extent should the speaker conform to the audience's "pattern of expectation for leadership"?

5. What are the effective speaker-audience relationships?

6. Hear a persuasive speech outside of class and write a report on the delivery, stressing the factors discussed in this chapter.

7. As the class delivers a round of persuasive speeches, write a brief letter to each class member, offering constructive suggestions for improvement of delivery. Hand in these letters to your instructor, for later distribution by him to the students to whom you are giving the advice. As you receive your own letters from other class members, correlate them carefully and note (*a*) the differing impressions you make upon different members of your classroom audience, and (*b*) the elements in which all or most of the members agree about your speech presentation. Draw up for yourself a set of guiding principles for improvement, based upon these critiques.

8. Students having special problems with their platform poise, presence, and effectiveness may be asked by their instructor to review chapters on delivery in standard textbooks for beginning courses. In addition, the following readings will be helpful in expanding the concepts set forth in this chapter:

Gordon W. Allport and H. Cantril, "Judging Personality from Voice," *Journal of Social Psychology,* V (February, 1934), 37-54.

K. C. Beighley, "An Experimental Study of the Effect of Four Speech Variables on Listener Comprehension," *Speech Monographs,* XIX (November, 1952), 249-258.

Janet Bolton, "The Garnishing of the Manner of Utterance," *Western Speech Journal,* 28 (Spring, 1961), 83-91.

W. K. Clark, "A Survey of Certain Audience Attitudes toward Commonly Taught Standards of Public Speaking," *Speech Monographs,* 18 (March, 1951), 62-69.

C. F. Diehl, R. C. White and K. W. Burk, "Rate and Communication," *Speech Monographs,* 26 (August, 1959), 229-232.

Paul J. Fay and Warren C. Middleton, "The Ability to Judge Sociability from the Voice as Transmitted over a Public Address System," *Journal of Social Psychology,* XIII (1941), 303-309.

———, "The Ability to Judge Truth-telling or Lying from the Voice as Transmitted over a Public Address System," *Journal of General Psychology,* 24 (1941), 211-215.

———, "Judgment of Spranger Personality Types from the Voice as Transmitted over a Public Address System," *Character and Personality,* VIII (September, 1939–June, 1940), 144-155.

Albert L. Furbay, "The Influence of Scattered versus Compact Seating on Audience Response," *Speech Monographs,* 32 (June, 1965), 144-148.

William I. Gordon, "A Comparison of Two Types of Delivery of a Persuasive Speech," *Southern Speech Journal,* 27 (Fall, 1961), 74-79.

K. A. Harwood, "Listenability and Rate of Presentation," *Speech Monographs,* 22 (March, 1955), 57-59.

E. A. Kretsinger, "An Experimental Study of Gross Bodily Movement as an Index to Audience Interest," *Speech Monographs,* 19 (November, 1952), 244-248.

William Michael and C. C. Crawford, "An Experiment in Judging Intelligence by the Voice," *Journal of Educational Psychology,* 18 (1927), 107-114.

Paul J. Moses, "The Study of Personality from Records of the Voice," *Journal of Consulting Psychology,* IV (1942), 257-261.

Alan C. Nichols, "Audience Ratings of the 'Naturalness' of Spoken and Written Sentences," *Speech Monographs*, 33 (June, 1966), 156-159.

Charles C. Noble, "A New Deal in Preaching," *Today's Speech*, V (January, 1957), 8-11.

W. M. Parrish, "The Concept of 'Naturalness'," *Quarterly Journal of Speech*, 37 (December, 1951), 448-454.

Edward Sapir, "Speech as a Personality Trait," *American Journal of Sociology*, 32 (May, 1927), 892-905.

Harold C. Taylor, "Social Agreement on Personality Traits as Judged from Speech," *Journal of Social Psychology*, V (May, 1934), 244-248.

R. C. Yarbrough, "The Preacher and His Vocal Equipment," *Today's Speech*, IX (September, 1961), 22-24.

PART V

Forms of Persuasive Speech

Intelligence is a slippery customer; if one door is closed to it, it finds, or even breaks, another entrance to the world. If one symbolism is inadequate, it seizes another; there is no eternal decree over its means and methods. ... At best, human thought is but a tiny, grammar-bound island, in the midst of a sea of feeling expressed by "Oh-oh" and sheer babble. ... The power of conception—of "having ideas"—is man's peculiar asset, and awareness of this power is an exciting sense of human strength. Nothing is more exciting than the dawn of a new conception.

—SUSANNE K. LANGER, *Philosophy in a New Key*

18.

The Speech to Convince

THE PERSUASIVE SPEECH HAS BEEN DESCRIBED AS A speech intended to change the beliefs, feelings, or actions of an audience. Such a definition suggests that there are actually three different types of persuasive speech, and this is, indeed, the prevalent judgment. The speech to convince aims to change an audience's belief. The speech to actuate tries to secure an immediate action. And the speech to stimulate enhances or deepens the feelings of the audience concerning the subject being discussed.

Typical differences among these three types of persuasion are often listed as follows:

Type of Persuasion	Type of Motivation	Type of Delivery	Type of Proposal
To convince	Facts and Reason	Judicial	To change belief
To actuate	Emotion and Rationalization	Impassioned	To secure action
To stimulate	Facts and Emotion	Dignified	To heighten feelings

Such generalizations as are represented in the preceding chart offer a satisfactory starting point for a consideration of the types of persuasive speech. The motivation and delivery factors are indicated as they appear in the chart because facts and reason, delivered with judicial calm, are normally more convincing than are emotion and rationalization delivered in an impassioned manner. Similarly, an impassioned presentation of emotion and rationalization is more likely to bring action than would a calm citation of facts. And the occasions on which speeches to stimulate are typically delivered tend more often than not toward dignity and formality. However, it is apparent that these factors are places for consideration to *start,* rather than to *end.* For "circumstances alter cases," and in many circumstances the charted factors must be changed. They are merely rough approximations, and should never be considered to be "persuasive formulas."

Speech of conviction defined

The goal of a speech to convince is to alter the beliefs of its audience. The proposal, then, is aimed at the convictions or opinions of the auditors. The speaker is not attempting to secure any special action, though it is obvious that in the long run actions will be modified or changed as beliefs are changed. For this reason we might restate our definition to read: The speech to convince seeks a delayed or long-range action rather than an immediate one.

George Washington's Farewell Address was a speech to convince. It laid down a set of principles that he believed the American people should follow. Assuredly, Washington sought to influence action—to cause some actions and to prevent others. But rather than an immediate reaction—such as a favorable vote on a specific proposal—he sought to inculcate a manner of thinking that would serve as a long-range guide to our national conduct. Thus, whatever action might result from his Address would be (1) delayed; (2) continuous or intermittent over a long period of time; and (3) varied in details to fit particular occasions, but consistent with the basic doctrines advocated by the speaker.

Many speeches have been delivered by many lecturers to convince audiences that Shakespeare's plays were written by the playwright from Stratford, or by Lord Bacon, or by someone else. In a sense, these speeches, too, have aimed at a kind of action, for to the extent that auditors were convinced, their reading habits, conversation, and the kind of books they would buy would be affected. It is, of course, impossible dogmatically to separate belief from action, but to the extent that a separation appears natural and proper, the speeches to convince are aimed to influence belief.

Still other speeches to convince are given by high school teachers and visitors who may recommend that the students should go on to college, or even to some particular college. Such talks, obviously, do aim at action—but the action is to be delayed. The student auditors may agree that they should go to college, but instead of getting up and going, they must return to their high school classes and complete the work before them. Even though a specific action is recommended, all that the speaker can really do is to affect the *belief* of the audience as to what should be done. If the action desired by the speaker finally does take place, it must be because the belief of the listeners is so vitally and profoundly affected that the auditors' own convictions will eventually lead them to act as the speaker desired.

From the illustrations that have been cited, it is apparent that speeches of conviction may be delivered on any of three planes:

1. To change opinions which will have little direct action-outlet;
2. To change opinions which will influence a general pattern of actions; or
3. To change opinions that will later result directly in some specific action.

When a conviction speech is being prepared it is of fundamental importance for the speaker to realize on which of these three planes he is to launch his motivation. The first type deals primarily with evidence, and thus (more than any other kind of persuasive speaking) tends to be subject-centered. It is the kind of persuasion of which it may most truly be said that "The facts speak for themselves." In the second type of speaking, the speaker intermingles with his facts earnest appeals for the audience to consider the general and far-reaching implications of what he is saying. And in the third type, the speaker phrases specifically and definitely the kind of action desired, and often injects a strong emotional appeal into the fabric of his facts and reasoning, with the hope of providing a motive-drive that will endure.

The use of exposition in conviction

Our attention is commonly directed to the difficulties of persuading individuals. But we should not overlook the fact that conviction often occurs with startling ease and from most casual causes. *On subjects that are relatively unfamiliar or with which we have little personal concern, our beliefs may be changed easily.* For example, in taking public opinion polls, the pollsters have to exercise extreme care to arrive at a neutral phrasing of the questions, for it has been found that even a slight "weighting" of the questions to suggest a particular answer will considerably change the result of the poll. It is evident that one characteristic of normal individuals is a *desire to agree,* unless they have some specific reason not to do so.

It is not true, of course, that normal individuals will believe anything that is told them. Sometimes the listeners will know facts which disprove what is said. Or they may have personal reasons for not wishing to believe it—which fact makes conviction much harder to achieve. And to the extent that the listeners are "sophisticated," they have acquired a general skepticism which leads them to resist belief as a matter of habit. It remains true, however, that a major reason for lack of belief is simply lack of understanding. We may have faith and confidence in the speaker, but we cannot accept what he says unless we understand what it is. Clear exposition, then, is a necessity when there is a predisposition on the part of the auditors to be convinced.

With neutral and even with hostile auditors, exposition also has a considerable persuasive function. Often we have seen an argument build up only to be extinguished by a careful explanation on one side or the other, with the result that the opponent says, "Well, I don't disagree with that." Sometimes a careful explanation will show that both sides actually do agree on the fundamentals. At other times, exposition of a point of view wholly devoid of argument presents it in so noncontroversial a character that no desire to oppose it is aroused.

Anyone who has seen two small boys or two dogs approach each other must have noticed how each eyes the other intently for the slightest signs of antagonistic behavior. If either of them shows a sign of belligerence, the other responds in kind, and soon a fight, on the verbal or physical level, is in progress. Adults are not so much different from the children or even from the dogs in their reactions. The feeling-tone of a speech—whether friendly, indifferent, or hostile—is far more readily communicated to an audience than are the speaker's ideas. When a speech proceeds in an argumentative vein, the audience reacts against the attack being made on their judgments, and conviction becomes increasingly difficult. On the other hand, when a speech proceeds as far as possible through exposition, this element of attack is lacking and the audience response of defensive withdrawal or counterattack is therefore not stimulated.

A major consideration, then, of the speaker who seeks conviction, on any one of the three planes, should be to develop as much of his persuasive approach as he can by means of simple exposition. A speech, for instance, to convince high school students that they should go to college might very well achieve a large part of its purpose by a simple explanation of what college is like and a description of how to select a suitable college. After this expository phase of the speech has prepared the students to view the speaker's proposal favorably, the speaker might then begin to press the point harder with reasoning, factual evidence, and emotional or rationalistic appeals. Exposition often cannot accomplish the entire work of conviction, but it is a valuable part of the process.

Motivation in the speech to convince

There obviously is a different persuasive problem when you seek to implant an idea designed to bear later fruit than when you try to sweep an audience into an immediate decision or action. Since the speech of conviction aims toward the future, it must be based upon motivation that will endure. The convincing speaker needs to present materials that will bear the test of later examination and consideration by the auditors, and that will be too substantial to be overturned by contrary arguments the auditors may later encounter. In order, so far as possible, to achieve these two effects, the speech to convince should normally consist of the following types of motivation:

1. *Facts and reason,* which conform so strictly to reality that the more the question is examined, the more evident it will be that the speaker's proposal is sound. Often this requirement demands that the speaker make a very thorough study of the subject, so that he will learn more about its various aspects than the members of the audience are likely to in their subsequent consideration of the question.

2. *Emotional or rationalistic* demonstration that the self-interest of the auditors is really served by acceptance of the proposal—or, at the minimum, that their self-interest will not be harmed by it. When this is done, the auditors becomes allies of the speaker and their subsequent consideration of the question will tend to support rather than undermine his proposal.

Delivery of the speech to convince

Since we have all learned to distrust emotional intensity, as a sure indication of a lack of clear thinking, it is well for the convincing speaker to cultivate a manner of judicious calm. He should seek to make it manifest to his audience that he has carefully and candidly examined all aspects of the problem, and that his own final choice of his stated proposal occurred only after an objective sifting of all the evidence. An impassioned manner may well prove more immediately interesting and persuasive; but in a speech to convince, the speaker is concerned not with the reaction ten minutes after he is through speaking, but ten days or perhaps ten years afterwards. He must be willing to sacrifice a heightened immediate effect in order to achieve a solid lasting effect.

This, of course, does not mean that the speech to convince should be either dull or lifeless. A speaker who is deadly in earnest, and who conveys his own sense of urgency to the audience, can still avoid the impetuosity that is a sign of loss of intellectual control. "Controlled power" is the impression he seeks to create.

In a speech to convince it is almost mandatory to speak with a tone of authority. If the speaker's status is lower (or at least not higher) than the status of his audience he will do well to enwrap this authority in a general note of respect for his auditors. But even if he is a clerk making a recommendation to the Board of Directors, along with the respectfulness of his presentation must be an authoritative indication that he does in fact know what he is talking about, and that he is venturing to urge his proposal upon them because he is sure that it is sound. A speaker who lacks this confidence in himself and his proposal can hardly expect the audience to develop a confidence that he himself has not achieved.

In summary, then, the speech to convince should be delivered with an air of judicious fairmindedness, earnestness, and authority. It follows as a matter of course that these characteristics can hardly be present until after the speaker has given his subject rigorous study in order to make sure that his proposal really does represent the answer his audience should accept.

The style of the speech to convince

The style of the speech to convince must, of course, conform to the spirit in which it will be delivered. This means that it will be characterized by judiciousness, fairness, and confident assertion. It will abound with expressions such as "on the other hand" and "as we examine these various aspects of the matter," indicating that the speaker has indeed taken all phases of the subject into account.

At the same time, another vital element in the style of the speech to convince is *vividness*. Since the speech of conviction aims at a lasting impression, it must contain elements that will be remembered. In part these elements consist of the subject matter itself, vitally related to the needs and interests of the audience. But also in part the memorable quality is achieved by vividness of style.

This vividness may be achieved by pointed anecdotes, by specific illustrations, by meaningful comparisons or contrasts, and by memorable phrasing. It inheres in such sentences as that spoken by Winston Churchill, which stuck like a burr in the conscience of the allied world: "Never before in human history have so many owed so much to so few." It is recurrent in the preaching of Jesus, as illustrated by his abbreviated parable: "Consider the lilies of the field, how they grow; they toil not, neither do they spin. And yet . . . even Solomon in all

his glory was not arrayed like one of these." Vividness of another sort
was accomplished by the repetitive insistence of Al Smith's campaign
phrase, "Let's look at the record." It was achieved by Roosevelt with
his key labels, "The New Deal" and "The Forgotten Man." Patrick
Henry achieved it with the vigor of his sentiment, "I know not what
course others may take, but as for me, give me liberty, or give me
death!" In the speeches of conviction that endure to carry on their
message long after they were spoken, vividness of style is one of the
merits that gave them success.

The audience for the speech to convince

   Throughout our consideration of persuasion, emphasis has been
placed upon the audience being addressed. For the speech to convince,
however, this concept has to be re-examined in terms of the ultimate
goal the speaker wishes to achieve. Often the immediate tendencies of
an audience are exceedingly transitory. A speaker who aims his speech
directly at the mood and desires of an audience before him may not
speak in a manner to create an impression that will prove lastingly
effective, when the mood of the moment has passed. Many a time a
speaker who wishes to establish a lasting conviction may have to say
to his audience, in effect, "I know that what I am saying to you now is
not what you care to hear; but remember my words, for in due course
you will find that they have weight." Thus, Winston Churchill for five
years refused to speak to the English Parliament in a reassuring
manner—during all the early days of Hitler's expanding power. But
when the crisis of Dunkirk arrived, the Parliament and people of England turned to him as their natural leader, for they found what he had
been saying had proved to be true.

   Again, it may happen that a speaker will want to appeal over the
heads of his immediate listeners to a larger audience beyond. This is
particularly true of many speeches delivered in official bodies by
minority speakers. Unable to shift the votes of the organized majority,
they aim their appeals beyond their auditors to the public, hoping to
achieve an effect upon public opinion. When this is the case, a convincing speech may deliberately alienate the immediate hearers and may

only serve to entrench their opposition the more deeply. But it is not really to them, after all, that the persuasion is addressed. The following stenographic summary, from *Hansard's Reports on the Proceedings in the British Parliament,* is an illustration of this kind of speech to convince.

On December 8, 1775, Charles James Fox delivered a denunciation of Lord North's bill to prohibit all trade with the American colonies. North's motion was carried by a vote of 143 to 38. But Fox, who knew he could not influence the vote, was aiming his appeal at the British public.

On Trade with the American Colonies

by
Charles James Fox

I have always given it as my opinion that the war now carrying on against the Americans is unjust; but, admitting it to be a just war, admitting that it is practicable, I insist that the means made use of are not such as will obtain the end. I shall confine myself singly to this ground, and shew that this Bill, like every other measure, proves the want of policy, the folly and madness, of the present ministers.

I was in great hopes that they had seen their error and had given over coercion and the idea of carrying on war against America by means of acts of Parliament. In order to induce the Americans to submit to your legislature, you pass laws against them, cruel and tyrannical in the extreme. If they complain of one law, your answer to their complaint is to pass another more rigorous than the former.

But they are in rebellion, you say; if so, treat them as rebels are wont to be treated. Send out your fleets and armies against them, and subdue them; but let them have no reason to complain of your laws. Shew them that your laws are mild, just, and equitable; that they therefore are in the wrong, and deserve the punishment they meet with. The very contrary of this has been your wretched policy. I have ever understood it as a first principle that in rebellion you punish the individuals but spare the country; but in a war against the enemy it is your policy to spare the individuals but lay waste the country. This last has been invariably your conduct against America.

I suggested this to you when the Boston Port Bill passed. I advised you to find out the offending persons and to punish them; but what did you do instead of this? You laid the whole town of Boston under terrible contribution, punishing the innocent with the guilty. You answer that you could not come at the guilty. This very answer shews how unfit, how unable, you are to govern America. If you are forced to punish the innocent to come at the guilty, your government there is and ought to be at an end. But, by the Bill now before us, you not only punish those innocent persons who are unfortunately mixed with the guilty in North America, but you punish and starve whole islands of unoffending people, unconnected with and separated from them.

Hitherto the Americans have separated the right of taxation from your legislative authority; although they have denied the former, they have acknowledged the latter. This Bill will make them deny the one as well as the other. "What signified," say they, "your giving up the right of taxation if you are to enforce your legislative authority in the manner you do. This legislative authority, so enforced, will at any time coerce taxation and take from us whatever you think fit to demand." The present is a Bill which should be entitled, a Bill for carrying more effectually into execution the resolves of the [American] Congress.

What success this and Fox's other similar speeches achieved is indicated in the judgment of the noted English historian, George Otto Trevelyan, who wrote in his *American Revolution* that Lord North would never have surrendered "if Washington had not been too strong for him abroad, and Charles Fox and his friends too many for him at home."

Occasions for the speech to convince

Occasions when speakers wish to influence the ultimate beliefs of their auditors rather than to achieve an immediate and transitory effect are legion. We could think of parents advising their children, teachers influencing their students, ministers preaching to congregations, politicians in all the speaking they do to the electorate between elections. We should add all the speakers in their home communities who are much more concerned with what will be thought of them and their proposals in the long run than they are with any specific immediate reaction. Even in the realm of business, where sales are the goal pursued, much of the speaking is to achieve a lasting good will. The business firm that is here to stay must give its major attention to building a lasting satisfaction with its goods and services. Thus, in all aspects of life, the occasions for the speech to convince are numerous.

Conclusion

The speech to convince is that form of persuasion that seeks to alter the beliefs or convictions of the audience. Because a change of belief inevitably influences action, such speeches also aim toward changing the conduct of the auditors. But the action they seek is sometimes indefinite, sometimes very general, and when the action is specific, the time for it to occur is delayed far beyond the date of the speech. Thus, the function of the conviction speech is to lay a sound basis of fact and reasoning, often buttressed by a demonstration that the self-interest of the auditors is involved, which will make a lasting impression until the ultimate action envisaged by the speaker may be achieved.

A cardinal principle of the speech to convince is that when practicable it should utilize simple exposition, thus implanting the desired ideas without danger of arousing the resentment and opposition often engendered by argument. Similarly, the delivery and style of the speech should be designed to create an atmosphere of reasonableness and fair-mindedness, rather than to suggest argumentative attack. When, however, the speaker is aiming "over the heads of his listeners" to a larger audience beyond, he may often find his cause aided by the more dramatic method of vigorous attack. Needless to say, the attack is not aimed against those whom he wishes to convince! Considering the general utility of the speech to convince, it is a form of persuasion that is widely and frequently used. The art of being truly convincing is a value we all may properly wish to attain.

Exercises

1. The class may discuss the validity of dividing speeches to persuade into three categories. To what extent do they overlap? Is it desirable to think of a particular speech you may be preparing as one or another of these types? Is it essential to maintain a strict separation among the categories?

2. Discuss the threefold division of the speech to convince, noting the differences among them.

3. Discuss the paradoxical fact that opinions on some matters are very hard to change; whereas other opinions are so easily changed that it

is difficult even to take an objective poll without "weighting" the results. What makes the difference? In exploring this question, you may find it advisable to reread Chapter 3, noting especially the influence of the ego and self-interest.

4. What are the values and dangers of suggesting (with qualification) that speeches to convince, actuate, and stimulate depend upon differing types of motivation and delivery?

5. To what extent today are speeches "delivered over the heads of the audience" to a larger group outside the immediate hall? How does this factor affect the persuasive task of the speaker?

6. List five occasions (realistically) on which you might have to convince an individual or an audience.

7. Select one of those five occasions and analyze the persuasive problems to be solved (involving the audience, the subject, the occasion, and the relations you as the speaker have with the total situation).

8. Prepare a five-minute speech to convince, based on the foregoing analysis. Inasmuch as the audience for which this speech is probably prepared is different from your classroom audience, your instructor may wish to have this speech written out rather than delivered orally. Or, by agreement, you may have your classmates "play the role" of the audience to which the speech should be directed.

9. For further reading on the formation of judgments and the development of conviction, the following readings are recommended:

John Dewey, *How We Think* (Boston: Heath, 1910).

William F. Dukes, "Psychological Studies of Values," *Psychological Bulletin,* 52 (1955), 24-50.

Elihu Katz and Paul F. Lazarsfeld, *Personal Influence* (Glencoe, Ill.: The Free Press, 1955).

Gardner Lindzey (ed.), *Assessment of Human Motives* (New York: Evergreen, 1960).

N. E. Miller and J. Dollard, *Social Learning and Imitation* (New Haven: Yale University Press, 1941).

Theodore Newcomb, *Personality and Social Change* (New York: Holt, Rinehart and Winston, 1957).

Milton Rokeach, *The Open and Closed Mind* (New York: Basic Books, 1960).

19

The Speech to Actuate

"To incite to action." thus do the dictionaries define the verb, to actuate. Persuasion falling within this category is speech aimed to induce an audience to carry out the specific request formulated in the speaker's proposal.

Be it resolved that this meeting endorses John Smith for Senator. Here the action requested is simply a definite and formal statement of a belief the audience is willing to register publicly.

Will each one here contribute a dollar to the cause? In this instance the audience is asked collectively a question that must be answered by the individual contributions of the separate members of the group.

Let us assemble now into groups of five to organize as teams to canvass the city. Now the speaker is asking for an immediate action which will be but a relatively easy step in a process that will lead to considerable later, and more difficult, activity. *I move that this meeting adjourn so we can go together to build the widow Jones's barn.* Such a proposal is a call for united and immediate group action.

In all the examples indicated, the speaker is asking for more than agreement with his views; he is requesting that such agreement be made explicit in the precise kind of action that he requests. In this respect, the speech to actuate is susceptible to the most rigorous of all tests of its effectiveness. When the speech concludes, it becomes evident whether, and to what degree, it has been successful.

Requirements for the speech to actuate

The speech to actuate is sufficiently broadly inclusive to accommodate all speeches requesting any specific overt action of any kind from its hearers, whether singly or as a group. The one thing such speeches have in common is that they do all lead up to a definite request for some precise form of explicit action to be promptly performed. If the action is not described explicitly, but is left to the judgment of the hearers (as in a speech calling on the group to do "something" about the problem presented) the speaker is trying to *convince* them of a need for action, rather than to *actuate* them. Similarly, if he recommends a future action (such as "when the time comes, you should go to college") the intent likewise must be to establish a *conviction* that will carry over into eventual action. Thus, inclusive as the speech to actuate is—ranging all the way from inciting a mob to lynch a helpless prisoner to a carefully reasoned sale of an insurance policy —it also has sharply defined limits: the limiting conditions being the fact that it leads to a request for carrying out a specific action.

A speech designed to actuate should: (1) formulate its proposal in terms of what the audience should, can, and will do; (2) point its appeal toward either group or individual action, whichever may be appropriate; (3) utilize methods of motivation best adapted to the audience and to the situation; (4) strengthen effective speaker-audience relationships; (5) be flexible enough in form and content to adjust to developing audience reactions; (6) express effective qualities of leadership in its delivery; and (7) be phrased in persuasively definitive style.

Stating these same requirements in different terms, the speaker seeking to incite an audience to action should:

1. Tell his audience what to do,
2. As individuals or as a group,
3. In terms suitable to the situation,
4. Based on the speaker's status,
5. With the purpose keyed to audience response,
6. As effected by the speaker's presentation,
7. Fortified by persuasive diction.

Formulating the proposal

The more definitely the speaker desires his audience to do some precise thing that he is recommending to them, the more necessary it is to phrase the proposal with utmost exactitude. Hence, there is probably no kind of speech that requires more care in formulating the proposal than the speech to actuate. Reference should be made by the reader back to Chapter 14. In addition to what is presented there, the following considerations should be kept in mind:

First, phrase the proposal in terms of what the audience *should* do. This phrasing represents the complete and unqualifiied goal of the speaker. It states what you believe this audience ought to do about the subject being discussed. Thus, when speaking on behalf of your annual church drive, you might say, "We should each give to the church one tenth of our annual income," and support this proposal with references to the biblical tithe, and to the needs of the church and the opportunities for service it would have if such donations were made.

Second, rephrase your proposal in terms of what your audience *can* do. This often represents a major but necessary qualification and limitation upon the original phrasing. It is a "whittling down" of the requirement derived from the subject, resulting from the speaker's turning of his attention to the primary consideration in all persuasive speech—the nature of his audience. Such a consideration may lead you to rephrase your proposal somewhat as follows: "We should all give as much as we individually can," and support this proposition with the assumption that some may be able to spare more than a tenth, whereas others might have to make real sacrifices in order to give half that percentage of their income.

Third, rephrase the proposal again in accord with your realistic appraisal of what the audience *will* do. To aim for more than your speech actually can accomplish is very much like firing over the head of a grouse. You frighten the quarry away without bagging it. Similarly, to request less of your audience than it might perform is to limit your persuasive effectiveness needlessly. The ideal is to phrase your proposal as close to what the audience *should* do as the limitations of *ability* and *willingness* permit. In terms of the example we have been using, you doubtless would confer with the minister, the members of the church board, and various members of the congregation before you decided just what the members might be willing to do. And after such consultation and careful thinking on your own part, you would phrase your proposal perhaps as follows: "Let us give as much more than we did last year as the demands upon the church have proved is required," and support this proposal by a reminder of the size of last year's budget, a detailing of desirable projects that had to be abandoned for lack of funds, and an estimate of the average percentage increase needed for all contributions.

It is readily apparent: (1) that phrasing the proposal for a speech to actuate is not easy; (2) that it usually represents a compromise between the demands of the subject and the willingness of the audience; and (3) that in speeches of consequence the speaker would do well to fortify his own judgment of how the proposal should be framed by consultation with others who are both interested and informed.

The reader is perhaps struck with the fact that in every chapter there has been considerable discussion of the *proposal*. The inference may fairly be drawn that there is no point of view from which persuasive speaking can be analyzed without the discovery being made of the proposal's primary importance. The proposal is to persuasion what the lead is to a bullet. You may have a fine gun, be an excellent marksman, have a cartridge containing a good charge of powder, and have a firing pin that always sets off the charge. But without the lead missile to be expelled by the explosion, all that would result when you pulled the trigger would be a harmless (though perhaps impressive) flash and noise. Similarly, a speech might be impressively delivered and might resound with fine phrases and appeals, but it would be only an ineffectively flashy performance unless the net effect were to drive the proposal home to the audience. To carry the analogy further, just as the hunter must match his bullets and his gun, so must the persuasive speaker match his proposal to an adequate array of supporting motivation. And as the hunter uses the right gun and shells for the game he seeks—a twenty-two for squirrels and a thirty-thirty for grizzly bears

—so must the speaker formulate his proposal in terms of what the audience to which he will speak *should, can,* and *will* perform.

The influence of the group

The reader's attention was earlier directed to the "individuality of the crowd"—to the fact that individuals may sit together in one audience, but that they listen and react one by one. It must be understood, of course, that the degree of individuality will vary in terms of: (*a*) the *polarization* of the audience; and (*b*) the nature of the proposal.

Anyone who has observed the frenzied concentration of a football audience into one compact emotional unity or has seen the surging power of mob action may well be convinced that there is such a thing as a "crowd mind." When individuals are crowded densely together, are deeply stirred to achieve one common goal, and are so aroused as to have abandoned all considerations except achievement of that goal, they become united by a strong bond of sympathetic interaction, which impels them to feel alike, think alike, and act alike. If the speaker's proposal calls for united group action, he may wish to heighten the polarization of his audience so that this crowd-mindedness will be dominant.

Group action resulting from such strong polarization can scarcely be of a complicated or thoughtful nature. It is most effective when the response desired is primarily one of submission to leadership—such as Hitler sought and achieved in his development of the Nazi program, or as when the auditors are being urged to submit themselves to the common current of popular feeling—as in speeches designed to strengthen the "war effort" or in appeals to party followers to maintain high loyalty to their party's candidates. In a sensitive and finely written novel, *The Ox-Bow Incident,* W. Van T. Clark relates how a group of ranchers turned into a lynch mob, and of how keenly they regretted the fact when their later restoration of individuality made it possible for them to contemplate what a savagely unjust act they had committed.

In the ordinary audience situation there is no such catastrophic loss of individual initiative and judgment. Yet it is true that we exist and develop as *social beings,* drawing our values and characteristics from the society in which we live. In a sense we cannot "be ourselves" as truly in solitude as we are in a friendly group. "We find the true man only through group organization," Mary Follett wrote in *The New State.* "The potentialities of the individual remain potentialities until they are released by group life. Man discovers his true nature, gains his true freedom only through the group." Wilson Ryland pointed out, in *Social Group Work Practice* that the individual's "social needs grow as his social experiences develop, and these needs are met in accordance with the accepted standards of his particular class groups." It should be no surprise, then, that (to quote Ryland further): "It is within the group setting that values and norms receive the greatest impetus to change.... Participation in the decision-making process of organized groups means that each individual's values are affected by the values of the others in the group, and the group-as-a-whole takes the responsibility of implementing these through the behavior required for membership."

Characteristics of the individual in an audience

Specialists in group dynamics have been reminding us that the very gathering of people into groups has deep-seated effects upon their reactions. Many of the effects are so variable that it is difficult to forecast what they will be in any specific situation. However, general factors of group influence may be noted—each needing to be particularly assessed in terms of each specific occasion.

1. The individuals in an audience are *conscious of belonging together*—much more so, for instance, than they would be if they were crowded together waiting for a streetcar. Sociologists are prone to call this consciousness the "we-feeling."

2. Being susceptible to one another's opinions, and likewise drawn together by natural feelings of homogeneity, the individuals *tend to act in unison,* each one having his normal tendencies to conform heightened by the audience situation. This tendency is usually known as "social facilitation."

3. *Patterns of relationships* become established in the audience, with all the members oriented toward the speaker, and with a few members in each part of the audience oriented secondarily toward some particularly responsive individual who becomes their "leader" and whose responses they tend to repeat or mimic. Throughout the audience there will be several (perhaps many) such centers. As auditors, the individuals do not all have the same status, but some are far more influential in determining the nature of the over-all audience response than are some others. This pattern of status relationships within the audience may be designated by the psychological term "configuration."

4. The emotional reactions of individuals vary from favorable to unfavorable, with a general and inexact tendency toward achieving an approximate balance. Thus, if they are strongly favorably inclined toward some aspect of what the speaker is saying, this may carry over to support for other aspects of his speech of quite a different nature; or, inversely, there may be an implicit urge for them to be unfavorably inclined toward other parts of it. For this pattern of *contrary emotional currents* the best available term is "ambivalence."

5. Since there is a *need for clarity of understanding and completeness of judgment* (as William Stern points out in "The Psychology of Testimony," *Journal of Abnormal and Social Psychology,* January, 1939, pp. 3-20) members of the audience feel impelled to reach some decision on the subject held before their attention by the speaker. Hans Vaihinger, in his penetrating book, *The Philosophy of 'As If,'* points out that the uncertainty of indecision "involves a condition of tension which must be exceedingly disagreeable to the mind. The mind has a tendency to bring all ideational contents into equilibrium and to establish an unbroken connection between them." This tendency toward completeness of judgment Vaihinger designates "the law of the resolution of psychical tension."

Significance of the individual-audience relationships

The five factors of relationship of the individual auditors to the audience as a whole, which have been identified, are of considerable significance to the speaker who wishes to incite the audience to some recommended action.

He should keep in mind the following facts:

1. The mere fact that the individuals have assembled together to hear his speech (or that they are listening to it together, regardless of their reason for assembling) insures a bond of unity—the "we-feeling" —among them. The stronger this bond is, the more likelihood that the auditors will make a unified response to his proposal.

2. Through the process of social facilitation, there will be a tendency for the group to increase its like-mindedness as the meeting progresses. The speed and degree with which this process operates depends to a considerable extent upon whether and how much the group may be polarized.

3. The need felt by all normal persons to "make up their minds" on any subject held before their attention leads the audience to resolve its psychological tension by adopting some definite point of view about the speaker's proposal.

4. Since the configuration within the audience indicates that leadership in reaching a decision will be exerted more by some auditors than by others, the speaker should make a definite effort to locate the dominant auditors and to direct his appeal especially to them. Usually they are evident, both because their responses (favorable or unfavorable) are more pronounced than are those of the rest, and because the auditors immediately around them tend to direct a part of their attention toward these leaders and to follow their lead.

5. Finally, since the auditors need and seek an ambivalent outlet for their feelings, the speaker should not only seek to direct favorable responses toward his proposal, but should provide intermittently for their attention to be turned to opposing forces or individuals whom they may regard unfavorably. Thus he may say, in effect, "My proposal offers such-and-such an advantage, which would be undermined if we adopted the contrary and harmful program." In other words, give the audience something to oppose as well as something to support.

Appealing to the individual or the group

As has been indicated, audiences vary in the degree to which the individuals are subordinated to the "group mind." The speaker should carefully phrase his proposal in terms of whether it calls for individual or group action. Knowing, then, which kind of response is required, he can strive either to heighten or lessen the group dominance. The more his proposal is individualized—by such terms as, "I know we cannot all give the same amounts," and "What each of us will wish to do will obviously depend upon his own individual needs"—the more readily can he keep the responses to his proposal varied. Moreover, since we are all more alike emotionally than we are intellectually, the liberal use of facts and reasoning individualizes the response more than when emotion and rationalization are freely used.

Such a proposal as "We should all support this organization by the best means we can individually" (some through administrative leadership, some by advertising its functions, some with funds, others through carrying out assigned tasks, and so forth) obviously calls for a maximum individualization of response. On the other hand, such a proposal as "Let us all sign this petition urging the withdrawal of our fraternity from its national affiliation" requires the utmost possible unanimity of response. The latter type of proposal, accordingly, will call for more polarization and operation of the group mind.

Adapting motivation to the situation

John Dewey and George H. Mead, authors respectively of *Human Nature and Conduct* and *Mind, Self, and Society,* two epochal books in the interpretation of motivation, both found it useful to think of personality as divided into two categories. These two aspects may be designated as "the person" and "the individual"—the former meaning the ways in which we conform to changing social situations (thus being a different *person* at the office, at the golf club, in church, in a night club); and the latter meaning the qualities which remain relatively permanent and unchanged under all circumstances (such as our tendency to view life cynically or naïvely or hopefully, our habits of precision or carelessness, whether our interests lie primarily in events, in personalities, or in ideas). Mead and Dewey distinguish these two aspects of the individual as the "me" and the "I." A clear view of these concepts helps illuminate the problems in the speech to actuate.

The "I" is defined by Dewey as "the reconstructive center of society." In other words, the "I" is the aspect of each of us that is assertive, that transcends the social situation, that makes its own dominance felt. When a group is engaged in discussion, it is the "I" element in a participant that impels him to speak out in disagreement with the others, to offer his own interpretation of the subject, to inject his own feelings, attitudes, and moods. By thus asserting itself, the "I" *reconstructs* the nature of the group—focusing attention on some new phase of the subject or inducing a new mood within which the subject is considered.

The "me," on the other hand, represents the submergence of the individual in the group, the tendency to conform, the reflection by the individual of the values and feelings, the attitudes and ideas, of the group as a whole. It is through the operation of the "me" elements in the whole group that a particular mood can be formed. Only as the "me" aspects of personality are predominant is there an aura of agreement, a generality of feeling, an over-all pattern of unity.

In terms of our earlier definition of leadership, the speaker who would lead his audience must exemplify enough of the "me" to be an integral part of the group, and enough of the "I" to transcend and dominate it. As was pointed out in the discussion of *configuration,* the members of the audience vary in the relative assertiveness of their "I" and "me" aspects. But, as was hinted in the brief analysis of *ambivalence,* each member of the audience needs an opportunity to display both sides of his personality.

From such considerations there emerges the problem of the speaker in adapting his motivation to the audience feelings. *The motivation should appear general enough to satisfy the members of the audience that it is directed to all of them alike.* In other words, each of the members should feel that the speaker is regarding him as a normal human being who reacts as do other normal individuals to arguments, facts, emotional pleas, and to the speaker's rationalization (which is effective only as the auditors interpret it as reason). This audience interpretation of the speaker's motivation gives to each of the members a full opportunity to enjoy the submergence in the group—the sense of "belonging"—which is required by his "me" feelings. At the same time, *the motivation should be susceptible of interpretation by each auditor as applying in certain respects peculiarly and individually to himself*—thus also satisfying each auditor's "I" feeling of being a unique individual.

How, we may wonder, can a speaker possibly aim his appeal in two different directions at once—to both the audience-as-a-whole and to the separate individuals in it? Fortunately, the problem is not so difficult as it may at first appear. It is rendered easier by the concurrent existence within each of us of two contrary tendencies—egocentricity (or the tendency to see everything from one's own point of view) and ego-identification (or the tendency to feel oneself an indissoluble and inseparable part of the group). Thus when a speaker says: "We want better educational facilities for our children because we all want them to have a chance to succeed in life. Some of us want our own children to have a better start in life than we had ourselves," a typical auditor will glow with the "me" feeling in the first assertion and is very likely to interpret the latter statement as applying in terms of the "I" particularly to himself. What the speaker should do is to insure that in his speech are statements of both kinds, thus giving to every auditor a chance to gain the satisfactions both of belonging to and of transcending the rest of the audience.

Emphasizing the speaker-audience relationship

The emphasis usually given to the "conversational style" in speaking is helpful in strengthening the common "in-group" relationship between the speaker and his hearers. Such a manner of speaking dissipates the barrier between speaker and audience; it tends to lessen the "social distance" between the dominant speaker and the passive auditors. It brings the speaker into the group, so that he can demonstrate that he is interpreting the subject from his audience's own point of view. As we have seen in the context of every preceding chapter, this element is one of the essential qualities of persuasiveness.

But as we have also seen, it is only one, and by itself would destroy the very persuasiveness it seeks to create. The more complete is the assertion of conformity, the less is there an element of transcendence or dominance; and for persuasion as for other forms of leadership both the conformance and the transcendence are required.

It follows, then, that the conversational manner has dangers as well as virtues. It fails of effectiveness when carried too far. The teacher who comes to be regarded by his class as "just like one of us" abdicates his function of leading the class to become something other than what it was when it enrolled in his course. The salesman or politician or preacher who enters fully into the mood, feelings, and beliefs of his listeners soon disqualifies himself as an influence capable of remaking them in the image of his own convictions and desires.

The very fact that an individual is invited (or, in the case of a house-to-house salesman, let us say, is *permitted*) to address an audience is to establish him in a position of partial and temporary dominance. This is the relationship which he must seek to enhance and utilize in order to get his own program of action adopted. The proper relationship of the audience to the speaker is that of followers to a leader. His norm of speaking, then, should strengthen—and certainly should avoid weakening—this pattern of relationship. The speaker has prestige from the very fact of being the speaker. His function as a speaker is predominantly the "I" function, with his conformance, or "me" function, expressed solely for the purpose of maintaining a close enough relationship with the group so that it will continue to regard him as giving superior expression to its own inherent characteristics.

If, then, you want your audience to take the action recommended in your proposal, you must indeed show that you belong to the group, that it is their interests and needs you are seeking to serve; but you must also utilize your temporary prestige as the speaker to be assertive, authoritative, confident, and positive in leading the group "out of its non-sense to your sense." Once again, the conclusion leads up to the reiterated principle that as persuasive speakers we must *conform* in order to be enabled to *transcend*.

Adjusting to audience reactions

A speaker-audience situation is dynamic. The speaker presents a definite subject matter and a definite proposal to his group of hearers. The thinking of the audience becomes focalized upon a field of inquiry selected by and relatively dominated by the speaker. Facts, opinions, attitudes, and emotions are mobilized by the speaker and are successively presented before the auditors for their consideration. The minds of the group are besieged with a series of demands for them to reorient what they already know, feel, and believe in terms of the new influences being exerted upon them.

With such a dynamic process under way, a speaking situation is not static. What an audience is willing to accept at the beginning of a speech is different from what it will accept at various stages as the speech progresses. An unskilled speaker may arouse antagonism and disagreements so that the auditors are actually less willing to proceed toward his conclusion half way through the speech than they might have been at its beginning. In any event, whether the speech is effective or not, the minds of the audience undergo changes in points of view and in intensity of feelings. If a speaker were perfectly capable of charting every such change in advance, he might be able to chart the complete course of his speech and to pursue it effectively without change to its conclusion. But it is obvious that no such power of absolute predetermination exists.

What must be accomplished, then, by the speaker who would be truly persuasive is to cultivate the sensitivity required to evaluate the predominant changes that take place in his audience's total reaction pattern. This is why, in Chapter 15, emphasis was placed upon organizing the persuasive speech through succeeding stages of "audience acceptance." The speaker should not think of his subject matter as consisting of so many "main ideas" (derived from the logical requirements of his topic), which are to be successively developed and presented in order to insure that his subject is adequately covered. Rather, he should conceive of his speech as attempting to lead his audience up a number of successive steps (from what it formerly wished to do to what he himself wants it to do). This view of the speaker's task presents him with two major responsibilities:

First, to adapt his remarks to audience reactions, so that he attempts to say just enough, of the right things, in the right way, to carry them along from one step to another. Adolf Hitler's emphasis upon this kind of continuing adaptation to levels of belief has previously been quoted, as illustrating the awareness of one very practical persuader to this type of responsibility.

Second, to have his proposal analyzed in his own mind in such a fashion that he may either diminish or enlarge it in accord with what proves to be the possibility of accomplishment. As one instance of this requirement, radio salesmen are generally instructed to direct the attention of their prospects first of all to medium-priced sets, meanwhile watching alertly for their reactions. Depending upon what the reactions may be, the next stage is to shift their attention (if such a change seems wise) either toward the higher or lower price ranges.

Whatever the subject matter of the persuasive speech may be, a speaker who has his audience physically seated before him should keep in mind the strong possibility that he may not have accurately predetermined precisely what degree of action he may be able to secure. His expectations, consequently, should be set upon a sliding scale, permitting him to ask for either less or more than he may initially have anticipated.

This does not mean, of course, that the speaker should willingly abandon or change his goal to conform to audience resistance. What it does mean is that in many instances the proposal cannot be established in one attempt, but has to be subdivided for future efforts. The persuasive speaker who follows the practice of trying to achieve the maximum possible effectiveness in every speech must be particularly alert to the necessity of paring down his expectations in many specific situations. "Let us do what we can do now, with the rest to be accomplished when opportunity offers later," is a good common-sense slogan for the persuasive speaker to keep in mind.

Presenting the speech to actuate

The speech to convince, as has been seen, is ordinarily best presented in a manner of calm judiciousness, with an air of restraint, so that the response of the audience will not be pushed far beyond a point that later reflection may maintain. When an immediate specific action is the goal of the speaker, however, he must not only win the intellectual agreement of his hearers but needs also to arouse and stimulate a positive effort to put that agreement into practical effect.

In order to achieve this kind of reaction, the proposal must be *forced,* not *avoidable,* and the manner of the speaker should fully reflect the same urgency that is represented in his words. The speaker's voice, posture, and physical activity should all combine to build toward a rising climax of decisiveness, all helping to implant in the audience's reaction the conception that a decision must be reached now.

One suggestive study of the actual presentation of a successful persuasive effort is contained in the book *Mass Persuasion, The Social Psychology of a War Bond Drive,* by Robert K. Merton and associates —a study of the audience reaction to a day-long series of appeals by Kate Smith to buy war bonds, made over the Columbia Broadcasting System, on September 21, 1943. From early morning until late at night, (8:00 A.M. till 2:00 A.M.) Miss Smith spoke a total of sixty-five times to an audience estimated at around twenty-three millions. Pledges to buy $39 millions worth of bonds were phoned in as a result of her appeals. With such a specific persuasive presentation to study, Merton and his helpers conducted exhaustive interviews with one hundred listeners to the broadcasts (seventy-five of whom purchased a bond, and twenty-five of whom "resisted") and nine hundred seventy-eight briefer supplementary interviews. The degree of interest Miss Smith aroused is indicated by the fact that of listeners who tuned in on her program before noon, 70 per cent listened more than ten times, 59 per cent more than twenty times, and 26 per cent more than forty times.

How compulsive the appeals became is indicated in the following statement by one of the listeners: "We never left her that day. We stood by her side. I didn't go out all day, except to go shopping. Even then, I was anxious to get back and listen. Of course my sister was holding down the post in the meantime and could tell me what had happened." A man who had been listening in a saloon reported: "One fellow wanted to have the radio turned off. Well, the reaction was that he was going to be thrown out. Nobody wanted it turned off." The nature of the reaction among many listeners is indicated by the testimony of one of them: "Kate Smith made me feel like an awful heel that I had not done more. This time, I mean it, nothing is going to stop me from buying a bond. I really need a dress and had sort of planned on getting it, but what the heck—I'm not walking around in the nude yet."

Miss Smith's delivery of course (over the radio) was limited to the qualities of directness she could put into her words and voice. Lacking the visual impact of a speaker before an audience, she yet was able to accomplish the following results:

1. The appeals were *personalized*.

Sample comments of listeners were as follows: "It seems that she's sitting in your kitchen and talking with you. The way it would be with a friend." "She was speaking straight to me." "You'd think she was a personal friend. I feel she's talking to me."

2. The appeals were pointed toward *direct action*.

"I listened all day and the phone was right in front of me. They gave me the number and so I called."

3. The appeals sounded *sincere*.

Sixty per cent of the listeners queried referred to Miss Smith's sincerity as a factor explaining her effects upon them. As one listener explained, "The words seem to come not from her mouth, but from her soul, from her heart. It wasn't anything she was being paid for."

4. The appeals invited *identification* of the auditors with the speaker.

As one listener reported, "She sounded so tired, her voice was trembling. I had tears in my eyes." Another reported, "I'm great for sharing with poor people; they can't help themselves. Kate Smith is great for charity; I done a lot of charity in my life. If you got twenty-five cents, you can share it. I see old men begging in the street. I take 'em into a restaurant. Kate Smith's got the same feeling about poor people like I do."

5. The appeals were *emotional*.

Aside from the emotional quality of sincerity, 39 per cent of the listeners referred to Miss Smith's evident philanthropy; 36 per cent to her patriotism; 26 per cent to the fact that she seemed to be "just plain folks"; and other large groups found her a "guide and mentor," "motherly," and "virtuous."

Such qualities, rather than judiciousness and restraint, seem to be factors of effectiveness for speeches designed to incite action.

Phrasing the speech to actuate

As the quality of vividness was found of value for the speech to convince, in order to implant an idea solidly enough so that its effects would last, just so is vividness an element of importance in the speech to actuate. Here its purpose is to make a sharp enough impact to induce an immediate response. The diction of the speech to actuate should have a *startling, challenging, unsettling* effect, so that prior attitudes and feelings will be shaken up to make a place for new impressions. Then the speaker's proposal should be presented in such a manner as to be *definite, personalized, desirable,* and *urgent.*

It should not be inferred, of course, that all speeches to actuate should be delivered in the same style. Much depends upon the status of the speaker, the tinsit of the audience, and the nature of the action proposed. The style of a high school sophomore urging a group of students to demand a holiday because of a sensational football victory and the style of an investment broker trying to persuade a board of directors to buy a block of stock would have many divergencies. In both speeches, however, there would probably be an effort to *unsettle* beliefs that the *status quo* should continue, and to challenge, direct, and urge the auditors to the action desired.

All are familiar with the impetuous, emotional, and challenging style of Patrick Henry's speech urging the Virginia House of Burgesses to support the revolutionary movement commencing in Massachusetts.

Of quite a different character, but still urgently persuasive, is the charge to the jury rendered by Judge Harold Medina, following the nine-months' trial of eleven communist leaders in New York. Judge Medina, as reported by *Time,* October 24, 1949, sought to narrow the thinking of the jurymen from the vast mass of irrelevant testimony they had heard down to the bare essentials which they should consider in reaching their decision. His persuasiveness, thus, was largely a dispassionate process of definition:

WHERE FREE SPEECH ENDS

... These defendants had the right to advocate by peaceful and lawful means any and all changes in the laws and in the Constitution; they had the right to criticize the President of the United States and the Congress; they had the right to assert that World War II, prior to the invasion of Russia by Germany, was an unjust war, an imperialist war and that upon such invasion it became a just war worthy of all material and moral support; and they had the right publicly to express these views orally and in writing. They had the right thus to assert that the Government was at all times exploiting the poor and worthy workers for the benefit of the trusts and monopolies.

They had a right thus to assert that what they call the democracy of Russia is superior in all respects to American democracy. They had a right thus to assert that the Marshall Plan was a mistake, that billions of dollars should be loaned to Russia and that legislation adversely affecting Communists should not be passed. Whether you or I or anyone else likes or dislikes such or similar and analogous views ... is ... not entitled to the slightest consideration in deciding this case. Unless a minority had a right to express and to advocate its views, the democratic process as we understand it here in America would cease to exist and those in power might remain there indefinitely and make impossible any substantial changes in our social and economic system. ...

I charge you that if the defendants did no more than pursue peaceful studies and discussions or teaching and advocacy in the realm of ideas you must acquit them.... Do not be led astray by talk about thought control, or putting books on trial. No such issues are before you here.

But no one could suppose nor is it the law that any person has an absolute and unbridled right to say or to write and to publish whatever he chooses under any and all circumstances.

Words may be the instruments by which crimes are committed, as in many familiar situations; and it has always been recognized that the protection of other interests of society may justify reasonable restrictions upon speech in furtherance of the general welfare. . . .

You must be satisfied from the evidence, beyond a reasonable doubt, that the defendants had an intent to cause the overthrow or destruction of the Government of the United States by force and violence . . . as speedily as circumstances would permit it to be achieved.

. . . I charge you that it is not the abstract doctrine of overthrowing or destroying organized government by unlawful means which is denounced by this law, but the teaching and advocacy of action for the accomplishment of that purpose, by language reasonably and ordinarily calculated to incite persons to such action. . . .

No such intent could be inferred from the open and above-board teaching of a course on the principles and implications of Communism in an American college or university, where everything is open to the scrutiny of parents and trustees and anyone who may be interested. . . . That is why it is so important for you to weigh with scrupulous care the testimony concerning secret schools, false names, devious ways, general falsification and so on, all alleged to be in the setting of a huge and well-disciplined organization, spreading to practically every state of the union and all the principal cities and industries.

Conclusion

The process of inciting an audience to action involves a sevenfold sequence. First, the proposal must be framed in terms of what the audience should do, as modified by what it can and will do. Second, the speaker must estimate the effects of the group situation upon its various individual members, and should aim his appeal either at the group-as-a-whole or at the individuals severally, depending on the kind of action desired. Third, the persuasive appeal must be tailored to the immediate requirements of the audience situation. Fourth, the speaker should present his speech in accordance with a realistic appraisal of his own relationship as a leader to the members of the group. Fifth, the proposal may have to be modified and limited in view of the nature of the audience response. Sixth, the presentation of the speech should exhibit the qualities of sincerity, personalization, specificity, identification of the speaker with the audience, and emotional depth. And seventh, the style, while geared to the nature of the speaker, audience, and proposal, should in any event implant a vivid sense of the meaning of the subject, an urgency to do something about it, and a definite indication of what is to be done.

Exercises

1. The class may discuss the influence of an audience situation upon the individuals who compose it, pointing out how individual thinking, feeling, and reacting are modified by inclusion in the group, and analyzing to what extent individuality of response is maintained.

2. Analyze the sevenfold task of the speech to actuate in terms of speeches you have heard or read.

3. To what extent do the principles discussed in this chapter also apply to other types of persuasive speaking?

4. Phrase proposals which incite to action for the following topics: The Cold War, The Federal Debt, Vocational Education, Tolerance, Price Support for Farm Products, Responsibilities of Citizenship, World Unity, Atomic Power, Study Habits, and Racial Integration.

5. Prepare and deliver a speech to actuate, based on one of your proposals.

6. For continuing study in the activation of human behavior, the following readings are recommended:

C. B. Ferster and B. F. Skinner, *Schedules of Reinforcement* (New York: Appleton-Century-Crofts, 1957).

Ernest R. Hilgard, *Theories of Learning* (New York: Appleton-Century-Crofts, 2nd ed., 1956).

Howard S. Hoffman, "Some Contributions of Behavior Theory to Persuasion," *Today's Speech,* VII (April, 1959), 15-17.

A. H. Maslow, *Motivation and Personality* (New York: Harper, 1954).

D. C. McClelland (ed.), *Studies in Motivation* (New York: Appleton-Century-Crofts, 1955).

Edward D. Steele and W. Charles Redding, "The American Value System: Premises for Persuasion," *Western Speech Journal,* 26 (Spring, 1962), 83-91.

W. S. Verplank, "The Control of the Content of Conversation: Reinforcements of Statements of Opinion," *Journal of Abnormal and Social Psychology,* 51 (1955), 668-676.

Franklin R. Weiss, "How the Lawyer Uses Rhetoric," *Today's Speech,* VII (September, 1959), 6-8.

✌ 20.

The Speech to Stimulate

CONSISTENTLY THROUGHOUT THE PRECEDING CHAPTERS reference has been made to the function of persuasive speech as changing beliefs, action, and *feelings*. It is with feelings that the speech to stimulate is concerned. The other two major types of persuasive speaking frequently require the use of feelings as a means—that is, employ emotional appeals in order to influence belief or action. But in the speech to stimulate, the whole intent of the proposal is to secure a change of feeling. Emotion in these speeches is aroused not as a means to some other effect, but as an end in itself.

The aim of the speech to stimulate is to make the audience emotional—or to make it *more* emotional—or to change its feeling tone from one emotion to another. Does this seem an unworthy motive for speaking? As we observed in Chapter 11, it is only necessary for a moment to review what a fundamental role emotion plays in human lives. Groups of people may be moved to the heights of self-sacrifice and loyal devotion to a cause, a leader, or an ideal; they may be helped to spiritual insight and a serene sense of identity with the all-pervasive will of the Divine; they may be inspired to unusual endurance, determination, and effort; they may be strengthened against adversity, heartened against fear, elevated above despair, and made generous in triumph. Moving speech has rendered some people contented with their lot and has aroused others to superhuman efforts for improvement and reform. The power of emotional utterance destroyed the

419

slave trade and abolished human slavery, brought emancipation to women, and freed children from factory labor. It has preached equality and brotherhood and pleaded for justice and mercy. And when spoken by men of another sort, it has aroused hatred and bitterness, intolerance and greed, cruelty and tyranny. Surely the power of emotional speech is a wondrous or a fearsome influence, neither to be ignored nor thoughtlessly used.

Definition of stimulating speech

Just as the speech to convince shapes certain beliefs that are implanted in the minds of the auditors, and the speech to actuate impels the listeners to perform the action proposed by the speaker, so does the speech to stimulate aim to change the audience's *sense of values,* its *emotional reactions,* its *mood,* or its *feeling tone.* The first two kinds of persuasive speech seek a particularized and carefully defined reaction: to have the audience believe or do something precisely defined and carefully differentiated. The speech to stimulate, however, aims at a much more generalized response. Its goal is not to win agreement that a certain proposal is just, but to induce its hearers to love justice; not to have them give ten dollars to the Red Cross, but to deepen their sympathetic and philanthropic dispositions. It asks its auditors not to *believe* or to *do* but to *become.* The goal of the speech to stimulate is broad and inclusive. It seeks not to change minds or actions, but lives. It re-creates the emotional power of its listeners to the end that they will have the will to self-generation of such thoughts and deeds as the speaker favors.

The function of the speech to stimulate is to lift its hearers out of the narrowness imposed by the practical demands of daily living, to free them from compromises and expediencies, to raise their vision from the immediate demands of the moment to the challenges and opportunities of broadened experience. As one of the greatest of stimulating speakers, Daniel Webster, declared in his justly famous Plymouth Oration, the speech of stimulation should elevate us from our own personal limitations and unite us in sympathy and a sense of brotherhood with all mankind.

It is a noble faculty of our nature, which enables us to connect our thoughts, our sympathies, and our happiness with what is distant in place or time; and, looking before and after, to hold communion at once with our ancestors and our posterity. Human and mortal although we are, we are nevertheless not mere insulated beings, without relation to the past or the future. Neither the point of time, nor the spot of earth, in which we physically live, bounds our rational and intellectual enjoyments. We live in the past by a knowledge of its history; and in the future, by hope and anticipation. By ascending to an association with our ancestors; by contemplating their example and studying their character; by partaking their sentiments, and imbibing their spirit; by accompanying them in their toils, by sympathizing in their sufferings, and rejoicing in their successes and their triumphs; we seem to belong to their age, and to mingle our own existence with theirs.

The speech to stimulate, then, liberates its auditors from their individual limitations and unites them in the broad interplay of the ideals, aspirations, desires, and fellow feeling of the larger group. Its effects are felt by individuals, who are conscious of the enlargement and release it provides for them. But far from turning the thoughts of the individuals inward upon themselves, it brings them out, shows them their basic unity with their fellows, and heightens the feelings that assure identity with their chosen society.

Types of the speech to stimulate

As has been indicated, the speech to stimulate includes three types:

1. To arouse an emotional response;
2. To deepen an existing emotional response; or
3. To substitute one emotion for another.

All three of these types seek to effect an emotional change in the auditors. But differences in the nature of the change that is sought result in three different kinds of speeches.

1. When the speaker has to arouse an emotional reaction toward his subject, it must be because the subject is either unknown to the audience or is a matter of indifference to them. Such a subject might be "American Policy Toward Indochina." Few in a typical audience would know or care even whether the United States had any policy at

all toward that almost unknown land. The task of the speaker would be to give them facts enough so they would begin to form a clear picture of the country, and to personalize those facts sufficiently so that the auditors would view the problems presented with real concern. Such a topic for a speech of stimulation may seem at first thought to be more difficult than it actually is. One prerequisite, of course, is that the speaker himself must know what he is talking about. But when he does so, it is not difficult to persuade the audience to place confidence in what he is saying. The superiority of his knowledge over theirs will be so evident that there will be little disposition to doubt or resist what he has to say. The next requirement for effectiveness is to find a means of showing the audience that what happens in regard to Indochina is of direct concern to them—perhaps either because of the fundamental human values involved, or because events there may affect the security or well-being of America. With any unfamiliar topic the problem of stimulating an emotional response involves two factors primarily: (1) having an abundance of specific factual materials to present; and (2) presenting them in a vividly personalized manner.

2. When the speaker's purpose is to deepen an existing emotional response, the problem is often quite different. The fact that the audience already is emotionally stimulated toward the subject may have "taken the edge off" its interest. In many instances the subject has become hackneyed and dull from frequent discussion. This is very likely to be the problem of a preacher who seeks to deepen the religious feelings of his congregation; or of an educator who tries to create a deeper appreciation for the values of learning; or of a citizen who tries to arouse a greater patriotic fervor, or more respect for the laws, or a more sympathetic concern for the poor. Auditors may respond to such speeches with the feeling, "This is old stuff; true, of course, but not very interesting." To overcome this handicap, the speaker who does not have a fresh subject should strive especially hard for a fresh point of view toward it, or for unfamiliar ways of developing it. And, as with any kind of persuasive speaking, he should so phrase his proposal and support it with materials that the audience

will feel that what he is saying is genuinely a matter of deep personal concern to themselves.

When Adlai Stevenson addressed a Democratic Party rally in New York City, on April 25, 1956, his persuasive problem was to deepen the emotional response of loyalty that his listeners already felt for his candidacy. The following passage from his introduction illustrates how he sought to stimulate their existing emotions:

> I spoke in Washington last Saturday of peace in the world.
> I want to speak tonight of freedom in America.
> Yet these are not really two issues, but rather two parts of one.
> There can be no lasting freedom in America unless there is peace in the world. And there will be peace in the world only when we here in America prove that freedom means what we say it means. We must show that freedom is the servant of the poor as well as the rich—for most of the world is poor—that it protects change—for most of the world is in revolution—that it is color-blind—for humanity knows no color lines. We must prove that freedom contains that full measure of justice without which it could be freedom for the strong to oppress the weak.
> I see freedom in the world today as the great life-giving river of which America is the source. It will be whatever we are, not more, not less. So if we hope to make the principles of freedom meaningful in the world, we must first make sure they have mighty meaning for ourselves. We must—in our land, in our own communities, and in our own hearts—live up to the values of individual freedom and individual right which are the basis of our American society.

3. Usually still more difficult is the third type of stimulating speaking, in which the speaker is attempting to change the nature of the emotional reaction of the audience. This is the problem, for example, confronting some professors who teach required courses: they must find some way of converting a distaste for the subjects into an enthusiasm for them. For another instance, consider the problem of a preacher trying to arouse a sense of reverence in a group of skeptics or cynics. The stronger the existing feelings, the harder they are to change; but it also is often true that the greater is the need to change them. Emotions wrongly oriented often do great harm to those who entertain the feelings (as psychiatrists are emphasizing in regard to persecution complexes, mother fixations, and feelings of guilt or

inferiority) and to all those who are subjected to emotional pressures (as are various minority groups). Since some existing emotional reactions are undesirable, speakers must labor to change them. In doing so, a long and patient process of re-education is often needed, such as is described in the following chapter. Whether the speaker attempts the task in one or in many speeches, however, the essential nature of the problem is the same: (1) to remove or weaken the reasons for the existing emotion; (2) to find a common ground upon which to appeal for a change to the desired emotion; and (3) to show the audience that what it fundamentally desires is best served by the new feeling which the speaker is seeking to arouse.

The attempt to change the emotional reaction of an audience is basically different from trying to change its belief (as in the speech to convince). If emotions are not involved, an audience may readily change its beliefs when proper factual evidence, reasoning or rationalization, and an emotional stimulus are provided to support the new conviction. But emotion involves a sense of personal attachment. We don't want to change emotions; we feel that a suggestion to change them is in the nature of a personal attack. Obtaining an emotional change requires an extremely careful handling of the egos of the auditors. Suggestions of how this may be done are presented in later sections of this chapter.

Occasions for the speech to stimulate

The number and diversity of occasions for speeches to stimulate indicate both the importance and the complexity of this kind of persuasive speaking. A few representative occasions will serve to show both the variety and the basic unity of this category of persuasion:

Rallies, pep meetings, and political conventions. Here like-minded individuals are gathered together, united in a common goal, with feelings strongly aroused, and wanting only for speakers to serve as spokesmen to reiterate what they already feel. The occasion is almost ritualistic, with whoops, yells, singing, and cheering interspersed with speaking, which in itself is conventionalized in pattern. The speaker is a mouthpiece for the group. He is scarcely "persuasive" in any sense, except as his skill in whipping up emotion may intensify feelings already dominant.

Evangelistic meetings. The purpose of these meetings is conversion or change, but under highly favorable circumstances, with most of the audience in full accord with the speaker, and with most of those who are to be "converted" also largely in accord so far as their general feelings are concerned.

Commencement addresses and speeches of commemoration. Anniversaries, graduation exercises, dedications, eulogies, presentations of gifts, farewell parties, and similar occasions are largely designed for public expressions of common feelings. Normally the tone is dignified and elevated, disagreement is at a minimum, and style of presentation is of major importance. Like the neoclassical poets, speakers on such occasions normally strive less for originality than for superior phrasing of "what oft' is said, but ne'er so well express'd."

Father-and-son banquets, Girl Scout and Boy Scout meetings. Like Sunday school sessions and other inspirational youth meetings, these talks seldom deal with controversial themes, but intermingle exposition of ideas, humor, specific examples, and moral teachings, all held together by a common theme of inspiration to high endeavor and dedication to fruitful living.

Sermons. While many sermons may be expository, convincing, or activating, many more are primarily inspirational. They seek to deepen existing religious sentiments and to give more meaning to emotions that have become relatively dimmed.

Community meetings are often held to celebrate Brotherhood Week, to promote charitable drives, to discuss international or community problems, to combat intolerance, and to clarify or consolidate feelings of civic responsibility. Stimulation of existing emotions or attempts to change prevailing sentiments are among the diverse purposes served in such meetings.

Good will speeches, promotional meetings, and "booster" sessions. Many large industries and industrial associations employ speakers to spend their time addressing groups primarily for the purpose of creating or maintaining the good will of the public. Similarly, Chambers of Commerce and many service clubs are organized principally to "boost" the merits of their communities or the activities in which their members engage.

Sales meetings, staff meetings, and special luncheons often have as their chief function the stimulation of the audience to better morale and greater effort in the work before them.

To offer a complete listing of occasions for the speech of stimulation would be impossible, for there are few types of gatherings in which speeches to stimulate are not sometimes presented. Since the emotions are the driving forces that unify, give meaning to, and intensify our efforts, speeches to arouse, deepen, or change our emotional reactions are in frequent demand. Few indeed are the speakers who find no occasion for this kind of public address.

Forms of support

In order to create, deepen, or change emotional reactions the speaker will need *materials,* as in any other type of speaking. There may be a considerable body of factual evidence, such as specific examples of emotion-stirring kinds, comparisons and contrasts, hypothetical instances, and testimony. Even statistics may be used for emotional effect, as in the somber reminder that one automobile driver or passenger in every three, on the average, is going to be involved in an accident. Analysis may be a medium of emotional stimulation, as in a careful examination of the psychology of a typical director of a Red concentration camp. Negative evidence may be used to arouse deep feelings, as in demonstrating a mother's unfitness to have custody of her children by showing their malnutrition, lack of cleanliness, and absence of any affection toward her.

Reasoning, too, may be used in the speech to stimulate. Frederick Douglass, the great Negro orator, for instance, wove a fabric of reasoning into an emotional pattern in his speech before the annual meeting in 1865 of the Anti-Slavery Society, in Boston, when he said:

I know that we are inferior to you in some things, virtually inferior. We walk among you like dwarfs among giants. Our heads are scarcely seen above the great sea of humanity. The Germans are superior to us; the

Irish are superior to us; the Yankees are superior to us; they can do what we cannot do, that is, what we have not hitherto been allowed to do. But while I make this admission, I utterly deny that we are originally, or naturally, or practically, or in any way, or in any important sense, inferior to anybody on this globe. This charge of inferiority is an old dodge. It has been made available for oppression on many occasions. It is only about six centuries since the blue-eyed and fair-haired Anglo-Saxons were considered inferior by the haughty Normans, who once trampled upon them. If you read the history of the Norman Conquest, you will find that this proud Anglo-Saxon was once looked upon as of coarser clay than his Norman master, and might be found in the highways and by ways of Old England laboring with a brass collar on his neck, and the name of his master marked upon it. You were down then! You are up now. I am glad you are up, and I want you to be glad to help us up also.

When Kaiser Wilhelm II on August 6, 1914, called the German people to arms, he used rationalization as his medium of emotional stimulation, as the following complete text of his speech illustrates:

Since the founding of the Empire, during a period of forty-three years, it has been my zealous endeavor and the endeavor of my ancestors to preserve peace to the world and in peace to promote our vigorous development. But our enemies envy us the success of our toil. All professed and secret hostility from East and West and from beyond the sea, we have till now borne in the consciousness of our responsibility and power. Now, however, our opponents desire to humble us. They demand that we look on with folded arms while our enemies gird themselves for treacherous attack. They will not tolerate that we support our ally with unshaken loyalty, who fights for its prestige as a great power, and with whose abasement our power and honor are likewise lost. Therefore the sword must decide. In the midst of peace the world attacks us. Therefore up! To arms! All hesitation, all delay were treachery to the Fatherland. It is a question of the existence or non-existence of the Empire which our fathers founded anew. It is a question of the existence or the non-existence of German might and German culture. We shall defend ourselves to the last breath of man and beast. And we shall survive this fight, even though it were against a world of enemies. Never yet was Germany conquered when she was united. Then forward march with God! He will be with us as He was with our fathers.

Emotion in the speech to stimulate

Although factual evidence, reasoning, and rationalization all are forms of support that the persuasive speaker uses for stimulating effect, the main substance of the speech must be impregnated with emotion. Chapter 11 may well be reread as a guide for the preparation and delivery of this type of persuasive speech. Among the methods recommended there are those arising from personality, choice of materials, language, bearing, voice, and relationships with the audience. All together they combine to effect a personalization, an urgency, and a vividness of impression. The net effect of such qualities is illustrated very simply and movingly in the following remarks made by Red Jacket, the great Chief of the Six Nations, in 1805, to a missionary who requested permission to establish missions among the Indians:

Friend and Brother:—It was the will of the Great Spirit that we should meet together this day. He orders all things and has given us a fine day for our council. He has taken His garment from before the sun and caused it to shine with brightness upon us. Our eyes are opened that we see clearly; our ears are unstopped that we have been able to hear distinctly the words you have spoken. For all these favors we thank the Great Spirit, and Him only.

Brother, this council fire was kindled by you. It was at your request that we came together at this time. We have listened with attention to what you have said. You requested us to speak our minds freely. This gives us great joy; for we now consider that we stand upright before you and can speak what we think. All have heard your voice and all speak to you now as one man. Our minds are agreed.

Brother, you say you want an answer to your talk before you leave this place. It is right you should have one, as you are a great distance from home and we do not wish to detain you. But first we will look back a little and tell you what our fathers have told us and what we have heard from the white people.

Brother, listen to what we say. There was a time when our forefathers owned this great island. Their seats extended from the rising to the setting sun. The Great Spirit had made it for the use of Indians. He had created the buffalo, the deer, and other animals for food. He had made the bear and the beaver. Their skins served us for clothing. He had scattered them over the country and taught us how to take them. He had caused the earth to produce corn for bread. All this He had done for His red children because He loved them. If we had some disputes about our hunting-ground they were generally settled without the shedding of much blood.

But an evil day came upon us. Your forefathers crossed the great water and landed on this island. Their numbers were small. They found friends and not enemies. They told us they had fled from their own country for fear of wicked men and had come here to enjoy their religion. They asked for a small seat. We took pity on them, granted their request, and they sat down among us. We gave them corn and meat; they gave us poison in return.

Identification

In many speeches to stimulate, the speaker is primarily a spokes-man for his audience, uttering feelings which they feel to be appropriate and desirable for the occasion. In these instances, there very definitely is an *identification* of the speaker with his audience. A speaker who is appealing to his auditors for a deeper patriotism, religious devotion, morality, or diligence can surely proceed in full confidence that he and his listeners are in basic accord, both in the goal sought and in the reasons for seeking it. Similarly, when a speaker is seeking to arouse an emotional reaction on a subject of present indifference to his audience, there is no reason for him to anticipate antagonism, and every reason why he should assume a basic agreement and speak in terms of that assumption. As has been pointed out earlier, the best way to win an argument is to avoid having one. In many speeches to stimulate, the avoidance of any argumentative tone is easy and almost inevitable.

However, in the speeches that attempt to substitute one emotion for another, the task of achieving identification is harder. There the very fact that a change of emotion is sought is an indication of a real difference between speaker and audience. What should be emphasized, however, is that this difference ought not to be permitted to assume any tinge of antagonism. Actually, the speaker has very little basis for an emotional appeal to his audience except where there is an essential like-mindedness. The task of the speaker is to penetrate behind the difference to a deeper segment of unity upon which he and his hearers feel alike.

Human beings, as was noted in Chapter 11, are much more alike emotionally than they are intellectually. It is generally possible to find an emotional tone in which all can unite, whatever the apparent differences may be. When this basis is found, the speaker can proceed with an "all in the same boat" approach, the secondary differences being minimized by the primary agreement. A celebrated instance of just this kind of procedure is the speech made by the Reverend Henry Ward Beecher at Liverpool, on October 16, 1863. With English textile mills closed by the Union blockade of Southern ports, Beecher was greeted by a mob so hostile the chairman had to threaten to call out the police before Beecher could even begin. His opening remarks indicate Beecher's method of shouldering his way through secondary (if keenly felt) disagreements down to a bedrock of identification with his listeners:

For more than twenty-five years I have been made perfectly familiar with popular assemblies in all parts of my country except the extreme South. There has not for the whole of that time been a single day of my life when it would have been safe for me to go south of Mason's and Dixon's line in my own country, and all for one reason: my solemn, earnest, persistent testimony against that which I consider to be the most atrocious thing under the sun—the system of American slavery in a great free republic. [*Cheers.*] I have passed through that early period when right of free speech was denied to me. Again and again I have attempted to address audiences that, for no other crime than that of free speech, visited me with all manner of contumelious epithets; and now, since I have been in England, although I have met with greater kindness and courtesy on the part of most than I deserved, yet, on the other hand, I perceive that the Southern influence prevails to some extent in England. [*Applause and uproar.*] It is my old acquaintance; I understand it perfectly [*laughter*], and I have always held it to be an unfailing truth that where a man had a cause that would bear examination he was perfectly willing to have it spoken about. [*Applause.*] And when in Manchester I saw those huge placards, "Who is Henry Ward Beecher?" [*laughter, cries of "Quite right,"* *and applause*]—and when in Liverpool I was told that there were those blood-red placards, purporting to say what Henry Ward Beecher had said, and calling upon Englishmen to suppress free speech—I tell you what I thought. I thought simply this, "I am glad of it." [*Laughter.*] Why? Because if they had felt perfectly secure, that *you* are the minions of the

South and the slaves of slavery, they would have been perfectly still. [*Applause and uproar.*] And, therefore, when I saw so much nervous apprehension that, if I were permitted to speak [*hisses and applause*]— when I found that they considered my speaking damaging to their cause [*applause*]—when I found that they appealed from facts and reason to mob law [*applause and uproar*], I said: No man need tell me what the heart and secret counsel of these men are. They tremble and are afraid. [*Applause, laughter, hisses, "No, no," and a voice: "New York mob."*] Now, personally, it is a matter of very little consequence to me whether I speak here tonight or not. [*Laughter and cheers.*] But, one thing is very certain —if you do permit me to speak here tonight you will hear very plain talking. [*Applause and hisses.*] You will not find a man [*interruption*],— you will not find me to be a man that dared to speak about Great Britain three thousand miles off, and then is afraid to speak to Great Britain when he stands on her shores. [*Immense applause and hisses.*] And if I do not mistake the tone and temper of Englishmen, they would rather have a man who opposes them in a manly way [*applause from all parts of the hall*] than a sneak that agrees with them in an unmanly way. [*Applause and "Bravo."*] If I can carry you with me by sound convictions, I shall be immensely glad [*applause*]; but if I cannot carry you with me by facts and sound arguments, I do not wish you to go with me at all; and all that I ask is simply fair play. [*Applause, and a voice: "You shall have it, too."*] Those of you who are kind enough to favor my speaking—and you will observe that my voice is slightly husky, from having spoken almost every night in succession for some time past—those who wish to hear me will do me the kindness simply to sit still and to keep still; and I and my friends the Secessionists will make all the noise. [*Laughter.*]

Brief as this passage is, it illustrates a number of important methods of achieving identification. Foremost, perhaps, is the very tone of the speech—a display of courage, of conviction, and of manly independence, which Beecher rightly felt would be appreciated and considered as British virtues even by those who resisted what he had to say. As another vital element, it will be observed that Beecher did not try to side-step the disagreements. Instead, he appeared even to aggravate and emphasize them, with his references to "Southern influence" and the placards, and with his direct challenge to the "minions of the South." But, as even this brief quotation reveals, Beecher took note of the disagreements only so that he could bring them out into the open and help the audience to see that they were of less significance than the commonalty of feelings that underlay them. Chief among these elements of common ground was Beecher's frank appeal for fair play; for the right of a manly man to disagree boldly and openly. Another element was his emphatic and reiterated reminder that attempts to prevent his speaking were tantamount to admissions that they would not dare to hear the truths he would utter. This kind of reasoning struck close home to an English audience whose ancestors had fought hard for free speech. A further common-ground element was Beecher's hint that they would hear "very plain talking"—a lure of excitement to which an excitable audience would be especially susceptible. Still another was his reiteration that he would appeal to them only with sound facts and arguments (which, of course, he did not do). It will also be noted that Beecher made skillful use of humor, always a good basis for uniting an audience in a common bond. And, in addition, he divided his auditors into two groups, the fair-minded who wanted to hear him, and the "slaves of slavery" who appealed from "reason to mob law" and who "tremble and are afraid." There could be no doubt as to which group it was most desirable to be in—so that the great bulk of the auditors hastily transformed their overt behavior in such a manner as to be included among the fair-minded. So definitely did this shift occur that Beecher was able to get predominant laughter, rather than hisses, when he made a humorous quip directed against the Secessionists—against, in fact, the very sentiment that had just previously been the dominant tone of the meeting.

It will generally be true, as it was for Beecher, that seeking identification does not mean an unrealistic or naïve pretense that no differences exist. Rather, more commonly, it means a highly realistic proposal to the audience to examine their own fundamental interests, wishes, and motives, so they will understand that what the speaker stands for is what they similarly stand for themselves. The speaker is trying neither to evade the issues nor weakly to compromise his own beliefs. Nor is he trying to delude the audience into momentarily forgetting its own contrary points of view. Rather, he is saying, in effect, "All right, on some things we don't agree. Maybe some time we can argue those matters out. But right now it is important for us to see where we do agree, and why. Let's look, then, at the fundamental principles for which you and I stand. This is the ground we must stand together to defend."

Style of the speech to stimulate

It is evident that there will be vast stylistic differences between the few remarks made by the football captain to the college all-student rally the night before the "big game" and the funeral eulogy preached in the St. Mark's Episcopal Church by the bishop. Both speeches are intended to stimulate, yet the range they represent is so broad as to indicate the difficulty of establishing any objective standards of style for this kind of speaking. Here, as in other forms of persuasive speech, the mood of the audience is actually the final test. The general principle to be followed, then, is that the speaker should use a style that is appropriate to the audience and the occasion.

In certain respects, however, there is a marked similarity among all kinds of stimulative speech—including the eulogy and the pep talk. There is a current of strong feeling flowing from speaker to audience, borne in the tones of the voice, in the manner, facial expressions, posture, and gestures of the speaker, and implicit in the content and language of the speech. To use again the term of De Quincey, speeches to stimulate make effective use of the "language of power." In speech books it has become customary to speak of such language as employing "loaded words."

"Oratory is the art of enchanting the soul," said Socrates, and perhaps this judgment applies more closely to the speech to stimulate than to any other kind. The words that help most to accomplish this aim are "loaded" with emotional connotations. Their meaning is *implicit* rather than *explicit, suggestive* rather than *prescriptive.* This is to say that "loaded" words (1) say more than they seem to say; and (2) say it in different ways to different auditors. They are, in sum, the kinds of words that inspire the hearer to elaborate their meaning in terms of his own experience.

House, for instance, is relatively an explicit and prescriptive term signifying an independently constructed dwelling unit. *Home,* on the

contrary, is an implicit and suggestive term, inviting the auditor to a
nostalgic recollection of his own family living quarters, enlivened with
the emotional overtones of the most intimate associations of his life.
The latter is a "loaded word," carrying upon its back all manner of
individualized meanings added personally by each listener.

Words become "loaded" both from the general background of the
auditors and from the immediate situation in which they are uttered.
These are two factors, both requiring of the speaker a close study of
his audience if he is to use language that will really move his hearers.
One audience will be stirred through memories and experiences associated with *corn pone,* another with *flapjacks,* and a third with *johnny-
cake,* but few hearers will be stimulated alike by more than whichever
one of them fits into his own background. Similarly, the same audience
that is aroused to a frenzy of emotion by the football captain's sturdy
assertion, "We're going out there tomorrow and rub our noses in the
mud to win that game for you and we expect to rub in a few noses
from the Bearcat team, too," would be startled and perhaps stimulated
(but hardly appropriately) by the same kind of language in the college
chapel. There is an appropriateness of time and place, of mood and
motive, to which effective speaking must conform.

The style of the speech to stimulate is most effective when it carries
to the audience the sincere feelings of the speaker phrased in terms of
the emotional needs of the auditors. The speaker's style is the elusive
quality of language by which he enters into and then to an extent
transforms the audience mood. "Speak to them as they are, in order
that you may lead them to become what you will," is the principle of
style the persuasive speaker should adopt.

Conclusion

Ranging very broadly through many different types of occasions,
and with seemingly many differing purposes, the speech to stimulate
actually has only one general goal: to secure a change of the audience's feeling tone. This change, however, may be any one of three
types, thus leading to three different kinds of stimulative speeches:
(1) to create emotional reactions on subjects to which the audience is

indifferent; (2) to intensify existing feelings; and (3) to change the nature of existing emotional patterns. While utilizing facts, reasoning, and rationalization to accomplish its aim, the speech to stimulate draws most heavily upon emotional appeals. This is done in part through establishment of a common ground of feeling with the audience, and in part through "loaded words" and other elements of moving style. In all kinds of stimulative speech, the speaker must be especially close to his audience. Sometimes, in effect, he serves primarily as the spokesman for what the auditors wish to have said. And even when he wishes to convert them from one feeling to another, he can do this only as he enters into their basic emotional patterns and seeks from that vantage point to achieve the changes he desires.

Exercises

1. Discuss the basic function of the speech to stimulate in terms of each of its three types. Note the similarities and differences between the third type and the speech to convince. Cite examples of each of the three types.

2. In view of the wide range of occasions for and styles of the speech to stimulate, there is special point to the need for a clear understanding of what they all have in common. How would you explain the statement, "It is with feelings that the speech to stimulate is concerned"?

3. Gather examples from your listening and reading to show how facts, reasoning, and rationalization are used for emotional stimulation.

4. Reread Chapter 11 to refresh your understanding of how a speech may be "impregnated with emotion."

5. Find a speech (other than Beecher's at Liverpool) in which the speaker made extensive use of *identification* to establish, deepen, or change an emotional response. Analyze the means by which this speaker-audience relationship was established.

6. Draw up a list of ten matching terms, one of each pair of which is emotionally "loaded," whereas the other is chiefly denotative (such as home-house, or brother-sibling).

7. Prepare and deliver a speech to stimulate, indicating on your outline the kinds of materials used.

8. Further guidance may be found in the following readings:

Joseph Gerard Brennan, "The Role of Emotion in Aesthetic Experience," *Quarterly Journal of Speech,* 40 (December, 1954), 422-428.

William Empson, *Seven Types of Ambiguity* (New York: Harcourt, Brace, 1931).

G. L. Thomas, "Oral Style and Intelligibility," *Speech Monographs,* 23 (March, 1956), 46-54.

Jack Matthews, "The Effect of Loaded Language on Audience Comprehension of Speeches," *Speech Monographs,* XIV (1947), 176-186.

Lester Thonssen and A. Craig Baird, *Speech Criticism* (New York: Ronald Press, 1948), "Emotion in Speech," 357-382, and "The Style of Public Address," 405-433.

9. The following speech illustrates not only the persuasive purpose *to stimulate* but also a combination of many qualities recommended throughout this book: realistic adaptation to the audience, not as a surrender of the speaker's aim but as a means of accomplishing it; an integration of humor and high seriousness; clarity of organization; nonargumentative progression toward the speaker's goal; and a fundamental *realism* of consideration of the problems involved. The speech well merits thoughtful analysis.

HIGHER EDUCATION AND THE MAINTENANCE OF AMERICAN FREEDOM

The Honorable J. W. Fulbright
United States Senator from Arkansas

Address presented at the Final General Session of the Tenth National Conference on Higher Education, sponsored by the Association for Higher Education, Chicago, March 2, 1955.

After the many taxing hours you've spent in discussion groups, I think I can best thank you for the invitation to speak here in this final hour by speaking briefly. I shall try to do just that. In fact, the heart of what I have to say is expressed in but one story.

Some time ago, so this story goes, a warden at the Joliet penitentiary played host to a conference of criminologists, called to consider ways and means of reducing the crime rate. One speaker seemed to carry the day with his thesis that the way to do this was by requiring all young people to study mathematics intensively. For the discipline gained in this way, so the speaker claimed, would lead the young to think logically, and so make them virtuous when they came of age.

There was great applause when he reached the end and sat down. The warden alone seemed unimpressed. He asked an aid to fetch a certain prisoner, introduced him to the meeting, and then at once sent the prisoner back to his cell. "That man you just saw," the warden explained to the criminologists, "is the most brilliant mathematician in the whole prison. So brilliant, in fact, that it took bank examiners ten years before they found that he was embezzling funds by juggling bank ledgers. That man was not deficient in mathematics. What he lacked was a sense of grammar and rhetoric. He simply didn't know the difference between the words 'mine' and 'yours.' "

You will agree, I think, that the criminologist who saw in the science of mathematics the means to create a nation of moral men and good citizens is not alone in his approach. He is joined by a chorus of voices, each with a special educational emphasis leading to the magic formula. To one person, it is training in physics, or medicine, or plant life. To another, it is training in business, or home-making, or athletics. Let this or that be the cornerstone for higher education—so they say—and the arrangement of its own force will meet every danger, solve every problem, remove every evil, and gain every good.

As for myself, I am inclined to favor the "Warden theory" of education, if I may call it that. I am inclined to favor it, subject to three qualifications.

First, no system of higher education, however arranged, can bear the whole load of cultivating what lies in the human spirit. For that spirit, as the ancients taught us long ago, is a mixed thing. It is formed and ruled not alone by reason. It is also formed, and it is all too often ruled, by the will and by the passions. And if there are those who may deny this ancient fact, the rule of Adolf Hitler in Germany, and Mussolini in Italy, and the careers of a variety of imitators in the United States—each in a land pre-eminent for its literacy and enlightenment—are case studies of how reason can be set on its head by willful men who know how to play on passions, and so make the worse cause appear to be the better one.

The second qualification follows from the first. It is that if the education of the individual is viewed in its entirety, then disciplined hearts must dwell in the same body as disciplined minds. And in this light, not the schools alone can carry the burden of the work that needs to be done. Nor can they be charged—as they now often are—with full responsibility for any defective products. Our homes, our churches, our political institutions, our economic enterprises—all our media of communication—are, and must be, considered a part of what educates the individual. None can absolve itself from the end result. All are jointly responsible for what it is like.

The third qualification is addressed to those who would have the schools and colleges emphasize this or that specialized science and art. Let me say here that I have the utmost respect for the specialist. It is plain, for example, that we urgently need scientists and technicians who can lend their expertness to the defense of America and the free world. So, too, as a further example, do we need men, skilled in the art of economic management, who can perfect the way we organize production and distribution. This work is of supreme importance; for though it is true enough that man does not live by bread *alone,* at least he lives by bread. And we need places specifically set aside for the purpose of cultivating the science and art of making bread, and defending it.

Yet divorced from all else, this specialization in art and science—and here I come to my point—is not an education for a *democracy.* There is nothing to distinguish it from an educational system in a totalitarian state. Men like Hitler, Mussolini, and Stalin may have boasted of a Nazi, or a Fascist, or a Communist science and technology. Yet these bits of knowledge are not political or moral by nature. The same textbooks dealing with them can be used by students in both democracies and tyrannies. For the subjects themselves are equally useful to free men and slaves alike; and indeed, in ancient times, they were cultivated chiefly by slaves.

I repeat that this specialization does not form an education for a democracy. It does not create an atmosphere in which the mind can be opened to every intimate impulse and voice, meshed with other minds of a like sort. Specialization, by definition, focuses on only a small part of the human battle line. It orients no one toward a view and a place in the battle line as a whole. It orients no one toward the whole intellectual life and tradition of a country. It orients no one toward an understanding of man as he appears in a particular moment of current history, and in the history of the ages.

And it is precisely at this point—as I shall try to make plain in a moment—that the comment of the Warden at Joliet seems to apply on all fours. Here, let me digress to say that from what I have seen of our colleges and universities, their key weakness is not that they breed Communists. It is arrant nonsense to say that they do. Not one of our enlisted men who went over to the Communist side during the Korean War and refused repatriation cited as his reason any Marxist indoctrination while in college. Many of them never went to more than the primary grades, and in fact, were illiterate. As for the officers who were court-martialed for aiding the enemy, not one of these pointed an accusing finger at some university professor under whom they had studied at West Point or elsewhere.

Yet there is a weakness in our colleges and universities. And now, in this hour of grace, when we do not have to spend all our strength in fighting back the McCarthy line of attack, we ought to turn our thoughts inward, and seek where this weakness lies. In my view, at least, it lies in our failure to teach grammar and rhetoric—to teach the difference between "mine" and "yours." In the largest sense for which this difference in words is but a symbol, it lies in our failure to keep intact as a unifying reference point for the undergraduate body, a common intellectual tradition, a sense of an intellectual community leading to a sense of the continuity of human experience.

One used to find all this in the old prescribed courses of the humanities before a rampant, free-for-all, excessively individualist elective system ripped everything apart. But now we live with a situation where doctors only know how to make their meaning plain to other doctors; or engineers to other engineers; or lawyers to other lawyers, or businessmen to other businessmen, and so on. Each of these talks, and talks well within the range of a profession. But they do not talk up and down and across their professions. They do not talk up and down and across the whole range of human experience, stimulating and stimulated by that experience, to perfect the spirit of their age in the light of the spirit of all ages. They do not and they cannot do this, because they do not have in common a vocabulary they all understand—a vocabulary that was once drawn from the common fund of knowledge embraced by the humanities.

All of this lends an air of paradox to our commitment to democracy. On the one hand, we assert our devotion to a system of government that is based on free and intelligible communication between citizen and citizen, and between the leaders and the led. On the other hand, we weaken the effectiveness of that system by a prevailing educational process that tends to narrow down communication by limiting it to an "Information Please" program and a *Reader's Digest,* or by rendering meaning altogether meaningless. This paradox, let me add, is made to order for exploitation by the demagogues. For I noticed that when our higher institutions of learning came under attack from that quarter, all too many of them were bewildered by what they were called on to defend. They seemed at times to flounder in an inner darkness of their own making, equal in density to the darkness the demagogues meant to impose on them from without. The best that many of them could do was to raise the rallying cry of academic freedom. Yet academic freedom, while of supreme importance in the educational process, is not the end-aim of the process. It is but a means to an end. And under conditions where so many of our institutions of higher learning lacked any coherent, general, and organized body of knowledge they meant to impart to their students, they were at a loss how to define the end they meant to preserve through academic freedom.

In saying this, I am not implying that our colleges and universities ought now to sit down in a solemn convention and agree on a body of doctrine which they will then impose as a new orthodoxy on their student bodies. In common with all of you, I see in any such proposal the death of all education; of an education, at least, whose aim ought to be the infusion of the spirit of learning among students, and whose method ought to be not indoctrination, but the constant exercise of the mind in meaningful arguments. In common with all of you, also, I see in any such proposal for orthodoxy, something of the ludicrous outlook of a university trustee who strongly objected to the text of a university president's commencement address. And when the president said to the trustee, "Well, don't you want your students to hear the truth?" the trustee answered, "Of course! But can't you print the truth on the back of the convocation program, and hand it to the graduates as they file out of the chapel?"

The tradition of the humanities, for whose restoration I am pleading as the heart of any educational system that can best serve democracy, is not a tradition of orthodoxy. It is a tradition of continuous disagreement between parties in a great dialogue extending back over the ages. All that these parties agreed upon was the topics they felt were worth talking about. And beyond this, the sense of unity that is present in their great dialogue was hinged to the fact that when they disagreed, they knew what they were disagreeing about. Today, by contrast, we are inclined to rush ahead pell-mell with our solutions, without first asking what the question is we want to solve. Today, also, it happens all too often that people disagree violently without recognizing that they are talking about different things in the first place.

In the long retrospect, I think it is fair to say that the strength of our political institutions is a strength drawn originally from men who shared the common heritage of education in the humanities. Indeed, in this respect there probably was no institution of higher learning in history equal to the community of men who formed the Constitutional Convention. All were pre-eminent in practical affairs. Yet they were also men who knew how to speculate, who brought a broad range of human experience to bear first on their thoughts and then on their practical work. This is not to say that they agreed with each other. They disagreed sharply. But when they did, they shared a common vocabulary which made the eventual agreement possible. So, also, in later years, a Thomas Jefferson and an Alexander Hamilton, whose thoughts form the basic fabric of our national life, disagreed sharply. Yet they were children of the same tradition. And because they were, each in the act of disagreeing, brilliantly served the nation so that we can now turn to Jefferson for guidance under one set of circumstances, and to Hamilton under a different set. And in this way, we profit from both.

I am saying here that tradition does not mean uniformity. It means diversity within an embracing unity. And it is to this end, I feel, that we must reconceive and reorganize the life that is lived in our schools of higher learning. We must make of those schools the home for a new spirit of learning. We must make them, as Woodrow Wilson pleaded in 1909, "a community of scholars and pupils—a free community but a very real one, in which democracy may make its reasonable triumphs of accommodation, its vital process of unity. I am not suggesting," Wilson continued, "that young men be dragooned into becoming scholars or tempted to become pedants, or have any artificial compulsion whatever put upon them, but only that they be introduced into the high society of university ideals, be exposed to the hazards of stimulating friendships, be introduced into the easy comradeship of the republic of letters. By this means the classroom itself might some day come to seem a part of life."

A final remark. I have no illusion that even if all this is done, all will be well with us in a present and future hour. For we face the fact that what we are educating is, after all, the son of Old Adam. And like his ancestor who rebelled against a teaching from the highest possible quarter, so can the son of Old Adam rebel against what he is taught, and reach for forbidden fruit. Yet this much, at least, can be hoped for: that a familiarity with what the many generations of man have talked about and experienced in their career on earth, can, by pointing up the consequences, reduce the danger of such a rebellion, though it may not eliminate it altogether. Indeed, without this heroic hope that education can inch humanity forward toward the vision of human perfectibility, life itself would have no purpose.

In all that touches existence, free men everywhere look to America for leadership. When we wobble, they feel unsteady. When we creak, they groan. When we slip, they fall. But when we act with the clarity of a great purpose, they feel braced and uplifted. Our schools of higher learning must view themselves as the heart within the heart of what it is that can enable America to give free men the leadership they want. Yet America cannot exercise that leadership if, within the borders of our own land, we are in danger of losing the ability to talk to one another. It is to the restoration of that lost art, in all its admitted difficulties, that I hope our schools of higher learning will bend their chief energies.

The Sustained Campaign

A MANUFACTURER WHO PRODUCES A NEW MAKE OF CAR has the problem of persuading the American public to buy it. This necessity confronts him with a problem that cannot be solved by a single persuasive appeal. What is required is a continuing campaign, to last as long as he has cars to sell. Similarly, in each community where he establishes a sales outlet, the dealer has to persuade the local public to come in and buy. He, too, has to conduct a sustained campaign.

Comparatively little persuasion that is concerned with subjects of importance can be accomplished in a single speech. Even when a momentary effect of an apparently satisfactory nature is achieved through one effort, the strong probability is that the effect will shortly be minimized or dissipated. Perhaps you have had the experience of "convincing" some friends that they should shift their political allegiance to the other major party—only to find that the next time you see them they have reverted to their former beliefs. Or maybe you have aroused what seemed like a burning enthusiasm for some cause or program, only to find that nothing has come of the plans to which everyone seemed to agree. The situation is typical: a group will meet in the evening, listen to stirring talk, agree that the time has come for them all to join in a real program of action—and by the next day they are again immersed in their daily affairs, with the enthusiasm cooled and the action postponed or forgotten.

So frequently is this condition encountered that many people come to doubt the usefulness of persuasive speech. "Nothing will come of it," they say, "it's only talk!" It is true that speech does not accomplish everything; but this is no reason for concluding that it accomplishes nothing. The fault lies not in the inefficacy of persuasion, but in expecting it to perform miracles.

Human beings are aggregates of habits: mental and emotional as well as physical. We know how hard it is to break such physical habits as smoking, swearing, or overeating. It is fully as difficult, or more so, to break mental and emotional habits, to change attitudes and fundamental convictions. One who likes conventional painting is not readily won to enthusiasm for modernistic art. A person who doesn't like to read is not easily made a devotee of mystery stories. It is hard to build up a sound conviction favoring prohibition among a group of habitual drinkers. Dozens of similar instances may readily be adduced. Wherever convictions are firmly established, they are difficult to change. If it were not for the general tendency toward stability of convictions, human nature would be far less dependable than it is; we should be unable to classify our friends; we should never know from one day to the next what attitudes and beliefs to expect.

The very structure of personality and the existence of organized society both depend upon a relative resistance to change. If the methods of persuasion set forth in this book were inevitably and promptly effective, society would be reduced to a chaotic fluidity, with attitudes, feelings, beliefs, and actions veering rapidly from one tendency to another in response to whatever persuasive influences might momentarily be operative. Fortunate indeed is it that persuasion is not so simple as in our more ardent moments we might wish it to be. Neither human nature nor society as we know them would be possible except for two conditions: first, that persuasion operates slowly and with difficulty, and second, that it can and does have a considerable effect. In sum, organized living would be impossible unless there were both the possibility of change and the virtual certainty that changes of importance must come slowly.

A typical persuasive campaign

In January, 1943, a decision was reached by the War Food Administration to initiate a nationwide campaign to reduce the waste of food. With 13 per cent of America's food production going to our armed forces and another 12 per cent allocated to lend-lease, the civilian populace was reduced to 75 per cent of the total supply. Moreover, food imports were almost eliminated, and the demands of our allies for additional food were steadily mounting. Food rationing had been inaugurated in the United States and in practically all the rest of the world the daily average food consumption was dropping toward, or even below, the starvation line. A drive for greater food production had proved successful beyond all expectations, but its effectiveness was greatly lessened by the extravagant waste of food in this country. The persuasive proposal that was formulated was simple: *reduce food waste!*

Step one in organizing a sustained food-conservation campaign was to discover the *facts*. In order to do so, the co-operation of four hundred forty-five hospitals, of thirty-nine colleges, of the American Restaurant Association, of the U. S. Bureau of Prisons, of the Army's Quartermaster General, of the U. S. Department of Agriculture's Bureau of Agricultural Economics, and of dozens of cities' sanitation and garbage disposal departments was secured. Data were gathered from all these and other sources on amounts and kinds of food waste.

Step two consisted of securing *agreement on the facts*. With data accumulated from many different sources, much of it not readily comparable, most of it sensational in its implications, and all of it susceptible to various interpretations, a major problem was to get the various experts to agree on what the facts were. This step depended upon collecting the data, correlating them, making preliminary interpretations, distributing them for consideration, and then calling the experts into a series of conferences to argue out their differing views as to what the facts really meant.

Step three was to *state the facts*. When agreements finally emerged, they had to be reduced to simple terms and stated in a seris of propositions: "We waste 20 per cent to 30 per cent of all the food we produce;" "The average person in the United States wastes two hundred twenty-five pounds of food a year;" "We waste 50 per cent of our vegetables, 29 per cent of our fruit, 7 per cent of our meat, and 14 per cent of our baked goods."

Step four was to *interpret the facts.* "Waste" had to be defined. It was shown to exist in careless methods of harvesting, in hasty and ill-considered methods of packing and distribution, in bad shopping practices, poor refrigeration, cooking methods, table manners, serving more food than people wished to eat, rejecting various kinds of food, and so forth.

Step five was to *formulate recommendations for saving food.* This involved consideration by experts in every phase of food handling, from marketing experts to nutritionists, to suggest better methods of storing, marketing, preserving, and serving foods. Specific suggestions varied from "eat potatoes instead of bread" campaigns during the potato harvest periods to demonstrations that three extra teaspoons of juice could be secured from each grapefruit half by squeezing it.

Step six was to *present the facts and recommendations to the public.* To accomplish this stage—in which the actual persuasion began to operate—an elaborate machinery of propaganda had to be set up. Twenty-four national women's organizations, with memberships totalling twenty million, were invited to co-operate, and special materials were prepared for them to distribute to their members. The Office of War Information secured the co-operation of national advertisers, newspapers, and radio broadcasting companies. Discussion guides and a public speakers' manual were prepared. Skits were written for grade school children to present and a study guide was prepared for use in the public schools. The Secretary of Agriculture and other national figures made nationwide radio talks. Through regional, state, and local organizations "Clean Plate Clubs" were established in hundreds of communities. The fact of food waste and suggested methods of reducing it were held before the mind of the public by concerted efforts of all mass media of information. Special groups—Negroes, Catholics, dock workers, restaurants, and dozens more—were deluged with information and appeals from their own organizations.

Step seven was to *personalize the facts*. When it was found that almost everyone agreed that *other people* were wasting huge quantities of food, it became necessary to find inoffensive means of showing that every one of us was a food waster. It was pointed out that much of the waste occurred through normal and accepted food practices in which all of us participate. It was not a matter of finding special villains to attack, but of changing some of our own habits.

Step eight, implicit in all stages of the campaign, was *to make the facts significant*. The wastefulness in America was contrasted with the starvation among some of our allies. Pictures of garbage cans were shown beside pictures of starving Greek children. The role of food in winning the war was explained. "Saving food will help save the life of American soldiers" was one of the themes developed.

The principal point of this brief explanation of one major persuasive campaign is to illustrate how far-reaching and complex the problem of persuasion actually is. The elaborate machinery of a national presidential campaign, of the effort to sell soap, or of the organized efforts to promote religion are other examples.

Typical good will campaigns

The sustained persuasive campaign is also well illustrated in the good will programs conducted by many businesses and associations. One such example is the Bell Telephone Company of Pennsylvania. The company has a virtual monopoly, under state regulations, and sells a product and service that are universally needed. Even so, the company officials see a variety of reasons why a continuing campaign of persuasion is required.

Basically, they want to keep the public satisfied that the company is doing a good job—for satisfied customers make the work far easier. Moreover, since the telephone company is a utility subject to governmental regulation, it naturally wishes the public to feel pleased with the mode of operation. In addition, telephone service is in direct competition with the telegraph and, in a sense, with the postal service.

Hence, it seems wise to the officials to keep emphasizing the point that there is no better way of maintaining fruitful contact with friends and business associates than frequent telephone conversations. And, of course, people can be persuaded to increase the number of telephone extensions in their homes, and to subscribe to such "extra" services as the monitoring of calls when they are out. For all such reasons, Bell of Pennsylvania does conduct a sustained persuasive campaign.

As Albert S. Barnes, the Public Relations Manager of the company, phrased it: "We have always worked on the basis that our service, no matter how good it may be, measured by the very strict standards we ourselves set up, is really no better than our public thinks it is." With this problem to solve, Bell depends not only on newspaper and magazine advertising, but also on a very extensive use of good will public speaking.

In 1954, for example, the company presented more than 3,300 talks before audiences totaling nearly 275,000 people. Three full-time lecturers were hired by the company to present talks in various sections of the state. As Mr. Barnes explains, "Most of these lecture-demonstrations deal with the newest and most interesting developments of our research laboratories, the Transistor, the Solar Battery, Nationwide Direct Dialing, NIKE—the guided missile—and the like, but they are all presented in layman's language."

In addition, Bell of Pennsylvania utilizes eighty part-time women lecturers, to speak largely before women's groups. These speakers are chosen for this part-time good will speaking from the ranks of the vocational and supervisory personnel. They speak chiefly on topics of interest to women—such as personality, color, music, and diamonds, all in relation to the telephone industry. Finally, supervisory personnel in all the local offices of the company are expected, as part of their job responsibility, to address local clubs about the nature of their own work and the service of the company as rendered locally.

Good will speaking is of importance not only to big business but to "big labor" as well. With seventeen million workers in the United States organized into two hundred seventeen national and more than a thousand state and city central federated unions, there exists a continuing task of creating and maintaining good will both among the members and in the general reaction of the public. In a graduate study conducted by Charles R. Petrie, Jr., in 1955, it was found that labor union leaders depend heavily upon public speaking to accomplish their good will function. Such labor leaders as George Meany, Dave Beck, Walter Reuther, James Carey, Martin Durkin, Harry R. Bridges, and John L. Lewis were found to be frequent speakers and strong advocates of the necessity for conducting sustained campaigns of good will speaking. It is significant, too, that although they speak on many different occasions to many kinds of audiences, a study of one hundred one speeches by twenty leading union speakers showed that they concentrated largely upon four themes—and were in general accord in the views expressed concerning them. In short, instead of speaking purely as individuals, they presented a "common front" to achieve a common understanding by the public.

Still another type of sustained campaign of great significance in our times is the extensive use of public speaking by the communist countries as part of their propaganda-control apparatus. A study of this type of "sustained campaigning" by the Communists showed that, in 1946, within the Soviet Union there were organized approximately three million "agitators" (as they call such speakers), or one for every sixty-five members of the population fifteen years old or over. Through weekly meetings conducted by these agitators, "Speech techniques of an unusually intimate nature are utilized systematically to insure that every member of the communist community feels he has a definite answer to his own personal questions—always, of course, within the strait jacket of the party line." As Alex Inkeles concludes in his *Public Opinion in Soviet Russia:* every agitator is told, "Do not hide from a puzzling, trenchant or even hostile question, but, on the contrary, give an answer that is straightforward and full of the stuff of the Party spirit."

This distortion of the uses of speech by the Communists to suit their own purposes suggests to us the far greater democratic values to be sought in achieving a solidarity of purposes and methods by the wise use of public discussion meetings in our own free society. As was concluded by Robert T. Oliver, in the foregoing study of speech in the communist countries: "For what is happening behind the Iron Curtain we should be seriously concerned. For what is not happening in the free world we should be even more deeply concerned. The tragic fact is that communism is advancing not alone through force of arms and extension of territory, but also by poisoning the living waters of democratic methodology and by administering this poisoned potion to undermine the individualist independence of peoples both inside and outside the Empire of the Hammer and Sickle."

In short, the sustained campaign is represented by a wide variety of uses, by many groups, for many purposes. In some of its uses it is evil and dangerous; in others productive of much good. In both instances, a large part of its power derives from the very fact that the persuasion is *sustained*—for as we all know, in constant repetition and unremitting effort there is great power of influence.

Problems in sustained persuasion

Whatever the persuasive campaign may be, certain kinds of problems have to be dealt with. In a general sense, these correlate with the eight steps listed in the food waste campaign. There is, of course, the basic task of motivation. This task, however, is complicated by the fact that the persuasive process is to be continued over a long period of time. Almost inevitably problems of sponsorship, joint planning, consistency of appeal, clarity of the goal, and means to be used will arise. Conducting or participating in a sustained campaign is far different from preparing and delivering a single persuasive speech.

1. *The Policy Line.* What is to be accomplished by the persuasion is, of course, the crucial question. This goal has been called "the proposal" for individual persuasive speeches. For sustained campaigns, it is usually known as "the policy line." Since continuing co-operation will have to be sought, some broader guiding statement is needed than a simple proposal. The policy line sets forth the goal to be achieved, indicates acceptable methods that may be employed,

and constitutes the ultimate test for determining whether all aspects of the campaign are actually contributing to its success.

As an example, the policy line for the food conservation campaign was phrased something like this: To secure the voluntary co-operation of all major publicity media; civic, religious, educational, social, and youth organizations; and appropriate governmental agencies to persuade the public to co-operate in securing the maximum benefit from available food supplies. With this policy statement before them, hundreds of participants in every part of the country knew in what manner they could co-operate. Advertisers, school officials, club officers, and all others within the categories named could be asked to contribute unpaid services to disseminate information and appeals designed to achieve the best utilization of available food. Sometimes this would require appeals to eat more of one food and less of another; sometimes to engage in a project to help harvest bumper crops or to co-operate in a mass fruit-canning program; and eventually it resulted in the abandonment of the conservation program as signs appeared that the supplies of food were once again becoming sufficient to meet all normal requirements. Within the broad limitations of this policy line, ample opportunity was left to all participants to devise their own methods for dealing with purely local and transitory phases of the broad campaign.

2. *Sponsorship.* Many sustained persuasive campaigns are originated by business concerns to achieve their own goals. Other campaigns are initiated by government agencies or by national organizations. In such instances, the sponsorship is predetermined. Many other sustained campaigns, on the other hand, are started by public-spirited individuals who wish to achieve some particular reform or program. When this is the case, the decision as to sponsorship becomes of vital importance. Some sponsoring agency must be found or set up that will have or win public confidence.

Prior to the attack on Pearl Harbor, two opposing persuasive campaigns were launched in the United States. One, intended to put this country into the war to destroy Nazism, was organized under the Committee to Save Democracy by Aiding the Allies. The other, seeking to keep us isolated from the conflict, was directed by the America First Committee. Each sought prominent and trusted Americans to constitute its Board of Directors and advertised this sponsorship prominently as one of its major persuasive devices. The American Red Cross seeks the best possible sponsorship by arranging for the President of the United States to serve as its Honorary President, and by persuading him to launch each year's campaign for funds with an appeal from the White House. When local community campaigns are launched, similar efforts should be made to secure effective sponsorship—perhaps by the Council of Churches, the Chamber of Commerce, the local labor unions, or other influential bodies.

Business concerns are very much concerned to keep the "good will" of the public, in order to keep their own sponsorship of their own products in good repute. The Ford Motor Company, for instance, suspended publication of the Dearborn *Independent* magazine when it became widely suspected of anti-Semitism. Early in the century the Standard Oil Company faced a possible loss of sales through the unfavorable reputation of John D. Rockefeller, and a public relations counsel was hired to persuade the public that Mr. Rockefeller was actually a kindly old man who delighted in giving dimes to children and who devoted his millions to charitable enterprises.

When any persuasive campaign is initiated, the question will soon arise, "Who is behind it?" To the extent that this question can be answered in terms that will win public confidence, the campaign is substantially aided.

3. *Spokesmen.* Who is to present the persuasive appeals to the public is a question closely allied with the sponsorship of the campaign. Persuasive speakers are often selected not so much for their speaking skill as for their standing in the community. Opponents of the "Welfare State" found effective spokesmen in ex-New Dealer James Byrnes and in General Dwight Eisenhower, who, of course, became President of the United States. Political party leaders hold many realistic conferences to decide on candidates who will appeal to the voters, even though these candidates may not have been loyal party workers. Thus, the Democratic party machine in New

Jersey, fearing defeat in the 1910 election, sought out Princeton's President Woodrow Wilson to run for the governorship, well realizing that he would oppose large parts of their program, but preferring a partial victory with him to complete defeat through election of a Republican.

Similarly, in planning local persuasive campaigns (such as raising funds for the home-town hospital) a question to be seriously canvassed is what speakers can be called upon who will have the most effect with the public. Sustained campaigning is distinctly teamwork, with each individual doing what he can properly do. Therefore, it frequently happens that those who plan the campaigns do little or no speaking themselves, but leave that job to those who can perform it most effectively.

4. *Resources.* What can be accomplished, and the means of doing it, must be dependent in large degree upon available resources. The size of the advertising budget is a major concern of business organizations. The extent and nature of every campaign are shaped partly by whether funds are available for printing leaflets, buying radio time, running advertisements, hiring clerical help, and paying for other services. If the program advocated is in the nature of a public service, and the sponsorship is of sufficient prestige, many volunteer participants can usually be found. Newspapers and radio stations will grant free space and time to raising funds for a public playground, but are far less likely to do so to aid a campaign for building a swimming pool in the Elks Lodge, to be used only by the members themselves.

5. *Audience.* Few campaigns are directed indiscriminately to the public at large. However general the campaign may be, it normally will succeed best if segments of the public are selected for particular and specialized appeals. The very fact that communities are organized into groups of various kinds indicates that there are differences in interests, in economic and social attachments, and in needs. Certain groups, such as church members, parents of school children, home owners, gardeners, sportsmen, labor union members, or the aged have logical interests in particular problems. Accordingly, a campaign to win higher pensions for the aged should not be addressed to the entire

community; the appeals will doubtless be most effective if they are phrased for the aged themselves and for family members having aged parents. One of the acute problems to be solved in planning a sustained campaign is to determine to what segments of the population it will primarily be addressed. The campaign may fail either by aiming at too broad an audience, thus trying to please everyone, and failing to be particularized enough to arouse the deep feelings of any; or by aiming at too narrow a segment and thereby missing the support otherwise forthcoming from other types of auditors.

6. *Motivation.* Determination of what kind of persuasion to use depends largely upon the preceding five considerations. For appeals that are to be directed over a long period of time to many different kinds of auditors, however, a general principle is to assume partial agreement with the policy line. In the food-conservation campaign, for instance, the assumption was that people do not *wish* to waste food, but that they do it carelessly or thoughtlessly. In a campaign to raise funds for a hospital, it is best to ignore the relatively few who distrust and despise hospitals, and to concentrate upon those who appreciate what they are doing, but have not realized the necessity of personal contributions to support the service. Those who are already fully convinced need no persuasion. And those who are strongly opposed or completely indifferent can hardly be persuaded without very direct and highly personalized appeals. In between these groups are many who need more motivation than the first group and who would be repelled by the assumption of hostility or indifference on their part. A cigarette company, for instance, aims its advertising primarily at those who already smoke, but have not yet discovered how superior is the brand being advertised.

7. *Mechanics.* In a campaign addressed to a broad public over an extended period of time, it is of great importance to determine just what the members of the public are expected to do, and to reiterate frequently how they are to do it. "How does all this affect me?" is a question no auditor ought to have need to ask. In the minds of the promoters of the campaign, two concurrent considerations need always to be present: (1) how to phrase appeals that will have an application

to all those who should be affected; and (2) how to indicate what each of them, as individuals, should do about it. Elaborate machinery of local committees may have to be set up for collection of funds, or of pledges, or to organize the efforts of volunteers who wish to help. Other devices consist of putting questionnaire forms in newspapers, to be filled out and mailed in; of requesting those who are persuaded to write letters to their Congressmen; of informing the auditors where the articles being sold can be bought; and of suggesting other appropriate actions to be taken as a result of the appeals.

Progressive stages of persuasion

The foregoing discussion has been concerned primarily with national or community-wide programs in which many individuals are participating. All of us have occasion for frequent experience with these kinds of persuasive campaigns, either as co-operative participants or as recipients of the appeals. Sometimes, however, we have occasion as individuals to carry on sustained persuasive campaigns of our own. Probably we do much more of this kind of persuasive speaking than we realize. When mother wants a new fur coat, son wants to go to a particular college, or daughter wishes to spend her vacation at a Western dude ranch, any one of them knows that a single abrupt appeal to father is dangerously likely to fail. What occurs is a long-range campaign, often far advanced before the recipient is aware of what is happening to him. Just this kind of approach would bring additional success to those who wish to effect a change of attitude, action, or belief in their communities. What we would like to accomplish in a single speech, and have done with, often in fact requires a sustained campaign over a considerable period of time.

Whenever you have a persuasive purpose to accomplish, it is wise to consider realistically whether you are likely to win full agreement with what you have in mind. If not, the practical procedure is to limit your goal, phrase a proposal that incorporates only a part of your ultimate aim, and try to get the audience thinking at least started in the direction you desire. As, in Chapter 15, it was advised to prepare successive stages within the persuasive speech to accord with anticipated audience responses, just so in a sustained campaign is there a series of proposals, each developed in terms of the speaker's anticipation of what degree of persuasion he may be able to achieve.

A woman, for example, who wished to persuade her fellow citizens to beautify their home town by planting flowers in vacant lots and parking strips, might commence her campaign with a series of talks on cities she had visited, taking care to direct attention to the attractive flower beds found in each. Or, using a different approach, she might give talks to various audiences on kinds of flowers, planting patterns, and other topics designed chiefly to arouse interest and build up understanding. After either type of introductory talks, she might well find that her indirect suggestion had stimulated one or many auditors to suggest of their own accord that "Perhaps a flower planting project could be started in our town." If no one else suggests it, she herself can introduce the idea; and if someone else does she is prepared to give it enthusiastic backing. It often is true that to inaugurate a campaign openly before there has been a period of preparation for it results in arousing doubts as to its practicality and opposition arising chiefly from lack of substantial interest. As in many other kinds of activities, persuasion, too, profits from having a sound foundation laid before the structure itself is erected.

Conclusion

Sustained persuasive campaigns are of many types, but for our purposes may be classified into two categories: those in which many persons participate, and those undertaken by a single speaker. The former type is dependent upon carefully integrated teamwork at every stage, including the decision to wage a campaign, the determination of a policy line, the selection of an appropriate sponsoring agency, the choice of spokesmen for various phases of the campaign, the acquisition of the resources deemed essential, the fitting of the motivation to various segments of the audience, and the provision of proper mechanics for achieving the action sought. When a single speaker is conducting an extended persuasive campaign by himself, the major consideration is the determination of the successive stages through which it will be carried, from simple exposition of background facts to tentative presentation of various aspects of the subject, until the time seems promising for urging adoption of the key proposal.

What is always to be kept in mind by every persuasive speaker is that for many problems it is impossible to achieve the totality of the desired persuasive effect in a single speech. An ancient proverb from Korea states the task of the persuasive speaker very well: "He who would make a mountain must carry every load of earth." Many a persuasive problem seems far less difficult of achievement after it has been subdivided into diverse phases, each to be taken up one at a time. The longer we deal with persuasion, the more we become convinced of the necessity and the utility of the sustained campaign.

Exercises

1. Select a subject concerning which you feel a desire to persuade your college associates (such as the need for better study habits, a more constructive school spirit, or more purposive selection of courses). Write out a program for a sustained campaign to accomplish your general goal, indicating the policy line, sponsorship, spokesmen, resources, audience to be reached, motivation to be employed, and the mechanics by which action is to be initiated. Try to plan a campaign that should succeed, keeping in mind the difficulty of effecting a change in any attitudes as deep-seated as you are likely to encounter on any significant campus problem.

2. After you have decided upon your campaign, indicate how it should be carried through each of the eight steps described for "A Typical Persuasive Campaign."

3. Analyze your campus audience to determine what natural groupings should be addressed by their own spokesmen (such as fraternities and sororities, professional societies, religious groups) and show what process would be required to select and win the co-operation of the most suitable spokesmen for each of the groups.

4. Indicate what methods other than speeches should be utilized in carrying on such a campaign.

5. Select any current sustained persuasive campaign (as carried on by a business firm, political party, church, or pressure group) and prepare a speech explaining to your class the methods by which the campaign is conducted.

6. Attend a meeting of some campus or town group that actually is conducting a sustained campaign, and report on how it is handling the "Problems in Sustained Persuasion." Present any suggestions you may have for improving the conduct of the campaign.

7. Select some current problem (such as American Policies in Asia, How to Improve College Education, or The Welfare State) and from *The New York Times, Vital Speeches of the Day,* and other sources, make a listing of speeches by different individuals all advocating the same "policy line" in reference to the problem. Write an analytical paper showing how well, or how poorly, these speeches conform to the requirements for carrying on a sustained campaign. What is needed to increase their effectiveness?

8. For further study of the sustained campaign, the following readings are grouped into topical categories:

A. Historic Movements

A. Craig Baird, "Opportunities for Research in State and Sectional Public Speaking," *Quarterly Journal of Speech,* 29 (October, 1943), 304-308.

Waldo Braden, "The Concept of Southern Oratory: A Selected Bibliography," *Southern Speech Journal,* 29 (Winter, 1963), 141-145.

Charles A. Johnson, *The Frontier Camp Meeting* (Dallas: Southern Methodist University Press, 1955).

Lawrence Lader, *The Bold Brahmins: New England's War Against Slavery (1831-1863)* (New York: Dutton, 1961).

John Lukacs, *A History of the Cold War* (New York: Doubleday Anchor Books, 1962).

Robert T. Oliver, *History of Public Speaking in America* (Boston: Allyn and Bacon, 1965).

Oscar Sherwin, *Prophet of Liberty: The Life and Times of Wendell Phillips* (New York: Bookman Associates, 1958).

Bernard A. Weisberger, *They Gathered at the River* (Boston: Little, Brown, 1958).

Earl W. Wiley, "State History and Rhetorical Research," *Quarterly Journal of Speech,* 36 (October, 1950), 514-519.

B. Political Campaigns

Barnet Baskerville, "Joe McCarthy: Brief-Case Demagogue," *Today's Speech,* II (September, 1954), 8-15.

Ernest G. Bormann, "Huey Long: Analysis of a Demagogue," *Today's Speech,* II (September, 1954), 16-20.

Lyndon B. Johnson, *A Time for Action* (New York: Pocket Books, 1964).

John F. Kennedy, *The Strategy of Peace,* ed. Allan Nevins (New York: Popular Library, 1961).

Robert F. Kennedy, *Rights for Americans: Speeches,* ed., Thomas A. Hopkins (Indianapolis: Bobbs-Merrill, 1964).

Richard M. Nixon, *Speeches, Remarks, Press Conferences, and Study Papers* (Washington: U.S. Government Printing Office, 1961).

Richard H. Rovere, *The Eisenhower Years* (New York: Farrar, Straus and Cudahy, 1956), particularly "The Vice-President," pp. 293-307.

Adlai E. Stevenson, *Putting First Things First: A Democratic View* (New York: Random House, 1960).

Theodore H. White, *The Making of the President: 1960* (New York: Atheneum, 1961).

————, *The Making of the President: 1964* (New York: Atheneum, 1965).

Russell R. Windes, Jr., "A Study of Effective and Ineffective Presidential Campaign Speaking," *Speech Monographs,* 28 (March, 1961), 39-49.

For group-studies of political campaigns, see also The Quarterly Journal of Speech, 34 (December, 1948), 421-438; 43 (February, 1957), 29-54; 46 (October, 1960), 239-252; 46 (December, 1960), 355-364; and 48 (December, 1964), 385-414.

C. International Persuasion

George N. Gordon, Irving Falk, and William Hodapp, *The Idea Invaders: International Propaganda and Mass Communication* (New York: Hastings House, 1963).

Robert T. Holt and Robert W. van de Velde, *Strategic Psychological Operations and American Foreign Policy* (Chicago: University of Chicago Press, 1960).

Walter Johnson, *The Battle Against Isolation* (Chicago: University of Chicago Press, 1944).

Paul M. A. Linebarger, *Psychological Warfare* (Washington: Combat Forces Press, 1955).

Robert T. Oliver, *Culture and Communication* (Springfield, Ill.: Charles C Thomas, 1962).

Charles Roetter, *The Diplomatic Art* (Philadelphia: Macrae Smith, 1963).

Barbara Tuchman, *The Guns of August* (New York: Macmillan, 1962), particularly Chapters I-IX, pp. 7-157.

D. Public Relations and Propaganda

Albert S. Barnes, "Bell's Talks to the Public," *Today's Speech,* IV (January, 1956), 9-11.

Herbert M. Baus, *Public Relations at Work* (New York: Harper, 1948).

Edward L. Bernays, *Public Relations* (Norman: University of Oklahoma Press, 1952).

Robert Haakenson, "Training for an Industrial Speakers Bureau," *Today's Speech,* XIII (February, 1965), 20-23.

W. Charles Redding and George A. Sanborn (eds.), *Business and Industrial Communication: A Sourcebook* (New York: Harper & Row, 1964).

Bruce L. Smith, Harold D. Lasswell, and Ralph D. Casey (eds.), *Propaganda, Communication, and Public Opinion* (Princeton: Princeton University Press, 1946).

Index

461